Retreat from Doomsday

RETREAT FROM DOOMSDAY

THE OBSOLESCENCE OF MAJOR WAR

JOHN MUELLER

BASIC BOOKS, INC., PUBLISHERS

NEW YORK

Library of Congress Cataloging-in-Publication Data

Mueller, John E.
  Retreat from doomsday.

  Bibliographical notes: p. 271
  Includes index.
  1. War.   2. World politics—20th century.   3. Military
history, Modern—20th century.   I. Title.
UA21.2.M84   1989   355'.02'0904   88–47899
ISBN   0–465–069398–1

To JAM and ESM,

to Karl, Michelle, Karen, and Susan,

and to the memory of Bernard Brodie

CONTENTS

ACKNOWLEDGMENTS

For helpful comments and suggestions I would like to thank Verna and Michael Cavey, Richard Dolan, Seymour Drescher, Stanley Engerman, MacGregor Knox, Karl Mueller, George Quester, Peggy Rosenthal, Kenneth Shepsle, Harvey Starr, and especially Robert Jervis. Dana Loud, virtuoso typist, weaver, and puzzle-solver, cheerfully fashioned a recognizable tapestry of my scrawls and endless emendations. At Basic Books, Martin Kessler helped greatly in shaping and improving the argument, and Sharon A. Sharp in shaping and improving the prose, while Charles Cavaliere ably guided the result through the production process. Research and writing were supported by the University of Rochester and by a John Simon Guggenheim Fellowship. Peace, now, to all.

Retreat from Doomsday

Introduction

History's Greatest Nonevent

ON MAY 15, 1984, the major countries of the developed world had managed to remain at peace with each other for the longest continuous stretch of time since the days of the Roman Empire. If a significant battle in a war had been fought on that day, the press would have bristled with it. As usual, however, a landmark crossing in the history of peace caused no stir: the most prominent story in the *New York Times* that day concerned the saga of a manicurist, a machinist, and a cleaning woman who had just won a big Lotto contest.

This book seeks to develop an explanation for what is probably the greatest nonevent in human history. For decades now, two massively armed countries, the United States and the Soviet Union, have dominated international politics, and during that time they have engaged in an intense, sometimes even desperate, rivalry over political, military, and ideological issues. Yet despite this enormous mutual hostility, they have never gone to war with each other. Furthermore, although they have occasionally engaged in confrontational crises, there have been only a few of these—and virtually none at all in the last two-thirds of the period. Rather than gradually drawing closer to armed conflict, as often happened after earlier wars, the two major countries seem to be drifting farther away from it.

Insofar as it is discussed at all, there appear to be two schools of thought to explain what John Lewis Gaddis has called the "long peace."[1]

One school concludes that we have simply been lucky. Since 1947, the *Bulletin of Atomic Scientists* has decorated its cover with a "doomsday" clock set ominously at a few minutes before midnight. From time to time the editors push the clock's big hand forward or backward a bit to demonstrate their pleasure with an arms control measure or their disapproval of what they perceive to be rising tension; but they never nudge it very far away from the fatal hour, and the message they wish to convey is clear. They believe we live perpetually on the brink, teetering on a fragile balance; if our luck turns a bit sour, we are likely at any moment to topple helplessly into cataclysmic war.[2] As time goes by, however, this point of view begins to lose some of its persuasiveness. When a clock remains poised at a few minutes to midnight for decades, one may gradually come to suspect that it isn't telling us very much.

The other school stresses paradox: It is the very existence of unprecedentedly destructive weapons that has worked, so far, to our benefit—in Winston Churchill's memorable phrase, safety has been the "sturdy child of [nuclear] terror."[3] This widely held (if minimally examined) view is, to say the least, less than fully comforting, because the very weapons that have been so necessary for peace according to this argument, also possess the capability of cataclysmic destruction, should they somehow be released. For many, this perpetual threat is simply too much to bear, and to them the weapons' continued existence seals our ultimate doom even as it perpetuates our current peace. In his influential best-seller, *The Fate of the Earth,* Jonathan Schell dramatically prophesies that if we do not "rise up and cleanse the earth of nuclear weapons," we will soon "sink into the final coma and end it all."[4]

This book develops a third explanation: The long peace since World War II is less a product of recent weaponry than the culmination of a substantial historical process. For the last two or three centuries major war—war among developed countries—has gradually moved toward terminal disrepute because of its perceived repulsiveness and futility.

The book also concludes that nuclear weapons have not had an important impact on this remarkable trend—they have not crucially defined postwar stability, and they do not threaten to disturb it severely. They have affected rhetoric (we live, we are continually assured, in the atomic age, the nuclear epoch), and they certainly have influenced defense budgets and planning. However, they do not seem to have been necessary to deter major war, to cause the leaders of major countries to behave cautiously, or to determine the alliances that have been formed. Rather, it seems that things would have turned out much the same had nuclear weapons never been invented.

That something other than nuclear terror explains the long peace is suggested in part by the fact that there have been numerous nonwars since 1945 besides the nonwar that is currently being waged by the United States and the Soviet Union. With only one minor and fleeting exception (the Soviet invasion of Hungary in 1956), there have been no wars among the forty-four wealthiest (per capita) countries during that time.[5] Although there have been many wars since World War II, some of them enormously costly by any standard, these have taken place almost entirely within the third—or really the fourth—world. The developed countries have sometimes participated in these wars on distant turf, but not directly against each other.

Several specific nonwars are in their own way even more extraordinary than the one that has taken place between the United States and the Soviet Union. France and Germany are important countries which had previously spent decades—centuries even—either fighting each other or planning to do so. For this ages-old antagonism World War II indeed served as the war to end war: like Greece and Turkey, they have retained the creative ability to discover a motivation for war even under an overarching nuclear umbrella if they really wanted to, yet they have now lived side by side for decades, perhaps with some bitterness and recrimination, but without even a glimmer of war fever. The case of Japan is also striking: this formerly aggressive major country seems now to have fully embraced the virtues (and profits) of peace.

In fact, within the first and second worlds warfare of *all* sorts seems generally to have lost its appeal. Not only have there been virtually no international wars among the major and not-so-major countries, but the developed world has experienced virtually no civil war either. The only exception is the 1944–49 Greek civil war—more an unsettled residue of World War II than an autonomous event. The sporadic violence in Northern Ireland or the Basque region of Spain has not really been sustained enough to be considered civil war, nor have the spurts of terrorism carried out by tiny bands of self-styled revolutionaries elsewhere in Western Europe that have never coalesced into anything bigger. Except for the fleeting case of Hungary in 1956, Europeans under Soviet rule have so far accepted their fate, no matter how desperate their disaffection, rather than take arms to oppose it—though some sort of civil uprising there is certainly not out of the question.[6]

Because it is so quiet, peace often is allowed to carry on unremarked. We tend to delimit epochs by wars and denote periods of peace not for their own character, but for the wars they separate. As Geoffrey Blainey has observed, "For every thousand pages published on the causes of wars there is less than one page directly on the causes of peace."[7] But now, surely, with so much peace at hand in so much of the world, some effort ought to be made to explain the unprecedented cornucopia. Never before in history have so many well-armed, important countries spent so much time not using their arms against each other.

To deal with this task, the book begins, in part 1, by tracing changing attitudes toward war in the developed world. As early as 1800 a few countries, like Holland, Switzerland, and Sweden, had begun to drop out of the war system, but war was still generally accepted as a natural and inevitable phenomenon. Beginning in 1815 the institution of war for the first time in history came under organized and concentrated attack. Opponents argued that war was repulsive, immoral, and uncivilized, and that it was futile, particularly economically. They remained a noisy minority for the next century and were often derided by those who still held war to be noble, thrilling, progressive, manly, and beneficial.

The holocaust of World War I turned peace advocates into a pronounced majority in the developed world and virtually destroyed war romanticism. Were it not for the astoundingly successful machinations of Adolf Hitler, just about the last European who was willing to risk major war, and for the anachronistic forays of distant Japan, World War I might have been the last major war.

Part 2 examines the long peace—the great nonevent—itself. Major war has been most likely to develop from the Cold War that has dominated postwar international history. The hostility of the era mostly derives from the Soviet Union's ideological—even romantic—affection for revolution and for revolutionary war. Although this ideology is expansionistic in some respects, it has never visualized major war as a remotely sensible tactic. The book traces the history of the Cold War, dealing particularly with the wars in Korea and Vietnam and with Cold War crises. It concludes that East and West have never been close to major war and that nuclear weapons have not been important determinants of this fact—insofar as a military deterrent has been necessary, the fear of escalation to a war like World War I or II has been sufficient. A large war, nuclear or otherwise, has never been remotely in the interest of the essentially contented, risk-averse, escalation-anticipating countries that have dominated world affairs since 1945 and, even allowing considerably for stupidity, ineptness, miscalculation, and self-deception, it is difficult to see how they could have gotten into one.

Because of economic crisis and persistent ideological failure, it appears in the late 1980s that the Cold War may be on the verge of substantial improvement as the Soviet Union, following the lead of its former ideological soulmate, China, abandons its quest for ideological expansion and quests after prosperity and a quiet, normal international situation.

Part 3 considers whether peace in the developed world is likely to linger or break down (the prospects for lingering look good as long as the quest for prosperity remains a popular goal). It also explores the possibility that major war has become, or is becoming, obsolete: without being formally renounced or institutionally superceded and without being undercut by notable changes in human nature or in the structure of international politics, major war may have gradually moved toward final discredit. In areas where war was once often casually seen as beneficial, noble, and glorious, or at least as necessary or inevitable, the conviction has now become widespread that war would be intolerably costly, unwise, futile, and debasing.

The book concludes by suggesting how the military strategists' concepts of deterrence and stability can usefully be broadened to include often crucial nonmilitary considerations. It also assesses the possibility that the apparent obsolescence of war in the developed world will eventually infect those portions of the globe where war remains endemic. And it examines the prospects that, in a world without war or warlike tension, the arms race will gradually atrophy and a general political settlement will be reached.

The Rising Costs of War

War is merely an idea. It is not a trick of fate, a thunderbolt from hell, a natural calamity, or a desperate plot contrivance dreamed up by some sadistic puppeteer on high. And if war begins in the minds of men, as the UNESCO charter insists, it can end there as well. Over the centuries war opponents have been trying to bring this about by discrediting war as an idea. In part, their message, which will be more fully assessed in the next chapters, stresses that war is unacceptably costly, and they have pointed to two kinds of costs: (1) psychic ones—war, they argue, is repulsive, immoral, and uncivilized; and (2) physical ones—war is bloody, destructive, and expensive.

It is often observed that war's physical costs have risen. World War II was the most destructive in history, and World War I was also terrible. World War III, even if nuclear weapons were not used, could easily be worse; and a thermonuclear war might, as Schell would have it, "end it all."

Rising physical costs do seem to have helped to discredit war. But there are good reasons to believe that this cannot be the whole story.

In 1889, Baroness Bertha von Suttner of Austria published a sentimental antiwar novel, *Die Waffen Nieder!*, that swiftly became an international bestseller—the *Uncle Tom's Cabin* of the nineteenth-century peace movement. In it she describes the travails of a young Austrian woman who turns against war when her husband is killed in the Franco-Austrian War of 1859. Now, in historical perspective, that brief war was one of the least memorable in modern history, and its physical costs were minor in comparison with many other wars of that, or any other, era. But Suttner's fictional young widow was repelled not by the war's size, but by its existence and by the devastating personal consequences to her. Opposition to war has been growing in the developed world because more and more people have come to find war repulsive for what it *is*, not simply for the extent of the devastation it causes.

Furthermore, it is simply not true that cataclysmic war is an invention of the

7

20th century.* To annihilate ancient Carthage in 146 B.C., the Romans used weaponry that was primitive by today's standard, but even nuclear weapons could not have been more thorough. And, as Thucydides recounts with shattering calm, when the Athenians invaded Melos in 416 B.C., they "put to death all the grown men whom they took and sold the women and children for slaves, and subsequently sent out five hundred colonists and inhabited the place for themselves."[8]

During the Thirty Years War of 1618–48 the wealthy city of Magdeburg, together with its 20,000 inhabitants, was annihilated. According to standard estimates accepted as late as the 1930s, Germany's population in that war declined from 21 million to under 13.5 million—absolute losses far larger than it suffered in either world war of the twentieth century. Moreover, and more importantly, most people apparently *thought* things were even worse: for centuries a legend prevailed that Germany had suffered a 75 percent decline in population, from 16 million to 4 million.[9] Yet the belief that war could cause devastation of such enormous proportions did not lead to its abandonment. After the Thirty Years War, conflict remained endemic in Europe, and in 1756 Prussia fought the Seven Years War, which, in the estimate of its king and generalissimo, Frederick the Great, cost it 500,000 lives—one-ninth of its population, a proportion higher than almost any suffered by any combatant in the wars of the nineteenth or twentieth centuries.[10]

Wars in the past have often caused revolts and economic devastation as well. Historians have been debating for a century whether the Thirty Years War destroyed a vibrant economy in Germany or whether it merely administered the final blow to an economy that was already in decline—but destruction was the consequence in either case. The Seven Years War brought Austria to virtual bankruptcy, and it so weakened France that the conditions for revolution were established. When the economic costs of war are measured as a percentage of the gross national product of the combatants, observes Alan Milward, war "has not shown any discernible long-term trend towards greater costliness."[11]

And in sheer pain and suffering wars used to be far worse than ones fought by developed countries today. In 1840 or 1640 or 1240 a wounded or diseased soldier often died slowly and in intense agony. Medical aid was inadequate, and

---

*To put things in somewhat broader perspective, it may be useful to note that war is not the century's greatest killer. Although there have been a large number of extremely destructive wars, totalitarian and extreme authoritarian governments have put more of their own people to death— three times more according to one calculation—than have died in all the century's international and civil wars combined (Rummel 1986). For example, the man-made famine in China between 1958 and 1962 apparently caused the deaths of 30 million people (see p. 165), far more than died during World War I. Governments at peace can also surpass war in their economic destruction as well: largely because of government mismanagement and corruption, the average Zairian's wages in 1988, after adjusting for inflation, were 10 percent of what they had been in 1960 (Greenhouse 1988).

since physicians had few remedies and were unaware of the germ theory, they often only made things worse. War, indeed, was hell. By contrast, an American soldier wounded in the Vietnam jungle could be in a sophisticated, sanitized hospital within a half hour.

Consequently, if the revulsion toward war has grown in the developed world, this development cannot be due entirely to a supposed rise in its physical costs. Also needed is an appreciation for war's increased psychic costs. Over the last century or two, war in the developed world has come widely to be regarded as repulsive, immoral, and uncivilized. There may also be something of an interactive effect between psychic and physical costs here: If for moral reasons we come to place a higher value on human life—even to have a sort of reverence for it—the physical costs of war or any other life-taking enterprise will effectively rise as cost tolerance declines.

It may not be obvious that an accepted, time-honored institution that serves an urgent social purpose can become obsolescent and then die out because a lot of people come to find it obnoxious. But this book will argue that something like that has been happening to war in the developed world. To illustrate the dynamic and to set up a framework for future discussion, it will be helpful briefly to assess two analogies: the processes through which the once-perennial institutions of dueling and slavery have been virtually eradicated from the face of the earth.

Dueling Ceases to Be a "Peculiar Necessity"

In some important respects war in the developed world may be following the example of another violent method for settling disputes, dueling, which up until a century ago was common practice in Europe and America among a certain class of young and youngish men who liked to classify themselves as gentlemen. When one man concluded that he had been insulted by another and therefore that his honor had been besmirched, he might well engage the insulter in a short, private, and potentially deadly battle. The duel was taken somehow to settle the matter, even if someone was killed in the process—or even if someone wasn't.[12]

At base, dueling was a matter of attitude more than of cosmology or technology: it was something someone might want to do, and in some respects was even expected to do, from time to time. The night before his famous fatal duel with Aaron Burr in 1804, the methodical Alexander Hamilton wrote out his evaluation of the situation. He could find many reasons to reject Burr's challenge—he really felt no ill will toward his challenger, he wrote, and dueling was against his religious and moral principles, as well as against the laws of New York (where he lived) and New Jersey (where the duel was to be held); furthermore, his death would endanger the livelihood of his wife, children, and creditors. In sum, "I shall hazard much, and can possibly gain nothing." Nevertheless, he still concluded he must fight. All these concerns were overwhelmed because he felt that "what men of the world denominate honor" imposed upon him a "peculiar necessity": his refusal to duel would reduce his political effectiveness by subjecting him to contempt and derision in the circles he considered important. Therefore, he felt that he had to conform with "public prejudice in this particular."[13] Although there were solid economic, legal, moral, and religious reasons to turn down the challenge of Vice President Burr, the prick of honor and the attendant fear of immobilizing ridicule—Hamilton's peculiar necessities—impelled him to venture out that summer morning to meet his fate, and his maker, at Weehawken, N.J.

Dueling died out as a general practice eighty years later in the United States after enjoying quite a vogue, especially in the South and in California. It finally faded, not so much because it was outlawed (like liquor—and war—in the 1920s), but because the "public prejudice" Hamilton was so fatally concerned about changed in this particular. Since dueling was an activity carried out by consenting adults in private, laws prohibiting it were difficult to enforce when the climate of opinion accepted the institution. But gradually a consensus emerged that dueling was contemptible and stupid, and it came to be duelers, not nonduelers, who suffered ridicule. As one student of the subject has concluded, "It began to be clear that pistols at ten paces did not settle anything except who was the better shot. . . . Dueling had long been condemned by both statute book and church decree. But these could make no headway against public opinion." However, when it came to pass that "solemn gentlemen went to the field of honor only to be laughed at by the younger generation, that was more than any custom, no matter how sanctified by tradition, could endure. And so the code of honor in America finally died." One of the last duels was in 1877. After the battle (at which no blood was spilled), the combatants found themselves the butt of public hilarity, causing one of them to flee to Paris, where he remained in self-exile for several years.[14]

The American experience was reflected elsewhere. Although dueling's decline in country after country was due in part to enforced legislation against it, the "most effective weapon" against it, one study concludes, "has undoubtedly been ridicule."[15] The ultimate physical cost of dueling—death—did not, and could not, rise. But the psychic costs did.

Men of Hamilton's social set still exist, they still get insulted, and they still are concerned about their self-respect and their standing among their peers. But they don't duel. However, they do not avoid dueling today because they evaluate the option and reject it on cost–benefit grounds—to use the jargon of a later chapter, they do not avoid it because it has become rationally unthinkable. Rather, the option never percolates into their consciousness as something that is available— that is, it has become subrationally unthinkable. Dueling under the right condi- tions—with boxing gloves, for example—would not violate current norms or laws. And, of course, in other social classes duel-like combat, such as the street fight or gang war, persists. But the romantic, ludicrous institution of formal dueling has faded from the scene. Insults of the sort that led to the Hamilton-Burr duel often are simply ignored or, if applicable, they are settled with peaceful methods like litigation.*

A dueling manual from 1847 states that "dueling, like war, is the necessary consequence of offense."[16] By now, however, dueling, a form of violence famed and fabled for centuries, is avoided not merely because it has ceased to seem "necessary," but because it has sunk from thought as a viable, conscious possibil- ity. You can't fight a duel if the idea of doing so never occurs to you or your opponent.

The Prussian strategist Carl von Clausewitz opens his famous 1832 book, *On War,* by observing that "war is nothing but a duel on a larger scale."[17] If war, like dueling, comes to be viewed as a thoroughly undesirable, even ridiculous, policy, and if it can no longer promise gains or if potential combatants no longer value the things it can gain for them, then war could fade away first as a "peculiar necessity" and then as a coherent possibility, even if a truly viable substitute or "moral equivalent" for it were never formulated. Like dueling, it could become unfashionable and then obsolete.

Slavery Abruptly Becomes a "Peculiar Institution"

From the dawn of prehistory until about 1788 it had occurred to almost no one that there was anything the least bit peculiar about the institution of slavery. Like war, it could be found just about everywhere in one form or another, and it flourished in every age.[18] Here and there, some people expressed concern about

*It is sometimes held that dueling died out because improved access to the legal system provided a nonviolent alternative. But most duels were fought over matters of "honor," not legality. Further- more, lawyers, hardly a group alienated or disenfranchised from the legal system, were frequent duelists—in Tennessee 90 percent of all duels were fought between attorneys (Seitz 1929, p. 30).

excessive cruelty, and a few found slavery an unfortunate necessity. But the abolitionist movement that broke out at the end of the eighteenth century in Britain and the United States was something new, not the culmination of a substantial historical process.

Like war opponents, the antislavery forces had come to believe that the institution that concerned them was unacceptable because of both its psychic and its physical costs. For some time a small but socially active religious sect in England and the United States, the Quakers, had been arguing that slavery, like war, was repulsive, immoral, and uncivilized, and this sentiment gradually picked up adherents.

Slavery's physical costs, opponents argued, stemmed from its inefficiency. In 1776, Adam Smith concluded that the "work done by slaves . . . is in the end the dearest of any" because "a person who can acquire no property, can have no other interest but to eat as much and to labor as little as possible." Smith's view garnered adherents, but not, as it happens, among slaveowners. That is, either Smith was wrong, or slaveholders were bad businessmen. Clearly, if the economic argument had been correct, slavery would have eventually died of its own inefficiency. Although some have argued that this process was indeed under way, Stanley Engerman observes that in "the history of slave emancipation in the Americas, it is difficult to find any cases of slavery declining economically prior to the imposition of emancipation." Rather, he says, "it took political and military action to bring it to a halt," and "political, cultural, and ideological factors" played crucial roles. In fact, at exactly the time that the antislavery movement was taking flight, the Atlantic slave economy, as Seymour Drescher notes, "was entering what was probably the most dynamic and profitable period in its existence."[19]

Thus, the abolitionists were up against an institution that was viable, profitable, and expanding, and one that had been uncritically accepted for thousands—perhaps millions—of years as a natural and inevitable part of human existence. To counter this time-honored institution, the abolitionists' principal weapon was a novel argument: it had recently occurred to them, they said, that slavery was no longer the way people ought to do things.

As it happened, it was an idea whose time had come. The abolition of slavery required legislative battles, international pressures, economic travail, and, in the United States, a cataclysmic war (but, notably, it did *not* require the fabrication of a functional equivalent or the formation of an effective supranational authority). Within a century slavery, and most similar institutions like serfdom, had been all but eradicated from the face of the globe. Slavery became controversial, then peculiar, and then obsolete.

War

Dueling and slavery no longer exist as effective institutions and have faded from human experience except as something one reads about in books. Although their reestablishment is not impossible, they show after a century of neglect no signs of revival. Other once-popular, even once-admirable, institutions in the developed world have been, or are being, eliminated because at some point they began to seem repulsive, immoral, and uncivilized: bearbaiting, bareknuckle fighting, freak shows, casual torture, wanton cruelty to animals, the burning of heretics, Jim Crow laws, human sacrifice, family feuding, public and intentionally painful methods of execution, deforming corseting, infanticide, laughing at the insane, executions for minor crimes, eunuchism, flogging, public cigarette smoking.*

In the remainder of this book the possibility will be explored that war is in the process of joining this list of recently discovered sins and vices. War is not, of course, the same as dueling or slavery. Like war, dueling is an institution for settling disputes; but it usually involved only matters of "honor," not ones of physical gain. Like war, slavery was nearly universal and an apparently inevitable part of human existence, but it could be eliminated area by area: a country that abolished slavery did not have to worry about what other countries were doing. A country that would like to abolish war, however, must continue to be concerned about those that have kept it in their repertoire.

On the other hand, war has against it not only substantial psychic costs but also very obvious and widespread physical ones. Dueling brought death and injury, but only to a few people who, like Hamilton, had specifically volunteered to participate. And although slavery may have brought moral destruction, it generally was a considerable economic success in the view of those who ran the system, if not to every ivory-tower economist.

In some respects, then, the fact that war has outlived dueling and slavery is curious. But there are signs that, at least in the developed world, it has begun, like them, to succumb to obsolescence. Like dueling and slavery, war does not appear to be one of life's necessities—it is not an unpleasant fact of existence that is somehow required by human nature or by the grand scheme of things. One can live without it, quite well in fact. War may be a social affliction, but in important respects it is also a social affectation that can be shrugged off.

*Where death and injury have only been by-products of an institution rather than consequences of its central intent, however, abolitionists have often failed to materialize. For a discussion about the potential value of abolishing the private passenger automobile, the cause of far more death and injury than most wars, see the Appendix.

I

THE DECLINE
AND PERSISTENCE
OF WAR BEFORE
WORLD WAR II

1

The Rise of Peace Advocacy Before World War I

As AN INSTITUTION, war had picked up a fair amount of discredit before 1914. Obviously the discredit was not enough to prevent the two tumultuous wars and the many smaller ones that have taken place since that time. However, those memorable events should not be allowed to obscure completely the fact that by the turn of the century some interesting and potentially significant patterns contrary to war were in operation and had been gathering momentum for a century or more.

This chapter focuses on four of these developments: (1) the beginning of a quiet retreat from war by some countries in the developed world, (2) the rise in the nineteenth century for the first time in history of an organized and vocal antiwar movement, (3) the occurrence of the first modern war—the American Civil War of 1861–65, and (4) the formation and propogation by antiwar activists of various remedies for and alternatives to war.

States Begin to Drift Away from War

Judging from the way they have strained to justify war, countries in the developed world over the last centuries have become somewhat uncomfortable with it. Some, in fact, have tried to drop out of the war system entirely, and here and there (as in North America) once-hostile neighbors have managed to establish conditions of perpetual peace.

War Becomes Rather Embarrassing.

In his insightful survey of war since 1400, *War in International Society*, Evan Luard describes an interesting change in the way war has been justified. In the first century or two of that period, no justification seemed necessary— war was seen as a "glorious undertaking" and a "normal feature of human existence, a favorite pastime for princes and great lords." By 1700 or so, however, attitudes had changed enough so that rulers found they were "expected to proclaim their own love of peace and their desire to avoid the tragedies of war"—although they still managed to concoct plenty of reasons to fight, and they continued to find war a "brilliant way to win glory," as Louis XIV of France put it.

The notion that war was normal, honorable, and in some respects desirable, persisted in the nineteenth century, as discussed more fully in the next chapter. But by then, as Luard observes, leaders "found it necessary to proclaim that war had been 'forced' on them." After World War I, leaders felt a heightened sense of necessity: even among those who were actively planning war, "affirmations of peaceful intent now became obligatory." Thus, Japan invaded China "to establish peace in the east without delay," Mussolini invaded Albania "to restore law and order" there, and Hitler invaded Poland because he claimed the Poles had committed "21 frontier incidents" which made the situation quite "intolerable."[1]

These shifts in justification suggest that changing attitudes toward war caused some of the twentieth century's chief warmongers to alter their rhetoric at least. They still managed to get into wars, of course. But no longer was it possible simply and honestly to proclaim like Julius Caesar, "I came, I saw, I conquered." Gradually this has changed to "I came, I saw, he attacked me while I was just standing there looking, I won." This might be seen as progress.

The Hollandization Phenomenon.

While some countries were questing after creative justifications for their wars, others were altering their whole international life-style and seeking to avoid war entirely.

World histories are preoccupied particularly with discussions of the comings and goings of those countries viewed as the "Great Powers." Determining exactly which countries in any historical period are Great Powers can be a bit tricky, because no one knows for sure what "power" is; therefore, deciding who has an especially large amount of it at any point calls for creativity. Nevertheless, a considerable consensus exists among analysts.[2] They tend to agree, for example, that Austria-Hungary was a Great Power in 1880 (although, perhaps, a "sick" one), only to be unceremoniously dropped from the register in 1918. Japan was once a rather sleepy place, but eventually it woke up, got its act together, achieved Great Power status early in the twentieth century, lost it in 1945, and, in classic Great Power terms at least, hasn't been heard from since. In 1880 the United States was far wealthier and potentially more potent militarily than almost any Great Power; but, oddly, it kept pretty much to itself, letting others "run" the world, and was not an accepted member of the club. (Soon, however, it began to find itself throwing its considerable weight around and has since gone on to become so awesome that its "power" status is now often designated by the comic-book prefix *super*.)

In general then, Great Powers are militarily significant countries that choose to engage in a game with other Great Powers in which each uses or threatens to use its military resources to advance its interests. Their interactions are often called a system (although *syndrome* might be a better word), and prowess in war is one of the chief indicators of Great Power status. "All historians agree," observed Leo Tolstoy in *War and Peace* in 1869, that states express their conflicts in wars and "that as a direct result of greater or lesser success in war the political strength of states and nations increases or decreases." Says Kenneth Waltz a century later, "The story of international politics is written in terms of the great powers of an era."[3]

As a chronicle of how the Great Powers roam the world arena, then, international history has tended to deal extensively with the preludes to, and consequences of, war, and to treat it as a fairly normal element of international life. As Hans J. Morgenthau declares (rather tautologically), "The history of nations active in international politics shows them continuously preparing for, actively involved in, or recovering from organized violence in the form of war."[4] But history also shows that some countries which had the means and potential to be Great Powers chose not to be "active" in his sense. Consequently, they go almost totally unmentioned in Morgenthau's influential textbook on international relations.

Some of these countries were Great Powers which came upon hard times and resigned themselves to existing as nongreatpowers rather than make the painful sacrifices necessary to regain their former exalted status. The Netherlands, for example, was a Great Power until 1713. A wealthy, central, even dominant, country, it got involved in the usual quota of conflicts. After 1713, however, it dropped out of the Great Power system and concentrated on commercial and colonial ventures. Although it has occasionally been swept into wider conflicts by others, for over two and a half centuries Holland has generally sought to avoid all international war in Europe, a pattern that can be called Hollandization.

Sweden, a Great Power—and a very warlike one—in the seventeenth century, lost that status by 1721 after a series of wars that left Russia as the dominant country in the Baltic area. Once, as one historian observes, "Sweden had been drunk with victory and bloated with booty"; but eventually, "in the grey light of everyday existence," the country decided to prepare for "a future of weight and dignity as a second-class power."[5] Swedish kings tried warfare again a few times between 1741 and 1814, sometimes being deposed by domestic opponents in the process. Thereafter, the Swedes largely lost whatever residual enthusiasm for war they could still muster, and they have now been at peace with the world for over a century and a half.

Spain was nothing if not a Great Power in most of the fifteenth through eighteenth centuries. Decline led to a fall from grace by 1808 at the latest, and the country has been content to be a nongreatpower ever since, avoiding all international war except for a few conflicts in the colonies and a brief, distant fracas with the United States in 1898.

There are also European countries that might have struggled into the Great Power club, or at least have gotten into the fringe of the war game, but simply chose not to. They were Hollandized in advance. The best case is Switzerland, a first-class military power in 1500. As one historian has observed, the Swiss have consistently shown a "curious indifference" to "political or territorial aggrandizement."[6] Curious, indeed: the Swiss merely avoided war and became prosperous. Denmark, often very warlike in some early periods, has followed a similar course, as, generally, has Portugal.

To be sure, most of these nongreatpowers were smaller and economically less impressive than, say, Britain or France over this period. But with enough effort some of them could have lingered for a while in the ranks of the Great Powers; enough, at least, to rival the less great Great Powers like Italy or Austria-Hungary. In 1710, when they were dropping out, Holland and Sweden each had armies bigger than those of Britain or Austria, and far larger than those of Prussia.[7] The sacrifices to remain in the club would probably have been proportionately no more than those the Soviet Union has borne in its costly effort to keep up militarily with the United States in the period since 1945 or those Israel has borne in seeking to pursue its destiny in the Middle East or those North Vietnam bore to expand its control into South Vietnam or those Japan paid to enter the club early in this century. But the Hollandized countries have concluded that the status simply isn't worth the cost and effort, and that the wars that go with the status don't really seem very interesting or enjoyable. (The aloofness, or neutrality, of these countries from war has sometimes been variously overseen by other, stronger countries. But that didn't cause their desire to leave the war system; it simply helped facilitate it. Moreover, at least two Hollandized countries, Sweden and Switzerland, have, in fact, armed themselves to the earlobes to maintain their neutrality.)

The Hollandized countries' responses refute two popular notions: first, that international war is endemic to human nature, and second, that war or "war fever" is cyclic. If either of these propositions is true, one would expect the Swiss, Danes, Swedes, Dutch, and Spaniards to be positively *roaring* for a fight by now.[8]

The Long Undefended Border.

Americans and Canadians are so accustomed to living peacefully side by side that it is easy to assume this has always been the case.[9] But once there was enormous hostility between the United States and British Canada, and it was registered in two wars: the American War of Independence of 1775–83 and the War of 1812–14. One cause of the latter was the desire of many Americans to take over their northern neighbor.

The war ended rather inconclusively and without a clear-cut winner largely because the Napoleonic Wars in Europe, to which it was a side show, came to an end. The United States and British Canada then lapsed into a period of wary coexistence. Impelled as much by economic exhaustion as anything else, the United States reduced its fleet of warships on the lakes between the countries and proposed that the British do likewise. The British, who were also in the process of reducing their fleet somewhat, eventually agreed, and the results were formalized in the Rush-Bagot Agreement of 1817, which placed exact limits on the number, size, and armaments of warships.

But there was no provision actually to destroy warships, and both sides kept some in dockyards where they could always be put into action should the need arise. Furthermore, there was quite a bit of evasion and technical violation over the next half century: the agreement's stipulation about ship tonnages soon became obsolete as iron ships were introduced, while the United States built "revenue cutters," and the British built merchant steamers that could easily be converted to military use if necessary. Both sides continued to build forts along the border (at one point the overzealous Americans accidentally built one in Canadian territory and had to abandon it), and the British created an extensive and expensive canal system in Canada as a military supply line.

These arms developments were accompanied by a series of conflicts between the two neighbors. There were border skirmishes in 1837, a crisis in 1839 in disagreement about the boundary between Maine and New Brunswick, continual war apprehension over the Oregon boundary (settled in 1846), and sporadic raids by Irish-Americans into British Canada. Meanwhile, many Americans were caught up in the romantic notion that it was somehow in their "manifest destiny to overspread the continent allotted by Providence for the free development of our yearly multiplying millions."[10] Because of heightened hostility during the American Civil War, the British sent 11,000 troops to strengthen its garrisons, and in 1864 there was a raid from Canada on a Vermont town by a band of Confederate soldiers that caused the United States to give notice that it was withdrawing from the Rush-Bagot Agreement (a notice that was itself withdrawn within a few months).

By the early 1870s, however, most of the claims and controversies had been settled. Canada was granted independent status in part because British taxpayers were tired of paying the costs of defending their large, distant colony, and with the Americans focusing on settling the West and recovering from their calamitous civil war, it seemed safe to begin to withdraw the British army from Canada. Without formal agreement, disarmament gradually took place between the two countries, and their forts became museums where rusting cannon still point accusingly but impotently in the direction of the nearby former enemy.

Peace came about mainly because both sides became accustomed to, and generally pleased with, the status quo. In simple fact, there no longer seemed to be any outstanding issue worth fighting over.[11] The idea of war between these former enemies faded, like dueling, beyond the realm of conscious possibility. If war is intrinsic to human nature, these two countries have somehow managed to suppress that instinct, at least as it pertains to their most likely target; and if countries can be expected to overcome their natural war-weariness after a period of peace, the Americans and Canadians seem to be singularly slow in doing so.

Today the Rush-Bagot Agreement has been hopelessly shattered in every way but spirit. As it happens, the two countries have found the Great Lakes to be convenient places to build, refit, and test warships, and by mutual agreement each maintains a naval arsenal there that dwarfs anything imaginable in 1817. If all the Canadian and American warships in the Great Lakes were to turn on each other and on each other's territory, the damage would be substantial. Each country lives with a tinderbox at its doorstep, but neither worries in the slightest about a dropped match. That's peace.

The Rise of the Liberal State.

It has amused a Canadian observer to note that relations between the United States and Britain were improved by any developments which served "to reduce the number of Americans who still thought of Britain in terms of King George III, and to multiply those who knew her as a sister democracy."[12] The phenomenon seems to be general: liberal democracies tend to get along with each other amazingly well. In fact, as Michael Doyle has shown, for the 200 years during which there have been liberal countries, no constitutionally secure liberal states have ever gone to war with one another.[13]

Building upon criteria and reasoning suggested by Immanuel Kant in his 1795 essay *Perpetual Peace,* Doyle defines a liberal regime as one that is externally sovereign, has a market and private property economy, gives its citizens juridical rights, and has a representative form of government with reasonably wide suffrage. There may be a few cases where one might quibble. Doyle determines that Britain became liberal only with the Reform Act of 1832, so the War of 1812 does not register as a war among liberal states. Moreover, the American Civil War might count as a war between two liberal entities, if not states, but Doyle considers the South to have been illiberal until 1865. There were also substantial elements of liberalism in Germany in 1914, particularly on domestic issues; but Doyle argues that Germany was essentially authoritarian on foreign affairs, a realm controlled by the kaiser and the army.[14]

With or without such caveats, the broad generalization is striking and provocative. Even though liberal countries have varied enormously in size, military strength, and economic effectiveness; even though they have had plenty of disagreements; and even though they have often gone to war against illiberal regimes, they have been remarkably good at staying out of war with each other. "Balances of power," colonial rivalries, fits of nationalistic ego, hegemonic and "power-maximizing" ambitions, seductive new weapons, dashing military doctrines—these have all come and gone, waxed and waned, over the last two centuries. Yet liberal countries have managed to carve out a separate, and apparently perpetual, peace among themselves.[15]

Part of the explanation for the phenomenon is that liberal countries subscribe to what Doyle calls a "basic postulate of liberal international theory": the notion that "states have the right to be free from foreign intervention."[16] If liberal states believe that—at least as far as it pertains to other liberal states—then no liberal state has much to fear from any other liberal state. Essentially, then, since liberal countries tend to regard each other as legitimate and unthreatening, wars among them are seen as immoral and unwise: immoral because they would involve intervention against a just state and unwise because there is no perceived threat to counter or contain.

That may put the liberal mystique into terms that are a bit too neat and syllogistic, but the evidence of two centuries strongly suggests that something like that has been going on. And it is an attitude or pattern of thought, not weaponry, that has prevented war within the liberal community. The liberal British, after all, could destroy American cities with nuclear weapons almost as readily as the Soviet Union could, yet the liberal United States does not worry about that prospect.

Of course it may be that war-avoiding liberalism is just a fad that will eventually fade or evolve into something else. In the broad sweep of history perhaps that is to be expected. But for now, and for some time to come, liberalism seems to be on an upswing. By Doyle's calculation there were only two liberal countries in 1800—Switzerland and the United States (and then only in certain cantons or states). There were twelve by 1900, thirty-three by 1950, and forty by 1980.[17] To that degree, at least, peace within large and important portions of the planet is likely to be around for a while.

The Rise of Antiwar Activism

The idea that war is foolish and contemptible is certainly not a recent one. Euripides wrote *The Trojan Women,* a play that is often taken to be a powerful statement against war, in 415 B.C.[18] In Roman days the Stoics were antimilitaristic, as were the early Christians—although after St. Augustine determined that war was a punishment from God administered by men, Christianity became, as Michael Howard has put it, "one of the great warrior religions of mankind."[19] The Dutch humanist Erasmus railed against war and its stupidities in such works as the satire *Praise of Folly* in 1509, and several other notable thinkers from that era and from somewhat later ones opposed war and proposed remedies: Sir Thomas More, John Colet, the Spaniard Juan Luis Vives, the French monk Eméric Crucé, the Duc de Sully, and Voltaire.[20] There have also been war opponents within Eastern religious movements, particularly the pacifist Jains of India.

The Quakers: War Is Immoral.

However, the first group that actively and persistently worked to reform war out of the human spirit seems to have been the Quakers. Formed in England in 1652 in the aftermath of the Thirty Years War and of the English Civil War, the Quakers stress in their faith that God can be found in, and speaks through, every person. This notion has led them to revere not only the human soul but also human life. It has also led them to renounce the taking of life. At the same time, Quakers have generally been devoted to social activism, and they have often been able to work from a secure and respected place in society because their principles of diligence, strict honesty, frugality, and deep respect for the humanity of others have very frequently caused them to prosper in business.[21] (It may be an exaggeration to characterize twentieth-century liberal democratic society as a Quaker invention, but the Quakers were among the very first to work actively for principles that form an important basis of that society. These principles include not only opposition to war and slavery but also religious tolerance; social concern for the poor, the insane, the infirm, and the imprisoned; equality by class, sex, and race; opposition to capital punishment and clericism; freedom of speech and assembly; and reverence for human life.)

While Quakers were creating such major businesses as Lloyd's of London and Barclay's Bank in England and founding the colony of Pennsylvania across the Atlantic, they were also beginning to use friendly persuasion to conduct what they like to call their "lamb's war" against social injustice. By the beginning of the nineteenth century their remarkably original and revolutionary idea that slavery was an evil was very much catching on (see pp. 11–18). But they had made little progress against war.

The Napoleonic Wars of 1803–1815, however, inspired substantial revulsion against war, and in 1814 and 1815 the first antiwar societies in history were formed in New York and London by Quakers and others. The movement spread throughout Europe and North America. Although it waned somewhat in the middle of the century, it was soon reinvigorated and was a political force of some potency by the end of the century—by no means dominant, but certainly noticeable. Books and pamphlets were published, international meetings were held, protests were registered, antiwar novels were penned, and dispute-solving mechanisms like international arbitration were advocated and organized.[22]

The Humanists: War Is Repulsive and Uncivilized.

In addition to those who, like the Quakers, renounced war for moral or religious reasons, there were many in the antiwar movement who opposed war

25

for reasons that were essentially aesthetic or humanistic: they found it repulsive and uncivilized. Moreover, as civilization advanced, they believed, war would wane.

Particularly inspiring to many were the writings in midcentury of the British historian Henry Thomas Buckle. After 1814, Europe experienced something new and remarkable: a long period free from significant war. Buckle discounted the peace-breaking Crimean War of 1854 because it was produced by the conflicting interests of Russia and Turkey ("the two most barbarous monarchies now remaining in Europe") and concluded that the "warlike spirit" was "steadily declining." The progress he hailed was intellectual, not moral: "As intellectual acquisitions of people increase, their love of war will diminish." War truly flourishes, he argued, only "in perfectly barbarous countries" where "the mind being a blank and dreary waste, the only resource is external activity, the only merit personal courage." As early as 1849, Ralph Waldo Emerson had expressed similar sentiments: "War is on its last legs; and a universal peace is as sure as is the prevalence of civilization over barbarism. . . . The question for us is only *how soon?*"[23]

Between 1854 and 1871 some of the more "civilized" countries of Europe managed to get into several wars with each other, and a massive civil war took place in the (at least semicivilized) United States. But the notion that peace was progressing and the warlike spirit declining in the civilized world survived these embarrassments.[24] And when Europe lapsed after 1871 into another period of peace that was to last over forty years, the notion gained renewed vigor. In 1889, Bertha von Suttner, who had been deeply influenced by Buckle's book, published her vivid, if stilted, antiwar novel, *Die Waffen Nieder!*, in which she shattered literary precedent by describing in detail the grotesque cruelties of warfare. The novel, which was exultantly compared to *Uncle Tom's Cabin* by pacifist Leo Tolstoy, and which has been called the "greatest Peace novel of all time," created a sensation—thirty-seven editions in over a dozen languages. It made Suttner into perhaps the most famous woman in Europe and helped enormously to fuel the antiwar movement. For all its handwringing and protest, however, the novel comes to an optimistic conclusion. It proclaims Europe to be "already standing at the gate of a new period" and edging away from "savagery, with its idols and weapons." "Hail to the future!"[25]

As the world advanced toward World War I through a period of crisis and near-war, the notion of progress remained bright. In 1911 the distinguished British historian G. P. Gooch concluded elegaically, "We can now look forward with something like confidence to the time when war between civilized nations will be considered as antiquated as the duel, and when peacemakers shall be called the children of God."[26]

26

The Economists: War and Conquest Are Futile.

Joining in the movement were a number of practical people who had concluded that war and conquest, which they took to be the chief goal of war, were economically counterproductive.

Versions of this idea had been around for some time. In 1795, reflecting a view of Montesquieu and others, Immanuel Kant argued that the "spirit of commerce" is "incompatible with war" and that, as commerce inevitably gains the "upper hand," states would seek "to promote honorable peace and by mediation to prevent war."[27]

Peace activists of the next century were quick to make a similar argument and often with a similar sense of optimism. Particularly prominent were two Englishmen, Richard Cobden and John Bright, a Quaker, who saw international peace as one of the benefits of free and unfettered trade. Buckle also considered the economic discoveries of Adam Smith to be one of the "leading ways" in which the "warlike spirit" had "been weakened by the progress of European knowledge," and in 1848 John Stuart Mill concurred: "It is commerce which is rapidly rendering war obsolete."[28]

As if to prove the economists correct, several important businessmen joined the movement by the end of the century. Andrew Carnegie funded an Endowment for International Peace in New York, and a Swede who had become rich by discovering how to handle nitroglycerin without being blown up funded the Nobel Peace Prize to honor people who were trying to discover how the nations of the world could handle their affairs without blowing each other up.

One of the most influential proponents of the economic position was an English journalist, Norman Angell. In 1908 he sought a publisher for a book he had written concluding that war and conquest were incompatible with economic progress and gain: "It is a logical fallacy," Angell declared, "to regard a nation as increasing its wealth when it increases its territory." Britain, he pointed out, "owned" Canada and Australia in some sense, yet it certainly did not get the products of those countries for nothing—it had to pay for them just as though they came "from the lesser tribes in Argentina or the USA." The British, in fact, could not get those products any cheaper than the Germans. Thus, he asked, "If Germany conquered Canada, could the Germans get the wheat for nothing? Would the Germans have to pay for it just as they do now? Would conquest make economically any real difference?" The popular notion that there were limited supplies in the world and that countries had to fight to get their share was nonsense, Angell argued. Indeed, he contended, "the great danger of the modern world is not absolute shortage, but dislocation of the process of exchange, by which alone the fruits of the earth can be made available for human consumption."[29]

Angell recalls that all the publishers he took the manuscript to "shied violently" from it on the grounds that "the public do not and cannot be persuaded to read books about 'peace'." As it happens, they were wrong. Angell cut the manuscript down and paid to have it published privately as a 126-page pamphlet; within a few months it had become the talk of London. Then, expanded and retitled *The Great Illusion,* it achieved formal publication and eventually went into several editions and many printings, selling over a million copies in at least seventeen languages.[30]

Critics, such as the prominent American naval historian Admiral A. T. Mahan, found two central problems with Angell's thesis. One was with his economics. Some wars, particularly short and cheap ones, could be economically beneficial, they said. Conquest could provide a place to send excess population, could establish a country in a predominant position, and could break down invidious tariff barriers by superimposing wider governments over pettier factions; after all, large businesses are often more profitable than small ones.

The other criticism concerned Angell's emphasis on economics. Mahan and others argued that even if it were true that war is economically unprofitable, nations mainly fight for motives other than economic ones; for example, for "ambition, self-respect, resentment of injustice, sympathy with the oppressed."[31]

Angell replied by continuing to stress that the inescapable economic chaos of war "makes economic benefit from victory impossible." And, while fully aware that motives other than economic greed very often impel countries into war, he argued that nations fight for "what they believe to be their rights, particularly the most elementary of all rights, the right to existence, the right of a population to bread and a decent livelihood." By stressing how war impinged on this "right," Angell hoped to reason with the warmakers, encouraging them to explore other, less costly, methods of reducing disagreement and pursuing their destinies.[32]

Angell helped to crystallize a line of reasoning that has been gaining in acceptability ever since. Even at the turn of the century proponents were hard-pressed to discover clear economic advantage in war. For example, Mahan conceded that "nations are under no illusion as to the unprofitableness of war in itself" and called it "a commonplace" to conclude "that war between two great nations injures both." That "commonplace" has since become even more common.[33]

Also very much gaining in credence is Angell's suggestion that nations with a "sense of proportion" should come to realize that "bread and a decent livelihood" are of paramount concern, not such vague and elastic goals as "honor" and "power" and "influence." A nation's "wealth, prosperity, and well-being . . . depend in no way upon its military power," argued Angell, noting that "the citizens of Switzerland, Belgium, or Holland, countries without 'control,' or navy, or bases, or 'weight in the councils of Europe,' or 'the prestige of a great Power,' are just as well off as Germans, and a great deal better off than Austrians or Russians."[34]

War is unlikely if countries take prosperity as their chief goal *and* if they come to believe that war is a poor way to achieve that goal. That line of thought has become quite popular since Angell's book was first published and is discussed more fully later.[35]

Other War Opponents.

Opposition to war was being voiced by other activists as well. Many feminists accepted world peace as a desirable goal, although their central concerns involved other issues. Socialists often shied away from the bourgeois peace societies and, indeed, often advocated revolutionary violence themselves; however, they tended to see international war as an evil fomented by capitalists and to that degree added their voices to the antiwar protest.[36]

Moreover, many of the wars of the era were protested on specific grounds by people who were by no means pacifists. Substantial opposition existed, particularly in New England, to the War of 1812; Abraham Lincoln criticized the Mexican War and therefore lost his seat in Congress in 1848 (he returned to politics later); and David Lloyd George (later to be Britain's prime minister) actively opposed the Boer War of 1899–1902.

An interesting development in military thinking in the nineteenth century also deserves mention. In 1832, *On War,* an analytic tome by a Prussian officer, Carl von Clausewitz, was published. As the title suggests, the book is largely an analysis of the problems and procedures involved in conducting war, but at center it is a concerted effort to demythologize and deromanticize war. "War," Clausewitz declares in his most quoted, and most misunderstood, aphorism, "is merely the continuation of politics by other means." For Clausewitz war did not have a life or existence of its own: it was not "something autonomous," but simply— merely—"an instrument of policy." To fight a war for the sake of war was for Clausewitz, if not for many of the dashing officers of his century, utterly ridiculous. As an analyst and theorist, Clausewitz had only limited impact on military thought in his own century, but he was to become quite influential in the next one.[37]

Resistance to the Antiwar Movement.

By 1914, then, war as an institution had for the first time in history inspired a significant amount of organized disdain and opposition on moral, ideological, and practical grounds. However, for all their zeal—indeed in part *because* of it—peace advocates had a substantial image problem. Although they sometimes caught the attention of prominent people—even the czar of Russia for a while—their protests and proposals were often frantic, muddled, and politically naive. The crusadingly idealistic Suttner was characterized by one observer as "a gentle perfume of absurdity," and the public image of her German Peace Society, as one analyst has put it, was of "a comical sewing bee composed of sentimental aunts of both sexes."[38] In England publishers had been unwilling to take on Angell's manuscript mainly because they were fed up with books about peace. Angell tried to assure them that his book was "about peace with a difference"—that it was, to use an anachronism, hard-nosed. The weary publishers waved him away with the suggestion that he try a Quaker publisher, and blunt friends advised him to "avoid that stuff or you will be classed with cranks and faddists, with devotees of Higher Thought who go about in sandals and long beards, live on nuts."[39]

As discussed in the next chapter, war opposition was far from a majority view in 1914; and, of course, the essential impotence of the movement was to be demonstrated with the cataclysmic war that began in August of that year—a war in which most peace activists soon found themselves taking sides. (Mercifully, perhaps, Bertha von Suttner died in June.)

But peace activism was on the march by 1914, and the marchers were winning converts and felt a strong, and not entirely unjustified, sense of progress. In his memoirs, Norman Angell even allows himself a wistful speculation about the incident that triggered the war: "If the fanatic's shot at Sarajevo had been delayed a few years, Western Europe might have acquired a mood which would have enabled it either to avoid the war, or if the war had come, to have made afterwards a peace that would not have led to the Second World War."[40]

Be that as it may, the people questing after that "mood" were about to be given an enormous boost by the very institution they so passionately opposed. World War I may have shattered their short-term hopes and clipped their myopic optimism, but it also established their respectability, vastly multiplied their numbers, and hardened their determination.

The American Civil War

For huge majorities in the developed world, World War I permanently discredited major war both as an appealing activity and as a potentially profitable instrument of national policy. Some of the experiences and results of that war, however, were anticipated in a war that took place half a century earlier—the American Civil War, a calamity that has often been called the first total war or the first modern war.

Great issues were at stake in 1861—slavery and the splintering of the Union—but it was not clear that these would necessarily lead to war. The fighting was begun by war-eager hotheads in South Carolina who were imbued, like many other Southerners, with a romantic, almost chivalric conception of war and honor—the "Sir Walter disease," Mark Twain called it, arguing that the immense popularity of the novels of Sir Walter Scott "had so large a hand in making Southern character, as it existed before the war, that he is in great measure responsible for the war."[41] War was triggered in an appropriately romantic fashion by an event that was both consequential and costless: the shelling and forced surrender of the federal garrison at Fort Sumter in Charleston harbor, a battle in which no one—no one—was killed. After the battle two federal soldiers were accidentally killed during a ceremonial salute, and they became the first fatalities in a war that eventually claimed the lives of 623,026 soldiers (one for every six slaves) and cost nearly eight times as much money as it would have taken to purchase the freedom of every slave in the country.[42]

After Sumter, men on both sides flocked excitedly to enlist for an adventure that was widely expected to be concluded quickly in one or two decisive encounters—enlistments were commonly for only three months.[43] This anticipation may have come close to fulfillment, because the first major battle, at Manassas in northern Virginia, was a clear success for the South. Had the victors pursued their advantage by capturing the nearby underdefended federal capital at Washington, the war could possibly have been settled at that point.

Instead, however, the adventure degenerated into four years of bitter attrition warfare characterized by huge battles that were both excruciatingly indecisive and unprecedentedly costly: in battle after battle more men perished than had been killed in all previous American wars. Eventually, one of the Northern military leaders, William Tecumseh Sherman, sometimes reckoned the first modern general, helped devise a strategy in which his troops were sent across Georgia and South Carolina sowing a wide path of devastation in order to hamper supplies and communication and to break the Southern will to resist. "We have made fine progress today in the work of destruction," he reported in 1863. "The inhabitants are subjected. They cry aloud for mercy. The land is devastated for 30 miles around." For Sherman war was "hell" and "cruelty," and he believed that "the crueler it is, the sooner it will be over."[44]

The purpose of Sherman's "fine progress" was not only to end the war as quickly as possible but also to teach a long-range lesson: As he explained it, "We cannot change the hearts of those people of the South, but we can make them so sick of war that generations would pass away before they would again appeal to it." And in a victory speech at the end of the war, he admonished, "For fifty years to come, at least, I never want to hear a word about war in America."[45]

The war resembled World War I in its casual ignition, in its opening enthusiasm, in its grindingly inconclusive battles, and in its bitter, catastrophic costs. But these alone were not enough to bring about the kind of visceral disillusionment with war that followed World War I: "No demythologizing of the soldier and of combat took place at that time, nor did any renunciation of war as a social experience, as occurred following the Great War," notes Gerald Linderman. Indeed, by the end of the century, as discussed in the next chapter, war was again being touted in many quarters of the United States as a great romantic adventure: as Twain grumbled in the 1870s, the "harms" committed by Scott's novels still lingered, and "in our South they flourish pretty forcefully still."[46]

Thus, as suggested in the Introduction, extensive physical costs in war are not enough alone to stamp out what Buckle called the "warlike spirit"; the sense that war is repulsive, immoral, and/or uncivilized must also be there. The American Civil War, despite its huge physical costs, apparently was too early historically for these combined forces to mesh and to have the impact in America that they were to have in the developed world a half century later.

But the war did create a bone-deep war-weariness, a pervasive sense of loss, and that has proved to be lasting at least as it pertains to the "war in America" that Sherman hoped might be put off for fifty years or for generations. Since 1864 there have been scores, possibly hundreds, of civil wars in the world, but unless one considers the conflicts with American Indians to be civil wars, none of these have taken place in the United States. After 1864 Americans, like the English two centuries earlier, became permanently sick of civil war. Neither the South nor any other section of the country has ever risen again—or, apparently, has ever even considered it seriously. On that score, Sherman proved to be a pessimist.* The experience of over a century suggests that the idea of civil war in the United States has become obsolete.

---

*This came largely from memories of the war experience itself, not from the persistent policing actions of the federal army. Indeed, that army, a million strong during the war, was soon reduced to a ghost: ten years after the war its authorized strength was 27,000, and in 1881 war opponent Andrew Carnegie was happily claiming that "the glory of America" lay in the fact that it had "no army worth the name" (Linderman 1987, pp. 272–73).

Remedies for War

By 1914 a great many people had given a great deal of thought to the issue of war and how it might be prevented or its effects mitigated and had proposed a wide variety of remedies or partial remedies. All of these proposed solutions are still with us, and it would be useful to summarize them.

Solve the Root Causes of War.

Quakers have taken the lead in advancing the proposition that all violence, including the organized violence of war, is wrong, immoral, and illegitimate, and they have sought to repudiate and banish it in part by refusing to participate in it. Others have seen the essential causes of war in poverty and injustice and believe war can be eliminated if those evils are eradicated. Some, like Angell, see an important root cause in the popular notion that one can profit economically from war; their solution is to appeal to reason to show the falsehood of this assumption and the futility of war for economic gain.

Buckle argued that the "warlike spirit" was being undermined by intellectual progress. Others, however, like the American intellectual and pacifist William James, found "reason" to be "one of the very feeblest of nature's forces" and proclaimed "our permanent enemy" to be "the rooted bellicosity of human nature." James's remedy, which he felt could be a "moral equivalent to war," was to conscript all youths, forcing them into armylike work battalions digging mines, building roads, constructing skyscrapers, and washing dishes. Others have proposed that commercial competition could serve as an equivalent—moral or otherwise—for the war spirit.[47]

A central cause of war, according to the nineteenth-century Italian writer Giuseppe Mazzini, was that state boundaries did not correspond to national boundaries. Peoples should be grouped according to their natural national aspirations (sometimes it might take war to do this), and governments should then be erected on these bases. Thus, harmony and peace would reign, because everybody would be essentially satisfied.[48]

Others have argued that war arises because certain kinds of states are naturally warlike. Many socialists saw the cause of war in capitalism and imperialism. Karl Marx determined that if "the conflict of classes within nations" were ended, "the hostile attitude of nations against each other" would be removed. He advocated both class war and some kinds of international war to bring about this state of tranquility. Others have characterized authoritarian states or states that are inter-

33

nally unstable as especially warlike or aggressive. Many, including Kant, have maintained that states with representative forms of government are "very cautious" about war because decisions about war are made by those who would have to bear the costs of the "calamities of war," rather than by the ruler who would not have to endure "the least sacrifice of the pleasure of his table, the chase, his country houses, his court functions, and the like."[49]

Change the State System.

Moving to another level of analysis, some commentators have focused on the state system itself, not on the nature of either people or the states themselves.[50] Some sort of world government or world federation has often been proposed as a solution. It would supposedly create an international police force to put down or to deter wars among component members or among warlike outcasts, and thus it would release the international arena from its essentially anarchic condition. Since crime and feuding have not exactly been eliminated even in societies with strong police forces, and since civil war is as frequent and often as costly as international war, this proposed solution with its facile analogy to domestic bliss has had its detractors. Nevertheless, many have seen it as a distinct improvement over what they take to be international anarchy.

Others, like Kant, Buckle, and the antiwar economists, have suggested that a prerequisite for international stability is world community. Although some truly massive wars have taken place between countries that knew each other only too well, they have proposed measures to enhance a sense of community and to eradicate misunderstanding and nationalistic rivalries and jealousies by increasing trade and communications links.

Provide a Substitute for War.

Some people who oppose war would admit that it has some positive effects in that it does generally settle disputes. For them the problem is that it does so in a singularly undesirable manner. Therefore, they propose other mechanisms to get the same result but without the terrible cost: systems of international law or, a very common theme in the last half of the nineteenth century, international arbitration. Also, proposals have been made for cooling-off periods when a dispute arises so that peaceful solutions can be invented and explored.

Control the Symptoms of War.

In part because they despaired of quickly controlling, or even really understanding, the basic or systemic roots of war, some individuals proposed in the late nineteenth century that the increasingly destructive instruments of war be controlled instead—a theme that, of course, came to dominate antiwar discussions after the invention of the atomic bomb in 1945. Some argue that the arms themselves can cause wars, perhaps through the mechanism of the arms race or through weapons accidents; others believe that countries that do not have arms readily at hand will at least have more difficulty getting into war and that, even if they do, the wars will be less destructive. Furthermore, arms control and disarmament measures can be used to reduce the advantage of a surprise attack, and they can reduce the control of munitions makers, whom some see as a sinister, self-interested force for war.

Most proponents of arms control and/or disarmament also hope that measures which restrict armaments will lead to more fundamental improvements—easing tensions and enhancing sympathetic understanding among potential enemies.

Make War Bearable.

If the calamitous nature of war could be somehow constrained, then war would at least be somewhat bearable, although perhaps still undesirable. Limitation of damage is, after all, something that might appeal to all combatants; therefore, it might well be more easily accomplished than an elimination of war itself, however admirable that might be as an ultimate goal.

In the late nineteenth century quite a bit of effort was made along these lines, leading to the establishment of the Red Cross, to the Geneva Conventions of 1864 and 1909 (further elaborated in 1925, 1929, 1949, and 1977), and to other agreements at St. Petersburg in 1868 and The Hague in 1899 and 1907. These efforts provided that prisoners of war and the wounded should receive humane treatment and that as much as possible killings should be limited to young men in uniform.

Make War Worse.

As discussed more fully in the next chapter, one reason peace advocates were so ineffectual at the turn of the century was that many people simply hadn't come to agree with their central premise that war is bad. The antiwar activists desperately needed to establish the soundness of this premise, because all their proposals and gimmicks and devices to deal with war sprang from that crucial axiom. They tried to handle their problem by declaiming their premise loudly, repeatedly, and with shrill urgency. But most people were deaf to, even contemptuous of, their cry.

Occasionally the idea surfaced in the years before the Great War that what the peace activists really needed was for war to become so much worse that their premise would in consequence become fully convincing and utterly inescapable. In the early 1890s, Alfred Nobel speculated to Bertha von Suttner, who had been his secretary and had helped to urge upon him the idea of a peace prize (which she later won), that "my factories may end war sooner than your congresses." But even as he expressed the hope that "the terrible effects of dynamite would keep men from war," he concluded to his "utter dismay" that his explosives were too limited "to be efficacious." He was "pessimistic about mankind" and decided that "the only thing that will ever prevent them from waging war is terror." What was needed, therefore, was a device that would threaten to destroy an army corps or a whole nation "in a second"—perhaps germ warfare, he speculated, could do the trick. Then "all civilized nations will recoil from war in horror."[51]

The combatants never got around to using germs in the war that followed, but Nobel's sardonic wish was largely fulfilled even without an ultimate weapon. The "civilized nations" of the world did come to recoil from war in horror.

2

A Recent Antiquity: War Advocacy Before World War I

IF WAR IS AN EVIL, it's a mitigated one. That sentiment may sound odd, even perverse, today; but if so, that very fact shows how far we've moved from the not-so-distant days when many people would quite firmly have declared that war was at worst a mitigated good. The great danger in casually assuming that war is unrelievedly evil is that this leads rather logically to the conclusion that wars can be started only by monsters or maniacs. But wars tend to be started by people who, while not necessarily careful of thought or clever of invention, are generally quite reasonable. Such people are far more numerous than monsters and maniacs; but it should be kept in mind by those who find this fact regrettable that reasonable people, unlike monsters and maniacs, are affected by reality and influenced by argument and experience.

In fact, it is possible to say some quite nice things about war. Consider the views of Mahatma Gandhi, probably the most famous pacifist in history. After declaring that "war is an unmitigated evil," he immediately contradicted himself by adding, "But it certainly does one good thing. It drives away fear and brings bravery to the surface."[1] If even war's most devoted enemies can find some limited good in it, its friends and lovers must discern much virtue. Before World War I, war had many such friends and lovers—they may have constituted something of a majority, in fact.

The Appeals of War

Military historian Michael Howard has observed that "before 1914 war was almost universally considered an acceptable, perhaps an inevitable and for many people a desirable way of settling international differences." And, lapsing into intentional hyperbole, he concludes, "The diplomats may have been desperately anxious to avoid a war, as were the businessmen, but . . . they were about the only people who were." It was not only curmudgeonly militarists who found virtue in war. In an extensive study of the attitudes of the era, Roland Stromberg was impressed by "the mountain of tracts and manifestos in which the intellectual elite of Europe embraced the war not merely as unpleasant necessity . . . nor even as potential excitement after many dull years, but as spiritual salvation and hope of regeneration." Bertrand Russell, a rare war opponent, also recalled the widespread support war enjoyed: "I discovered to my amazement that average men and women were delighted by the prospect of war."

It is important, therefore, to appreciate how very long ago 1914 was. In terms of war attitudes it was a different era. Bernard Brodie quotes composer Alban Berg: "Believe me, if the war ended today, we should be back within the same old sordid squalor within a fortnight. . . . The war's great surprise will be in the guns, which are going to show a frivolous generation their utter emptiness." As Brodie concludes, "It would probably be the last time that anyone with pretensions to being a civilized European would express such views." War opponents like Norman Angell—whose lectures at German universities in 1913 were often broken up by rioting students and professors—may have felt history, progress, and logic were on their side; but they were well aware of their difficulties. As Bertha von Suttner acknowledged wistfully in 1912, "War continues to exist not because there is evil in the world, but because people still hold war to be a good thing." And William James pointed out, "The plain truth is that people *want* war."[2]

Despite the Civil War's horrors and trauma, war—at least international war—regained its appeal in the United States by the end of the century. There had been something of a period of war quietism until about 1880—there were few Civil War novels, membership in veterans' organizations was small, and the army fell into low esteem. With a revival of interest in the Civil War came a revival of enthusiasm for things martial, so that by the 1890s war-devastated America was about as war-eager as undevastated Europe. Astoundingly, this change even affected war-is-hell William Tecumseh Sherman. By 1890 he had concluded that war was almost heaven: "Now my friends, there is nothing in life more beautiful than the soldier. A knight errant with steel casque, lance in hand, has always commanded the admiration of men and women. The modern soldier is his legitimate successor. . . . Now the truth is we fought the holiest fight ever fought on God's earth."[3]

Many of the most fervent war supporters seemed beyond logical or practical appeal because they were so intensely romantic about their subject. Others were attracted to war because they believed it to be beneficial and progressive, and many, including some who loathed war, considered it to be natural and inevitable. Most of these views, particularly the romantic ones, were encouraged by the widespread assumption that war in the developed world would be short and cheap.

A consideration of these views is a journey into a recent antiquity, for virtually none of these lines of thinking has serious advocates today, particularly as far as they pertain to international war in the developed world. Indeed, for vast majorities, these patterns of thought, so popular and attractive in 1914, had lost all appeal by 1920, two decades before science had split its first atom.

War Is Noble, Uplifting, Virtuous, Glorious, Heroic, Exciting, Beautiful, Holy, Thrilling.

Gandhi was far from alone in observing that war can bring out admirable qualities like bravery. For example, the distinguished American jurist Oliver Wendell Holmes, Jr., told the Harvard graduating class in 1895 that a world without the "divine folly of honor" would not be endurable. At a time in which he felt he was witnessing "the collapse of creeds," the one thing Holmes found to be "true and adorable" was "the faith . . . which leads a soldier to throw away his life in obedience to a blindly accepted duty, in a cause which he little understands, in a plan of campaign of which he has no notion, under tactics of which he does not see the use."* Winston Churchill, writing in 1900, observed that in civilization "joy" is sacrificed to "luxury," whereas in the field of battle life is "at its best and healthiest" as one "awaits the caprice of the bullet." The great French social scientist Alexis de Tocqueville concluded that "war almost always enlarges the mind of a people and raises their character," and Frederick the Great observed, "War opens the most fruitful field to all virtues, for at every moment constancy, pity, magnanimity, heroism, and mercy shine forth in it;

---

*Holmes's saga was a microcosm of the war spirit in America. He had gone into the Civil War filled with romantic enthusiasm and had become severely disillusioned, referring to battles as "butchery" and praying he might lose a foot to escape further combat. By 1895 he was telling college students that war's message was "divine" (see Linderman 1987, pp. 281–82).

every moment offers an opportunity to exercise one of its virtues." In Britain, Adam Smith held the "art of war" to be "certainly the noblest of all arts," and the nineteenth-century German general Helmuth von Moltke found that war "developed the noblest virtues of man." When the trustees voted in 1898 to admit women to the University of Rochester, local dignitary Susan B. Anthony was elated and called it even "better news to me than victory over Spain." In England the Reverend Father H. I. D. Ryder observed in 1899 that war evokes "the best qualities of human nature, giving the spirit a predominance over the flesh," and he found this true not only for the actual belligerents but also for "all those who care for them at home."[4]

The historian Heinrich von Treitschke in his carefully followed lectures in Germany before the turn of the century assured all listeners that war inspired great selflessness and self-sacrifice, and in that lay war's "sublimity" and "grandeur": "It brings out the full magnificence of the sacrifice of fellow-countrymen for one another . . . the love, the friendliness, and the strength of that mutual sentiment." Treitschke readily acknowledged that war had its unpleasant side, but these defects, he held, were overwhelmed by its many virtues: "War, with all its brutality and sternness, weaves a bond of love between man and man, linking them together to face death, and causing all class distinctions to disappear. He who knows history knows also that to banish war from the world would be to mutilate human nature." In 1913 the German Youth League called war "the noblest and holiest expression of human activity" and found it to be "beautiful" because "its august sublimity elevates the human heart beyond the earthly and the common."[5]

In 1866 the English essayist and art critic John Ruskin delivered a lecture to soldiers at the Royal Military Academy. Ruskin (whose military experience, speculated A. A. Milne, "must have included several drawing-room renderings of *The Charge of the Light Brigade*") expressed his hope that "you love fighting for its own sake," and then went on to assure them that war is the "foundation of all the high virtues and faculties of men."[6]

The thrill, adventure, and sheer excitement of war brought out many paeans in its praise. A popular rhetorical piece by Edward Carpenter, published in the 1880s, concluded with a flurry of exclamation points and capital letters: "From this hour, War! Ever more splendid and glorious War!" The Futurists proclaimed, "There is no beauty except in strife" and proposed to "glorify war." In the United States the usually skeptical folk pundit Finley Peter Dunne, creator of the sage Mr. Dooley, believed "the good reporter, like the good soldier, must look upon war as the supreme adventure in the great drama called Life."[7]

Pacifists often found such exclamations to be profoundly unsettling, gloomily concluding with Bertrand Russell that "the impulse to danger and adventure is deeply ingrained in human nature, and no society which ignores it can long be stable." (So much, as usual, for the Swiss.) Similarly, the American pacifist philosopher William James argued in 1910 that "military feelings are too deeply grounded to abdicate their place among our ideals until better substitutes are offered." War, which he called "supremely thrilling excitement" and "the supreme theater of human strenuousness," has "so far . . . been the only force that can discipline a whole community." His somewhat desperate hope was that the "martial virtues," which he called "absolute and permanent human goods," could be "bred without war" by conscripting all young men into work battalions—a device he claimed could be a "moral equivalent to war." After that experience, he concluded, "they would tread the earth more proudly, the women would value them more highly, they would be better fathers and teachers of the following generation."[8]

War Is Manly.

As his solution suggested, James had concluded that war and the preparations for it were a sort of natural passage for men. He found that war apologists considered peace and the "pleasure-economy" to be "feminism unabashed," and he thought it important that a substitute for war "must make new energies and hardihoods continue the manliness to which the military mind so faithfully clings."[9] That is, it was widely held that militancy and war appeal to real men and peace only to mere women.

In the United States, Homer Lea made a parallel in a 1909 book: "As manhood marks the height of physical vigor among mankind, so the militant success of a nation marks the zenith of its physical greatness." And President Theodore Roosevelt, who was to win the Nobel Peace Prize in 1906, observed in 1901, "We do not admire the man of timid peace. We admire the man . . . who has those virile qualities to win in the stern strife of actual life." Ruskin had gone even further in his discussion in 1866 of "manly war." For him, apparently, even *women* who disliked war were effeminate: "All healthy men like fighting, and like the sense of danger; all brave women like to hear of their fighting, and of their facing danger."[10]

It followed from this that lovers of peace must be effeminate. The 1913 editorial from the German Youth League crowed, "Let us laugh as loud as we can at the old women in men's trousers who are afraid of war and therefore complain that it is ghastly or ugly." By the time he published his memoirs in 1951, Norman Angell found it difficult to explain this prevailing prewar attitude to his readers: "It is perhaps impossible to bring home to one age or generation the intellectual and moral odor of a previous one. At the turn of the century, it was not merely the implication of crankery which made it difficult for any man to state a cause for the avoidance of war. There was the implication of a want of manliness, virility, in such an attitude." But, Angell noted with some satisfaction, "nearly all of this now has, of course, disappeared."[11]

Peace Is Immoral, Decadent, Corrupt, Materialistic, Base.

While war opponents were arguing that war is immoral and economically futile, war advocates were arguing that *peace* is immoral and that to preoccupy oneself with economic concerns is base and corrupt. Thus, said Treitschke, "war is both justifiable and moral. . . . The ideal of perpetual peace is not only impossible but immoral as well." He contended, furthermore, that "it is a false conclusion that wars are waged for the sake of material advantage. Modern wars are not fought for the sake of booty. Here the high moral ideal of national honor is a factor handed down from one generation to another, evoking something positively sacred, and compelling the individual to sacrifice himself to it." The German general Friedrich Bernhardi was of the opinion that "all petty and personal interests force their way to the front during a long period of peace. Selfishness and intrigue run riot, and luxury obliterates idealism. Money acquires an excessive and unjustifiable power, and character does not obtain due respect." Although not a proponent of war, H. G. Wells in 1908 saw considerable virtue in military organization: "When the contemporary man steps from the street of clamorous insincere advertisement, push, adulteration, underselling, and intermittent employment, into the barrack-yard, he steps on to a higher social plane, into an atmosphere of service and co-operation and of infinitely more honorable emulations."[12]

For some it followed that periodic wars were necessary to cleanse the nation from the decadence of peace. Bernhardi approvingly quoted the German philosopher Hegel on this: "Wars are terrible, but necessary, for they save the State from social petrifaction and stagnation." Treitschke noted "the corroding influence of peace" on the Dutch, who once were "a glorious people." War, he found, "fosters the political idealism which the materialist rejects." According to Friedrich Nietzsche, "It is mere illusion and pretty sentiment to expect much (even anything at all) from mankind if it forgets how to make war," and Von Moltke declared "perpetual peace" to be "a dream and not even a beautiful one. . . . Without war, the world would wallow in materialism." Similarly, J. A. Cramb, a British professor of history, characterized universal peace as "a world sunk in bovine content," and, waxing eloquent, considered it "a nightmare which shall be realized only when the ice has crept to the heart of the sun, and the stars, left black and trackless, start from their orbits." Five years before writing his treatise, *Perpetual Peace,* Immanuel Kant had held that "a prolonged peace favors the predominance of a mere commercial spirit, and with it a debasing self-interest, cowardice, and effeminacy, and tends to degrade the character of the nation." It was the German poet Schiller who intoned

> Man is stunted by peaceful days,
> In idle repose his courage decays . . .
> But in war man's strength is seen,
> War ennobles all that is mean.

At Yale, William Graham Sumner identified peace with "selfishness," a time "when men look with indifference upon wickedness and injustice"; war, however, proves that men "have a deeper horror of falsehood than of bloodshed." The president of the Naval War College found peace to be "more degrading" than war's "simple savagery."[13]*

For art critic John Ruskin, war is "the foundation of all great art." "As peace is established . . . the arts decline," and they become costly, "lose their life," and wallow in "luxury and various corruptions." In fact, "among wholly tranquil nations" the arts "wither utterly away," remaining only in "partial practice among races who, like the French and us, have still the minds, though we cannot all live the lives, of soldiers." Peace, he finds, is historically associated not with "loving," "plenty," and "civilization," but rather with "sensuality," "selfishness," "corruption," and "death."[14]

The notion that war could be a purifying, cleansing experience was extremely popular among European intellectuals at the turn of the century. English writer Hilaire Belloc enthusiastically declared, "How I long for the Great War! It will sweep Europe like a broom." A German lawyer, Karl von Stengel, compared war to storms that "cleanse the air and throw decayed and putrid trees to the ground." Georg Heym, a German poet, longed, "If only there were a war, even an unjust one. This peace is so rotten." Stromberg, in his study of intellectual thought of the era, *Redemption by War,* concluded that there was a "similarity of the war mood in all the belligerent countries. The structure of bellicosity was the same in London (or, indeed, Dublin) to Moscow." War was seen "as restoration of community and as escape from a trashy and trivial way of life," even "as salvation." When war finally came, "the commonest images around . . . were the cleansing fire or flood."[15]

*Gerald Linderman argues that the revival of militarism in the United States at the end of the nineteenth century was in part impelled by the desire of ordinary ex-soldiers and others to protest rampant industrialization and to capture some of its popular esteem (1987, pp. 287–90).

War Is Beneficial, Progressive, Necessary.

As noted in the previous chapter, the notion that war is economically profitable was in substantial dispute by 1914. Many saw virtue in conquest, colonization, hegemony, dominance, and expansion, but these were valued at least as much for their beneficial impact on a country's international status and self-respect as for any potential economic advantage.[16]

Still, it was sometimes argued that war, and the preparations for it, acted as a stimulus to economic and technological innovation. In 1908, Wells found commercial advances to be "feeble and irregular" compared to the "steady and rapid development of method and appliances in naval and military affairs." He noted that the household appliances of his era were "little better than they were fifty years ago" but that the "rifle or battleship of fifty years ago was beyond all comparison inferior to those we now possess."[17]

Beyond any short-term economic advances war might stimulate, many found war to be a key element in promoting broad-scale historical development. In severe contradiction to H. T. Buckle and others who argued that progressive forces were on the side of peace, Treitschke proclaimed that "the great strides which civilization makes against barbarism and unreason are only made actual by the sword." "Brave people alone have an existence, an evolution or a future; the weak and cowardly perish, and perish justly. The grandeur of history lies in the perpetual conflict of nations, and it is simply foolish to desire the suppression of their rivalry." Therefore, "the appeal to arms will be valid until the end of history, and therein lies the sacredness of war." Bernhardi maintained that war was a "powerful instrument of civilization" and "a political necessity . . . fought in the interest of biological, social and moral progress." For him it had "a necessary place in historical development" because it was "a regulative element in the life of mankind which cannot be dispensed with." "Without war," Bernhardi asserted, "inferior or decaying races would easily choke the growth of healthy budding elements, and a universal decadence would follow."[18]

In this Treitschke and Bernhardi were reflecting the views of some Social Darwinists like the British statistician Karl Pearson, who felt he had discovered a correlation in 1900: "The path of progress is strewn with the wreck of nations . . . who found not the narrow way to great perfection. These dead peoples are, in very truth, the stepping stones on which mankind has arisen to the higher intellectual and deeper emotional life of today." In 1869, Walter Bagehot, in his book *Physics and Politics,* announced a "law" central to his theory: "Those nations which are the strongest tend to prevail over the others; and in certain marked peculiaries, the strongest tend to be the best." In 1886 a Russian sociologist maintained, "Nature is a vast field of carnage. . . . No cessation is possible.

. . . International policy is the art of conducting the struggle for existence between social organisms." In 1871 a French intellectual, Ernest Renan, called war "one of the conditions of progress, the cut of the whip which prevents a country from going to sleep, forcing satisfied mediocrity itself to leave its apathy"; and in 1899 British intellectual H. W. Wyatt argued, "The only means, revealed to us by past experience, whereby the vigorous people has supplanted the weaker, has been war, without which change and movement must have ceased." In 1891, Émile Zola found war to be "life itself. . . . We must eat and be eaten so that the world might live. It is only warlike nations which have prospered: a nation dies as soon as it disarms." In America, Henry Adams concluded that if war made men "brutal," it also made them "strong" and "called out the qualities best fitted to survive in the struggle for existence"; and Admiral Stephen Luce declared that "war is one of the great agencies by which human progress is effected." One German writer worked himself into ecstasies on the theme in 1907: "War is the great chiming of the world clock . . . the opening of new paths for human culture; the expulsion of stagnation by progress; the struggle of the stronger and more vigorous, with the chance to create new cultural values of a richer existence; a necessity that cannot be eliminated." Or, as Russian composer Igor Stravinsky put it simply, war is "necessary for human progress."[19]

Even some war opponents bought the notion that war could be progressive; they tried to argue, however, that while war may once have been productive and necessary, it was no longer so. In a lecture published in 1849, the American essayist Ralph Waldo Emerson concluded that "in the infancy of society" war was "part of the connection of events, and, in its place, necessary." This was because "war educates the senses, calls into action the will, perfects the physical constitution, brings men into swift and close collision in critical moments that man measures man." But, he felt, "it is the ignorant and childish part of mankind that is the fighting part"; and he argued that since civilization was now maturing and entering "higher stages," war was in "decline"—indeed, "on its last legs." All to the good, opined Emerson, as he approvingly quoted the French scientist and man of letters, Fontenelle: "I hate war, for it spoils conversation."[20]

Herbert Spencer, a prominent Social Darwinist, came to a similar conclusion. Writing in 1908, he argued, "From war has been gained all that it had to give" and "no further benefits are to be looked for." Although "indispensible" as a "process by which nations have been consolidated, organized, and disciplined," and by which "certain traits of individual human nature" have been developed, war had done its work. Since "the peopling of the Earth by the more powerful and intelligent races is in great measure achieved," said Spencer, all that remains is to allow the workings of "the quiet pressure of a spreading industrial civilization on a barbarism which slowly dwindles."[21]

45

War proponents, however, would have none of this. Observed Homer Lea, an American military analyst, in 1909, "Commercialism grows as militancy deteriorates, since it is in itself a form of strife," but it is a "debased one—a combat that is without honor or heroism."[22] No matter how much peace might aid polite conversation, they concluded, it tended to cause crass materialism to take precedence over higher matters.

War Is Natural and Inevitable.

The argument was commonly heard that whether war was progressive or not, it was natural. An American major general, J. V. P. Story, was one of many who held this view: "A few idealists may have visions that with advancing civilization war and its dread horrors will cease. Civilization has not changed human nature. . . . Armed strife will not disappear from the earth until human nature changes." In 1895, Oliver Wendell Holmes maintained that "now, at least, and perhaps as long as man dwells on the globe, his destiny is battle, and he has to take the chances of war." Even William James agreed that bellicosity was "rooted" in "human nature"; and Leo Tolstoy, who was to become an ardent pacifist at the end of the century, concluded in 1868 that men killed each other by the millions to fulfill an "elemental zoological law." Thus, as Story was quick to conclude, "The nature of man makes war inevitable." Cramb found war "a permanent factor in the life of states" and approvingly quoted Frederick the Great: "Running over the pages of history I see that ten years never pass without a war. This intermittent fever may have moments of respite, but cease, never!"[23]

It does not follow, of course, that war will materialize on a particular date just because there is a general feeling that it is inevitable. But, as Robert Jervis has observed, "a major cause of past wars was the belief that armed conflict could not be avoided." That belief was widespread in 1914, fed not only by the notion that war was natural (which Angell tried to counter, ineffectually, by observing that dueling and religious warfare had once also been so regarded), but also by the continuing international tension, imperial rivalries, and the prewar arms competition. Furthermore, because of this belief James Joll has concluded, "the protagonists in 1914 often felt that they were the victims of objective forces which they could not control."[24]

War Is Cheap.

If many people found that there was a great deal to be said in war's favor at the turn of the century, most of them also believed that war's benefits could be achieved at a cost that was bearable. Bernhardi saw only gain: "The appropriate and conscious employment of war as a political means has always led to happy results." Conclusions like these rested largely on the widely held assumption that while war might be nasty and brutish, subsequent wars would be short—and therefore cheap. As Michael Howard has observed, any future war was generally foreseen to be "brief—no longer, certainly, than the war of 1870 that was consciously or unconsciously taken by that generation as a model."[25]

As Emile Driant, a member of the French parliament put it, "The first great battle will decide the whole war, and wars will be short." In 1906 a French general predicted that "the outcome of the next war will be decided in less than a month." When war came in August 1914, the kaiser told departing German troops, "You will be home before the leaves have fallen from the trees." Others in the German camp predicted the war would last six to ten weeks; one anticipated a "short, cleansing thunderstorm," another a "brisk and merry war." In Russia they debated whether the war would take two months or three; the few who guessed six were derided as pessimists and defeatists. The English, too, anticipated a conclusion within a few months.[26]

The short-war thesis was supported by two lines of reasoning, one military, the other economic.

Most military thinkers had come to the conclusion that wars would be short because the fast-paced offensive technically dominated the stodgy defensive. A massive, well-equipped army properly concentrated at the right point could rout the defense: "The best strategy consists in being very strong, first everywhere and then at the decisive point," as one important German commander summarized it. Other Germans chimed in: "Attack is the best defense"; "the offensive mode of action is far superior to the defensive mode." The French declared that their army "no longer knows any other law than the offensive"; and British generals assured all listeners that the offensive "will win as sure as there is a sun in the heavens" and that "the defensive is never an acceptable role to the Briton, and he makes little or no study of it."[27]

The few responsible leaders who took issue with this notion were ineffective in advancing their argument. General Helmuth von Moltke of the German general staff at times said he feared a "long, wearisome struggle" (but at others predicted a short one); and General Joseph Joffre, his counterpart in France, said the war might be of "indefinite duration." However, both continued to plan for a short war and made no allowance in these plans for the possibility that a long war of attrition might occur. More forceful was Lord Kitchener in Britain, who became war minister early in the war. He not only insisted that "we must be prepared to put armies of millions in the field and maintain them for several years," but he acted as if he believed it. Foreign Secretary Edward Grey reports that the British War Council largely discounted Kitchener's startling prediction because he was utterly unable to disclose "how or by what process of reasoning he made this forecast." They concluded it arose simply "by some flash of instinct rather than reasoning." Grey also reports that Kitchener was as perplexed as any when static trench warfare developed later in the war, declaring: "I don't know what is to be done; this isn't *war*."[28] Thus, the council was very likely right about Kitchener, if not about the war.*

Variously characterized as the cult of the offensive, the mystique of the offensive, the exaltation of the offensive, the ideology of the offensive, or the offensive syndrome, the basic line of thought derived from certain selected military experiences. All the wars in mid-Europe over the preceding 100 years had been short and had been attended by costs that were considered bearable: The First Schleswig-Holstein War of 1848 had lasted a few months and cost 6,000 lives, the Franco-Austrian War of 1859 had lasted seventy-four days and cost 22,500 lives, the Second Schleswig-Holstein War of 1864 had lasted three months and cost 4,500 lives, the Seven Weeks War of 1866 had actually lasted only six weeks and cost 36,100 lives, and the Franco-Prussian War of 1870–71 had lasted seven months and cost 187,500 lives. To be sure, there had been recent wars where the strength of the defensive had proven substantial, causing the wars to be far longer and far more costly than originally anticipated: the American Civil War of 1861–65 (650,000 lives), the Russo-Turkish War of 1877–78 (285,000 lives), the Boer War of 1899–1902 in South Africa (22,000 lives), and the Russo-Japanese War of 1904–05 (130,000 lives). But these were all *elsewhere*, were on very different kinds of terrain, and generally seemed rather primitive to the sophisticated Europeans of 1914. Germany's chief general characterized the American war as "armed mobs chasing each other around the country, from whom nothing can be learned." Anyway, the Russian troops lacked the true "spirit of the offensive," it was pointed out, and the British finally won the Boer War once they got onto the offensive. Furthermore, even in these outlying areas there had been wars that fit the offensive model: the Sino-Japanese War of 1894–95 (eight months and 15,000 lives), the Spanish-American War of 1898 (four months and 10,000 lives, mostly from disease), as well as a number of quick colonial wars.[29]

In 1898, Ivan Bloch, a rich Polish-Jewish entrepreneur, vehemently took exception to these conclusions. After eight years of research he published a six-

---

*Grey himself is sometimes considered to be a prophet of the impending horrors, because on the eve of the war he tellingly remarked, "The lamps are going out all over Europe; we shall not see them lit again in our lifetime." The remark has become famous, although Grey apparently can't recall ever saying it and simply reports in his memoirs, published eleven years later, that a friend remembers him making the remark. But, assuming everyone has the quote correct, it probably stems from Grey's frustration over his inability to stop the momentum toward war in 1914 rather than from any knowledgeable anticipation that the war would be long and costly, for Grey also makes it clear that he as much as anyone expected the war to be short (1925, pp. 20, 71).

volume study of these same wars and of advances in weaponry, tactics, munitions, and logistics. As he saw it, the defense now had the advantage, and he envisioned the next war as one in which soldiers would dig in and, using rapid-firing, long-range firearms, simply mow down those on the offensive: "The spade will be as indispensable to the soldier as the rifle. . . . Battles will last for days, and at the end it is very doubtful whether any decisive victory can be gained." Furthermore, he argued, the "increased slaughter" on the stalemated battlefield would lead to "a long period of continually increasing strain upon the resources of the combatants," then to "entire dislocation of all industry and severing of all the sources of supply by which alone the community is enabled to bear the crushing burden," and ultimately to famine, the "bankruptcy of nations," and "the break-up of the whole social organization." Thus, war—by which he meant all-out war among the major European countries—"has at last become impossible": it could not be carried out "except at the price of suicide." Nonetheless, he gloomily concluded, "I do not for a moment deny that it is possible for nations to plunge . . . into a frightful series of catastrophes which will probably result in the overturn of all civilized and ordered government."[30]

Bloch's argument had little impact on military planners. They had already been considering the effect of such developments as the machine gun. In France, Colonel Ferdinand Foch argued that improved firepower could benefit the offense; if accomplished in large enough numbers and in appropriate coordination with artillery, the offensive charge could still succeed. In Germany, Bloch was read seriously by the military establishment, but his arguments were dismissed as those of a dilettante and "an ignorant theoretician." His lack of firsthand military experience caused him, the critics held, to focus exclusively on material matters of machines and weaponry, ignoring the great importance of human and moral factors. Troops on the offensive were in a morally superior position—they had the initiative and were spurred on by a sense of emotional superiority. Furthermore, even if war became protracted, which few believed, it would simply be a more extended test of a nation's highest qualities. Sacrifice and human resourcefulness would keep the war machine functioning.[31]

We now know that many of Bloch's predictions came true: the war that began in 1914 turned out to be a long, slogging war of attrition costing some 9 million lives in which the defense proved dominant. Nevertheless, a reasonable case can be made for the proposition that the offense cultists were almost proved right. As Howard has observed, in some areas the offensive worked as planned: "On the eastern front . . . battles of this kind did occur. Fronts did crumble. The victorious cavalry did pursue."[32] Furthermore, on the western front where many things went wrong from the start, the Germans nonetheless came close to defeating the French within two months, as planned. The French, in fact, call the

49

battle that stopped that victory "the Miracle of the Marne." Had the Germans done a few things better or the French a few things worse, the miracle might have struck on the other side, and history books would now conclude in their brief section on the War of 1914 that it proved the offensive cultists had had their exaltations right.[33]*

Moreover, although Bloch was certainly right about the stalemate and trench warfare on the western front, he vastly underestimated the ability—amazing even in retrospect—of embattled economies to cope with the adversities of a long war. Economic collapse never happened, and famine never ensued. But he was not unusual in making this error. Because of the quick exhaustion of available capital, "the war could not last much more than a year," economist John Maynard Keynes informed his friends, one of whom recalls that "it was a great relief to have Maynard's assurances on this point." Peace activist Andrew Carnegie confidently informed people that if war were to occur, "We won't give them any money."[34]

In fact, the widely accepted notion that a long war would bring severe economic strain or even collapse, far from discouraging enthusiasm for war, often perversely nourished the notion that war would be short and, consequently, cheap. The work of Norman Angell, to his lifelong dismay, has often been taken to suggest that "war is impossible." Angell, like Bloch, specifically and repeatedly stated that although war would be futile and absurd, it was entirely possible that countries could be foolish enough to get into one. However, one could conclude from his argument that, while countries might be able to get into a war, the dawning economic calamity would keep them from allowing the war to become very large. One of Angell's followers, David Starr Jordan, president of Stanford University, argued exactly this way in 1913 when he denied the possibility of a large-scale war, although not necessarily of a small, short one: "What shall we say of the Great War of Europe, ever threatening, ever impending, and which never comes? We shall say that it will never come. Humanly speaking, it is impossible. . . . The bankers will not find the money for such a fight, the industries will not maintain it, the statesmen cannot. . . . There will be no general war."[35]

It is clear, in fact, that much of the colossal martial enthusiasm that war glorifier Treitschke was able to muster stemmed from his conclusion that economics would keep the war from becoming too unpleasantly costly: "Wars will become rarer and shorter, but at the same time far more sanguinary." He ex-

*Things might have been much different, for example, if the Belgians had decided, following the German plan, to let the Germans cross their territory without opposition. Instead, they decided to be "crushed gloriously." Another possibility, debated endlessly since 1914, concerns what would have happened if the German commanders had not decided to move troops from the right wing of their advancing army to shore up the left wing, thereby undercutting their own plan and disastrously weakening the offensive dynamic in a key area.

plained his reasoning this way: "Civilized nations suffer far more than savages from the economic ravages of war, especially through the disturbance of the artificially existing credit system, which may have frightful consequences in a modern war. . . . Therefore wars must become rarer and shorter, owing to man's natural horror of bloodshed as well as to the size and quality of modern armies, for it is impossible to see how the burden of a great war could long be borne under the present conditions."[36]

This sort of economic reasoning was a basis on which German general Alfred von Schlieffen fashioned his dynamic strategy of conquest: "In an age in which the existence of nations is based on the uninterrupted progress of trade and commerce . . . a strategy of exhaustion is impossible." Therefore, he anticipated a war in which the will of one side or the other would be quickly shattered. Interestingly, however, while denying that war would be lingering, Schlieffen provided for the possibility that he might be wrong and Bloch correct. He believed that if the aggressive sweep into France failed and got bogged down, Germany should immediately seek a negotiated peace rather than continue to slog onward with a costly and unproductive war. As Bernard Brodie has noted, "To the enormous subsequent cost not only of Germany but of the whole world, such a thought never entered the heads of those who finally executed the plan and saw it fail."[37] Had the thought done so and had they acted on it, the war would probably have been fully as short as almost all the pundits were predicting.

Deterrence and the Lessons, If Any, of World War I

As has often been noted, World War I was an event that really should never have happened: there was not really a great deal to fight about because important territorial issues like the unification of Germany and Italy had been solved, most colonial rivalries had been worked out, and there were no severe economic problems.[38] The lesson most commonly derived from the calamity of 1914 has been that war could have been prevented if the leaders of the rival nations had understood each other better and if they had been more sweetly reasonable and accommodating with each other. As discussed in the next chapter, this lesson was to inform the 1930s policy of appeasement, which was such a spectacular failure at preventing the next world war.

However, war in 1914 might also have been prevented—deterred—if the antagonists had been able credibly to threaten that the war would be as disastrously destructive and costly as it in fact turned out to be. But as Michael Howard has observed, armies in 1914 were not particularly conceived of as deterrents, but rather simply as "instruments for fighting a war which was widely regarded—and not by soldiers alone—as being inevitable, necessary, and even desirable." Moreover, most historians agree that Germany was impelled by a strong desire for expansion and hegemony and was quite prepared to use military means to achieve this. They anticipated that their goals could be accomplished quickly and cheaply, but a few even welcomed a long war.[39] A guarantee that they would lose would have deterred them, but little else.

The international political climate of the post-1945 period is often compared with that of the pre-1914 period. There are quite a few similarities. In both eras, large well-armed nations have jockeyed for position in an atmosphere fraught with rivalry, hostility, distrust, misperception, confusion about intent, and appeals to patriotism. There have been alarming crises in both periods; and in both, arms races or competitions have taken place, built around weapons systems that have been held to give significant advantage to the side that starts the war.

But there are also pronounced differences that make the comparison strained at best. In the post–World War II period there have been conscious efforts at deterrence built around some important and comparatively unambiguous alliance commitments. Moreover, since 1945 it has been very difficult to find anyone who seriously maintains that war, particularly war among advanced countries, would be an interesting test of manliness or that it would be profitable, desirable, virtuous, ennobling, cleansing, beautiful, heroic, glorious, uplifting, necessary, progressive, romantic, redemptive, beneficial, or, certainly, cheap. The maneuverings and posturings and fulminations and crises that took place before 1914 were carried out in an atmosphere where such views were the prevailing wisdom. A central theme of this book is that a profound—and consequential—change in the climate of opinion about war has occurred since that time.

In 1987 in the Algonquin Hotel's Oak Room in New York City, a talented young cabaret performer, Michael Feinstein, was rendering a series of songs by Irving Berlin. As he delivered the 1911 song "Alexander's Ragtime Band," Feinstein came to the line announcing that the way the band plays a bugle call is "so natural that you want to go to war." Struck by the line's odd sentiment, he remarked to his audience in wistful explanation, "It's an old song." Indeed. They don't write 'em like that anymore.

3

World War I: Major War Becomes an Anachronism

ALTHOUGH THE intervening experience of World War II tends to cloud more distant recall, it should be remembered that a most powerful effect of World War I on the countries that fought it was an overwhelming—and so far, permanent—desire for international peace in the developed world. Had the only countries capable of starting another major war been Britain, France, the United States, Canada, Spain, Czechoslovakia, Poland, the Soviet Union, Austria, and probably even Italy, World War I might well have been the war to end war—at least war of that scope and type. Almost the entire developed world had been Hollandized.

This chapter examines the desperate quest for peace after World War I and the simultaneous drive for war by some of the few remaining war advocates in the developed world.

The Impact of the Great War

The Great War (as it was to be called for over two decades) was greeted with considerable jubilation—even euphoria—in Europe in 1914.[1] To many, it seemed a noble and inevitable clash of national wills that would quickly and dramatically settle old scores and determine new destinies. Impelled by the excitement of the hour and by the conviction that the war would be short, men all over the continent rushed to enlist to get in on the action before the war was over.* Remarkably, support for the war persisted even when it began to prove to be a long, costly, static war of defense. With the combatants locked in brutal, unending, and decidedly unromantic warfare, millions of young men continued to enlist for the slaughter, and the economies at home rose to the unprecedented challenge as each side strained to outlast the other. As Bernard Brodie suggests, what kept them going was a "fierce dedication to the goal of victory . . . at whatever price and however long it might take."[2]

By 1916, however, discontent appeared, and in 1917 there were mutinies within the French army and a collapse of the Russian forces to mutiny and revolution. After the entry of the United States into the war, the Germans tried a major offensive and, upon its eventual failure and degeneration into mutiny, sued for peace. An armistice between the exhausted combatants took effect on the eleventh hour of the eleventh day of the eleventh month of 1918. Some 9 million soldiers, as well as millions of civilians, had died in the war.[3]

At the end of the war and during its immediate aftermath, bitterness, disillusionment, recrimination, and revulsion blossomed. As Roland Stromberg notes, "Romantic illusions vanished in the grimness of trench warfare and mass slaughter." "Mechanized slaughter," he observes, "was to destroy forever the heroic image of war." Michael Howard refers to the war as "a dark scar across the history of Europe," and Barbara Tuchman calls it a "band of scorched earth" dividing time. While the war obviously did not change attitudes enough to make further conflicts impossible, it did mark, as Arnold Toynbee has observed, the end of a "span of five thousand years during which war had been one of mankind's master institutions"; or in Brodie's words, it brought about "a basic historical change . . . in the attitudes of the European (and American) peoples toward war."[4] For most, war was no longer supreme theater, redemptive turmoil, a chess game for high stakes, a riveting diversion, a natural progression, or an uplifting affirmation of manhood. It was what the first modern general, William Tecumseh Sherman, had called it a half century earlier: hell.

People who had often praised war and eagerly anticipated its terrible, determining convulsions now found themselves appalled by it. Within half a decade,

---

*Said one British recruit, "I will dash into the great adventure with all the pride and spirit an ancient race has given me." A German poet, Ernst Lotz, declared, "At last war! All the people are wildly enthusiastic, and so am I." The British poet Rupert Brooke effused, "It's all great fun"; and another British poet, Julian Grenfell, proclaimed, "I *adore* war. It is like a picnic without the objectlessness of a picnic." When a friend in the army wrote that he found war to be "something, if often horrible, yet very ennobling and very beautiful," English diarist Vera Brittain replied, "Women get all the dreariness of war, and none of its exhilaration." (Fussell 1975, p. 21; Miesel 1978, p. 11; Stromberg 1982, p. 50; Mosley 1976, p. 239; Brittain 1934, p. 104.)

war opponents, once a derided minority, had become a decided majority: everyone now seemed to be a peace advocate. War, just about everyone in the developed world now seemed to agree, was repulsive, immoral, uncivilized, and futile.*

That World War I was a watershed event in attitudes toward war in the developed world is clear. Exactly why is less clear. The war's physical costs were, of course, enormous. But the Americans suffered far worse in their civil war of fifty years earlier and, while civil war fever never revived there, a degree of romanticism about war in general did rise again. The suffering and destruction of World War I were proportionately not all that much different from that borne during the Napoleonic Wars of a century earlier, and they were far less than that borne in the Thirty Years War of the seventeenth century, at least according to accepted wisdom. Contrary to prewar predictions, the major combatants were able to handle the unprecedented strains and disruptions economically; and rather than descending into the economic barbarism Ivan Bloch had predicted, most had substantially recovered from the war's ravages within a few years. The war toppled political regimes in several countries, but it was certainly not new in that respect.

The impact on war attitudes of the Great War's physical devastation and of its horrifying weaponry should not be discounted, nor should the impact of the war's evident political pointlessness. But the bone-deep revulsion it so widely inspired and the very substantial blow it administered to the war spirit so prevalent just a few years earlier should be credited at least in part to the insidious propagandistic efforts of the prewar peace movement. The war proved to be a colossal confirmation of its gadfly arguments about the repulsiveness, immorality, and futility of war and of its uncivilized nature. Of course, the war also shattered the peace movement's airy optimism, and it certainly undercut its proposition that Europe was becoming progressively more civilized; but that was nothing compared to what it did to the notion that *war* was progressive—as well as glorious, manly, and beneficial.[5] For those who now wished to believe that war was neither natural nor inevitable, the antiwar movement had already conveniently formulated a set of arguments and alternatives. Since the peacemakers of 1918 were substantially convinced that the institution of war must be controlled

---

*A. A. Milne crisply characterized the change this way: "In 1913, with a few exceptions we all thought war was a natural and fine thing to happen, so long as we were well prepared for it and had no doubt about coming out the victor. Now, with a few exceptions, we have lost our illusions; we are agreed that war is neither natural nor fine, and that the victor suffers from it equally with the vanquished" (1935, pp. 9–10). Some young men might still see excitement and adventure in war, but a visceral change in romanticism clearly took place: as Linderman has observed, the "honorable wound" of the American Civil War became in World War II the "million-dollar wound" because it removed the victim from the war theater and from the theater of war (1987, p. 12).

or eradicated, they tried to apply some of the devices and approaches the peace movement had long been advocating.

For reasons that seem in reflection to have been special, it didn't work out so well. In Germany a leader arose who almost single-handedly brought major war to Europe, while Japan, a country that had not substantially participated in World War I nor learned its lessons, set itself on a collision course in Asia that was to lead to national cataclysm.

The Desperate Quest for Peace

In his 1914 book, *The War That Will End War,* H. G. Wells argued that "this, the greatest of all wars, is not just another war—it is the last war!" Likewise, an American historian dared to hope in 1921 that, because "public opinion is now turning against war," the age "is witnessing the dawn of universal peace." Others were far less confident. Associated with the revulsion against war, however, was a deeply felt and widely held conviction that, as a British historian recalls, "all wars were unnecessary." Many, in Britain and elsewhere, simply refused to countenance the possibility of another major war and assumed that no sane person could possibly ever want to experience one.[6]

As the victors convened in Paris to fashion appropriate punishments for Germany and to dismember the Austro-Hungarian empire, they also sought to keep the Great War from recurring. War, they now assumed, was no longer an inevitable fact of life; it could, and should, be prevented. As the militarily trained King George V of Britain put it, "I *will* not have another war. I *will not.*"[7]

Peace Devices and Institutions.

Several of the devices peace advocates had long been promoting were adopted, at least in part. A sort of world government, the League of Nations, was set up to speak for the world community and apply moral and physical pressure on potential aggressors. As fabricated, the league hardly superceded the warring nation-state system, but it did create an international organizational apparatus that could in time be gradually strengthened and developed.

Legal codes and bodies that might be able to deal peacefully with international disputes were also set up. A Permanent Court of International Justice was established at The Hague in war-avoiding Holland in 1922. And in 1928 fifteen nations signed the Kellogg-Briand Pact, a document that "outlawed" war and declared its signatories' intent to seek peaceful remedies to disagreements. By 1934 sixty-four nations had signed up—virtually all the countries in the world at the time. The pact is still theoretically in effect, although it has garnered a fair amount of ridicule over the decades.

Efforts were also made to deal with the issue of armament. First, Germany, officially branded the sole cause for the war by the victors, was substantially disarmed. Then, in an effort to deal with the burgeoning strength of the Japanese, the United States, Britain, France, and Italy worked out an agreement with them in 1922 to limit the strength each would enjoy in battleships and cruisers.

Quite a bit of thought, in fact, went into the issue of arms control during the postwar period, in part because of the theory that the Great War, like lesser ones before it, had principally been caused by the greed of munitions makers. Conferences were held in 1919 and 1925 in an effort to establish procedures for restricting or eliminating the private arms trade. The munitions-maker theory was particularly popular in the 1930s in the United States, where many concluded that a conspiracy of arms makers had dragged the country into that appalling war; this led to calls for unilateral arms reductions and for isolation from the quarreling Europeans and their contemptible foreign wars.[8]

Visions of Doomsday: War Becomes the Enemy.

The Great War caused revulsion not only for the extent of the casualties that were suffered but also for the *way* they were suffered. The war was remembered not for dashing cavalry charges or for heroic individual displays of derring-do but for a method of warfare in which masses of men swarmed out from muddy defensive trenches to slaughter each other in huge numbers with new mechanized devices like machine guns and tanks. And above all there was the war's most ghastly innovation of all: chemical warfare.

The Germans introduced gas into the war in 1915. The greenish-yellow chlorine gas they used killed in a peculiarly agonizing manner that could take up to two days: the victim suffocated—or, really, drowned—as his lungs filled with fluid. Gas caused panic in the British troops on whom it was first used, and very shortly three lines of activity were set in motion: (1) the use of gas in retaliation (the British did so in five months); (2) the hasty development and distribution of protective masks; and (3) as part of the ongoing British program to entice the United States into the war on its side, intense propaganda efforts to stigmatize the Germans as inhuman monsters for introducing chemicals into the art of war. (It is estimated that for effect the British quintupled their gas casualty figures from the first German attack.)[9]

Innovation in gas technology continued throughout the war—some thirty different gases and at least seven different kinds of gas masks were tested in combat. Until July 1917 defensive measures proved dominant: since all the gases had to be breathed into the lungs to be effective, they could be neutralized by masks. But then the Germans introduced mustard gas, an agent that works by coming into contact with the skin. It took a year before Germany's opponents had their own supply of this gas, and both sides used it extensively during the last portion of the war. The British, for example, suffered 20,000 gas casualties before July 1917 and over 160,000 during the last sixteen months of the war. Gas accounted for over 34 percent of all American casualties in the last month of the war.[10]

Thus, although chemical weapons accounted for only a small portion of the war's total injuries and an even smaller portion of its deaths, they were becoming progressively more effective at the war's end. Delivery systems were also rapidly improving: by 1918 half of the German artillery shells were filled with gas, and war plans for 1919 anticipated massive applications of chemical weapons. Further improvements in effectiveness were certainly to be expected. As Winston Churchill put it in 1925, "As for Poison Gas and Chemical Warfare in all its forms, only the first chapter has been written in this terrible book."[11] And, used in combination with aircraft—another rapidly developing innovation of the Great War—the weapons could easily be used against not only military forces but also civilian populations far behind the lines.

Soon quite a few people (though by no means all) were envisioning doomsday. Paris could be "annihilated" in an hour by 100 airplanes each carrying a ton of gas, some claimed, and a former British War Ministry official told the House of Lords that forty tons could "destroy the whole population of London." Others claimed that twenty large gas bombs could destroy Chicago or Berlin, or that "one air force group . . . could completely paralyze all activities in a city the size of New York for any protracted period." Some military theorists, especially the influential Italian general Giulio Douhet, concluded from the experience of the Great War that any ground war would quickly and necessarily degenerate into a stalemate while air power would determine the outcome. He calculated that 500 tons of bombs, mostly gas, could destroy a large city and its inhabitants. The effects of gas could be lingering as well as devastating: gas dropped on an area could remain disabling for several weeks and might cause or aggravate later illnesses. Thus, one report concluded, a potential combatant could anticipate "the depopulation of large sections of the country, as to threaten, if not destroy, all that has been gained during the painful centuries of the past."[12] In Britain many concluded that an air attack could deliver a "knock-out blow" to the country, particularly to London. As one prominent politician recalled in 1966, "We thought of air warfare in 1938 rather as people think of nuclear warfare today."[13]

Where war was once seen as progressive, many people now concluded that they had had about all the progress they could tolerate. Churchill concluded that war was now "the potential destroyer of the human race. . . . Mankind has never been in this position before. Without having improved appreciably in virtue or enjoying wiser guidance, it has got into its hands for the first time the tools by which it can unfailingly accomplish its own extermination." Psychoanalyst Sigmund Freud concluded his 1930 book, *Civilization and Its Discontents,* by expressing his own discontent with the way civilization had developed: "Men have brought their powers of subduing nature to such a pitch that by using them they could now very easily exterminate one another to the last man." British Prime Minister Stanley Baldwin was one of many who declared, "When the next war comes . . . European civilization [will be] wiped out." It was also widely assumed in the West that (assuming anything was left standing) a major war would lead to a worldwide depression.[14]

We have no experience with atomic war to judge the predictions of what it would be like, but we do have World War II to judge the predictions of those who envisioned major war before 1939. Obviously, doomsday and apocalypse in the sense of the extermination of the human race did not occur; bombing was far less decisive than many anticipated; and, for reasons discussed in the next chapter, gas was scarcely used at all. But the central notion that the next Great War would be vastly more horrible than the first one (which, of course, was already sufficiently horrible for virtually everybody) certainly did come to pass. There were some 15 million battle deaths, and, following the interwar predictions, civilians became important targets; consequently, the total destruction of human life in the war probably reached 35 million or more.

For many, then, the real threat and the true enemy had become war itself. In a study of fictional accounts of future war, I. F. Clarke notes that World War I produced a pronounced change, which World War II and atomic weapons were later only to embellish: "Since 1914 the literature of imaginary warfare has seen a constant retreat from the old, heroic, and aggressive attitudes. The chief enemy is no longer some foreign power; it is the immense destructiveness of modern weapons. . . . All that has been written about future wars since Hiroshima merely repeats and amplifies what was said between the two world wars."[15]*

Now, if it is a choice between two evils, the enemy and war, and if the enemy is the lesser of the two evils, then anything the enemy wants must be preferable

---

*Typical was a 1931 novel, *The Gas War of 1940,* which envisioned a war begun by a German attack on Poland that escalated to worldwide ruin from poison gas and high explosives. Other British works of the era have such titles as *The Poison War, Empty Victory, War upon Women, People of the Ruins, The Last Man, The Collapse of Homo Sapiens, Invasion from the Air, Last of My Race, At the End of the World, Day of Wrath,* and *The World Ends.* Similar tales were penned in Germany and France. The Germans even had a name for the genre: *Weltuntergangsroman*—world-downfall novels.

to war. In the 1936 motion picture *Things to Come,* with a screenplay by H. G. Wells, an English character observes on Christmas Day 1940, as cataclysmic war is about to break out, "If we don't end war, war will end us." Britons were at war by the end of 1940, as Wells had predicted; but they went into the war saying, essentially, "If we don't end Hitler, Hitler will end us." It was not an easy transformation to make.

The Lessons of 1914.

Throughout, all were haunted by the 1914 experience. As suggested in the previous chapter, there were two ways that the Great War might have been prevented. One of those was through calm negotiation—talking things over in an accommodating manner. Grievances might have been ironed out, and hostilities, many of them based on misperception or simplistic mindsets, might have been lessened. There are historians who doubt this process would have been successful in 1914, because in their view Germany was looking forward to a fight and anticipating a victory that would greatly expand its area of control and firmly establish it as the dominant country in the area.[16] But it was often touch and go in 1914, and a few wise moves could have averted war at that time. And perhaps, given some breathing space, the protagonists might have eventually abated or diverted the momentum toward war. The lesson is not unreasonable, and it was the one principally derived by Western peace-preferrers from the political and military maneuvers that led to catastrophe in 1914.

The other method for preventing World War I would have been to make it clear to any would-be aggressor that war would be exactly as counterproductive and horrible as, in fact, it proved to be. Given the overwhelmingly common assumption that war would be short and cheap, this deterrence process was probably simply not feasible in 1914. But after the war it might have been accomplished through either of two methods: (1) the development of weapons that could promise mass destruction or (2) the creation among the peace-preferring nations of a firm alliance that could promise quick, enveloping escalation.

If after World War I the peace-preferring nations had assiduously sought to develop chemical and similar weapons and the methods for delivering them, they might have been able eventually to create a force capable of massively retaliating against the civilian population of any aggressor nation in Europe.[17] To use the jargon of a later era, they would have had an effective countervalue capability: even if they had been attacked first, they could have responded with a severely punishing retaliatory strike.

There are several reasons why the peace seekers of the interwar period never tried to develop this capability. One clearly was that the other side could have, and in all probability would have, also developed such a capability. Thus, the fear was that in any major conflict chemical warfare would be used by both sides against civilian targets, causing death rates far beyond those suffered in the Great War. Furthermore, the purposeful targeting of civilians was a notion that no one was yet willing to accept. When civilian targets were bombed at Guernica in 1937 during the Spanish Civil War and at Warsaw and Rotterdam early in World War II, great horror and outrage were registered. (One of the most notable developments of World War II was that, by its end, this moral concern had been fully overcome: the cities of Hiroshima and Nagasaki were considered to be military targets by the people who bombed them in 1945.)[18] In addition, chemical warfare had picked up a particularly negative onus, in part because of the effective British propaganda branding its initiator, Germany, as morally degenerate. Somewhat trapped by their own argumentation, the British took the lead in seeking to ban this method of killing in favor of more old-fashioned ones like bullets, bayonets, and shrapnel. There was also strong hostility to gas among military establishments, which found chemical warfare to be disgustingly mechanistic, uncivilized, and dishonorable, as well as extremely messy to use on the battlefield; accordingly, they never really assimilated it into their military plans. Among those who had a personal aversion to gas was Adolf Hitler, who had been temporarily blinded by a British gas attack in 1918.[19]

However, even if the peace preferrers of the interwar period were unprepared to develop weapons of unprecedented civilian destruction as a deterrent, they could have sought to deter by banding together in a firm alliance that would have threatened a potential aggressor with another massive, multiple-front war like World War I. In other words, deterrence might have worked if the countries opposing war had credibly threatened to coalesce into exactly the sort of alliance they actually did form once the war began. Suggestions that this be done were common enough at the time, particularly as the threat from Germany grew in the 1930s. But neither small nor large countries could bring themselves to fashion such an alliance. The lessons of 1914, in fact, seemed to suggest that alliances could actually drag a country into a pointless war. And there were other barriers to alliance. The Soviet regime, with its advocacy and promotion of worldwide violent revolution, was often considered in the West to be even more threatening than the Nazis. And effective alliance within the West was hampered by several factors, including economic crises in Britain and constant political turmoil in France, as well as disillusioned isolationism in the United States.

Thus, the experience of 1914 taught those questing for peace after the Great War that the best way to prevent war was to be accommodating and unthreateningly reasonable. Three countries had leaders who were prepared to exploit such attitudes: Italy, Germany, and Japan.

Mussolini's War

Although Benito Mussolini may not occupy an exalted place in the pantheon of warmongers, he is in there somewhere. Mussolini came into authority in Italy in 1922 and seized dictatorial, or near-dictatorial, control in 1927. By then he had formulated a plan—even a kind of theory—of conquest. Italy, he felt, deserved a more prominent place in world affairs. To achieve this status, he proposed an expansionistic policy—but, conveniently, in a direction away from the major military countries of Europe. Italy had managed to fight on the victorious side in the Great War, and most border issues with the nations to the north had been settled. It was Mussolini's notion that his country's destiny—its "national mission"—now lay in the reestablishment of the Mediterranean as "the sea of Rome" which Italy ought to control "by right of its geographical configuration and the maritime traditions of its race." Furthermore, he felt, war could unite his country and could promote the process of revolution he was trying to further there.[20]

Mussolini was one of those few souls after the Great War who still thrilled at the thought of war. His Fascist philosophy believed "neither in the possibility nor the utility of perpetual peace," he once wrote, and he found pacifism in its "renunciation of the struggle" to be "an act of cowardice," because "war alone brings up to its highest tension all human energy and puts the stamp of nobility upon the peoples who have the courage to meet it."[21]

Impelled in part by such anachronistic ravings, Mussolini cast about for a war he could wage courageously and energetically to win his nobility stamp. His schemes had to be kept manageable, however, because of economic, industrial, and military weakness, and because of the memory of the Great War that haunted too many Italians. By October 1935, with Germany rearmed and encouraging, France catatonic over internal disunity and the growing German threat, and Britain and the United States bogged down in a major economic depression, Mussolini found his target: Ethiopia, a weak, backward, landlocked, underpopulated, tribal/feudal country in Africa that was of little or no interest to other European colonizers.

Even then Mussolini had to struggle to win acceptance of his distant war. The army, the monarch, the conservative establishment, and even prominent members of his own Fascist party were extremely reluctant to take what they saw as "a great gamble." The venture did get some support from the Roman Catholic Church, which was looking forward to converting and civilizing the Ethiopians, and it also enjoyed a fair amount of public popularity because it would avenge a humiliating defeat that the Italians had suffered there in 1896 and were still smarting over.[22] It took seven months, but with the aid of aerial bombing and poison-gas attacks, the Italians defeated the Ethiopians.

Mussolini was emboldened by this popular victory in a land whose value was apparent to no one else in Europe, and he was greatly encouraged by the unwillingness of the peace-preferring nations to do much of anything about his aggression. Accordingly, he tinkered onward, more or less following his old theories of advance. In 1938 he sent arms and troops to help the Fascist cause in the Spanish Civil War; in 1939 he annexed Albania; and on June 10, 1940, he joined Germany in war against France and Britain.

But he dragged his country kicking and screaming every step of the way. Glorious plans to attack Egypt were scuttled by the army, and the generals and admirals went along with his war declaration only after it was obvious that the Germans had defeated France (Italy quickly flew over a few planes to get in on the kill) and only after Mussolini had tricked them with assurances that there actually would not be any war to fight thereafter. "The generals," he complained disgustedly later, "didn't want to make war." And although a superior demagogue, Mussolini was unable to generate in the Italian people the sort of enthusiasm for war that had been so prevalent in Europe in 1914. As MacGregor Knox has observed, he "struggled in vain for years to prepare the day when the Italian public would rise to its feet and demand war."[23]

It would be scant comfort to the families of the 20,000 Ethiopians who died fighting the invader, but even under the leadership of a charismatic, self-deluded, and fairly crafty war enthusiast, Italy was hardly the model of a modern major aggressor. As their early collapse in World War II was to demonstrate, the Italians had little stomach—that is, were too civilized—for war. Without the coordinated machinations of their German ally and, later, master, the puffed-up, self-conscious adventures of Mussolini and his reluctant Italians would have been only a minor blot on the peace that broke out in Europe at the eleventh hour in 1918.

Hitler's War

It is not true that no one in Europe besides Adolf Hitler wanted war, or at any rate the gains of war. Obviously, he found enough residual war spirit to inflame, and others found his vision of an expanded Germany attractive. It does seem true, however, that after 1918 Hitler was the only person left in Europe who combined the requisite supreme political skills with a willingness to risk major conflagration to quest after his vision. Not only did he manufacture a reason for war, but against great internal and external opposition, he crafted a military strategy that promised to achieve these gains without repeating World War I; and for a decade he experienced an amazing record of success against his timorous opponents.

There was great discontent with the status quo in Germany after the defeat of 1918 and after the punishing, often gratuitously insulting terms that were imposed upon it, and there was enormous frustration with the enervating domestic combat between the political left and right, and with the waffling, ineffectual center. In places the war spirit lingered: in the 1920s Germany produced not only Erich Maria Remarque's famous antiwar novel, *All Quiet on the Western Front,* but also Ernst Jünger's popular and blood-curdling, if less well-remembered, *The Storm of Steel.* Moreover, there was economic chaos, political instability, class hostility, and ethnic turmoil throughout Central and Eastern Europe. Some limited military clashes might have developed out of the various festering national resentments and rivalries—perhaps some border conflicts or land seizures, bitter but brief. However, given the overwhelming horror of major war that prevailed throughout the continent, and the profound exhaustion with it, the idea that another world war would somehow have naturally evolved out of the conflict and chaos in Europe is singularly unconvincing. A spectacularly skilled, and unusually lucky, entrepreneur was necessary for war.

Hitler needed the chaos and discontent to work with—although he created much of it, too. And surely he needed assistance—colleagues who were worshipfully subservient; a superb army that could be manipulated and whipped into action; a population capable of being mesmerized and led to slaughter; foreign opponents who were confused, disorganized, gullible, myopic, and faint-hearted; neighbors who would rather be prey than fight—although he created much of this as well. Hitler took the conditions of the world as he found them and then shaped and manipulated them to his own ends. He created the machinery to allow him to carry out his war plans and then ran the machinery himself. To a considerable degree, World War II came about because one man wanted it to occur and, with astonishingly single-minded and ruthless guile and craft, made it happen.

Hitler's Centrality.

Hitler was central to the Nazi system both creatively and operationally. As Norman Rich observes, "The point cannot be stressed too strongly; Hitler was master of the Third Reich." Hitler received "dictatorial powers" within his own party in 1921; and after seizing control of the country in 1933, he moved quickly and decisively to persuade, browbeat, dominate, outmaneuver, downgrade, and, in many instances, murder opponents or would-be opponents. He possessed enormous energy and stamina, exceptional persuasive powers, an excellent memory, strong powers of concentration, an overwhelming craving for power, a fanatical belief in his mission, a monumental self-confidence, a unique daring, a spectacular facility for lying, a mesmerizing oratory style, and an ability to be utterly ruthless to anyone who got in his way or attempted to divert him from his intended course of action.[24] Although he could be laughable with his struttings and fulminations and Chaplinesque moustache, he was, as historians like Rich, Allan Bullock, and Hugh Trevor-Roper have suggested, "a political genius." Because he was a moral criminal, a monster, it is easy to conclude that he must also have been an irrational fanatic with little grasp of reality. Trevor-Roper calls this the error of "extrapolating low intelligence from moral degradation."[25] To conclude that he could not recognize reality and manipulate it to his benefit would be to continue the underestimation of his talents that helped drag his contemporaries into history's most terrible war.

Hitler, in short, was neither symptom nor figurehead. He invented Nazism, he made it work, and he caused World War II.

Hitler's Theory of Conquest.

Although he was quite capable of seizing political opportunities when they arose, Hitler was at core a man with a plan that derived from a cosmic, if appalling, theory. The German people, he had convinced himself, were destined to dominate the world—with himself, of course, at the helm. As he figured it, this destiny derived from their racial superiority. As the master race, they naturally needed something to master; and the races to the east, which Hitler had concluded were inferior, seemed to him ideal for this role. The essence of Hitler's thought, according to Rich, was that "the German population was too small and its territorial base too limited to guarantee the survival of the racially superior Germans in the world arena of racial competition; if the German race was to survive, both its population and territorial base would have to be extended—at once and on a vast scale." It was therefore necessary for the German people to gain land, particularly in the east, for agricultural settlement and industrial development. The inferior people on the newly conquered territories would in no sense be assimilated; instead, they would be used for labor, expelled, or exterminated.[26] There was substantial enthusiasm in Germany for Hitler's demand that Germans in Central Europe all be incorporated into a single state, and the major countries in Europe proved to be sympathetic to that demand. What brought war was Germany's quest to occupy and control non-German lands, and that idea appears to have occurred to no one but Hitler.

Hitler's Military Strategy.

Conquest, therefore, was central to Hitler's theory. Although war was obviously ultimately necessary as a means to this end, it is not clear that Hitler was enamored of war for its own sake: unlike Mussolini, he does not seem to have been all that romantic about it. As Gerhard Weinberg has suggested, if the peoples Hitler wanted to conquer offered him "subservience" rather than "defiance," he was quite willing to accept it.[27] To be sure, Hitler had been a war enthusiast in his youth. In his autobiographical and ideological testament, *Mein Kampf*, he recalls a childhood fascination with books on military subjects and says he "raved more and more about everything connected with war or with militarism." He also relates that when war broke out in 1914, he was "overwhelmed by passionate enthusiasm" and fell on his knees to thank "Heaven" from his "overflowing heart" for granting him "the good fortune of being allowed to live" during those times. But these attitudes, as suggested in the previous chapter, were far from unusual at the time.* And Hitler also relates that as the Great War continued "the romance of battle had turned into horror. The enthusiasm gradually cooled down and the exuberant joy was suffocated by the fear of death."[28] Hitler certainly sought war, he apparently enjoyed being commander-in-chief during World War II (at least when things were going well for him), and he sometimes voiced Social Darwinist ideas at the time, arguing, for example, that a war every fifteen or twenty years was "good for the German people." But these unofficial pronouncements were often in the context of providing justification for the sacrifices he was demanding of his country. He saw expansion as racially invigorating and necessary, and wars that accompanied such expansion were therefore desirable. However, since war tends to call out "the best racial elements," too much of it could lead to the "slow bleeding away of the best, most

*Compare the 1914 comment of a British radical reformer: "I feel nothing but gratitude to the gods for sending [this war] in my time" (Joll 1984, p. 183).

valuable elements of a nation." Therefore, war should never become the "aim of the life of the people, but only a means for the preservation of this life."[29]

Given the realities of the situation, war was clearly necessary because the peoples he wanted to conquer were hardly likely to join his foreign, racist regime by their own will. In seeking to gain an effective consensus within Germany in support of his policy, however, Hitler inevitably came up against the argument put forward by not only his military chiefs but just about everybody else: However desirable his goals might be, any effort to achieve them by force would ultimately devolve into a long, eviscerating war of attrition like World War I or worse.

Hitler's response was to argue that the wrong lessons were almost universally being adduced from the experience of the Great War. He agreed that Germany could never win a war of attrition from its present position. His policy was for rapid rearmament and for a series of separate isolated wars, avoiding the multi-front war that overextended and ultimately doomed Germany in World War I. The mobility of airpower and tanks would be stressed in these wars, and upon the success of each, more geography would be added to the empire. Should total war eventually evolve out of this process (which Hitler may have expected and certainly was planning to be ready for), Germany would be in a good position to win, given its vast new territorial base.[30]

Hitler's Successes.

Hitler invented, then, not only a theory of expansion and conquest but also a military methodology for carrying it out. Then, riding over internal and external opposition, he proceeded to put it into action. Under his leadership and through the direct application of his will Germany regained the Saarland in the west; rearmed; reintroduced conscription; reoccupied the Rhineland between Germany and France; took over Austria and then the Sudetenland section of Czechoslovakia; invaded the rest of Czechoslovakia; and invaded, in succession, Poland, Denmark, Norway, Holland, Belgium, Luxembourg, and France.

All these ventures were successful, and all were accomplished at remarkably little cost. It was a truly virtuosic performance. Given the experience of 1914–18, it might not be unreasonable to consider Hitler's deft destruction of Dutch, Belgian, British, and French forces in 1940 to be the most spectacular military success in history. At each step there were doubters and opponents within the regime; but, impressed by Hitler's steadily lengthening record of unalloyed success, they became fewer and fewer, and the objections gradually focused less on strategic judgment and more on minor matters of tactics.[31]

The German people seem to have reacted similarly. Hitler had achieved great popularity by the mid-1930s because he had reestablished domestic order and because he seemed to have gotten the lurching economy to function productively. But, in great contrast with 1914, there was no widespread enthusiasm for war. Conscription was not popular, and the public reacted to one of Hitler's greatest triumphs, acquiring by bloodless intimidation the Sudetenland section of Czecho-slovakia, by cheering the English peacemaker, Neville Chamberlain. And they watched silently and sullenly as Hitler publicly oversaw the sending of motorized units to Czechoslovakia, causing Hitler to reportedly mutter, "With these people I cannot make war." Hitler's military advances into Poland in 1939 or into the Low Countries and France in 1940 did not inspire enthusiasm, although the Germans did apparently permit themselves an optimistic victory celebration when their old enemy, France, fell with such amazing quickness.[32]

The war, then, was Adolf Hitler's personal project. As Weinberg has put it, "Whether any other German leader would indeed have taken the plunge is surely doubtful, and the very warnings Hitler received from some of his generals can only have reinforced his belief in his personal role as the one man able, willing, and even eager to lead Germany and drag the world into war."* Hitler himself told his generals in 1939 that "essentially all depends on me, on my existence, because of my political talents." "In all modesty," he boasted, he was "irreplace-able. Neither a military man nor a civilian could replace me."[33]

Opposing Hitler

Given Hitler's plans and ideological need for geographic expansion and conquest, it seems likely that he could have been stopped only if his opponents had banded together either by militarily restraining him early in his path of adventure (when he was assuring all listeners that his appetite was moderate, conventionally nation-

---

*As Hitler biographer Allan Bullock puts it forcefully, "It is no good saying that it was 'the machine' that did this, not Hitler. Hitler was never the prisoner of 'the machine.' If 'the machine' had been left to decide things, it would never have taken the risk of attacking the West. . . . If it had been left to 'the machine,' German rearmament would never have been carried out at the pace on which Hitler insisted, or on the blitzkrieg pattern which proved to be as applicable to war with the Western powers as to the limited Polish campaign." It was "Hitler, not the German military leaders or the German people" who "decided that enough was not enough, that war must go on," and "the one thing no one thought of except Hitler was to attack Russia." "Of course he could not have done this without the military machine and skill in using it which the German armed forces put at his disposal, but the evidence leaves no doubt that the decision where and when to use that machine was in every case Hitler's, not his staff's, still less that all Hitler was doing was to react to the initiative of his opponents" (1972, pp. 241–43).

alistic, and entirely satiable) or by putting together a truly effective alliance with the Soviets and others that could have credibly threatened Germany with an immediate multifront war, thereby undercutting the very premise upon which Hitler's strategy rested. And, of course, major war in Europe could in all probability have been prevented if at any time Adolf Hitler had gotten in the way of a lethal germ, a well-placed bullet, or a speeding truck.[34]

But Hitler's opponents in Europe were horrified by the experience of the Great War and appalled by the prospect of going through anything like that again. They had concluded that only a monster or a lunatic could want, or even want to risk, another Great War, and they paid Hitler the undue compliment of assuming that he did not fall into those categories. As Williamson Murray puts it, the British were "firmly convinced that wars were something that twentieth-century statesmen did not consider." There was thus broad consensus—shared even by the curmudgeonly Winston Churchill, then out of office—that great efforts should be expended to reach a general peaceful settlement of any remaining grievances in Europe.[35]

Hitler exploited this desire like the master orchestrator and consummate liar he was. It is true that in *Mein Kampf*, written in the mid-1920s, he had envisioned a vast German empire through expansion toward the east; but now as the responsible and undisputed leader of Germany, he claimed that he only sought a settlement in which Germany would embrace all the various Germanic factions scattered around Central Europe in the Saarland, the Rhineland, Austria, and the mostly German Sudetenland section of Czechoslovakia. This last acquisition was, he assured his appeasers, the "last territorial claim I have to make in Europe." Moreover, he repeatedly proclaimed his peaceful intentions. He said he regarded "the forcible amalgamation of one people with another alien people not only as a worthless political aim, but in the long run as a danger to the internal unity and hence the strength of a nation. . . . Our racial theory therefore regards every war for subjection and domination of an alien people as a proceeding which sooner or later changes and weakens the victor internally. . . . Germany wants peace because of its fundamental convictions. . . . Germany has nothing to gain by a European war of any kind" (1935); "There is not a single German who desires war. The last war cost us two million dead and seven and a half million wounded. Even if we had been victorious, no victory would have been worth the payment of such a price" (1936); "We have no interest in breaking the peace" (1938); "For years past I have expressed my abhorrence of war and, it is true, also my abhorrence of war-mongers. . . . I love peace" (1939).

The British and French reluctantly approved his demands in hopes that Hitler really had moderated the visions expressed in *Mein Kampf*. As archappeaser, Chamberlain observed wishfully at the time, "In spite of the hardness and ruthlessness I thought I saw on his face, I got the impression that here was a man who could be relied upon when he has given his word." Meanwhile, the Allies belatedly began to build up their military forces and anticipated that in a war they could rely on the dominance of the defensive (a lesson, they thought, of the Great War) and on a sea blockade. After the Sudetenland agreement at Munich in 1938, Hitler showed his truer colors in 1939 by taking over the rest of Czechoslovakia. The British and French then guaranteed the safety of Poland and, when that country was invaded by Germany in September, declared war after thinking it over for a few days. Even at that, however, war was purely declaratory: Britain and France hunkered down behind their defensive fortifications and did no actual fighting until Germany invaded France eight months later—an idea that was Hitler's alone. It seems entirely possible that had Hitler remained content with his conquests to that point, no general war would have taken place, and Hitler and his racist Reich might still be there now, festering in Central Europe.[36]

Most of the smaller countries of Europe were even less effective in dealing with Hitler. Instead of seeking to ally themselves with larger and stronger countries, many of them responded to the German menace by trying to become as unthreatening as possible in hopes, apparently, that they might become invisible to him. Thus, Holland decided to remain quiet and neutral, Belgium broke off its alliance with France, and Denmark disarmed, while Poland and Yugoslavia strained to remain on good terms with the Germans. Hitler, of course, encouraged these developments, solemnly pledging that he would respect the small countries' neutrality.[37]

When the menace became fully manifest, many countries were so horrified by the prospect of presumably fruitless battle that they simply capitulated. Thus, Austria opened its gates to the Germans in 1938; Czechoslovakia, which was well armed, gave up without a fight in 1938 and 1939; and Denmark, which wasn't, surrendered precipitously in 1940. Those who fought—the Poles, the Norwegians, the Dutch, and the Belgians—collapsed quickly, as did the divided and demoralized French. Although the British, armed with Winston Churchill's inspiring rhetoric, managed to hold out behind their English Channel moat, their armies in France mostly reacted to Hitler's advances with retreat, and in Malaya a year and a half later their army of 100,000 meekly surrendered to an invading Japanese army of 30,000. To a notable degree, Europeans had lost all will for waging a substantial war. The only ones besides Germany that seem to have been fully willing to fight were Poland (which held out rather well for a while against impossible odds), Finland (which battled the lumbering Soviet Union in 1939–40), and Switzerland.[38]

After the fall of France in 1940, Hitler continued to pursue his visions. With the war stalemated in the west at the Channel, he turned his attention to the east, where he had always wanted to carry out his dreams of expansion. Impressed by the Soviets' incredible ineptitude in their war with tiny Finland, and noting that Soviet dictator Josef Stalin had recently killed off most of his best officers in a typical fit of paranoia, Hitler abrogated his 1939 nonaggression pact with the Soviet Union and invaded in June 1941, a decision the German people greeted with dismay.[39] As anticipated, initial victory was swift and sure, but as the brutal winter hit, the Soviets had not collapsed. It is probably not going too far to suggest that by Nazi standards the invasion of the Soviet Union was the first visible and consequential mistake Hitler had made in at least ten years.

But now he was bogged down in a war with enemies, including eventually the United States, on all sides. He had his empire, and he also had a total multifront war. Gradually the tide turned against him, but the Germans fought tenaciously for him, and the war raged on until May 1945, when Adolf Hitler finally removed himself from the scene by pointing a pistol into his mouth and pulling the trigger.

It seems a reasonable, if depressing, prediction that hundreds of years from now when the twentieth century for most people will have been reduced to a few catch words, the name that will represent it in the popular imagination will not be Winston Churchill, Pablo Picasso, George Balanchine, Franklin Roosevelt, Albert Einstein, or even Fred Astaire. Our best-remembered figure will be Adolf Hitler.

Japan's War

In the 1920s and 1930s struggles for power in Italy and Germany were won by fanatical, antidemocratic groups whose programs included territorial expansion. The idea of expansion was fairly popular even outside the newly ruling factions; but because of the memory of World War I, few in any segment of the society, including the military, were willing to risk a major war to achieve this expansion. Expansion came about only because dynamic individual leaders in each country were able, in part through deception, to convince the others that a general war could be avoided.

During the same decades a similar group, also yearning for expansion, seized power in Japan. It differed from its European counterparts, however, in that the willingness, even the eagerness, to risk a major war was quite widespread. In that respect Japan was a throwback to pre-1914 Europe. This distant, less developed country had barely participated in World War I, and it could still enthuse over war in a manner that had become largely obsolete in Europe: it was, as Alfred Vagts points out, the only country where old-style militarism survived the Great War.[40]

Japan Expands.

Beginning in 1868 a major change had taken place in Japan. Ending two centuries of seclusion from the rest of the world, Japan opened outward and at the same time shifted its domestic priorities. Henceforth, the previously despised merchant class was allowed to develop and was granted new prestige, whereas the feudal samurai class, a warrior elite steeped in mystical militarism and parasitical idleness, was cut off from support.

It seemed clear that a modern army was needed in the new Japan—one open to all classes. Many from the samurai class, seeking a place of honor, migrated into this army, taking their militaristic mentality with them. Prussian officers were brought in as trainers, and very soon Japan's army had racked up two impressive victories—one against China in 1895 and, most strikingly, one in 1905 against a major European country, Russia.

By the 1920s the new Japanese army had become the center of a militant, romantic ideology that stressed nationalism and expansion. Scorning materialism—which they associated with the classes they despised as well as with the nation they found most threatening, the United States—the ideologues latched onto the mystical notion that it was Japan's historic mission to expand into East Asia, thereby securing peace in the area and preserving their hundreds of millions of fellow Asians from imperialist oppression. By 1936 people with these ideas had achieved control of the country. Opponents in government, business, and the universities had been removed from influence and authority—many of them by assassination—and responsible ministers were inspiring arrogant slogans: "It is the holy mission of Japan to establish peace in the Orient"; "The day will come when we will make the whole world look up to our national virtues"; "Our supreme mission is to make a paradise in Asia"; "Light comes from the East!" War, the Japanese war ministry proclaimed, was "the father of creation and the mother of culture." In earthier context, sentiments like these were taken to mean that Japan was determined to use military means to dominate the world, or at least that very significant portion of it which eventually was to be dubbed the Greater East Asia Co-Prosperity Sphere.[41]

Like Hitler and Mussolini, the Japanese had formulated a sort of theory of conquest; but unlike them, they had no plan of action and achieved war mainly by wandering into it. The first move in this direction occurred in 1931 when portions of the Japanese army stationed in Manchuria, acting largely on their own authority, essentially took control of the area. As the army and its civilian allies gradually tightened control within Japan, they cast about for new territories upon which to bestow their benevolent, if uninvited, stewardship; at the same time, they sought to prepare the Japanese people for all-out war should that eventually prove necessary to maintain the national ambition. As early as 1932 many felt that a war against the Soviet Union was inevitable.[42]

In 1937, after several military incidents in China as well as a series of ill-considered policy lurches, Japan decided that it was "irrevocably committed to the conquest of China." "Holy war" was on, and within half a year the Japanese peacemakers had committed tens of thousands of rapes in China and over 200,000 murders of civilians and prisoners of war. Even Hitler, a Japanese ally, was dismayed at the aggression. The Japanese army had entered this war boasting that a successful conquest of China would take a mere three months. The Chinese retreated but continued to fight, and the conflict in China lasted eight years, cost Japan 250,000 battle deaths, and eventually evolved into a broader war that cost an additional million.[43]

Toward War with the United States.

With the China "incident," Japan went onto a war footing, both economically and psychologically; but the costs of the vast war in China soon brought economic strain, even as the prosecution of the war itself brought deteriorating relations with the British, Americans, and Soviets (with whom Japan had two costly border clashes in 1938 and 1939). Japan reacted by forming closer ties with the Germans and Italians, by tightening the grip at home, and by calling for "sacrifices upon sacrifices." After all, suggested Japan's premier in 1940, "no nation has ever become powerful by devoting itself to luxury and pleasure," a proposition that the history of post-1945 Japan would eventually contradict.[44]

In the early summer of 1940, Germany defeated Holland and France and had Britain, to put it mildly, severely preoccupied. With Dutch, French, and British control over their colonies thus substantially weakened, Japan soon formulated amazing plans to establish, by conquest if necessary, a "New Order" in East Asia which would include, in addition to China and Manchuria, the French colonies in Indochina and the Pacific, the Dutch colonies in the East Indies, independent Thailand, and the British colonies in Malaya, Burma, Borneo, and India. To this degree, Hitler's victories were a contributing cause of the war in Asia and the Pacific.[45]

To establish bases to the south of China that could be used in the war effort there, Japan intimidated the French colonials to assign them areas in northern Indochina. Some of the hopelessly outnumbered French defenders thought they ought to go down fighting; that view did not prevail.[46]

Japan was peculiarly susceptible to economic pressure because it had to import so many of its vital resources: in 1936, for example, 66 percent of its oil came from the United States, a country which had become increasingly concerned, and threatening, over Japan's foreign adventures during the decade. In sympathy with China, the United States began signaling its concerns and potential military involvement by variously restricting trade with Japan and by moving its Atlantic fleet first to San Diego and then, in spring 1940, to Pearl Harbor in Hawaii. The Japanese got the message and then decided to continue their quest to establish the Greater East Asia Co-Prosperity Sphere.[47]

As the first stage, bases were forcibly established in southern Indochina in the summer of 1941, a move that drew a sharp reaction from the United States: an economic embargo. The Japanese and the Americans negotiated for five months on this issue, but it soon became clear that there would be no agreement; the United States would continue its embargo until the Japanese backed down on its imperial ambitions. Japan's oil stocks and other supplies necessary for war were rapidly dwindling, so a decision was made to seize the necessary raw materials and to establish the New Order by a coordinated attack on possessions of Holland, France, Britain, and the United States. Included was a lightning raid on December 7 on the U.S. fleet reposing so temptingly within range at Pearl Harbor.

The general feeling, as a Japanese minister explained it to the skeptical emperor, was that Japan was like a patient who was wasting away on an operating table. An operation was necessary to prevent death, although there was no guarantee the operation would be successful. To give in, they felt, would be equivalent to national suicide.[48] Death here was being equated both with the abandonment of the imperial aims that had been so central to Japanese thinking for a decade or more and with the acceptance of a gradual military decline to second- or third-rate status.

The United States did not see it that way. Rather than prescribing "death," the Americans stood ready to assist the patient, once it had abandoned its military ambitions, peacefully to secure "all the desiderata for which she allegedly started fighting—strategic, economic, financial, and social security," as Joseph Grew, the American ambassador, put it at the time.[49] In fact, after the war the United States had an opportunity to carry out that promise, and eventually the Japanese did gain awesome influence, if not direct control, over exactly the areas they had lusted after in 1941 (and, it seems, over quite a few additional ones, like California).

Romanticism and the War with the United States.

However, the American plan for Japan was an idea whose time had not yet come; and almost all the Japanese leaders agreed that although they actually preferred peace to war, under the circumstances war was the only honorable, or even conceivable, course of action. (On the Japanese decision for war, see pp. 229–30). The Japanese may have been less willing than Hitler to countenance total war, but they seem to have been equally willing to risk it rather than give up on their grand schemes. They maneuvered themselves into a position of desperation, which developed "into a determination to risk all," as Grew described it. When War Minister Tojo assessed the prospects, he opined that at some point in a lifetime one might find it necessary to make a dangerous jump with eyes closed—a romantic pronouncement, Robert Butow observes, that was in "the tradition of the samurai" from whom Tojo was descended, where "willingness to take up any challenge, regardless of the odds, was legendary."[50]

Unlike in Germany, the Japanese willingness to take risks went rather deep into the society. No one was asking the Japanese people for their opinion on these matters, but quite a few groups within the army and within the civilian population were noisily crying for immediate war, and some were threatening to assassinate any leaders who might disagree. Connected to this was a widespread, rather mystical, belief in a sort of apocalyptic final victory. As Tojo, now the premier, put it in a speech early in the war, the "key to success" lay "firmly in believing in the certainty of victory." Japan was impelled by an intoxicating, romantic, semireligious faith that victory could come out of spectacular, glorious battle and that spirit could miraculously triumph over material force. This very old-fashioned belief persisted throughout the war, especially in the army, and was still being voiced after the atomic bombings of Hiroshima and Nagasaki.[51]

Opposing Japan

The Japanese drive for status and empire in East Asia was a thoroughly accepted premise of its policy by the end of the 1930s, and it is difficult to see, short of a radical change of leadership, how they could have been dissuaded or deterred from war.

Of course, one method that would have worked, at least in the short run, would have been to let them have what they wanted. They seem to have been sincere in their repeated proclamations that they didn't really desire war and felt it their mission to bring peace to the area through a sort of paternalistic conquest. Already bogged down in a costly, lengthy war in China, they were not really hankering for more of the same. Although their imperial ambitions even included the notion of bringing India into their embrace, the strain of managing an empire might have tempered such far-flung ambitions eventually.

Another alternative for the United States—using jargon formulated in a later era—would have been to apply containment to the Japanese, rather than rollback. In their negotiating proposals of late 1941, the Japanese said they would withdraw from southern Indochina if the United states would lift its embargo and allow them to continue with their "holy war" in China.[52] The United States could have accepted this while seeking to contain further expansion by militarily shoring up areas on the periphery of the empire and continuing to aid the Chinese. Japan would then have been left with its enervating war in China, but it would not have been faced with collapse. Thus contained, Japan might have mellowed its ambitions in time. Instead, the oil embargo cut off something vital to the Japanese, giving them a choice of starting a war to regain it or committing "national suicide" by abandoning cherished goals. (In the postwar era the American embargo might be equivalent to cutting the Soviet Union off from the Ukraine, leaving the Soviet leadership with the choice of war or, as they might see it, terminal decline.)

Containment might not have worked with the Japanese in 1941. They planned to escalate their demands if the United States accepted their negotiating proposals,[53] so they might have doggedly pursued a policy that would have eventually led to war anyway. And, of course, given the poor state of America's military preparedness and the strength of its isolationist movement, the United States did not really have the military force or the political will to harden a containment perimeter around Japan, although it certainly could have increased its aid to China, where Japan's chief imperial problems lay.

Another method for deterring the Japanese might have been to disrupt their short-range plans, which were so resolute and optimistic. If near-term victory had been unlikely, myopic Japanese decision makers might have considered their schemes more carefully.[54] But, again, the United States simply didn't have the military strength or the political unity to carry out such a policy before Pearl Harbor.

Although nuclear weapons do not seem to have been crucial to developments in the post war world, as discussed later, American possession of atomic weapons in 1941, coupled with the credible threat to use them, might have effectively deterred the Japanese—particularly if Japan did not also have them. Such a dramatic threat of destruction in the short run might have been vivid enough to puncture Japanese romanticism. But it might just as well have caused them to moderate their aggression by moving on British, French, and Dutch possessions and avoiding the triggering attack on Pearl Harbor.

For Japan was in general a backward country in 1941—one where major or total war was still seen to be a possible benefit or an honorable necessity, and where imperial status was held to be crucial.[55] It took a cataclysmic war for the Japanese to learn the lessons Europeans had garnered from World War I, and which Holland and a few other countries had grasped centuries earlier. But the Japanese were to learn the lesson well.

Toward a World of Milnes

In the 1930s A. A. Milne, the author of *The World of Pooh,* was one of many writing in advocacy of peace. Milne firmly contended that war does not come about by some ineffable cosmic process, but rather that "war is something of man's own fostering and if all mankind renounces it, then it is no longer there." Since he rejected war himself, it followed that "if everybody in Europe thought as I do, there would be no more war in Europe. If a few important people thought as I do: if Ramsey MacDonald were Milne, and Mussolini were Milne, and Stalin were Milne, and Hitler were Milne, and anybody who might at any moment be in a French Cabinet were Milne: then, however tolerable the prospects in other ways, there would be no more war in Europe." At the same time Milne rejected the notion that threats of war could be used to prevent war: war was a poison, he felt, and "we should not roll it meditatively round the tongue and wonder how to improve the taste."[56]

Regretfully for Milne's cause, a few people in his world, including a couple on his little list, still savored the unimproved poison. It took another conflagration to get rid of them and of like-minded leaders in Japan, but when it was over, the developed world was significantly closer to Milne's ideal state: the futility and repulsiveness of major war became even more evident and was accepted about as universally as any idea can be. Even Germany and Japan became Hollandized. But at the same time, the somewhat paradoxical notion that the threat of war should be used to prevent—to deter—war achieved credibility and viability. It soon became an important—but possibly an anachronistic—part of diplomatic policy.

II

COLD WAR, NUCLEAR WEAPONS, AND THE LONG PEACE

4

Implications of the World War II Experience

BY THE END OF 1941, world war had been achieved. In June, Hitler launched his long-planned advance to the east by invading the Soviet Union, and on December 7, Japan attacked the United States at Pearl Harbor as part of a drive to take over various British, Dutch, and American possessions in Asia and the Pacific. The United States had been gradually moving toward war with Germany and Italy, and Hitler and Mussolini, seeing war with the Americans as an ultimate inevitability and wishing to curry favor with their Japanese ally, linked the war in Asia with the one in Europe by declaring war on the United States on December 11.[1]

This chapter focuses on four somewhat disconnected aspects of the World War II experience that relate to broader themes developed in this book: (1) the astounding performance in the war of the American economy and its potential as a deterrent to a future aggressor even in the absence of nuclear weapons; (2) the curious avoidance of chemical weapons in the war, suggesting that even major conflicts do not necessarily escalate to incorporate all available weapons; (3) the atomic bomb's dubious impact on the Japanese surrender of 1945 and its less than fully obvious military value in future conflicts; and (4) the remarkable absence, or near absence, of armed civil opposition to Nazi occupation, suggesting that by the 1940s most people in the developed world had lost all stomach not only for international war, but for civil war as well.

Detroit and Deterrence

The United States went into the war with enormous reluctance—Robert Sherwood called it "the first war in American history in which the general disillusionment preceded the firing of the first shot." Allan Nevins characterized the national mood during the war as "grimly somber," and in general the war was cheerlessly accepted as "but one more task that must be done to quench the flame that would engulf our world," as an amateur poet put it in the *New York Times* on the day before Pearl Harbor.[2]

The Americans carried out this "task" with methodical dispatch. They built a large army (in 1940 they had about as many men under arms as Belgium, which had just crumbled before the Nazi invasion), but it was their economic contribution that was probably their most impressive achievement. Engaged now in large wars on two separate continents, the United States decided to hold off one major enemy, Japan, while concentrating with its allies on knocking off the other first. Meanwhile, it needed to supply both itself and its far-flung allies.

The economy was put into gear. Even with 8 million of its ablest men out of the labor market, industrial production increased 15 percent per year, and agricultural production rose 30 percent overall. War production, which stood at 2 percent of total output in 1939 and 10 percent in 1941, was 40 percent in 1943, and by 1944 the United States was producing 40 percent of all the armaments in the world and as much steel as the entire world had produced before the war.[3] When President Franklin Roosevelt called upon American industry to produce a totally unprecedented 50,000 aircraft in 1942, he was scoffed at, and, to a degree, the scoffers proved right: the United States turned out only 48,000 aircraft in 1942. Then it produced 86,000 in 1943 and nearly 100,000 in 1944. In the course of the war the United States produced about as many aircraft as the Germans, Japanese, and Soviets combined, and the American total included a far higher proportion of large, technically advanced bombers.[4]

Some of this can be attributed to the sheer size of the American economy, but much of it was due to its quality as well. Industrial labor productivity increased 25 percent between 1939 and 1944, and wartime output per worker was twice that of Germany and about five times that of Japan. The yield per harvested acre of the major crops rose by over 26 percent between 1940 and 1942 and by another 13 percent in 1945. Ingenuity and experience with mass production also helped. The prototype of a complex new gun had taken 450 man hours of highly skilled labor to produce in Sweden; when mass production techniques were applied, the

Americans found ordinary workers could turn out a gun in 10 man hours. The U.S. Maritime Commission hoped a large merchant ship could be constructed in six months; shipbuilder Henry J. Kaiser figured out how to do it in twelve days. A factory in Michigan, scheduled to produce 160 machine guns between March 1941 and March 1942, found it could just as easily produce 28,728, and did.[5]

As early as 1943—only two years after Pearl Harbor—some munitions plants were being closed down in anticipation of postwar surpluses. It was already too late. When the war ended, the United States had on its hands $90 billion in surplus war goods. If the government could have sold this stuff to somebody, it could have lived for a year and a half on the proceeds: national expenditures in the first peacetime year were only about $60 billion. Moreover, while producing all this war material, while paying taxes with an appended 5 percent "Victory Tax" surcharge, and while plowing billions of dollars into U.S. War Bonds, Americans increased their consumer spending by 12 percent between 1939 and 1944.[6]

Of course, there were inefficiencies and necessary sacrifices. The war cut off supplies of rubber, an important commodity, and Americans had to conserve. Gasoline was severely rationed in order to save on tires, and the country switched to synthetic rubber: 1 percent of consumption in 1941, 80 percent in 1944. (A terrible girdle shortage ensued, and bubble dancer Sally Rand felt it her patriotic duty to turn over sixty-one of her sixty-three rubber bubbles in the big midwar rubber drive.)[7]

By any standard it was an impressive, even astonishing, performance. As the amazed British historian Denis Brogan put it at the time, "To the Americans war is a business, not an art."[8]

The Soviets also stood to be impressed. Roosevelt liked to refer to his country as the "arsenal of democracy," but the United States also effectively supplied one of the world's largest nondemocracies. Getting supplies to the beleaguered Soviets was no easy task, but somehow 15,234,791 long tons (that's 17,062,965 regular tons) got there. Included were 409,526 trucks (81 percent of them 1½-ton trucks or larger), 12,161 tanks and other combat vehicles (more than the Germans had in 1939), 32,200 motorcycles, 1,966 locomotives, 11,075 railroad cars, 112,293 submachine guns, 15,000 aircraft, 2,670,371 tons of petroleum products, 16 million pairs of boots (in two sizes), and more than one-half pound of food for every Soviet soldier for every day of the war (much of it Spam).[9]

In all, these imports represented a substantial portion of Soviet war material. Even assuming that Stalin's postwar statistics about Soviet war production were not exaggerated, the West supplied him with 10 or 15 percent of his heavy equipment. Although the Soviets were often reluctant to acknowledge this aid and sometimes even manipulated the figures to make the aid seem smaller, they must have been well aware of what the war-wary Americans could produce once they set their minds to it.[10]

The Soviets no doubt carried at least some measure of appreciation for U.S. accomplishments into the postwar world. The United States possessed the bomb after the war, and it also had Detroit. *Either* weapon could be an effective deterrent.

Restraints on Escalation: The Case of Gas

That gas was not used in World War II is curious. As Frederic Brown has noted in his study of chemical warfare, "For the first time since the advent of the nation at arms a major weapon employed in one conflict was not carried forward to be used in a subsequent conflict."[11]

Several reasons account for this unprecedented phenomenon. Many people, including Roosevelt, found the weapon morally repugnant. Furthermore, most military establishments, while readily accepting two other innovations from World War I—the tank and the airplane—into their arsenals, never really incorporated the chemical weapon into their thinking. Some felt it was militarily ineffective because it could be countered by masks and other defensive measures. They were also disconcerted by the fact that gas often tended to wound rather than kill. In World War I, for example, gas may have caused 1.3 million casualties, but only 91,000 of these people died; the rest eventually recovered.[12]

Others saw it as all too effective, carrying with it many unpleasantly complicating effects. Some American army maneuvers in 1936 with simulated mustard gas produced estimates of 80 or 90 percent casualties among combatants, raising massive problems of recovery and medical treatment. Moreover, no one liked the idea of trying to operate and communicate while wearing those ghastly masks, and the notion that one's tactics would depend on which way the wind happened to be blowing at the moment added more uncertainty to the situation than most commanders liked to contemplate. There was also the extremely messy problem of decontamination. Soldiers who were exposed needed to bathe in motor oil and then in hot soapy water; metal articles had to be washed in kerosene, treated with bleaching powder for hours, washed with water, and then dried and oiled; clothing had to be steamed for four hours. The task of decontaminating a one-mile stretch of road was deemed to be "a stupendous undertaking."[13]

But probably the most important reason gas was not used in World War II

84

was mutual deterrence, the fear of retaliation. Everybody had stocks of the stuff and could deliver it. Therefore, although some short-term gains existed from introducing the weapon into combat, the other side was likely to retaliate in kind, leading to a pointless escalation of destruction.[14]

Throughout the war the leaders of the combating nations issued explicit and vivid threats of retaliation. Roosevelt, while declaring that the United States would never use the weapons first, pledged that "any use of gas by any Axis power" would "immediately be followed by the fullest possible retaliation." Germany and Italy issued similar proclamations, and British Prime Minister Winston Churchill was, as usual, the most piquant: "We are, ourselves, firmly resolved not to use this odious weapon unless it is used first by the Germans. Knowing our Hun, however, we have not neglected to make preparations on a formidable scale." The tendency for each side to overestimate the chemical warfare capabilities of the other enhanced the effectiveness of such declarations.[15]

The British, despite their bold assertions, apparently planned to use gas as a weapon of last resort if the Germans invaded. Whether Britain would actually have done so, given the significant likelihood of German retaliation on British population centers, is questionable. The Germans, after all, eventually were invaded and were pushed to their last desperate innings, yet they never made use of their chemical warfare capabilities. Hitler at the end apparently did order that gas be used, but either his underlings talked him out of it, or they managed to undermine the implementation of his orders.[16]

Despite Roosevelt's explicit warning that "any use" of gas would "immediately" lead to "the fullest possible retaliation," minor Japanese violations did not trigger an escalatory chain reaction. Another violation apparently occurred, this time by accident, in Italy, where German artillery struck some stocks of American chemical weapons. As the cloud of toxic gas drifted toward the nearby Germans, the American commander sent a message to his German counterpart explaining what had happened. The German commander believed the message and did not retaliate.[17]

Obviously, then, effective restraint in the use of weapons can occur even in a war that is otherwise "total" and even when minor or accidental violations of the constraints occur. Thus, as Brown suggests, there is no reason to assume that escalation must be inevitable.[18] One should not casually extrapolate from the World War II experience with gas to conclude that nuclear weapons could necessarily be kept out of World War III. Nuclear weapons are more militarily impressive, easier to use, and have entered far more deeply into military and political war planning. But, as argued more fully in chapter 10, enough aspects of the dynamic that kept chemical weapons from being used in World War II apply to the nuclear case to suggest caution in accepting the widespread (and quite possibly beneficial) assumption in the postwar world that escalation to doomsday is inevitable, or nearly so, if the United States and the Soviet Union ever get into serious direct military conflict.

The Atomic Bomb and its Military Implications

Although the United States had firmly pledged not to use chemical or biological weapons, the inclusion of these weapons in the invasion of the main Japanese islands was given passing consideration. The idea was quickly rejected because of moral and political concerns, because the military was poorly equipped and trained to use the weapons, and because of fear that the Japanese might retaliate both against the invaders and against America's Chinese allies.[19] Obviously, no such restraints were effectively operative in the decision to use the new atomic bomb.

The Decision to Drop the Bomb.

Before the bomb was dropped, the Americans, British, and Chinese issued the Potsdam Declaration of July 26, 1945, calling once again for Japanese surrender and warning that the alternative would be "the complete destruction of the Japanese homeland." The Japanese cabinet, stalemated by a tie vote on getting out of the war, adopted a wait-and-see attitude, hoping for Soviet mediation. But the public response, as expressed by the Japanese prime minister and official newspapers, was that the declaration was not of "great value" and that it would be "killed with silence" or "treated with silent contempt." So rebuffed, the new American president, Harry Truman, anxious to end the war as soon as possible and therefore to minimize American casualties, ordered that the new weapon be dropped on Japanese cities to help the enemy come to its senses.[20]

Although World War II will probably be remembered most for the Nazi death camps and for the atomic bomb, neither element was well known or appreciated at the time by the people who actually lived through the war. Some general information circulated about the death camps, but much of this was discounted as exaggerated rumor, in part because of the wariness induced by propagandistic lies that had been floated about German atrocities during World War I. More-over, the extent of the systematic slaughter of Jews and other groups by the Nazis—totaling perhaps 12 to 20 million—could not be fully grasped until the invading armies overran the camps, and this happened only at the end of the war.* And, of course, the existence of the atomic bomb was known only to a few before it was dropped on Hiroshima and Nagasaki.

That the weapons might be crucial was by no means obvious to all of those who knew about them. The American Chiefs of Staff treated the atomic bomb as "just another weapon." Admiral William Leahy was doubtful that it would be effective, and General George Marshall anticipated that it would primarily be useful as "protection and preparation for landings" on Japan.[21]

For the most part, the atomic bomb differed from earlier weapons only in that a single explosion could cause vast damage. Using conventional bombing meth-ods, tens of thousands had been killed in the German city of Dresden, and raids of Tokyo in March 1945 had killed about 100,000. It was anticipated that the bombs dropped on Hiroshima and Nagasaki would kill 20,000 each. While the actual death toll turned out to be 110,000 or greater, the atomic bombs could cause no more damage than the United States was already fully capable of inflicting with its total command of the air, though now the Japanese had to scurry for cover when just a couple of bombers appeared.[22]

Japan's Decision to Surrender.

The Americans' chief hope was that the new weapon would somehow have a beneficial shock effect on the Japanese. The evidence that it had this impact is less than fully convincing. No vote in the Japanese cabinet was changed by the two bombings, nor did the Japanese modify their surrender terms—the crucial demand that the emperor and the imperial institution be retained. The most that can be said for the bombs is that they helped to undercut the Japanese army's romantic pretensions that victory could somehow be salvaged in a last glorious battle for its never previously conquered homeland, and that they helped the

*In a 1943 poll only half the American population said they though the death-camp "rumors" were true. By the end of 1944 this proportion had risen, but few respondents guessed that the death toll would be greater than "thousands." Polls also suggest that in 1943 American hatred of the Japanese was substantially greater than that of the Germans. This difference may be partly due to racism, but it also reflects special hostility to the Japanese because of their known mistreatment of American prisoners of war—1 percent of American prisoners in German hands died, as compared with 57 percent of those in Japanese hands (NBC 1986)—and because of the "sneak attack" at Pearl Harbor (Hitler at least had declared war before fighting the Americans—if not the Poles). Moreover, since the Japanese had no clear Hitler figure to hate, Americans tended to blame the general populace for the war. However, by 1946, after the death camps had been discovered, this difference between hatred of the Japanese and of the Germans was almost eliminated (Mueller 1973, pp. 64–65, 173–74).

emperor, who had been on the side of surrender for months, to exert himself in the cabinet debates. That is, while they may have helped to tip a balance, they were effective only because a delicate balance happened to exist.[23]

Had the Americans refused to keep the emperor, or had the emperor wanted, like the craven Hitler, to preside over a final drawn-out, suicidal conflagration, the war would have continued, bomb or no bomb.[24] When the emperor went on the radio a week after the atomic bombings to announce surrender, the reaction of the Japanese people was almost universally one of astonishment and shock: it was generally expected that he would urge them on to greater efforts or to fight to the last.[25] Many in the leadership wanted to do exactly that, and had the emperor agreed, the United States might *still* be fighting on the Japanese islands, at least against urban guerrillas and rural outposts. The Communists in Vietnam have been fighting one enemy or another (including two different nuclear powers) almost continuously since 1940; the Japanese certainly might have been capable of similar fanaticism.

Hatreds were intense in the Japanese-American war, and many Japanese fully believed they would be tortured and killed by the American occupiers.* Fed in part by that anticipation, Japanese soldiers had fought to the death or committed suicide rather than give up: usually less than 5 percent surrendered.† Moreover, the last year of the war had seen thousands of attacks by suicidal kamikaze bombers and shinyo boats, as well as mass suicide among civilians.[26] On Saipan, hundreds of Japanese civilians, forced to a cliff by advancing American forces, killed themselves and their children by exploding hand grenades or by leaping onto jagged rocks or into the sea. On Okinawa, civilians were pressed into military service; and hundreds of others, particularly children and the elderly, turned over their food to the Japanese army and then killed each other with razors, hatchets, and sickles. "We will fight," the Japanese had vowed, "until we eat stones." Or as the war minister exhorted to the army *after* Hiroshima and Nagasaki, "All that remains to be done is to carry through to its end the holy war for the protection of the Land of the Gods. We are determined to fight resolutely although that may involve our nibbling grass, eating earth, and sleeping in the fields. It is our belief that there is little in death." Had the emperor actively supported the idea, the popular Japanese slogan "One hundred million die together!" might well have eventually been translated into vivid reality.[27] Even without his blessing, a

---

*Their belief was not entirely without foundation. Asked what should be done with the Japanese after the war, 10 to 15 percent of Americans in various polls conducted during the war volunteered the solution of extermination. After the war was over, 23 percent said they regretted that many more atomic bombs had not "quickly" been used on Japan before they "had a chance to surrender." For analysis, see Mueller 1973, pp. 172–73.

†In the battle for the Philippines, only 7,236 surrendered out of a garrison of 317,000, and on Okinawa 107,000 were killed and 10,600 were taken prisoner (Batchelder 1961, p. 149).

few Japanese soldiers, refusing to believe surrender had ever occurred, held out for decades in isolated caves.*

As this suggests, the timing of a war's end is determined more by the loser than by the winner; that is, it is probably more sensible to think of wars being lost than won. In this respect they are more like street fights than sports matches: they are over when one side gives up. This could be quickly—before a blow is even struck—or it could be days, weeks, years, or decades if both sides (or avenging friends or relatives) want to continue the dispute.

The Atomic Bomb as a Weapon.

For the most part, the atomic bombings had an electrifying impact on world opinion. Like gas, the bombs were seen to have put warfare on a new and even more terrible plane. And, also like gas, nuclear weapons were seen to be horrible not only for the damage they caused but for the way they inflicted it: lingering deaths and sickness from radiation poisoning, burns, and cancer, plus long-term genetic damage. In part because of these especially insidious effects, nuclear weapons, again like chemical ones, soon picked up a peculiar onus that led in the postwar era to continuous efforts to ban them in favor of more conventional methods of destruction.

People now had new and even better reason to envision apocalypse and dooms-day. But some believed that this weapon, which seemed by sheer terror to have brought World War II to a precipitous end, might through similar means prevent the next one by vividly promising consequences that no one—not even a Hitler—could possibly want to contemplate. And so, at least in some quarters, hope survived horror.

At the same time, some analysts were skeptical about the revolutionary nature of the atomic bomb. One military commentator, Major Alexander de Seversky, after inspecting the two bombed cities in 1945 at the request of the U.S. Secretary of War, reported to him and then to the public in lectures, books, articles, and congressional testimony that although destruction in the two cities was extensive, the damage was far less than popular accounts often indicated. De Seversky concluded that the bomb could not conceivably do damage on that scale to a modern city, and he calculated that the destruction could have been du-plicated by 200 bombers loaded with conventional weapons (the official estimate,

---

*The U.S. Strategic Bombing Survey concludes that Japan would have surrendered by the end of 1945 even if the bombs hadn't been dropped and even if the Soviets had not entered the war (1946b, p. 13). But this conclusion derives from postwar interviews with Japanese leaders detailing political progress toward surrender in the cabinet and indicating the emperor's position on the issue. It is not based on the notion that Japan would have been physically incapable of fighting by that time.

which came out after de Seversky's estimates, was 210 for Hiroshima and 120 for Nagasaki). Furthermore, he concluded that it would have taken at least 5,000 atomic bombs to accomplish the widespread damage that conventional bombers had inflicted on Germany and its occupied territories.[28]

De Seversky and others were impressed by several facts: many modern buildings of steel and concrete survived the attack, even when they were close to the blast center; no nonwooden bridges were destroyed; and railroad tracks, streets, and underground water lines were largely undamaged. Destruction was so great, they concluded, because of the exceptional vulnerability of most of the buildings with their thick tile roofs on light, flammable wooden frames. It was also impressive that electrical service was restored within one day, railroad and trolley service within two, telephone service within seven, and that the debris was largely cleared up within two weeks. As for casualties, many were due to fires in these tinderbox cities and were high both because of the peculiarly flammable nature of the building construction and because an unusually large number of people happened to be outside, were lightly clothed, and took no shelter. Moreover, only superficial wounds were received by those two-and-a-half miles away even when fully exposed, and the 400 people at Nagasaki who managed to be inside cavelike bomb shelters were uninjured even though they were close to ground zero.[29]

Thus, some concluded, hysteria was not called for: the bomb could be dealt with. Added to this was the fact, known to just a few at the time, that only small numbers of bombs were potentially available.[30] In some important respects, then, the exact military value of the atomic bomb was not entirely obvious. If it couldn't even destroy bridges and if only a few were available, reasoned some, the atomic bomb might be useful only to terrorize people or blast cities. Its future as a battlefield weapon was questionable.

The Soviets, meanwhile, were playing it cool. When Truman told Stalin of the bomb's existence, the Soviet dictator seemed unimpressed. Soviet journalists visited Hiroshima and Nagasaki and reported that the bomb's destructiveness was much exaggerated in American reports.[31] At the same time, however, Stalin launched a crash program to break the American atomic monopoly.

World War II and the Decline of Civil War in the Developed World

Europe's last free-standing civil war occurred in one of its least developed corners, Spain, between 1936 and 1939. A horrific experience in which massacre was common and in which several hundred thousand people died, it was also notable for a complex clash of ideologies: fascist, anarchist, liberal, socialist, democratic, communist, religious. Outside countries aided the side they favored: Hitler and Mussolini helped the Nationalist side; Stalin and (intermittently and unofficially) the liberal democracies aided the Republican side. The Spanish civil war thus became in part a surrogate war for larger contestants on the world scene—a form of indirect conflict that became fairly common in the Cold War that emerged after 1945. The only civil wars that have taken place in Europe since the Spanish Civil War have been connected to World War II in one way or another. And there have been remarkably few of these.

One might have expected that widespread civil warfare would erupt against the occupation forces of the hated Nazis who controlled most of Europe during much of the war. But civil warfare truly developed only in Yugoslavia, where visible, indiscriminate mass murder by the occupying Nazis and their local allies became commonplace, creating the impression that no one could possibly be safe from slaughter; thus legions were driven into desperate armed opposition.[32] The Nazis perpetrated plenty of mass murder elsewhere in Europe, of course, especially of the Jewish population. But in general, the Nazis exerted great efforts to make those murders invisible (target populations were "relocated" to secluded camps) and discriminate: anyone who did not belong to a specifically identified enemy group of the occupying forces or who did not break certain specific rules could have hopes of living in a reasonably normal fashion.

And while deeply resenting the occupiers, that's what just about everybody did. Particularly in the early years of Nazi rule, subject populations kept out of trouble by cooperating in the sense of carrying out their normal occupations and functions. This, as Norman Rich has observed, "kept the routine business of government and the economy going and thereby enabled the Nazis to rule, and to exploit, the occupied countries with a minimum investment of German personnel."[33] Indeed, the Germans often found that occupation, contrary to the dicta of Norman Angell, could be quite profitable. The people of the occupied territories continued to turn out products necessary for Germany's war, and the occupiers levied taxes, charged "occupation costs," and engaged in other financial devices to obtain revenue. The sums so received were far higher than the actual costs of maintaining the occupying army; the occupation of France was particularly profitable.[34] The Soviets were to find something similar after World War II when they occupied some of the areas formerly controlled by Nazi Germany.

To be sure, the Germans (and the Soviets) could be extremely ruthless with opponents, and underground resistance movements existed throughout the Nazi empire, particularly as German authority began to wane toward the end of the war. There were also a few armed uprisings, and often there was nonviolent opposition to the occupiers—work slowdowns, obstruction of orders, mass non-cooperation, symbolic protests, social boycotts, economic sabotage, underground efforts to maintain national cultural traditions that were banned by the authorities, even efforts to spread contagious diseases among occupying troops.[35] But, in general, the occupied territories, particularly those in the west, were populated by people who had lost all appetite for armed opposition. Tales about resistance fighters may inspire adventure novels and films, but resistance activities rarely constituted an important part of the war. Indeed, in all the occupied territories only two Nazi leaders were assassinated: one of these was an easy target because he rode the same route to the office every day in an open car guarded only by his chauffeur, and the other was murdered by his mistress.[36] Outside the developed world, things were different. In Japanese-occupied areas of Asia and the Pacific extensive guerrilla opposition movements often appeared—in Manchuria, China, Indochina, and the Philippines, for instance. The Japanese were capable of being brutal and vindictive like the Germans in seeking to put down such rebellions, but their efforts were not nearly as effective in stifling the war spirit.

This experience suggests that in an important area of the world armed rebellion has widely come to be accepted as futile and unwise. Between 1945 and 1980, forty-three clearly identifiable civil wars were begun in the world, and there have been many more since that time. Over the same period there have also been numerous other events that might be considered civil wars by some standards: anticolonial wars, bloody coups, armed uprisings, violent communal conflicts, regional wars within a country. Unless one counts the Hungarian rebellion of 1956 as a secessionist civil war and unless one considers terrorism in a few places like Northern Ireland to have reached warlike levels, none of these hundreds of events (so far, at least) have taken place in the developed world.[37] Clearly, this is a regularity that cannot be explained as a statistical quirk. Something deeper has been going on.

5

Cold War, Containment, and the Irrelevance of Nuclear Weapons

H ISTORY'S most destructive war concluded with the annihilation of the war-endorsing regimes that had started it and with the rise to central international prominence of the United States and the Soviet Union. Once wary wartime allies, the two big countries—superpowers, they were quickly labelled—gradually became contesting and often hostile opponents. For a major war to break out in the postwar era, the United States and the Soviet Union would have to be central participants. Accordingly, the nature and evolution of their conflict are important concerns in the remainder of this book. That conflict has generated crises and surrogate wars, but it appears that direct war between the US and the USSR has never been close and has become decreasingly likely as time has passed.

This chapter deals with the early years of the Cold War between West and East when the outlines and basic premises of the conflict were established and when the two sides formulated their basic strategies for dealing with each other. World War I, it has been argued, shattered what H. T. Buckle had once labelled the "war-like spirit" in the developed world and made large majorities there into unapologetic peacemongers. World War II, it appears, was regrettably necessary to reinforce that lesson in Europe and to convert the less advanced Japanese in Asia. When the rubble had settled, the notion that appeal and wisdom existed in a direct war between developed countries had been about as discredited as any idea can be.

Nevertheless, some sort of conflict between East and West was inevitable. While the violence of *major war* may have come generally to be accepted as repulsive, immoral, uncivilized, and/or futile, the Soviet Union still subscribed religiously to the notion that the violence of revolution and of revolutionary war was necessary, progressive, beneficial, natural, inevitable, heroic, glorious, beautiful, cleansing, thrilling, noble, virtuous, exciting, and, at least in their own special ideological sense, holy.

Furthermore, the Soviets and their supporters believed that the virtues of revolution would spread worldwide and that they were morally bound to aid in this natural and inevitable process. This worldview and its explicit and endlessly repeated threat did not go entirely unappreciated in the capitalist world. That anyone wishing to preserve the capitalist system would seek to prevent Communist revolution and its violence was obvious.

This contest carried with it the potential for war. Before World War I, Soviet Communism's founding guru and patron saint, Vladimir Lenin, had declared that "war is progress, irrespective of the victims and the suffering it entails" if it liberates the proletariat from the capitalist "yoke."[1] The problem for the war-averse West, then, was to figure out how to deal with people like that. Major international war was not central to Lenin's theory, the way it was to Hitler's, but it was in there someplace and could, in theory at least, bubble to the surface if conditions seemed favorable.

During the late 1940s, the West worked out a half-dynamic, half-restrained policy to deal with the Soviet threat by seeking to contain it—to hold it where it stood in hopes that in time the Communists would lose their evangelistic, threatening, revolutionary spirit. This chapter deals with the evolution of that policy as well as with simultaneous Soviet maneuverings and with post-Lenin developments in Communist theorizing about war.

It also discusses nuclear weapons, which seem to have been essentially irrelevant to these processes. It is difficult to see how either side could find a nuclear war remotely in its interests, but it is no easier to envisage how the cautious, war-sobered countries that have dominated the postwar era could possibly look upon a repetition of World War II with any sort of glee either. Insofar as a military threat has been necessary, it is the fear of escalation that has deterred and has kept international behavior restrained, not the special peculiarities of the horror that awaits at the end of the escalatory ladder.

The chapter begins by evaluating the way things looked as the world emerged from that well-remembered cataclysm.

The Losers: Acquiescence

Among the losers of World War II, the first to go was Italy. The Italians never managed to work up much enthusiasm for dying for Mussolini's vainglorious visions of a Mediterranean empire, and they constantly had to be propped up by their exasperated German allies. Prop or no prop, however, the Italians collapsed by 1943, and Mussolini ignominiously retreated to the protection of German forces. At the end of the war he was captured by Italian partisans and shot.

The Germans fought much harder for their leader, who had brought about precisely the kind of two-front war of attrition he had proclaimed to be the central mistake of German policy in World War I. But, pushed back on the ground and incessantly bombed from the air, the Germans finally capitulated after Hitler's suicide. The victors then proceeded to dismember the country and to eradicate the remnants of Hitler's once-triumphant Nazi party.

In an astounding transformation, the Japanese abruptly changed under their emperor's leadership from militaristic fanaticism to compliant docility. They ceased fighting almost completely and allowed the hated and feared Americans to defile their precious homeland by becoming the first conquerors in Japan's history. The Americans quickly disproved the wartime contentions of Japanese propagandists by ruling with neither viciousness nor vindictiveness.* In a remarkable display of magnanimity and enlightened self-interest, they kept their promise about retaining the emperor, while deposing and in a few cases executing the rest of Japan's war leadership.[2] Then they set about unleashing the country's powerful commercial instincts. To the fanatics' slogan of "One hundred million die together" the emperor implicitly countered with "One hundred million live together." On the whole the Japanese seem to have found that it's worked out pretty well the emperor's way.

Unlike the situation at the end of World War I, the losers were thoroughly and unambiguously defeated. Nevertheless, the peoples of any of the defeated countries could have sunk into bitter resentment, finding appeal in political entrepreneurs who endorsed forceful revenge, as had happened in Germany after 1918. But this didn't occur. There was plenty to be bitter about, but the notion that one might risk another major war in order to rectify the consequences of

---

*By contrast, widespread murder, rape, kidnapping, and pillage were committed by Soviet troops invading Japanese-held Manchuria and Korea in the last days of the war. Of the 1,300,000 Japanese soldiers and civilians who surrendered to Soviet forces, 300,000 were never seen again (Ienaga 1978, pp. 233–34; Dower 1986, pp. 298–99, 363).

World War II has never gained a following in the defeated countries. In the developed world, casual warmongering, so common before 1914, was shattered by the First World War and extinguished by the Second. The Germans resigned themselves, at least temporarily, to accepting the carving up of their country into rival zones of occupation. The Japanese, as John Dower points out, "were sick of death"; for them, "purification through self-destruction now seemed absurd," and "the goal became instead to cleanse Japan of corrupt traditional, feudalistic, militaristic elements."[3] At long last and at great cost Italy, Germany, and Japan became Hollandized.

The Victors: Contentment

The victors were also substantially exhausted by the war. Although the British and French managed to suffer fewer battle deaths than in World War I, they were physically and economically debilitated in 1945. They had sought desperately to avoid the conflict and found that the costs even of victory were prohibitive, just as they had anticipated. Weakened and worn, they limped into the postwar era still proud, but second-rate.

The big victors, the United States and the Soviet Union, had also sought to avoid the war, and when it came they suffered considerably—far more than they had in World War I. But if international status is of value, they also gained a great deal, because they emerged from the war as by far the most important countries in the world. Thus, as Kenneth Waltz has observed, they "have more reason to be satisfied with the status quo than most earlier great powers had."[4]

The United States, unscathed at home, was to dominate the international economy for decades, even as it was gradually drawn into political and military leadership of the West. The Soviet Union paid a colossal price for victory—estimates often run to 20 million dead—but it also emerged dominant over a vast area of the globe.[5] It directly annexed new chunks of ground on its fringes in Europe and Asia and dominated the territory overrun by the Red Army—which happened to include most of Eastern Europe and a substantial portion of Germany. Except, of course, for the dismemberment of Germany, even a war-exhausted Hitler might have been content with the empire his archenemy Josef Stalin controlled at the end of World War II.

Thus, despite their visceral enmity, both the United States and the Soviet Union have had good reason to be essentially comfortable with the status quo—that is, each has a lot to lose. Although each can imagine a world that would be even better—a world in which the other regime did not exist, for example—no responsible leader on either side has seen major war as a sensible or viable method for bringing about an improved state of affairs.

Renewed Visions of Doomsday, Renewed Schemes to Avoid It

Although World War II did not bring about the annihilation of the human race or of European civilization that many had anticipated, it came far closer than any previous war and certainly closer than anybody could reasonably find comfortable. The war also generated the atomic bomb, which promised destruction on a new and heightened scale. Doomsday became an even more vivid nightmare.

For many, the war and the bomb engendered a profound sense of despair: Not only had the human race invented new and even more effective methods for devastating itself, but it also seemed utterly incapable of controlling its own destiny. The Great War, for all its horror, had often seemed to carry with it the potential for an equally great postwar healing. By destroying militarism and the warring nation-state system, thought many, it might be "the war that will end war," as H. G. Wells, the popular British writer and futurist, entitled a 1914 tract. Never in the course of human affairs has a prophecy proved to be so spectacularly in error. For despite the experience of that costly conflict, despite the revulsion with war that it inspired, and despite the deep yearnings for peace felt by practically all enlightened people at its conclusion, the human race, and particularly civilized Europe, managed to plunge into an even worse war a mere twenty years later.

In the last years before his death in 1946, Wells, ill and deeply embittered, abandoned his lifelong celebration of human progress and prophesied inevitable and inescapable doom. In his last writings he declared that "the end of everything we call life is close at hand and cannot be evaded," and that mankind was "the most foolish vermin that have ever overrun the earth." His epitaph, he told friends, should read: "God damn you all: I told you so." Arnold Toynbee reached a similar conclusion but phrased it more delicately: "In our recent Western history war has been following war in an ascending order of intensity; and today it is already apparent that the War of 1939–45 was not the climax of this crescendo movement."[6]

In general, there seems to have been a popular, if glib, belief that since some twenty years separated the first and second world wars, World War III would come to pass about twenty years hence (opaquely ignoring the fact that the world war previous to World War I had occurred a hundred years earlier). Public opinion polls conducted in the United States in the mid-1940s characteristically found 30 to 75 percent opining that the next war would occur within twenty-five years.[7] Among those holding this opinion was Stalin, who said he anticipated that Germany would revive fairly rapidly, after which Germany and the USSR would fight again: "We shall recover in fifteen or twenty years and then we'll have another go at it."[8]

With some desperation, schemes were formulated at the war's end to try to invalidate such fatalism. Some Western scientists, apparently consumed with guilt over having participated in the development of a weapon that could kill with new efficiency, helped found the *Bulletin of the Atomic Scientists* in 1945. It soon sported its "doomsday clock" on the cover, suggesting that there was hope of preventing Armageddon, but only if one were quick about it.

Led by the legendary Albert Einstein, many of these scientists took time out from their laboratories and studies to consider human affairs. They quickly came to conclusions expressed with an evangelical certainty they would never have used in discussing the physical world. Although he had done his greatest work in physics while a citizen of the sovereign nation of Switzerland, Einstein proved as immune to the Swiss example as everyone else: "As long as there are sovereign nations possessing great power," he declared, "war is inevitable." Moreover, he wrote in 1950, "Unless we are able, in the near future, to abolish the mutual fear of military aggression, we are doomed." Fortunately, he and other scientists had managed to discover the one device that could solve the problem: "Only the creation of a world government can prevent the impending self-destruction of mankind." Or, as Edward Teller, a physicist who was later to be instrumental in the development of the hydrogen bomb, put it in 1946, world government "alone can give us freedom and peace." Philosopher Bertrand Russell was equally certain: "It is entirely clear," he declared, "that there is only one way in which great wars can be permanently prevented and that is the establishment of an international government with a monopoly of serious armed force."[9]

If world government was both an "absolute" and an "immediate" necessity, as Einstein proclaimed, a problem arises: How does one get there from here? Einstein hoped that world government might emerge naturally out of the United Nations.[10] Others in the West, while less visionary about world government, also hoped that somehow the victors of the war could band together in the world organization to establish and to police a lasting universal peace. The United States had been a major holdout from an earlier device, the interwar League of Nations; but it was now willing and eager to participate in, and even to host, the new venture. The idea was that the productive wartime cooperation between West and East could be preserved and harnessed to everybody's mutual benefit. For the most part, however, the Soviet Union viewed the UN with contempt, and in 1947 a committee of Soviet scientists informed Einstein with as much politeness as they could muster that his idea of a world state was a "mirage" and a "political fad." Nevertheless, many in the West hoped that grand self-interest and a process of international domestication of the Soviets would eventually bring basic agreement and general, if not genial, cooperation. Renewed efforts were also made on disarmament, focused particularly at the atomic bomb. Proposals were made, meetings were held, and hands were wrung.

It was a worthy try perhaps. But viscerally opposing policies and interests of the major members kept the United Nations from ever functioning in the way its idealistic founders intended, and disarmament proposals never got off the drawing board. Nevertheless, enthusiastic support for the UN continued for decades in the West: in 1961 President John F. Kennedy called it "the only true alternative to war" and "our last best hope."[11] Disarmament and arms control schemes continued to be formulated with ever-increasing ingenuity and debated with ever-increasing sophistication. As it happens, peace between the major countries has been maintained, but the United Nations deserves little credit for it, and disarmament and world government deserve none at all.

War and Soviet Ideology

Although the Soviet Union on one level was essentially content with the postwar status quo, on another it was viscerally opposed to it.

According to the ideology on which the regime had been founded in 1917, world history is a vast, continuing process of progressive revolution. In a theory propounded by Karl Marx and Friedrich Engels, updated and pragmatized by Lenin, and modified and enshrined by Stalin, the Communist revolution in Russia was only the first step in a process of terminal world Communization. Steadily, in country after country, the oppressed working classes will violently revolt, destroying the oppressing capitalist classes and aligning their new regimes with other like-minded countries. Eventually the world will be transformed, all class and national rivalries will vanish, and eternal peace and utopian bliss will inundate the earth. As noted, Lenin speculated that even war might be used to assist in the overthrow of decadent capitalism.

This theory can seem a little hostile to those it brands oppressors, and from the start it has inspired enmity: as Gaddis observes, "Moscow's commitment to the overthrow of capitalism throughout the world" has been "the chief unsettling element in its relations with the West since the Russian revolution." In the civil war that followed the Russian Revolution of 1917, capitalist states sent aid and military expeditions in an unsuccesful effort to topple the new Communist regime. Even when capitalist states decided to deal with the regime in terms of formal equality, they did so with great wariness. In recognizing Stalin's Soviet regime in 1933, President Franklin Roosevelt exacted from it a solemn, if empty, assurance that it would "respect scrupulously the indisputable right of the United States to order its own life within its own jurisdiction in its own way and to refrain from interfering in any manner in the internal affairs of the United States, its territories and possessions."[12]

If the Soviet Union subscribed to an ideology that seemed threatening and subversive, it also developed a social and political system that was singularly repugnant to liberal Westerners. Under Stalin after 1928 a massive tyranny was established in which a vicious totalitarian government systematically visited brutalities and spectacular economic mismanagement upon its own citizenry. During Stalin's tenure tens of millions were shot, sent to death camps, or deliberately starved to death. In terms of domestic human destruction, mounting evidence suggests that, corpse for corpse, Stalin may have outpaced Hitler as a monster.* In the words of the Yugoslavian Communist Milovan Djilas, Stalin may well have been "the greatest criminal in history."[13]

But if Stalin's regime can brook comparison with Hitler's in some respects, the Soviets, however dynamic and threatening their ideology, have never—either before or after the invention of nuclear weapons—subscribed to a Hitler-style theory of direct, Armageddon-risking conquest. The regime was born in part because a world war brought about the collapse of the czarist dynasty in Russia; and from this experience, as William Taubman has pointed out, the revolutionaries learned the "crucial lesson" that world war "can destroy the Russian regime."[14]

In 1919, Lenin wrote that before international capitalism collapsed, "a series of frightful collisions" between the Soviet Republic and the capitalist states was "inevitable," and Stalin repeated this notion in the late 1920s and early 1930s. However, the Soviets have expected that a major war between the Communist and capitalist world would arise only from an attack on them by

---

*One estimate of those killed or intentionally starved to death in 1930–37 alone comes to 14.5 million—comparable to the number killed in all of Hitler's death camps (Conquest 1986, p. 306). As MacGregor Knox puts it, both systems "required the pitiless elimination of groups: the class enemy for Marxism, the racial enemy for Nazism" (1984, p. 11).

the enemy, citing continually the example of Western intervention in their civil war.*

But by 1935 at the latest, official proclamations had abandoned the notion that such wars were inevitable and had decided that the solidarity of the international working class and the burgeoning strength of the Soviet armed forces had made them avoidable. Thus, to reduce the danger of attacks, the Soviets have sought refuge in their own military preparations and in various subversive and diplomatic methods designed to keep the capitalist world confused and disunited. They also hold a hope, stemming from their ideological perspective, that the capitalist states will be deterred by the realization that, as Stalin put it in 1934, "the numerous friends in Europe and Asia of the working class of the USSR will endeavor to strike from the rear their oppressors who have started criminal war against the Fatherland of the working class of all countries."[15]

For decades then, Soviet doctrine has consistently held that a major war between the capitalist and Communist worlds would have to be started by the capitalists. As Nikita Khrushchev remarks in his memoirs, "Our military objectives have always been defensive. That was true even under Stalin. I never once heard Stalin say anything about preparing to commit aggression against another country. His biggest concern was putting up antiaircraft installations around Moscow in case our country came under attack from the West."† The Soviets have noted that major wars can agreeably carry a harvest of revolutions in their wake, but as they see it, these revolution-advancing wars would have to be begun by the capitalists. For their own part, as Taubman has observed, they have advocated exploiting various conflicts *among* the capitalist states "to avert war by playing off one set of capitalist powers against another and to use the same tactic to expand Soviet power and influence without war."[16]

Unlike Taubman, some scholars and analysts have argued that Soviet designs are essentially benign and defensive. But even those who are the most hostile to

---

*There was some toying in the early days with the idea that Red Army troops might be sent to aid revolutions in neighboring countries. In 1919 the army was ordered to help out with a revolution in Hungary, but these orders were retracted when the troops were needed at home. In 1920 Soviet troops actually launched an invasion of Poland for this purpose, but the invasion failed and Lenin reportedly concluded that the Red Army should never again be sent directly to aid a revolution abroad. There was also some Red Army intervention in northern Iran for a while in 1920 and 1921 (Hosmer and Wolfe 1983, p. 185; Taracouzio 1940, pp. 88–89; Spector 1959, pp. 90–93). As late as 1925, Stalin was still holding the option open: "The question of our army, of its might and preparedness, will certainly face us as a burning question in the event of [revolution] arising in the countries around us. . . . Our banner is still the banner of *peace*. But if war breaks out we shall not be able to sit with folded arms. We shall have to take action, but we shall be the last to do so" (Stalin 1954, pp. 13–14).

†Khrushchev 1974, p. 533. Khrushchev is obviously thinking of major war here, not incursions against South Korea in 1950 or against various border countries in the years before World War II (see p. 137).

the Soviet regime have concluded that the Soviet Union has never seen major war as a productive, viable, useful, or remotely sensible procedure for advancing what the Soviets view as an eminently desirable and beneficial process of revolutionary development. Thus, Soviet defector Arkady N. Shevchenko, while stressing that "the Kremlin is committed to the ultimate vision of a world under its control," gives an "unequivocal no" to the question of whether "the Soviet Union would initiate a nuclear war against the United States"; instead, the Soviets "are patient and take the long view," believing "that eventually it will be supreme—not necessarily in this century but certainly in the next." Similarly, Michael Voslensky asserts that Soviet leaders desire "external expansion," but their "aim is to win the struggle between the two systems without fighting." He notes that Soviet military ventures before and after World War II have consistently been directed only against "weak countries" and only after the Soviets have been careful to cover themselves in advance—often withdrawing when "firm resistance" has been met. Richard Pipes says, "Soviet interests . . . are to avoid general war with the 'imperialist camp' while inciting and exacerbating every possible conflict within it."[17]

Although some may see the USSR as striving toward some sort of Hitlerian world domination, outright conquest, while not completely ruled out by the ideology, is neither central nor necessary to it. Instead, subversive internal revolution in the capitalist world and opportunistic exploitation of conflicts among competing capitalist states are stressed.

Moreover, Lenin's methodology contains a strong sense of cautious pragmatism: A good revolutionary moves carefully in a hostile world, striking when the prospects for success are bright and avoiding risky undertakings. As Nathan Leites has pointed out, three central rules for Soviet leaders have been "avoid adventures," "do not yield to provocation," and "know when to stop."[18]

Lenin and particularly Stalin developed a distinctly non-Marxist vision of the Soviet Union's role. As Stalin put it in 1945, they envisioned "socialism in one country"—the USSR—where "the dictatorship of the proletariat" would be consolidated, "using it as a base for the overthrow of imperialism in all countries."[19] The notion, then, was that while holding the capitalist world at bay by defensive military preparations and ingenious political maneuvers, the Soviets would aid and inspire subversive revolutionary movements throughout the world. With luck, capitalism could lurch to its inevitable demise without ever getting around to invading the "Socialist Fatherland." Aggressive, conquering Hitlerian war by the Soviets themselves would foolishly risk everything; it does not fit into this scheme at all.

The West Reacts: Containment

Western observers in the aftermath of World War II found at least two notable problems in concluding from Soviet ideological pronouncements that they were not inherently aggressive. First, despite all his talk about fraternal relations among Communist parties around the world, Stalin insisted on tight organizational control from Moscow. Thus, should a country succumb to Communist revolution, it would probably become a puppet colony and a military ally of the Soviet Union, not an independent ideological partner in a socialist commonwealth. Second, in areas where Stalin's Red Army gained control as the war ended, the overrun territories were forcefully dominated by Moscow and gradually but firmly brought under its direct and apparently perpetual control. As Stalin put it blandly in conversation with fellow Communists at the end of the war, "Whoever occupies a territory also imposes on it his own social system . . . as far as his army can reach. It cannot be otherwise."[20]

The West was alarmed. Stalin's regime, like Hitler's, was totalitarian and revolutionary. In the case of Hitler (and Japan) those characteristics were associated with armed aggression and ultimately with world war, and it now seemed that Stalin might well have similar dreams of expansion. Accordingly, Harry Truman's United States came up with a policy to deal with the Soviet threat that might have worked to oppose Hitler: it was called containment.

While reluctantly conceding that it would be difficult and dangerous to push the Soviets out of the territories they occupied in Eastern Europe after the war, containment stresses that the West should do everything possible to hold the Soviet Union where it stands, allowing it no further expansion.

The policy was strongly influenced by lessons derived from the interwar experience and summed up in the one-word slogan, "Munich." Before World War II the peace-preferring states had timorously allowed Japan, Italy, and Germany to take over peripheral areas in hopes that the acquisitions would satiate the appetites of those discontented countries for territory. Instead, it was concluded, their cravings "grew with the feeding" and made them ever more daring; eventually this culminated in the very conflagration the peace-preferring states were so desperate to avoid. Appeasement, which reached its pinnacle with the agreement at Munich to give Hitler major portions of Czechoslovakia, was therefore seen to be a spectacularly counterproductive method for dealing with an aggressor. Instead, it was crucial to oppose the aggressor early and everywhere, even in areas that objectively have little military, political, or economic importance, because if the aggressor is not confronted there, the battle will only have to be fought later under less favorable circumstances and in locales of greater significance.[21]

Containing Indirect Aggression.

In applying this lesson to the Soviet Union, Western policymakers were aware that the Soviet expansionist threat was likely to be expressed primarily in what they called "indirect aggression": subversion, diplomatic and military pressure, revolution, and armed uprising—all inspired, partly funded, and heavily influenced by Moscow.

The policy of containment was formally set in motion as the United States responded to crises that suggested indirect aggression was afoot on the periphery of Europe. In Greece, Communists were waging a civil war against a Western-oriented monarchist government, and in Turkey pressures were being applied on the government by the Soviet Union to gain various territorial and naval rights. Both threatened countries needed help, and the United States came through with military and economic aid accompanied by the ringing declaration of the Truman Doctrine of March 12, 1947, that "it must be the policy of the United States to support free peoples who are resisting attempted subjugation by armed minorities [Greece] or by outside pressures [Turkey]."[22]

In putting forth this policy, Truman made it clear that no crisis was an island unto itself. If "Greece should fall," the effect on Turkey "would be immediate and serious." Then "confusion and disorder might well spread throughout the entire Middle East." Moreover, this would have a "profound effect" upon important countries in Europe which were already "struggling against great difficulties to maintain their freedoms and independence while they repair the damages of war."[23]

This was an early expression of what would later be called the domino theory, and it derives directly from the Munich experience. It was also free of explicit limits. If all else failed, U.S. combat troops could quite possibly be sent over as part of the aid package—although nothing in the Truman Doctrine guaranteed this would occur. (As it happened, however, that decision never had to be made because troops were never required: the Greek Communists were defeated by 1949, and the Turks were able successfully to stand up to Soviet pressures.) The policy pronouncement also seemed to suggest that containment would be applied in any place in the world where, in the American judgment, international Soviet-linked Communism was on the march.[24]

A more insidious form of "indirect aggression," one with chillingly wide-ranging potential, was internal subversion in the West. In part, such subversion had allowed Hitler to take over Austria in 1938 and Japan to take over Manchuria in 1931. Then, in 1948 a coup by the Moscow-supported Communist party in Czechoslovakia brought that country into the Soviet camp—a development that, it was feared, might soon be repeated in other countries like France and Italy where there were large and well-organized Communist parties.

Even the small Communist party within the United States seemed a potential threat. Ideologically committed to the violent overthrow of sitting governments and allied with a hostile foreign country, domestic Communists had a subversive agenda that included agitation, conspiracy, sabotage, and espionage. Fears rose as evidence from defecting American and Canadian Communists in 1945 and 1946 suggested that the operatives of the Communist party generally really did believe in the conspiratorial revolutionary ideology that filled their speeches, directives, and publications.[25]

The Truman Doctrine also saw economic stability as important in opposing the spread of Communism. This lesson too was derived in part from the experience of the 1930s, because it was concluded that economic chaos had spawned Hitler and thus eventually world war. As Truman put it in 1947, "The seeds of totalitarian regimes are nurtured by misery and want. They spread and grow in the evil soil of poverty and strife. They reach their full growth when the hope of a people for a better life has died. We must keep that hope alive. . . . If we falter in our leadership, we may endanger the peace of the world."[26]

Containing Direct Aggression.

Confronting Soviet indirect aggression was therefore a multifaceted, improvisatory business, but within Western establishments the consensus gradually grew that it was wise and necessary. The issue of direct aggression by the Soviets, however, was more problematic. Following Leninist precepts (as outlined earlier), if a Communist leader could be convinced that war might safely speed up the revolution and more quickly undermine international capitalism, war would become an acceptable means.[27] Such wars in the colonial areas—wars of national liberation, they called them—were explicitly seen to be desirable and inevitable by Communist ideologues. If the opportunity arose, why not one in Europe? Policies for countering indirect aggression in its various forms were designed to nip destabilizing developments in the bud, before they could escalate to the point where military action might seem called for; but suppose Stalin with his huge postwar army decided simply to skip over various revolutionary stages and launch a direct invasion of Western Europe?

Many people felt that likelihood to be exceedingly small. George Kennan, one of containment's chief architects in the U.S. State Department, concluded, as he put it in 1948, that "we do not think the Russians, since the termination of the war, have had any serious intentions of resorting to arms."[28] But no one, of course, could be sure. Stalin had what seemed to many to be an enormous military advantage in Europe, brought about in part by the alacrity with which the American government had responded to an overwhelming sentiment (strongly encouraged by the American Communist party) to "bring the boys home" after the war. Might not the clearly hostile Stalin be tempted to use his advantage? With the Communist takeover of Czechoslovakia in the spring of 1948, Truman concluded that "we are faced with exactly the same situation with which Britain and France were faced in 1938–39 with Hitler." Responsible American officials in Europe warned that war could come with "dramatic suddenness," and the Central Intelligence Agency concluded that war was improbable only for sixty days or so. Even Kennan conceded that war might come about if Soviet "political fortunes were to advance too rapidly in Europe and they were to become dizzy with success" or if "they were to become really alarmed for security of their power in eastern Europe and take foolish and precipitate action to prevent its dissolution." In March 1948 he mused that recent Soviet actions suggest "there is something of both those elements."[29]

In the summer of 1948 the Soviets confronted American military forces directly in Germany: they blocked off Western land access to the capital city of Berlin, which lay deep within their zone of occupation. Challenged, Truman concluded, "We are going to stay. Period." The area of Berlin controlled by the West was supplied by air until the Soviets lifted the blockade a year later.

The Berlin blockade was neither war nor a clear instance of direct aggression, but it was close enough: American and Soviet troops were only a step or so away from shooting at each other. Even Kennan was willing to agree that war must be regarded "if not as a probability, at least as a possibility, and one serious enough to be taken account of fully in our military and political planning."[30] By 1949 the United States and eleven of its anti-Soviet allies had created the North Atlantic Treaty Organization. This alliance is not a traditional one that exists merely on paper or on call. Rather, all members contribute troops and put them under a joint military command, and each pledges to come to the aid of any member, no matter how small or distant, if it is attacked. An alliance like that, people argued at the time (quite probably accurately), might even have deterred Hitler from his aggressions. With NATO, containment took on its most important military component and faced up to the possibility of direct Soviet aggression in Europe. In 1950, with the Korean War, the subject of the next chapter, this possibility became truly vivid.

Containment over the Long Term.

As a policy for dealing with the Soviet expansionary threat, containment stressed, as an American secretary of state put it at the time, "patience and firmness."[31] In the long run, it was hoped, the Soviets, frustrated in their drive for territory and expanded authority, would become less hostile and more accommodating. Diplomacy would encourage that desirable development and remain open to it.

How long it might take for this to occur was not predictable, of course, but Kennan apparently believed that it wouldn't take too long. Even if Stalin, clearly the kingpin of the Soviet system, was able to maintain rigid control until his death, important changes were likely at that time. Stalin turned seventy in 1949, and Kennan anticipated that any transfer of power might well "shake Soviet power to its foundations." In general, Kennan concluded, there was a "strong" possibility that Soviet power "bears within it the seeds of its own decay, and that the sprouting of these seeds is well advanced."[32]

Moreover, the Soviets were not likely to find maintaining control over Eastern Europe easy; in 1947, Kennan proclaimed it "unlikely" that the 100 million Soviets could permanently hold down not only their own minorities but also "some 90 millions of Europeans with a higher cultural level and with long experience in resistance to foreign rule."[33] As early as 1948 some of this seemed to be coming true: an important schism in the Soviet empire developed when Stalin sought to bring Yugoslavia, led by a loyal but independent Communist party, under tighter control. Rather than coming to heel, however, the Yugoslavs pulled out of the empire. Although the Yugoslav party had been ideologically even more aggressive and belligerent toward the West than the Soviets, this breach in Communist solidarity was quickly welcomed with offers of aid and friendship by American policymakers, who nevertheless have often since been accused of being insensitive to differences among members of the international Communist movement.*

Perhaps, then, the crumbling from within had already begun by 1950. But in that year Kennan argued that even if it took an extremely long time—like thirty years—for the "defeat of the Kremlin" to occur, the "tortuous and exasperatingly slow devices of diplomacy" were surely preferable to a "test of arms" which was unlikely to bring about "any happy or clear settlement" of international differences.[34] Actually, as it turned out, the "defeat of the Kremlin" still had not

---

*President Truman declared, "There isn't any difference in totalitarian states. I don't care what you call them—you call them Nazi, Communist or Fascist, or Franco, or anything else—they are all alike" (Gaddis 1982, p. 66). Yet his actions showed Truman to be much more flexible and less doctrinaire than such statements suggest.

occurred even by 1980, and the Soviets had no more difficulty maintaining control over resentful, sophisticated people than the Nazis had.

Alternatives to Containment

By the end of the 1940s a substantial consensus had been forged among American decision makers around the policy of containment as a method for dealing with the Soviet threat. However, the policy had plenty of critics who advocated other approaches—some more accommodating than containment, others much more belligerent.

Isolationism.

In the United States after the war there was substantial sentiment for a return to the sort of isolationism that had dominated American foreign policy in the 1920s and 1930s. The Europeans, who seem so regularly to stumble somehow into massive self-destructive wars, should be allowed to stew in their own juice, it was argued, while the United States should withdraw behind its oceans, relying on its military and economic potential for protection.

Most Americans, however, felt a sense of guilt about the war, concluding that irresponsible American isolationism was exactly what had brought it about, giving aggressors the illusion that they could strike without having to take on the American colossus.[35] Furthermore, since the United States was now by far the strongest nation on the globe, it should grow up and take its rightful place in international politics. As the perceived Soviet threat began to loom over war-torn Europe, it also became clear to most that the United States was the only country capable of leading an effective opposition.

Internationalism.

Another alternative, discussed earlier, was for the United States to subordinate itself to the international commonwealth, seeking to build peaceful accord through world law and through an effective world government of which the United Nations was the first step.

Visceral disagreement with the Soviet Union, which cropped up even as the war was ending, suggested to most that such a policy was too idealistic, however desirable in principle. But internationalists often argued that perceptions of the Soviet threat were exaggerated or even hysterical, and that Soviet leaders, however hostile their ideology, were realists with limited world aims who could best be worked with if their suspicions about the encircling capitalist world were not constantly confirmed by Western belligerence. Clearly, the Soviets had the same selfish, long-term interests in peace, contended the internationalists; and by opposing them at every turn and blowing each disagreement up to crisis proportions, containment-inspired confrontation could bring about the very war the policy was designed to avoid. Einstein viewed "the phobia against the Soviet Union" as "a threat to world peace."[36]

Rollback.

Some found containment outrageous and immoral because it blandly seemed to accept Soviet domination of Eastern Europe. The war against Hitler, after all, was triggered by his invasion of Poland in 1939. In this view, casually consigning the very people over whom the war was fought to control by a totalitarian regime as unwanted and more or less as brutal as Hitler's would suggest that World War II had been pointless. The West should never accept this appalling stance and should instead use firm diplomacy, the threat of force, and perhaps even force itself to roll the Soviet conquerors back and to make them live up to their wartime agreements about preserving the integrity and independence of the small countries of Eastern Europe.

Containment advocates, of course, were not at all pleased by the Soviet grasp in Eastern Europe, but they tended to feel that the territory through which Russia had been attacked twice in this century was, realistically, part of its natural sphere of influence. If pushed too far, the Soviets might well fight to maintain their control over this vital piece of real estate that separates them from their traditional enemy in Germany. Thus, direct efforts to loosen the Soviet grasp in the area were imprudent.[37]

Preventive War.

As early as 1945, Ambassador Joseph Grew, one of America's most perceptive diplomats, had reached the conclusion that "a future war with the Soviet Union is as certain as anything in this world." If war between West and East was inevitable, a few argued, the best time to fight would be sooner, rather than later, while the United States still possessed a monopoly on the ultimate weapon. Among those who advocated a policy like this during the first few years of the Cold War were the occasional businessman and retired general as well as one philosopher—Bertrand Russell, who was later to be highly active in various disarmament and antiwar movements.[38]*

Most recoiled from the preventive war policy because it seemed so monstrous and because, as George Kennan argued urgently in *Reader's Digest* in early 1950, its central assumption that war was inevitable was not sufficiently convincing. Moreover, this policy vastly overestimated both the effectiveness of the new atomic bomb and the size of the atomic arsenal. In 1949 the United States had only about 100 atomic bombs. As some noted, even if all of these were used and actually landed on their targets, they could not really be expected to do much more damage on the vast Soviet Union than conventional bombing had done on the much smaller Germany: physicist Ralph Lapp estimated in 1949 that it would have taken 75 atomic bombs to duplicate the damage conventional bombs had inflicted on concentrated targets in Germany. Of course, this bombing might somehow have snapped the Soviet willingness to resist, but there was certainly no guarantee about that. Russell had based his proposal for preventive war on the assumption that it would result in "quick victory for the United States and its allies." But as General Omar Bradley, chairman of the Joint Chiefs of Staff, pointed out in 1949, the atomic bomb "cannot win a war by itself," and therefore "we cannot count upon it to be quickly decisive." He found the notion of preventive war to be "an absurdity," because after the bombs had fallen, the United States would probably find itself bogged down in something *really* terrible—"an extended, bloody, and horrible" conflict like World War II.[39]

The Essential Irrelevance of Nuclear Weapons

As this suggests, the precise military usefulness of the atomic bomb was not entirely clear in the years following its invention. Nevertheless, it is widely assumed that nuclear weapons have had a major impact: Morgenthau calls their

*It could be argued that, logically, this proposal followed quite directly from the pronouncements of some of the atomic scientists. Einstein had concluded that "unless peace is secured by a supranational organization, a general war of annihilation is inevitable"; had determined that "once stockpiles of atomic bombs have been accumulated by two national blocs in a divided world, it will no longer be possible to maintain peace"; and had announced that this kind of war "will surely destroy our civilization." If only world government can prevent this calamity and if, as Einstein himself gradually came to admit, the "hope" for world government was "slender," then the West ought to fight quickly, before the Soviets developed their bomb and brought the world to inevitable, cataclysmic atomic war (Einstein 1960, pp. 560, 411, 395, 470–71, 562).

introduction "perhaps the first true revolution in foreign policy since the beginning of history."[40] Those who take this position are engaging in "might have been" analysis. If there had been no atomic bomb, they suggest, history would have taken a much different course. In the immediate postwar period atomic weapons are often given credit for three effects: deterring the Soviet Union from invading Western Europe; importantly moderating the behavior of the major countries in their interactions, particularly in crises; and shaping the contending alliances that were forged in the first years of the Cold War.

On examination, none of these supposed effects seems likely. Since Hiroshima the bomb has inspired a great deal of cosmic pronouncement and desperate hand wringing; it has certainly affected defense budgets and planning; and it has expanded our visions of apocalypse and made them even more vivid. But it does not appear to have been very important in shaping the course of international history, and this is first evident in an examination of the bomb's supposed impact in the immediate postwar era.

The Soviet Noninvasion of Western Europe.

In 1950, Winston Churchill pronounced the "melancholy thought" that "nothing preserves Europe from an overwhelming military attack except the devastating resources of the United States in this awful weapon." Truman felt the same way at the time, and the notion that the Soviets could and would sweep across Western Europe but for the bomb has continued to have advocates for decades ever since. As Robert Art and Kenneth Waltz put it in 1983, "The probability of war between America and Russia or between NATO and the Warsaw Pact is practically nil precisely because the military planning and deployments of each, together with the fear of escalation to general nuclear war, keep it that way."[41] This notion does not stand up well under careful examination.

To begin with, it is not clear that the Soviets think of Western Europe as a prize worth taking risks for. As discussed earlier in this chapter, Soviet ideology, insofar as it is expansionistic, emphasizes subversive revolution, not adventuristic outright military invasion. Hugh Thomas characterizes Stalin's postwar policy as "conflict which should not be carried into real war. . . . Thus, though expansion should be everywhere attempted, it should not come too close to fighting in zones where the United States, and probably Britain, would resort to arms." Furthermore, the Soviets, particularly in the immediate postwar period, were having enough trouble consolidating their hold at home and on Eastern Europe; they had no immediate need for more turf to oversee (among their problems was a major famine in the Ukraine in 1946 and 1947). And as they tried to recover from the ravages of war, the Soviets were hardly in a mood for more: Stalin's declaration of war on Japan three months after the defeat of Germany was met with great dismay within the Soviet Union. To launch an adventuristic war in the West might have risked discontent to the point of insurrection in Eastern Europe and revolution at home: Stalin could hardly be expected to forget that many Soviet citizens, particularly in the Ukraine, had initially welcomed the invading Germans as liberators. Although Kennan was not prepared to dismiss the danger of war in postwar Europe completely, he found it highly unlikely; and in reflection he wrote in 1987, "I have never believed that [the Soviets] have seen it in their interests to overrun Western Europe militarily, or that they would have launched an attack on that region generally even if the so-called nuclear deterrent had not existed."[42]

Secondly, if Western Europe was weakly defended in the immediate postwar period, this was partly because the United States pulled many of its troops out, and the Americans did so in part because they felt they could count on the atomic bomb as a deterrent. Accordingly, if the bomb had not existed, it is likely there would have been more American troops in Europe, and a Soviet invasion would have been militarily more problematic.

Most importantly, however, it is extremely doubtful that the Soviets actually had the strength to be successful quickly and overwhelmingly in a conventional attack. Some Western intelligence estimates in the late 1940s concluded that the Soviets could sweep to the English Channel and to the French-Spanish border in a matter of weeks.[43] They calculated that arrayed against less than 20 Western divisions were some 175 Soviet divisions plus 75 more from Eastern Europe.

In a study of these estimates, however, Matthew Evangelista has found them far too high for several reasons: they include understrength divisions, a Soviet division was only about half the size of a Western one, most of the East European divisions might well have revolted rather than fought, and many of the Soviet troops were needed to occupy East Europe or were involved in political work or basic manual labor. The number of Soviet troops actually available for attack was probably not much greater than the West had for defense. Furthermore, the Soviet troops had morale problems, were ill-equipped for rapid thrusts, and were backed by primitive transport, communications, and logistic systems.[44]

Thus, there is good reason to believe that the Soviets would not have attacked even in a nuclear-free world. But suppose (1) that the atomic bomb had never been developed, (2) that Stalin was anxious to add Western Europe to his empire, (3) that even without the atomic bomb to rely on, the United States would have substantially disarmed as it did, and (4) that the Soviets actually had the military strength to overrun Western Europe quickly in a conventional attack. Even under those circumstances, the United States would *still* have possessed an effective deterrent: Detroit. Even if the USSR had had the ability to blitz Western Europe, it could not have stopped the United States from repeating what it had done after 1941: mobilizing with deliberate speed, putting its economy onto a wartime footing, and in due course wearing the enemy down in a protracted conventional major war of attrition massively supplied from its unapproachable rear base.

After a successful attack on Western Europe the Soviets would have been in a position similar to that of Japan after Pearl Harbor: they might have had gains aplenty, but they would have had no way to stop the United States (and its major unapproachable allies, Canada and Japan) from eventually gearing up for, and then launching, a war of attrition.* All they could have hoped for, like the Japanese in 1941, would have been that their victories would cause the Americans to lose their fighting spirit. But the United States was propelled into war by Japan's Asian and Pacific gains in 1941, it would surely have found a Soviet military takeover of Western Europe—an area of far greater importance to it—to be alarming in the extreme. Not only would it have been outraged at the American casualties in such an attack and at the loss of an important geographic area, but it would very likely have concluded (as many Americans did conclude at the time even without a Soviet attack) that an eventual attack on the United States by the USSR was inevitable. Any Hitler-style protests by the Soviets that they had no desire for further territorial gains would not have been very credible, especially with their dynamically expansive ideology. Thus, even assuming that the Soviets had the conventional capability to take over Western Europe easily, the American ability credibly to threaten a long, continent-hopping war of attrition from south, west, and east would probably have been highly effective in deterring them—even in the absence of nuclear weapons.[45]

The astonishing American economic contribution to World War II was discussed in the previous chapter. That Stalin was fully aware of the American achievement—and deeply impressed by it—is clear. Adam Ulam has observed that Stalin had "great respect for the United States' vast economic and hence military potential, quite apart from the bomb." Furthermore, "Stalin's whole career as dictator had been a testimony to his belief that production figures were a direct indicator of a given country's power."[46]

It is extremely difficult to imagine Stalin willingly taking on the somewhat lethargic, but ultimately hugely effective, American juggernaut. As a member of the Joint Chiefs of Staff put it in 1949, "If there is any single factor today that would deter a nation seeking world domination, it would be the great industrial capacity of this country rather than its armed strength." Or as Thomas has concluded, "If the atomic bomb had not existed, Stalin would still have feared the success of the U.S. wartime economy." In 1953, Averell Harriman, a former

---

*Interestingly, one of Hitler's "terrible anxieties" before Pearl Harbor was that the Americans and Japanese might work out a rapprochement and unite against Germany (Rich 1973, pp. 228, 231, 246).

ambassador to the Soviet Union, observed that Stalin "was determined, if he could avoid it, never again to go through the horrors of another protracted world war."[47] Even if Stalin had had the conventional superiority to win quickly in Europe and even if the atomic bomb had never been invented, he could not have attacked Western Europe with any reasonable confidence that such horrors could be avoided.

Conflict Behavior.

Because of the harrowing image of nuclear war, it is sometimes argued, the major countries have been notably more restrained than they might otherwise have been, and thus crises that might well have escalated to dangerous levels have been resolved safely at low levels. Thus, Robert Gilpin credits the "existence of nuclear weapons" for the "restraint" the United States and the Soviet Union have shown in avoiding confrontation where their "vital interests" might be directly at issue, and John Lewis Gaddis notes the "sobering effect" of nuclear weapons which has "served to discourage the process of escalation that has, in other eras, too casually led to war."[48] There is, of course, no definitive way to refute this notion; we cannot replay events without the nuclear weapons. And it is certainly true that decision makers have been well aware of the calamities of nuclear war and cannot be expected to ignore the possibility that a crisis could lead to such devastation.

However, this notion that the fear of nuclear war has kept behavior restrained looks far less convincing when its underlying assumption is directly confronted: the idea that the major contestants would have allowed their various crises and disagreements to escalate if all they had had to fear at the end of the escalatory process was something like a repetition of World War II. Whatever the rhetoric in these crises, it is difficult to see why the unaugmented horror of repeating World War II, combined with a considerable comfort with the status quo, wouldn't have been enough to inspire restraint.

Nor does it appear that a nuclear threat is likely to be more potent than a threat to repeat World War II. In 1946 the United States pressured the Soviet Union to remove its troops from northern Iran, and Truman later claimed that an American "ultimatum"—presumably nuclear-backed—had driven the Soviets out of Iran. However, careful assessments of this claim have led James Thorpe and McGeorge Bundy to conclude that Truman's "ultimatum" is a "myth": notes delivered to the Soviets were extremely mild in tone and, in any event, the maneuverings of the Iranian government in negotiations with Stalin were far more important in determining the outcome. But even if one assumes the threat *was* important, it is not at all clear why it had to be *nuclear* to be effective—a threat to commit hostilities on the order of World War II would also have been notably unpleasant and dramatic. Much the same could be said about other instances in which there was a real or implied threat that nuclear weapons might be brought into play, such as the Berlin blockade of 1948–49. Although the horror of a possible nuclear war was doubtless clear to the participants, it is certainly not apparent that they would have been much more casual about escalation if the worst they had had to visualize was a repetition of World War II.[49]*

Stalin may have found the bomb impressive—he once called it "a powerful thing, pow-er-ful!" But it is certainly not clear that it intimidated him or peculiarly limited his behavior, particularly in the crucial area of Eastern Europe; Ulam argues that it would be difficult "to specify what more the USSR would have gotten had the United States *not* had the bomb."[50] Insofar as Stalin was restrained from greater provocations, it seems likely that the spectre of another World War II was a sufficient influence on his behavior.

Cold War Alliance Patterns.

Since the Cold War was an outgrowth of various disagreements between the United States and the USSR over ideology and over the proper destinies of Eastern, Central, and Southern Europe, much of the reaction of the United States in this period to the perceived Soviet threat mainly reflects prenuclear thinking. In particular, the formation of the North Atlantic Treaty Organization and the division of the world into two alliances centered on Washington and Moscow suggest that the participants were chiefly influenced by the experience of World War II, because in general, the alliances include a group of nations that contribute little to nuclear defense but possess the capability unilaterally of getting the alliance into trouble.

That is, the structure of the alliances reflects political and ideological opposition rather than sound nuclear strategy. As military economist (and, later, defense secretary) James Schlesinger noted, "The U.S. decision to organize NATO . . . was based on some rather obsolescent notions regarding the strength and importance of the European nations and the direct contribution that they could make to the security of the United States." Or, as Warner Schilling has observed, American policies in Europe were "essentially pre-nuclear in their rationale. The advent of nuclear weapons had not influenced the American determination to restore the European balance of power. It was, in fact, an objective which the United States would have had an even greater incentive to undertake if the fission bomb had not been developed."[51]

*As Michael Mandelbaum has put it (oddly enough, in a book entitled *The Nuclear Revolution*), "The tanks and artillery of the Second World War, and especially the aircraft that reduced Dresden and Tokyo to rubble might have been terrifying enough by themselves to keep the peace between the United States and the Soviet Union" (1981, p. 21).

The Memory of World War II as a Deterrent

By 1945, it seems clear, a reality had become overwhelmingly obvious: Apart from any moral or aesthetic considerations, major war was spectacularly costly, destructive, and counterproductive—that is, as Norman Angell would have it, it was futile by just about any standard. Few with the experience of World War II behind them could contemplate a repetition with anything other than horror. Nuclear weapons have compounded and further dramatized this central reality, but without them, the memory of World War II would still stand as a vivid and effective deterrent: to be able to threaten nuclear war may be impressive, but to threaten a repetition of World War II (or for that matter World War I) is not that much less impressive, especially if the would-be aggressor is basically content with the status quo.*

None of this, of course, is to deny that nuclear war is appalling to contemplate and mind-concentratingly dramatic, particularly in the speed with which it could bring about massive destruction. Nor is it to deny that decision makers, both at times of crisis and at times of noncrisis, are well aware of how cataclysmic a nuclear war could be. It is simply to stress that the horror of repeating World War II is not all that much *less* impressive or dramatic, and that leaders essentially content with the status quo will strive to avoid anything that they feel could lead to *either* calamity. A jump from a fiftieth-floor window is probably quite a bit more horrible to think about than a jump from a fifth-floor one, but anyone who finds life even minimally satisfying is extremely unlikely to do either.

Of course, nuclear weapons have added a new element to international politics—new pieces for the players to move around the board, new terrors to contemplate. But in counter to Einstein's oft-quoted remark that "the atom has changed everything save our modes of thinking," it appears that nuclear weapons have changed little except our way of talking, gesturing, and spending money.[52]

---

*Observed George Kennan, "The atom has simply served to make unavoidably clear what has been true all along since the day of the introduction of the machine gun and the internal combustion engine into the techniques of warfare—what should have been clear to people during World War I and was not: namely, that modern warfare in the grand manner, pursued by all available means and aimed at the total destruction of the enemy's capacity to resist, is, unless it proceeds very rapidly and successfully, of such general destructiveness that it ceases to be useful as an instrument for the achievement of any coherent political purpose" (1961, p. 391).

6

Korea and the Demise of Limited War

BY 1950 the Cold War had begun, with Europe as its chief focus. Eschewing isolationism, the United States reacted to the challenge posed by the Soviet Union's ideological dynamism and to the threat posed by its expansionary assertiveness in Eastern Europe, Czechoslovakia, and Berlin.

The Americans sought to counter the threat of indirect aggression in Europe by sending economic and military aid to shaky regimes in Greece and Turkey, as well as economic aid to the rest of Western Europe to help stabilize economies that were still reeling from the effects of the war.

As for direct aggression there, the containment policy sought to trigger deterrence through the threat of escalation—to use jargon that was not yet in vogue in 1950. By integrating itself into a supranational alliance, the United States was pledging that even a minor military incursion on the smallest of its allies could very well lead to world war. As a policy, it was thus the polar opposite of appeasement.

It was the kind of arrangement, people thought, that could have prevented Hitler's aggression; and countries like Holland, Denmark, and Belgium, which had meekly sought to avoid entangling alliances in the 1930s, eagerly became charter members of NATO a decade later. Stalin's schemes, expansionary visions, and willingness to risk major war were quite a bit different from Hitler's perhaps, but enough similarities existed to suggest that it would be wise to err on the safe side and to prepare for the worst.

When Stalin, or at any rate international Communism, launched direct aggression in Korea in June 1950, it seemed that the worst had come to pass, or was about to. Although Stalin probably saw the Korean venture as a limited and rather safe military probe, the West reacted as if everything it stood for was being put to the test.

The Korean War, quite possibly the most important event since World War II, capped the Cold War: it demonstrated to the West that the danger of direct aggression was very real, and thus the military component of containment was vastly expanded.

At the same time it reduced even further the prospects for major war between the United States and the Soviet Union. A direct, frontal, Hitler-style war between East and West has never made much sense to anybody, as discussed in the previous chapter. Korea demonstrated that even peripheral military ventures by surrogates were unwise because they could too readily escalate to something fearsome and counterproductive. As discussed more fully in the next chapters, some kinds of warfare remained in the Communists' repertoire—particularly domestic revolution and civil war against colonial overlords or against anti-Communist elites outside the developed world. The use of international crisis—a sort of warlike behavior—also had yet to be abandoned. But Korea ended any thoughts of flirting with old-fashioned, direct, over-the-border war as a method for advancing the international Communist cause and it has never been tried again.

This chapter explores these issues, and it further develops the notion that nuclear weapons—pointedly unused in Korea—have been quite irrelevant to these important historical developments.

The View before Korea

By early 1950 things were looking fairly good for American policy in Western Europe. To begin with, threats in Greece and Turkey had been overcome without having to consider sending American troops.[1] There had been great concern about the activities of the large Communist parties in France and Italy, which were loyal to Moscow; in 1948, in fact, it briefly seemed possible that the Italian Communists would actually be elected to power. But by 1950 the influence of Communist parties had diminished considerably in France and Italy as well as elsewhere on the continent.* Most countries in the region were enjoying the

*For example, in elections in 1948 and 1949 the Communists lost a quarter of their seats in Finland, over half their seats in Sweden, and all of their seats in Norway. One event that undercut Communist party support in the West was the statement in 1949 of Maurice Thorez, general

beginnings of a very pleasant economic resurgence; the non-Soviet portions of Germany had been melded into a viable, pro-Western unit; and NATO was off the drawing board—if not exactly on the march.

Some of these favorable developments can be attributed to the skills of fore-sighted American statecraft. But they were also a reaction to Stalin's brutal behavior in Eastern Europe, his subversive takeover in Czechoslovakia, and his belligerent policies over Germany, which had culminated in the provocative blockade of Berlin. That the acquisitive Stalin might next send his armies march-ing west seemed a possibility too likely to be ignored prudently.

The loss of Yugoslavia can also primarily be credited to Stalin's policies. Once booted out of the fraternity, Yugoslavia quickly turned from an ardent and even aggressive advocacy of international Communism to a circumspect, pragmatic nationalism. It no longer had much interest in exporting revolution or in destabil-izing the capitalist world. Although its domestic political system at first remained as unpalatable to Western democratic tastes as ever, Yugoslavia's major foreign policy change was enough to cause the United States to embrace the renegade. (A very similar development was to occur in Sino-American relations in the 1970s.)

There were also challenges to be met outside Europe. In China a civil war between Communist and anti-Communist forces was raging, while anticolonial rebellions, many of them led by well-known Communists, were under way in Burma, Indonesia, Indochina, Malaya, and the Philippines. In principle the policy of containment, as announced in the Truman Doctrine, suggested that applications would be vigilant and worldwide—an implication that suggested unrealistic extension and alarmed contemporary critics such as the influential political columnist Walter Lippmann.[2] In practice, extension was pragmatic, wary, and often tentative, particularly outside Europe.

In China the anti-Communist forces received a great deal of support. In large measure it was sympathy with these Chinese that had dragged the United States into its war against the aggressive Japanese. In their postwar battles with Commu-nist forces, however, the Nationalist Chinese proved increasingly inept, ineffec-tual, and corruption ridden. It seemed clear that they could be saved only by direct American military intervention, and nobody felt eager to venture into that particular quagmire.[3] Consequently, the Nationalist Chinese were cut from the dole, and in 1949 they fled the mainland in defeat, setting up a rump government on the large offshore island of Taiwan.

---

secretary of the French Communist party, that in a war between France and the Soviet Union, the party would support the Soviet Union. The statement was reprinted by Communist parties through-out the world (Shulman 1963, pp. 58–61, 290; Starobin 1972, pp. 209–12).

American policy toward the new Communist regime was wary and standoffish at first, but not exactly hostile. The administration announced in early 1950 that it would stay out of the ongoing Chinese conflict and would not provide military aid or advice to the regime on Taiwan, and it was widely believed that Taiwan would fall to the Communists fairly quickly. In early 1950 the United States declared that it was not "irreconcilably opposed" to letting the Communists occupy the China seat at the United Nations.[4]

In Indochina the French were combating an anticolonial rebellion led by the Communist Vietminh whose leader, Ho Chi Minh, had helped found the French Communist party in the 1920s and had been an international Communist agent for decades. Despite this, the United States was less than eager to see colonialism return to that part of the world and began to support the French in earnest only after 1949, when aid to the Vietminh from the triumphant Chinese Communists connected the rebellion in Indochina more directly to the international Communist movement.

In Indonesia anticolonial insurrection seemed unlinked to international Communism. There the Americans strongly, and eventually successfully, pressured their Dutch allies to turn control over to the rebels. Meanwhile in the Philippines, where the United States was itself decolonizing, a Communist rebellion was under way. Extensive assistance was given by the Americans to the new Philippine government, much as in Greece. By 1954 the rebels had been put down and, as in Greece, no American troops were ever required. The British and their local allies achieved similar anti-Communist successes in Burma and Malaya.

At the end of the 1940s, then, some of the urgency about world affairs that had attended the early postwar disagreements, particularly over the fate of Europe, had diminished. The developed world had been carved into two ideological and economic spheres, and a coexistent, if competitive, peace seemed a real possibility. At the time of the Czech coup in early 1948 some 75 percent of the American public said it felt a major war was less than ten years away. By mid-1949 this had dropped to a (comparatively) comfortable 48 percent, and even the successful Soviet test of an atomic bomb later that year pushed it up only some ten percentage points.[5]

Within a year, however the percentage shot up to a near-unanimous 83 percent. This surge was caused by the first, and thus far only, full-out conventional war between the forces of East and West.

Stalin and the Origins of the Korean War

By 1950, Soviet foreign policy had mostly experienced discouragement or at least a form of stalemate as the West became alarmed and united against it. There was little sign either of the harvest of revolutions that Stalin may have expected to occur after the war or of the internecine rivalries among capitalist states that Communist doctrine had long held to be inevitable.[6]

In 1950, Stalin was led to experiment with outright warfare—but in Korea, a comparatively safe corner of the world, where united Western opposition seemed unlikely. According to Nikita Khrushchev, the idea was broached in late 1949 by Stalin's close ally, Kim Il-sung, the leader of Communist North Korea. If he prodded South Korea with the "point of a bayonet," Kim asserted, an "internal explosion" in South Korea would be touched off. Although Stalin had some misgivings, Kim was "absolutely certain of success" and promised that South Korea would quickly fall into the Communist camp before the West even had much of a chance to react. Eventually, both Stalin and the Chinese Communists gave their blessings to the scheme.[7]

In approving Kim's plan, Stalin may have been encouraged by American secretary of state Dean Acheson's declaration in January 1950 that defined America's "defense perimeter" in the Pacific to include the Aleutian Islands, Japan and the Ryukyu Islands, and the Philippines, and therefore to exclude South Korea and Taiwan. Even earlier the Joint Chiefs of Staff had concluded that "Korea is of little strategic value to the United States" and that "any commitment to United States use of military force in Korea would be ill-advised and impracticable." And in May 1950, Senator Tom Connally, chairman of the U.S. Senate's Foreign Relations Committee, suggested in an interview that the Soviet Union could overrun Korea "whenever she takes a notion" to do so. Stalin may also have hoped a dramatic victory in Korea would have a demoralizing impact within the capitalist world, exacerbating disagreement and confusion, and that it would encourage the Japanese to pay more respectful attention to Soviet desires in Asia.[8]

What Stalin approved was a distant war of expansion by a faithful ally, a war that was expected to be quick, risk-free, and cheap. In Khrushchev's view Stalin had no choice: "No real Communist would have tried to dissuade Kim Il-sung from his compelling desire to liberate South Korea from [political leader] Syngman Rhee and from reactionary American influence. To have done so would have contradicted the Communist view of the world." Stalin may have been a "real

Communist" in those terms, but he also took precautionary steps to limit the war by withdrawing from North Korea not only Soviet military advisors but also most Soviet equipment.[9]

The West Reacts: War Fears and Rollback

For the most part, leaders in the West also viewed Stalin's actions as those of a "real Communist," and they saw them as confirming their worst fears of what that meant: A "real Communist" would start a war—commit "direct aggression"—any time and any place it seemed advantageous. As President Harry Truman concluded at the time, "The attack upon Korea makes it plain beyond all doubt that Communism has passed beyond the use of subversion to conquer independent nations and will now use armed invasion and war."[10]

A direct analogy with the 1930s was readily applied. In Truman's words, "Communism was acting in Korea just as Hitler, Mussolini, and the Japanese had acted ten, fifteen, and twenty years earlier." All of his advisers agreed that to fail to meet the challenge in Korea would be appeasement, which, experience had shown, would lead ultimately to war. "I felt certain," Truman recalled, "that if South Korea was allowed to fall Communist leaders would be emboldened to override nations closer to our own shores. . . . If this was allowed to go unchallenged it would mean a third world war, just as similar incidents had brought on the second world war."[11] Accordingly, less than five years after the end of World War II, the United States, acting through the United Nations, entered another full-out shooting war.

There was some fear that an American military response in Korea could be "the beginning of World War III," but it was generally concluded that this likelihood was "rather remote," particularly since there seemed to be few, if any, Soviet troops among the invaders. In attempting to probe Stalin's reasons for starting the Korean War, however, most Western decision makers felt it was part of a "Soviet strategic master plan," and they became concerned that it might be merely a diversionary tactic or, as General Omar Bradley once characterized it, a "softening-up operation." While the military forces of the West were deployed in Korea, an area of little strategic value to anyone, the Soviets might launch a major attack in an area that mattered more—Iran, or perhaps even Europe.[12]

There was no evidence at the time that Stalin actually had anything like this in mind, nor has any come to light since. The Soviet leader remained extremely cautious about risking anything that might bring on a major war, and in his

Korean venture he seems at most to have been, in Ambassador Phillip Jessup's words, "probing for a soft spot." Nevertheless, at least some American officials became worried that a big war might be imminent. Even George Kennan, who had never seen the Soviet challenge in military terms, speculated that "armed action by German units, along the Korean pattern" was not out of the question, and the Central Intelligence Agency thought Stalin might soon "deliberately provoke" a general war.[13]

Even in retrospect, this concern seems justifiable. Stalin remained in full control of the Soviet system until his death in 1953, and although he had always been exceedingly wary about getting into a war with the West, his last years became "ones of increasing madness and sterility," as Kennan, the American ambassador in Moscow in 1952, put it. A lunatic war was certainly conceivable. Milovan Djilas, who met with Stalin in 1948, was alarmed by "conspicuous signs of his senility" and found Stalin's intellect to be distinctly in "decline": where Stalin in 1945 had been "lively, quick-witted, and had a pointed sense of humor," he "now laughed at inanities and shallow jokes." Khrushchev has described the intense loneliness and suspiciousness of Stalin's last years. Stalin was surrounded by sycophants, and at his "frightful" dinner parties, Stalin would require his colleagues to sample all food and drink before he would taste them. He would then lead them in drinking bouts in which he "found it entertaining to watch the people around him get themselves into embarrassing and even disgraceful situations." Although "when he was well and sober, he was still a formidable leader," Stalin had started "to be not quite right in the head" during the war, Khrushchev recalls, and every year after he seemed to be "weakening mentally," showing "eclipses of mind and losses of memory."[14]

Moreover, Stalin was given in his last years to believing that he could control nature at will. In 1949 he grandly issued a "Stalin Plan for the Transformation of Nature" which set out extravagant schemes for weather-controlling irrigation and forestation projects; massive dam, canal, and power installations; and the construction of skyscrapers in Moscow to rival those in New York City. He also repudiated Darwin and Mendel, declaring that the evolution of plant and animal life could be fully controlled by environmental manipulation.[15]

In 1950, with the recent establishment of a congenial Communist regime in the world's most populous nation, China, it was easy to believe that the aging Stalin might come to imagine himself presiding over an apocalyptic worldwide revolutionary upheaval, with war as its midwife, in which capitalism would finally be destroyed. After all, Stalin was, in Djilas's characterization, "one of those rare terrible dogmatists capable of destroying nine tenths of the race to 'make happy' the one tenth."[16] Under the circumstances, to ignore the possibility of some sort of Soviet military action in Europe would have been irresponsible.

Because Korea could have been the prelude to, or the opening phase of, World

War III, more people, including a few influential ones, now urged the United States to beat Stalin to the punch by launching preventive war. As the United States and other members of the United Nations sent troops to Korea to help turn back the North Korean offensive, Secretary of the Navy Francis P. Matthews, reflecting, he later said, a view common in the Navy, publicly proposed that the United States become an "aggressor for peace." Major General Orvil A. Anderson, commandant of the Air War College, agreed, as did *The Pilot,* the official newspaper of the Archdiocese of Boston; and Secretary of Defense Louis Johnson is reported to have been proposing the same thing privately. The Truman administration, however, was not interested in the least in getting into a major war, so Matthews's statement was immediately repudiated and he was shuffled off to Ireland as ambassador, while Anderson was retired.[17]

But then an opportunity arose for expanding the war in a more limited manner. In October 1950 the North Koreans had been pushed back in disarray across the thirty-eighth parallel into their own territory by UN, U.S., and South Korean forces, and it was decided that the retreating forces should be pursued, the Communist regime in the north destroyed, and the country unified under the anti-Communist southern regime.

There were warnings from the new Communist regime in China that it would not stand idly by and watch as its North Korean friends were crushed, but these warnings were generally dismissed as bluff. With that, Western forces launched a counterinvasion into enemy territory in the first, and the only significant, effort at rollback ever attempted. It proved to be a major mistake.

China Enters the War

As Western and South Korean forces surged northward toward the Chinese border, the Chinese apparently became convinced that despite repeated protestations to the contrary by Truman and others, the invaders were planning to continue pressures on China and perhaps even to attack it. In the early autumn of 1950 they issued various warnings, but these were often ambiguous or contradictory: in September they told the Indian ambassador they would not intervene and then, two weeks later, said they might take retaliatory measures; later they sent some contingents of Chinese troops into North Korea but then abruptly withdrew them.[18]

All this was consistent with the Western estimate that the Chinese regime, which had been in office for only a year after a long, costly civil war, had no stomach for a new war in Korea. Indeed, at the time these estimates may well have been correct: Khrushchev reports that in the autumn the Chinese had consulted Stalin on the matter and both agreed that "it was fruitless for China to intervene."[19] Eventually, however, the Chinese changed—or made up—their minds, and at the end of November they sent in masses of troops, overwhelming the overextended U.S. and UN forces and pushing them into costly and ignominious retreat.

With that, Americans entered into deadly combat against the forces of the Soviet Union's largest and most important ally. Many important officials in the United States became utterly convinced that the one remaining escalatory step would soon be taken: the Soviet Union would institute general war through a major attack in Europe. Public opinion polls at the end of 1950 registered a similar alarm: 40 percent said they expected a world war within one year, 56 percent within two, and 83 percent within 10, the highest ratings ever recorded on that question.[20]

Pessimistic prognoses like those proved unsound, because both sides had a substantial interest in staying out of a wider war. Indeed, the war had already become far larger than anyone had intended. The Soviets apparently anticipated that a sharp punch by the North Koreans could bring a quick decision; the West expected that they could bring the war to a favorable conclusion by Christmas 1950; the Chinese were impressed by assurances from their highly respected commander that the enemy could be quickly crushed and finished off by decisive flanking strikes.[21]

As the Chinese sent his troops reeling in retreat, General Douglas MacArthur issued calls for an expansion of the war into China itself by bombing and blockading it, and possibly by launching "diversionary" actions from Taiwan. Expansion was the last thing the administration in Washington wanted, and when MacArthur disobeyed orders by making his views public, Truman fired him. General Omar Bradley summed up the administration position about the strategy of enlarging the conflict to China in some oft-quoted words: "Red China is not the powerful nation seeking to dominate the world. Frankly, in the opinion of the Joint Chiefs of Staff, this strategy would involve us in the wrong war, at the wrong place, at the wrong time, and with the wrong enemy." The "right" enemy, obviously, was Stalin's Soviet Union, and the "right" place was Europe. It was important for the United States to be prepared for that war and to limit its investment in the enervating and distracting conflict in Korea. Accordingly, although there were signs that Chinese forces were on the brink of collapse in mid-1951, their opponents quickly agreed when the Communists suggested peace talks. There followed two bitter, frustrating years of negotiations while the war dragged on, but at a substantially reduced pace.[22]

Korea and the Atomic Bomb

Throughout the war, the United States kept reign on its ultimate weapon, the atomic bomb. As it had often been assumed after World War I that war's most dramatic weapon, gas, would be freely used in the next war, it was often assumed after World War II that atomic explosions would be a commonplace in the next big conflict. Yet the weapon remained tethered in the Korean War, although the two nuclear countries were arrayed on opposite sides in fierce, if indirect, combat.

In discussing this issue, Bernard Brodie lists several reasons why the bomb was not used. In descending order of importance these were the desire to reserve this scarce weapon for the potential major war in Europe; the prevailing belief by military planners that the bomb was useful for destroying cities but had few viable battlefield applications; the intense opposition to the use of the bomb by an important ally, the British; the fear that the Soviet Union might conceivably retaliate with one of its small number of atomic bombs; and possibly the concern about "racist overtones," because the bomb had thus far been dropped only on Orientals.[23]

The possibility that atomic weapons might be used was, of course, always present.* But only near the end of the war did the Americans make semiexplicit atomic threats. When he came to office in 1953 after the United States had endured a year and a half of frustrating negotiations with the Communists, President Dwight Eisenhower says he sought to formulate "definite measures" to end "these intolerable conditions." One approach was "to let the Communist authorities understand that, in the absence of satisfactory progress, we intended to move decisively without inhibition in our use of weapons, and would no longer be responsible for confining hostilities to the Korean Peninsula." He says "we dropped the word, discreetly, of our intentions," feeling "quite sure" that it reached "Soviet and Chinese Communist ears."[24]

His bluff was never called, but it is clear that Eisenhower was deeply impatient, that he was making ready to expand the war, that he was at least seriously contemplating the use of atomic weapons in this venture, and that various

*The Indian ambassador in Peking reports that one Chinese general, in phrases later to be used by Mao, was quite casual about this issue: "They may even drop atom bombs on us. What then? They may kill a few million people. Without sacrifice, a nation's independence cannot be upheld. After all, China lives on farms. What can atom bombs do there?" (Panikkar 1955, p. 108; see also Whiting 1960, pp. 134–36).

American contingency plans designed to force an end to the war incorporated atomic weaponry into their calculations—although Gaddis concludes that Eisenhower was "more eager to *talk*" about possibly using the weapons "than actually to do so."[25]

It is far less clear that it was the atomic threat that impelled the Communists to agree to the armistice which was finally concluded in July 1953. By then the Chinese and the North Koreans seem to have been eager for a full year to bring the costly, pointless war to an end, and Stalin seems to have been coming to the same conclusion by late 1952 and early 1953. Stalin's death on March 5, 1953, broke any lingering impasse, and his successors in Moscow quickly sought to liquidate the war. Chinese representatives returning from Stalin's funeral dramatically issued conciliatory statements, and truce talks were productively reopened. These important maneuvers on the Communist side all took place before Eisenhower's veiled atomic threats were even uttered.[26]

In the late spring of 1953 there were jockeyings for position and various disagreements over truce details that often brought new frustrations. American threats to expand the conflict were indirectly renewed. But for the Communists by now it was mainly a matter of getting the most favorable possible settlement; they had no intention of seriously reopening the war.

Thus, although many Americans, including then Vice President Richard M. Nixon, were to conclude from this experience that it was Eisenhower's atomic threat that had bludgeoned the Communists into accepting peace terms, it seems more likely that things were moving toward resolution anyway and that if anything was crucial, it was the death of Stalin, not American threats. But even if we assume that the threats *were* important, it is not at all clear why they had to be peculiarly *nuclear*—a credible threat to reopen the war and commit hostilities on the order of World War II would also have been notably unpleasant and dramatic.[27] Once again nuclear weapons do not seem to have been vital in shaping the course of history.

The Impact of the Korean War

With the Korean War the Cold War became fully engaged. Alarmed by the apparent Soviet willingness to revert to direct aggression, the West felt an urgent necessity to rearm in order to deter the Soviet Union from trying similar ventures elsewhere. The American defense budget quadrupled—something that previously had been thought to be politically and economically infeasible—and NATO was rapidly transformed from a paper organization (big on symbolism, small on actual military capability) into a viable, well-equipped, centrally led multinational armed force.[28]

At the same time the United States expanded its commitment to anti-Communist ventures throughout the globe. If it was important to keep South Korea out of Communist control, then perhaps the same applied to Taiwan. Accordingly, the American Seventh Fleet was sent to patrol the waters that separate that island from the threatening Communist Chinese mainland. American aid to the embattled French in Indochina also increased, until by 1954 the United States was paying 75 percent of the financial cost of the war. Potential dominoes were everywhere.

In the United Nations, China was officially branded an aggressor, and Sino-American relations remained deeply sour for twenty years. There was also a strong inclination in the West to see the Sino-Soviet bloc as a monolith—in part because an important effect of the Korean War was precisely to drive the USSR and the Chinese into tight fraternal alliance.[29]

Within the United States the Korean War substantially heightened concern about domestic subversion. Since there was an international linkage among Communists, and since Communism now seemed to be willing to use aggressive warfare as a tool, many concluded that U.S. Communists were devoted to a system dedicated not only to the revolutionary overthrow of the American government but also ultimately to a direct invasion of the American homeland. Several spectacular espionage cases heightened this concern. Before Korea, a respected former State Department official, Alger Hiss, was accused of having sent huge quantities of classified documents to the Soviets. Hiss denied this allegation under oath and was then convicted of perjury. The Hiss conviction was (and remained) controversial, but other State Department officials were also accused of such dealings and confessed to them, so the basic issue of spies and traitors in high office was never really at issue; in the immediate postwar period, over 200 State Department officials were fired or eased out of office on security concerns.[30]

Then as the Korean War was about to begin, a former Communist, British physicist Klaus Fuchs, admitted that he had sent atomic secrets to the Soviets. The trail from Fuchs soon led to the arrests of others in his spy ring and ultimately to the celebrated trial of two Americans, Julius and Ethel Rosenberg, who were convicted as atomic spies. Their execution in 1953 would probably never have taken place had the Korean War not occurred.[31]

Public opinion poll data strongly suggest that it is a substantial exaggeration to refer to the anti-Communist apprehensions of the early 1950s as "hysteria."* But the issue was extensively and successfully exploited by various politicians, of whom Senator Joseph McCarthy is the best remembered, and it reflected a genuine concern that the experience in Korea made alarmingly palpable.

Korea and the Concept of Limited War

The Korean experience also impelled the development of the concept of "limited war," the notion that the major countries could wage a war that could be restricted in geography, weaponry, and goals—that, as Brodie puts it, they could "test each other's strength and resolution with limited rather than unlimited commitments to violence." As he notes, "Following World War I it became axiomatic that modern war means total war," and that notion seemed to be confirmed by World War II. General Matthew Ridgway, the commander in Korea after MacArthur, has recalled that before Korea "the concept of 'limited warfare' never entered our councils"; all planning assumed that "the next war involving the United States would be a global one."[32]

But as Brodie notes, "The total-war idea, which seemed so overwhelming in its logical simplicity, was a fairly novel one historically."[33] In fact, of course, before 1914 there were many instances of wars between major countries that were fought within very substantial constraints, and there is no particular reason to assume modern countries are so passionate that they are utterly incapable of operating under similar self-interested limits.

---

*Recent examples include Kaufman 1986, p. 36; Foot 1985, p. 246. In 1954, in the depths (or heights) of the McCarthy era, one major survey found that its respondents seemed to be utterly unworried either about Communism or about threats to civil liberties. Asked "What kinds of things worry you most?" less than 1 percent mentioned either the threat of domestic Communism or concern about civil liberties. Even when specifically asked for their worries about "political or world problems," only 6 percent mentioned the Communist threat and only 2 percent mentioned concerns about civil liberties. When asked "Do you happen to know the names of any of the Senators or Congressmen" taking "a leading part" in "investigations of Communism," 30 percent could name no one, and only 13 percent volunteered the name of more than one (Mueller 1988a, p. 21).

Korea as a Stabilizing Event

If war can be limited, it may become "possible" again: if the combatants tacitly or explicitly agree to stay within tolerable constraints, they can test national will and military prowess while keeping damage within bearable bounds. The Korean experience, however, suggests two flaws in this line of thinking that have kept the notion of a limited conventional war from ever gaining much practical appeal. First, there is no guarantee the limits will hold. No one intended Korea to escalate as far as it did, and a future limited war of Korean size could escalate to an even more destructive level. Second, the Korean War, no matter how quaintly effective the limits on its mayhem, wreaked widespread destruction: some 2 million died in battle.

If that's a limited war, East and West have decided ever since to avoid limited conventional conflicts, and thus the Korean War may well have been an extremely important stabilizing event that vividly constrained the methods each side could use in pursuing its policy.

For the Soviets the lessons of the Korean War must have enhanced those of World War II: once again the United States was caught surprised and underarmed, once again it rushed hastily into action, once again it soon applied itself forcefully to combat—and in this case, for an area it had previously declared to be of only peripheral interest. The Korean invasion may simply have been a somewhat tentative probe of Western resolve, but the Soviets apparently heeded the lesson the Truman administration intended to impart. Unlike Germany, Japan, and Italy in the 1930s, they have not tried direct aggression again, even in a probing manner: there have been no Koreas since Korea.*

Taubman characterizes the pattern of Stalin's foreign policy as "cautious but persistent probing that was only safe if the Americans were not spoiling for a fight"; Korea clearly showed that there was a point at which the Americans would fight. As Ernest May has suggested, "A quick success in Korea might have emboldened 'hawks' in the Kremlin." As "real Communists," they would surely at least have been encouraged serously to consider toying with the technique elsewhere—perhaps, they might have mused, only a few more "prods with the

---

*As discussed more fully in chapter 9, Soviet military intervention in Afghanistan in 1979 was an effort to prop up a faltering pro-Soviet regime. As such, it was not like Korea, but rather more like American intervention in Vietnam in 1965 or like the Soviet interventions in Hungary in 1956 or Czechoslovakia in 1968. China's brief war against India in 1962 (discussed in chapter 8) also does not fit the Korean pattern because its territorial goals were severely circumscribed.

bayonet" would send the whole capitalist world into the inevitable, apocalyptic collapse that Communist theory had so long confidently predicted. The Korean experience severely undercut the appeal of that line of reasoning. As May observes, even with decades of hindsight "one cannot confidently second-guess Truman's decision."[34]

That is, it is conceivable that the USSR, in carrying out its ideological commitment to revolution, might have been tempted to try step-by-step, Hitler-style probes leading ultimately to military action if it had felt that these would be reasonably cheap and free of risk. The policy of containment, of course, was designed precisely to counter such probes, carrying with it the threat of escalation. If the USSR ever had any thoughts about launching military probes, the credible Western threat that these probes could escalate—demonstrated most clearly in Korea as well as in such episodes as the Berlin crisis of 1948–49—would be significantly deterring, whether or not nuclear weapons awaited at the end of the escalator ride.

The Korean experience may have presented a somewhat similar learning experience for the United States. In 1950, amidst talk of "rolling back" Communism and sometimes even of liberating China, American-led forces invaded North Korea. This venture led to a costly and demoralizing, if limited, war with China and resulted in a considerable reduction in enthusiasm for such maneuvers. Had the United States been successful in taking over North Korea, there would probably have been noisy calls for similar ventures elsewhere—although, of course, these calls might well have gone unheeded by the leadership.

It is not at all clear that the major countries needed the Korean War to come to the visceral belief that direct, conventional probes can be intolerably costly and that escalation can be easy. But the war may well have reinforced those beliefs for both of them and, to the degree that it did, Korea was an important stabilizing event.

7

Khrushchev and the Demise of Crisis

ALTHOUGH there have been no Koreas since Korea, the Cold War continued after the end of that conflict and after the death of Stalin, both of which transpired in 1953. Under new leaders in Moscow international Communism continued to seek to fabricate and perfect techniques to advance its cause. This chapter deals with these methods as they were developed and variously deployed in the decade after 1953 and with the Western reaction to them.

The relevance of war and warlike activity in the Communist arsenal receive special attention. The Communists rejected certain kinds of wars and were wary of others; but they still embraced some forms as progressive, desirable, necessary, and inevitable. Although they apparently never intended their preferred wars to lead to major war, the potential was always there. The potential for escalation to major war also accompanied other devices in their arsenal, such as crisis and military threat, and this era of the Cold War is particularly memorable for a series of tense international crises mostly engineered by the new Soviet leader, Nikita Khrushchev. During these, it often seemed, the world teetered precariously on the brink of thermonuclear cataclysm. In retrospect it does not appear that major war was at all close, but in one of his ploys—an escapade that led to the Cuban missile crisis of 1962—Khrushchev managed to bring war much nearer than he, or anyone else, considered desirable. That experience led to some important tactical changes in the competition. In particular, it seems to have permanently discredited crisis as a methodology. And, to the degree that crisis is necessary to precipitate war, the experience reduced the likelihood of major war to levels that were even lower than before.

The Arsenal of Struggle

After Stalin's death, his successors still clung to Marxism-Leninism as their operative theory and theology. It purported to explain the workings of the world, and in it the new leaders sought explanations for the past and guidelines for the future. History, they confidently believed, was on their side; but as committed conspirators and revolutionaries, they took it as their duty to try to hustle history along by probes, prods, schemes, and fancy footwork. "Struggle," they called it.

Capitalism, the old enemy, was still out there uncooperatively lingering on, oddly unappreciative of its own theoretical decadence. Indeed, in direct consequence of Stalin's clumsy misadventure, the Korean War, the capitalist world was looking more hostile and more threatening than ever—in good shape economically and armed now to the earlobes. Particularly unsettling was the addition in 1955 of a rearmed West Germany to the anti-Soviet NATO alliance.

Still, there was the remarkable triumph of like-minded revolutionaries in China in 1949. In one sweep this development had quadrupled the number of people basking under the theoretical Marxist glow. Although the Chinese Communists could be peskily independent at times, their costly heroics in the Korean War and their ferocious hostility to the capitalist world showed them to be right thinkers and valuable members of the camp.

The basic shape of things was clear, then: History and the Chinese were the allies, capitalists were the shifty-eyed opponents, struggle was the order of the day. Given the heavily armed condition of the world, the problem was figuring out how to struggle without suffering too many punishing setbacks: History may be moving generally in a favorable direction, but one doesn't want to struggle in a manner that causes one to be blown off the face of the globe while gingerly seeking to speed the process up.

In the immediate aftermath of Stalin's death there were several pressing problems to attend to: keeping the Eastern European colonies in line, stifling any potential uprising at home, and settling the issue of which of the terrorized sycophants who fluttered around Stalin's deathbed was going to step into the blood-stained boots at the bedside. By 1956 or 1957, Khrushchev had clambered over several others into the chief leadership role in the Soviet Union, and he remained the dominant personality in the Sino-Soviet camp until he was bloodlessly deposed in November 1964. As the method of his exit suggests, he never attained Stalin's monolithic control domestically.

Moreover, he was soon to be challenged within the bloc as the Chinese increasingly criticized his policies and his leadership. In the assessments of the time, these challenges began as a dialogue, soon became a debate, developed into a dispute, escalated to a conflict, graduated to a schism, progressed to a rift, and ended as a split. An important matter at issue was how best to struggle—how best to nudge History along. Under Khrushchev's leadership, the Soviets were inclined to be cautious, if pious, about worldwide revolution. The Chinese found Soviet wariness callow and contemptible, and they even came darkly to suspect at times that the timorous Soviets might treasonously bolt from the bloc to form an anti-Chinese alliance with the capitalist world.

Of central concern to international Communists, then, were the wisdom and efficacy of methods that might be used in the struggle to confront and undermine the egregious, degenerate capitalist world. Various possibilities were available: major war, military probes, revolution and subversion in capitalist countries, revolution and revolutionary war in the third world, example and seduction, and crisis and bluster.

Major War

When musing about major war—war among developed countries—Marxism-Leninism distinguishes two kinds: war between the capitalist and Communist worlds, and war among capitalist countries.

As discussed earlier (pp. 100–102), the Soviets have not seen much value in the notion of starting a substantial war with the surrounding capitalist world. However, they have been very concerned that the capitalists might attack *them*, and no less a figure than Lenin had proclaimed such eventual "frightful collisions" to be "inevitable." By 1935, however, the Soviets had pretty well decided that Soviet armed strength and international working-class solidarity made such wars potentially avoidable—although still dangerously possible, as Hitler's invasion of 1941 was to confirm.

After the war authoritative publications reaffirmed that "the new world war now being prepared by the imperialists can be averted," and in an important speech in 1956 Khrushchev added his weight to the argument: "As long as capitalism survives in the world, the reactionary forces . . . may try to unleash war. But war is not fatalistically inevitable. Today there are mighty social and political forces . . . to prevent the imperialists from unleashing war."[1]

Although sometimes implicitly accused by the Soviets of desiring a world war, the Chinese fully acknowledged "the possibility of stopping the imperialists from unleashing a new world war." However, the Chinese and the Soviets did seem to disagree about the *consequences* of a major war between the two camps. In 1954 a prominent Soviet leader, Georgi Malenkov, echoing a sentiment common in the West, declared that a war between the camps would result in "the destruction of world civilization" because of the "present means of warfare." He was forced to recant this gloomy prognosis because of its theoretical unorthodoxy and because it could be convenient only to Western "war-mongers" who "calculate to intimidate people by atomic blackmail." By 1960, however, Khrushchev and other Soviet leaders had accepted Malenkov's heresy, concluding that a nuclear war would "bring immeasurable disaster to the whole of humanity" and would therefore be "madness."[2]

The Chinese found this admission to be chicken-hearted and, like Malenkov's former critics, potentially encouraging to the war-eager capitalists. Accordingly, they liked to argue that although a major war between the camps would "impose enormous sacrifices," the result would be progressive: "On the debris of a dead imperialism, the victorious people would create very swiftly a civilization thousands of times higher than the capitalist system and a truly beautiful future for themselves." After all, mused their leader, Mao Zedong, in 1957, "The First World War was followed by the birth of the Soviet Union with a population of 200 million. The Second World War was followed by the emergence of the socialist camp with a combined population of 900 million. If the imperialists should insist on launching a third world war, it is certain that several hundred million more will turn to socialism; then there will not be much room left in the world for the imperialists."[3]

In giving his estimate of the postwar housing crunch for imperialists, however, Mao insisted that the war would have to be started by the imperialists: "We are against it," but "we are not afraid of it." Thus, although they may have been somewhat nonchalant about the consequences of a major war between the camps, the Chinese, as Frederic Burin has observed, never found wars between Communist and capitalist states to be inevitable, nor did they ever advocate them. On the contrary, their position, as expressed in 1960, was that "no Marxist-Leninist party advocates that the socialist countries resort to war between states to spread revolution. . . . [To contend otherwise] is nothing but nonsense in the service of imperialism." And in 1963 they reiterated that "no Marxist-Leninist ever held or ever will hold that revolution must be made through world war."[4]

Apart from his "frightful collisions" remark, Lenin had little to say about wars between the Communist and capitalist camps. He had a great deal to say, however, about the other kind of major war—war *among* capitalist states. Indeed, it was central to his whole theory of imperialism. He had become enamored of the notion that as capitalist countries greedily carved the world into colonies, they would increasingly clash with each other over questions of turf. These conflicts, he felt, would eventually lead to wars among them: "Imperialist wars are absolutely inevitable *as long as* private property in the means of production exists."[5] These wars were capitalism's ultimate "contradiction," and he felt they could be transformed by crafty and agile revolutionists into massive civil wars that would ultimately lead to capitalism's final collapse.

Since Lenin, Communist thinkers, ever opportunistic, have vigilantly sought evidence of conflict and contradiction among capitalist states. One interpretation of Stalin's foreign policy of the 1930s is that he tried to encourage capitalist states to give in to their natural tendency to make war among themselves, while he lurked idly on the sidelines, ready to capitalize (as it were) on the resulting cataclysm.[6]

From the Soviet perspective, World War II began in 1939 as a war among capitalist states that turned lamentably sour with the invasion of the Soviet Union by Germany in 1941. Clearly, manipulating capitalist contradictions was a bit trickier than Lenin had anticipated. Nonetheless, in his last major tract, published in 1952, Stalin continued to insist that, while intracapitalist rivalries were currently being held in check by the "jackboot of American imperialism," one could look fondly forward to the day when temporarily inconvenienced capitalist states like Germany and Japan would rise again and "try to smash the U.S." To hold otherwise is to "believe in miracles" for Stalin thundered, "the inevitability of wars between capitalist countries remains in force."[7]

In his 1956 speech Khrushchev apparently intended to include intracapitalist wars among those that he had decided were no longer "fatalistically inevitable," because he went out of his way to argue that Lenin's dictum about the inevitability of war was now out of date. Khrushchev maintained that Lenin had formulated the dictum when "imperialism was an all-embracing system" and forces in favor of peace were "weak" and "poorly-organized." Now, claimed Khrushchev, "the situation has changed radically" because the "world camp of socialism" has become "a mighty force" possessing "not only the moral, but the material means to prevent aggression." By 1961 he had become quite explicit on this issue: While "acute contradictions and antagonisms between the imperialist countries . . . still exist," they "are compelled to heed the Soviet Union and the entire socialist camp, and fear to start a war between themselves." Therefore, "the likelihood is that there will not be wars" between them, "although this eventuality cannot be ruled out."[8]

In principle, Khrushchev presented a radical new idea: Soviet strength should be used to prevent the very kind of war that Leninist theory argues is most likely to spread revolution and bring about the collapse of capitalism. In their debate with Khrushchev and the Soviets, the Chinese largely continued to cling to the Lenin-Stalin view on this issue.[9]

Thus, Communist states have taken varied stances on intracapitalist wars—from encouraging (Stalin) to discouraging (Khrushchev) to exploiting (Lenin, the Chinese) them. But all Communists believe that they can do little to instigate such wars, because they see such wars as springing from the peculiar competitive nature of avaricious capitalism. Conceivably, such wars could lead to a harvest of revolutions or even to the final revolutionary collapse of the capitalist system, but capitalist states must begin them.

Military Probes

Although Communist states have never been able to see much sense in initiating, or even in risking, major war with the capitalist world, and although they generally see intracapitalist war as something that arises from the nature of international capitalism itself and not from their own efforts, they have been willing at times to use limited military force to advance their interests. Marx and Lenin did not have much to say on this issue. Neither did Stalin actually, but his actions suggested that he had given it thought.

In the prelude to World War II, Stalin's Soviet Union used limited military force to expand its borders at several spots. After the Germans defeated the Poles in September 1939, the Soviets moved in with German approval, annexing major portions of eastern Poland and, a bit later, portions of Rumania. They also expanded into the tiny Baltic states of Estonia, Latvia, and Lithuania, first by demanding "mutual assistance pacts" and then, in 1940, by sending in troops.[10] Similar demands on Finland got out of hand and led to a brief but rather costly war with that country in 1939–40. At American urging the Soviets also joined the war against Japan in August 1945 by invading Manchuria. And after the war, of course, the Soviets incorporated into their empire several East European states they had overrun in the course of the war, and they also tried to cling to portions of northern Iran.[11]

These ventures might suggest that the Soviets have something of a penchant for opportunistically exploiting perceived weaknesses in their environment and a willingness to use military force for limited aims where they think they can get away with it. As discussed in chapter 5, a nagging suspicion that this might be the case led, in part, to the countering policies in the West of containment and deterrence—policies carrying the threat that even limited incursions by the Soviets could escalate to costly confrontations with militarily advanced countries. Despite these policies the Soviets were willing in 1950 to try out a surrogate war in Korea—remote terrain that may have looked like a chink in the enveloping containment curtain to them. As noted in chapter 6, the failure of this probe seems to have permanently discredited the notion that limited military action is a sensible method for advancing revolution or other interests, although the Soviets have been willing to use troops to prevent portions of their contiguous empire from seceding in Hungary in 1956, Czechoslovakia in 1968, and Afghanistan in 1979.

The Chinese also underwent the souring Korea experience. Despite quite a bit of verbal bluster, they too have been distinctly reluctant since then to risk direct military action with the major capitalist states, although they have used force to shore up their empire (particularly in Tibet), and they did successfully launch one bit of military action—a lightning advance and orderly retreat in border regions of neutral India in 1962.

Revolution and Subversion in Capitalist Countries

By the Khrushchev era, then, major war and direct military action against the capitalist world had largely been abandoned—insofar as they had ever been accepted—as methods for promoting revolutionary progress and/or Sino-Soviet interests in the world. But this certainly didn't mean that international Communism had given up the contest. Khrushchev proclaimed "peaceful coexistence" to be his policy, but he candidly explained that the phrase meant "intense economic, political, and ideological struggle between the proletariat and the aggressive forces of imperialism in the world arena."[12] Although Khrushchev carefully omitted *military* struggle from his catalogue, he remained committed to methods that involved violence, the threat of war, and real, if theoretically limited, warfare.*

*In his memoirs, Khrushchev expresses it this way: "Both history and the future are on the side of the proletariat's ultimate victory. . . . We Communists must hasten this process by any means at our disposal, *excluding war*. . . . There's a battle going on in the world to decide who will prevail over whom. . . . To speak of ideological compromise would be to betray our Party's first principles— and to betray the heritage left us by Marx, Engels, and Lenin" (1974, pp. 530–31, emphasis in

Among these was revolutionary class warfare which Marx saw as the crucial method for removing capitalists from their dominant position in Western society. The problem was that revolutionary forces in the capitalist centers didn't seem to be doing so well by the mid-1950s. In the aftermath of World War II, Communist parties in Western Europe enjoyed a fair amount of credibility and good will. They had been admitted to cabinets in France and Italy, but their influence had declined considerably as suspicion of, and then coordinated opposition to, international Communism grew in the West. Unsuccessful efforts by French and Italian Communists in the late 1940s to use extralegal means like strikes and riots to improve their political position served to undercut some of their appeal, and various maneuvers by their Moscow allies—the Czech coup of 1948, the Berlin blockade, and the Korean War—also produced that effect.[13]

In approaching voters and constituents, Communist parties in Western democracies were constantly belabored for their theoretical adherence to a doctrine that exalted revolutionary violence as the only method for gaining political control. That notion seemed a tad undemocratic, detractors were led to suggest, and many Western democracies instituted policies and procedures designed to check domestic Communists. In the United States these ventures have often been designated "McCarthyism" after the most virulent and demagogic of the anti-Communists of the time. But anti-Communism both preceded and followed Senator Joseph McCarthy's time on the stage of American politics, and it reflected a widespread concern that domestic Communists were linked to an international movement which had as one of its chief goals the eradication of democratic capitalism and which espoused violence as the prime method for achieving that end.[14]

In 1956, Khrushchev sought to make life a little easier on this score for his Communist allies in democratic countries. While acknowledging that in a number of capitalist countries the "violent overthrow" of the capitalist system is "inevitable," he declared that "violence and civil war" are not "the only way to remake society," and that this could possibly be accomplished by the "winning of a stable parliamentary majority backed by a mass revolutionary movement." (The Chinese rejected this position, arguing in 1960 that "revolution means the use of revolutionary violence by the oppressed class," and quoting Lenin: "Not a single great revolution in history has ever been carried out without a civil war and no serious Marxist will believe it possible to make the transition from capitalism to socialism without a civil war.")[15]

However, when Khrushchev made this declaration, he also denounced Stalin

---

original). Also, he says, "peaceful coexistence among different systems of government is possible, but peaceful coexistence among different ideologies is not" (1970, p. 512).

with a long speech frankly cataloguing some of the crimes committed by the man he had once praised as "our inspired leader and teacher." Party members and functionaries throughout the world were shocked and startled by these revelations, which argued that the man they had once worked for and worshipped was a monster of monumental proportions. In the West in particular the result was a substantial exodus from the Communist party, already weakened by electoral decline and political persecution. Further defection occurred later in the year when the Hungarians, inspired in part by Khrushchev's revelations, attempted to withdraw from the Soviet empire and were forcibly brought back into the fold by a Soviet military invasion.[16]

Thus, the outlook for revolution, peaceful or otherwise, in the capitalist world during the Khrushchev era was not very good, whatever the theory might have to say about its desirability and inevitability.

Revolution and Revolutionary War in the Third World

If revolution was having a rather rocky time of it in the major capitalist areas, international Communism could cast its eye with more pleasure on the less developed areas of the world where dozens of new nations were emerging, most of them carved out of colonial empires that were gradually dismantled in the postwar era. Warfare accompanied the birth of some of these new nations. A successful anticolonial war in Indochina against the French brought in a congenial-minded Communist regime in North Vietnam in 1954, and a similar war against the Dutch brought a potentially congenial regime into control in Indonesia in 1949, as did a civil war in Cuba in 1959 and an anticolonial war against the French in Algeria in 1962. Violence, if not always full-scale war, accompanied the emergence of other new nations as well—Kenya, India, the Congo, Israel, Cyprus, Malaysia, Pakistan, Burma, and the Philippines.

The Soviets have always encouraged such developments.* After they came to power in 1949, the Chinese saw all sorts of resemblances to their own civil war experience, and they loudly and persistently declaimed that wars in colonial and

---

*As in Andrei Zhdanov's famous 1947 call for worldwide opposition to the "imperialist and antidemocratic" camp in which he saw the Indochina war as an example of "a powerful movement for national liberation in the colonies and dependencies" (Hosmer and Wolfe 1983, pp. 3–4; Rubinstein 1985, pp. 60–62).

post-colonial areas were, as Burin puts it, not merely one element in the "struggle," but "the driving forces of the world revolutionary process." In 1965, Chinese defense minister Lin Biao became positively elegiac on this matter. Although he was bound to admit that "for various reasons" revolution had been "temporarily held back in the North American and West European capitalist countries," he was not struck glum by this fact because "the people's revolutionary movement in Asia, Africa, and Latin America has been growing vigorously." Thus, "the whole cause of world revolution hinges on the revolutionary struggles" in these areas. Therefore, the Chinese urged, "all revolutionary Marxist-Leninists should support these just struggles resolutely and without the slightest reservation."[17]

For their part, Khrushchev and the Soviets actually had a slight reservation, which arose from a fear of escalation: the problem with "local wars," as they called them, was that one could "develop into a world thermonuclear and missile war." Eventually, they distinguished "local wars," such as the invasion of Egypt by Britain, France, and Israel in 1956, from "national-liberation wars," like those in Algeria and Vietnam, which were "uprisings of colonial peoples against their oppressors." The latter, as Khrushchev put it in 1961, are "not only justified, but inevitable" and should be supported "wholeheartedly and without reservations."[18]

However, these statements often came infused with a distinct wariness about wars of national liberation. One Soviet commentator hopefully suggested that the "rapid stream" of historical progress might finally make "any war" impossible, and another thought it wise to ensure that "internal processes in particular countries do not lead to military clashes of the two anti-podal systems." Furthermore, in practice the Soviets under Khrushchev were remarkably careful about getting too close to exemplars like the "heroic Algerian people" who were "fighting for freedom and national independence." Instead of extending them the promised "fullest material assistance," the Soviets were much quicker with verbal valentines extending "heartfelt greetings and support." As Thomas Wolfe concludes, "Khrushchev talked a strong line of support for such movements, but when concrete cases arose which might have involved the Soviet Union in a direct confrontation with United States military power, he generally refused to tender Soviet aid in any form that would have entailed the unpredictable danger of widening war."[19] Soon the Chinese were burlesquing Khrushchev's caution: "Certain persons," they crowed in 1963, "have been spreading the argument that a single spark from a war of national liberation or from a revolutionary people's war will lead to a world conflagration destroying the whole of mankind." The facts, they assured all listeners, "demonstrate the absurdity of this argument."[20]

In the West the prospect of dealing in the third world (as it came to be called) with revolution and revolutionary civil war was seen as an important challenge. Under the policy of containment, of course, efforts to expand the Communist system were to be confronted wherever they might crop up; to give in would only encourage more aggression elsewhere.

Actually, the Greek civil war, which largely triggered containment, had been a sort of war of national liberation.* The side supported by the United States there had prevailed, and a similar success was racked up in a war against Communist insurgents in the Philippines between 1946 and 1954. The locals and the British also successfully waged a war against Communist guerrillas in Malaya between 1948 and 1960. On the other hand, the Communists won in Indochina: the United States gave the French extensive financial support, but when the embattled colonialists requested American air support in 1954, the United States was unwilling to go that far, and the French caved in.

It seemed sensible to believe the evangelists for international Communism and to assume that such wars would proliferate in the future. Nuclear weapons had little relevance in such encounters, so considerable efforts were made in the United States in the late 1950s and early 1960s to study guerrilla and insurgency warfare and to develop military techniques to deal with the challenge. By the 1961–62 "season," observes participant-historian Arthur Schlesinger, "counter-insurgency was the rage in Washington."[21]†

In the Khrushchev era the United States found itself sending assistance to several third world nations that were battling real or potential Communist insurgencies. In 1958 the United States even landed troops—some 14,000 marines— to assist the government of Lebanon in a civil war situation. As it turned out, the troops managed to leave within a few months without actually fighting much, but no guarantee of that agreeable outcome had existed when they were sent— sheer luck accounted in part for the failure of the situation to escalate into a substantial conflict.[22] Then violence broke out when the Belgians abruptly withdrew from their large central African colony of the Congo in 1960 and the new country began to splinter into several warring factions with various ideological allegiances, drawing the concentrated interest of both the United States and the USSR. The United States particularly feared that the Soviets might gain a "foothold" in Africa if the country broke apart. Over five years, in a complicated series of scrapes accompanied by various forms of warfare, the Congo (renamed

---

*An even earlier instance might be the Spanish civil war of 1936–39 in which the Soviets actively aided and influenced one side.

†Of course, during its military history the United States had already fought quite a few counterinsurgency wars—against Pancho Villa in Mexico in 1916–17, against guerrillas in the Philippines at the turn of the century, against rebels in Nicaragua in the 1920s and 1930s, against Indians in Florida and the American West—but these had largely been forgotten. On this issue, see Weigley 1984, Sarkesian 1984.

Zaire) remained whole and became basically neutral in the ideological conflict. Neither side seemed very interested in getting into a direct fight in that chaotic corner of the world: despite Khrushchev's fears—or perhaps because of them—escalation was held in check.

One of the other areas in which the United States became involved was Laos, a sparsely populated chunk of what had once been French Indochina. A shifting, triangular civil war was going on there in which one side was being actively supported by the Soviets, Chinese, and North Vietnamese. By 1961 the new Kennedy administration had reluctantly concluded that the United States was overextended in this backward country, and in 1962 a face-saving agreement was worked out under which Laos was effectively partitioned. The United States shifted its attention to South Vietnam, where another Communist insurgency was under way, and where the anti-Communist side seemed to have better prospects for eventual victory.

For all the competitive evangelical bellowing that emerged from the Communist disputants about the value and efficacy of wars of national liberation, the remote Laotian plain gained in the partition of 1962 was the only territory in the world that such wars directly delivered to the Communist side between 1954 and 1975.

Example and Seduction: The Space Race

Besides revolution and revolutionary war, another method existed for advancing Communism in the third world. Most of the new states and many of the old ones in the area had leaders and leadership elites who, although not Communists in the classic sense, bubbled over with ideas about economics, politics, and society that could comfortably be labelled "progressive" by Communist ideologues. Through example, aid, persuasion, and perhaps a bit of judicious subversion, the ideologues hoped to lead these countries toward ever more enlightened ways of thinking and eventually perhaps into the Communist camp.[23] As an approach, this seemed at least as promising as revolutionary warfare—and quite a bit less risky. The West became duly alarmed and attempted to refocus its containment efforts to counter the challenge.

Stalin had experimented with a policy something like this in China in the 1920s and in Spain in the late 1930s; but after the war Soviet theoreticians argued that it would take "proletarian revolution" to solve "colonial slavery," and they tended to dismiss leaders of such newly independent countries as India, Indonesia, and Egypt as "lackeys."[24]

Khrushchev changed this. He found the approach enormously appealing, and in 1955 he ostentatiously toured India, Burma, and Afghanistan and began courting the new Egyptian leader, Gamal Abdel Nasser, by sending him military aid, even though Nasser often persecuted local Communists. When Khrushchev proclaimed in 1956 that Communist movements could sometimes flourish under parliamentary circumstances, he spoke not only of developed capitalist states but also of "former colonial countries." The idea apparently was to assure the new leaders that the international Communist movement could be on their side rather than simply plotting revolution or violent coups, as Leninist and late-Stalinist theory would suggest.[25]

In pursuit of his strategy, Khrushchev was not above rattling the occasional rocket to show his eternal friendship and concern to third world countries. During the Suez crisis of 1956 when British, French, and Israeli forces launched a joint attack, Khrushchev not only threatened to send Soviet volunteers to help the Egyptians but also implied that he might rain nuclear devastation on the attackers: "What would be the position of France," the Soviets coyly queried, "if she were attacked by other states having at their disposal modern and terrible means of destruction?" Khrushchev made similar veiled threats a year later when he became concerned that Turkey was planning to attack Syria.[26] And in 1958 he loudly let it be known that he was not pleased by American military intervention in Lebanon or by other Western maneuvers in Middle East trouble spots at the time.

He was, of course, to take full credit later for preventing war and turning back the imperialist tide in these instances, but he had actually moved with extreme caution. For example, he swung into verbal action on Suez only after it was clear that the United States wasn't involved in the attacks and, in fact, opposed them; also, he quietly withdrew some of the Soviet advisers and technicians from Egypt and ordered the others to stay out of the fighting. During the Lebanon events, he did nothing more substantial than announce some Soviet military maneuvers near the border with Turkey—something that bitterly disappointed the Arabs to whom he had been waxing eloquent about his all-embracing and all-protecting regard.[27]

In general, Khrushchev seemed to be more comfortable supporting congenial third world countries with methods that were less blatantly military or quasi-military. Aid, judiciously applied, seemed a potentially useful lever, and other countries besides Egypt soon found themselves to be the beneficiaries of Soviet largesse, especially Indonesia, Syria, Iraq, Afghanistan, North Yemen, India, Guinea, Morocco, the Congo, and Algeria.[28]

Economic and military aid, while useful, was not likely to be the surest route to influence, however; the United States and Western Europe were also busily pursuing that particular game, and they had a lot more money.[29] It was cheaper—and safer—to rely on hype and one's persuasive and seductive skills.

Seduction helped with Khrushchev's only significant acquisition for the Communist camp during his tenure in office: Cuba. A radical reformer, Fidel Castro, fought his way into control there at the end of 1958, and he proved to be most receptive to Soviet blandishments. He soon declared himself a reborn ideological Marxist-Leninist, cut off ties with nearby imperial America, rolled his revolution into the Communist camp, and found it in his heart to accept graciously the very substantial Soviet aid that was necessary to keep his regime afloat economically. Castro also became very interested in furthering the interests of the Soviet Union and of international Communism in Latin America, a third world area that had yet to be fully exploited ideologically and where revolutionary progress proved most pleasantly to be highly irritating to capitalist America. Intensely concerned, the United States in 1961 tried and failed to eliminate Castro and to roll back Communism by putting together an invasion by anti-Castro exiles at Cuba's Bay of Pigs—one of the great foreign policy fiascoes in American history.

Although aid, seduction, subversion, and military posturing all had their benefits from the Soviet point of view, the best way to lead the world was by example. After all, if the path they were taking could clearly be seen to be the quickest and surest road to paradise, all would soon be led to follow along by their own free will. By the late 1950s and early 1960s Khrushchev had convinced himself at least (as usual, the propagandist principally propagandized himself) that things were moving along very well indeed. "The victory of socialism on a world scale, inevitable by virtue of the laws of history, is no longer far off," he enthused in 1960. Other Soviet spokesmen also extolled "the power of example" and calculated that because of its "irreversible process" of "expansion," the Communist camp would embrace a majority of the world's population by 1980, while its share of the world's industrial production would undergo an 83 percent increase from 33 percent to 60 percent, even as the share contributed by the capitalist world tumbled from 56 percent to 29 percent.[30]

If victory was indeed in sight, the Soviets felt this was due not only to the manifest virtues of their system but also to the fact that the "world capitalist system" was at that very moment "going through an intense process of disintegration and decay."[31] Nothing seemed to exemplify this better than the space race.

In 1957 the Soviet Union had startled the world by launching into orbit the first artificial satellite, *Sputnik*. Impelled in no small degree by the public relations blitz Khrushchev launched immediately afterward, many came to believe that the remarkable Soviet achievement in space said something tangible about the basic comparative worth of capitalism and Communism. Beginning from a woefully backward position in 1917, the Soviets had, on the fortieth anniversary of their revolution, surpassed the decadent capitalists in one of the most highly technological areas. The Soviets also had a related advantage—most frightening to the West—in intercontinental ballistic missile technology (and, Khrushchev erroneously claimed, in ballet). To the Soviets the Communist camp was clearly the wave of the future and would soon outdistance the capitalist world in every field of endeavor—"We will bury you," Khrushchev exuberantly crowed. (He explained, however, that what he meant by this famous, offensive phrase was that "we will be present at your funeral"—the capitalist system, he felt, would inevitably dig its own grave.)[32]

The impact of the space race can hardly be overstated. For the better part of a decade the Soviets scored triumph after triumph as the United States struggled desperately to get into the game. Not only did the Soviet Union launch the first satellite, but their satellites were much heavier (Khrushchev liked to refer to American satellites as "oranges and grapefruits"). Then, in 1959 the Soviets launched the first satellites outside the earth's orbit; one of these circled the sun—the first artificial planet—and another went around the moon and sent back pictures of the moon's far side, an accomplishment a British survey called "an astonishing demonstration of Soviet technological skill" and "a feat of enormous propaganda value."[33] In 1961 the Soviets put into orbit the first man in space, in 1963 the first woman, and in 1964 the first multiman satellite. (At that point, however, the Soviets began to fall back in the race, and the United States forged ahead to score the ultimate triumph in 1969: putting a man on the moon. Few in the Khrushchev era would have expected the race to end this way.)

These developments made some Americans feel like losers. The Communists seemed to be on the march everywhere: winning hearts and minds left and right in the third world, and outclassing the West in important areas of technology. Furthermore, while the Soviet and Chinese economies appeared to be soaring, the American economy, though far larger, was bogged down in a recession.

Thanks to their ideology, the Communists seemed to know where they were going, but the materialistic United States lacked focus, or as the slogan of the late 1950s put it, it didn't seem to know what its "national purpose" was. Accordingly, the nation underwent a period of semimasochistic self-examination centered on these issues, and President Dwight Eisenhower became so concerned that he took a supremely daring step: he appointed a committee of august Americans to find out what the national purpose was.

The President's Commission on National Goals responded in the expected manner: it issued a report. The document, which ran 372 pages in book form, concluded that the country was in "grave danger" from the "Communist-oriented world." This "deadly menace" rested on "the Soviet Union's great and swiftly growing strength," on "the industrial and military progress and potential of Red China," on the Communist camp's "great capacity for political organization and propaganda," and on the "specious appeal of Communist doctrine to peoples eager for rapid escape from poverty" whose "historic resentments, inadequate economies, inexperience in self-government, and excessive expectations offer fertile ground for Communist persuasion and conquest."[34] But despite all those horrors, concluded the commission, the situation was not hopeless.

It urged the country to get cracking to meet the "Communist challenge," and came out firmly in favor of the family, spiritual health, physical health, equality, individual rights, liberty, education, art, science, progress, growth, the United Nations, foreign aid, military strength, the study of disarmament, and tax reform. In 1960 presidential candidate John F. Kennedy embraced the theme of alarm, expressed horror at America's declining prestige abroad, and promised to get the country "moving again."

If the political, economic, and technological progress of the Communist camp buoyed Khrushchev and depressed the Americans, it launched the Chinese into the ozone layer. Always confident of the ultimate success of Communism, Mao declared a month after the *Sputnik* launch that "the international situation has now reached a new turning point. . . . The East wind prevails over the West wind. That is to say, the socialist forces are overwhelmingly superior to the imperialist forces." As early as 1946 he had voiced his view that American reactionaries and their atom bomb were "paper tigers"—terrifying in appearance, but "not so powerful" in reality. He repeated that assertion now with even more confidence.[35]

While Khrushchev and Mao agreed on which way the wind was blowing, they drew notably different lessons from this observation. Since "the victory of socialism on a world scale" was obviously "no longer far off," it seemed to the Soviets that the judicious policy of "struggle" known as "peaceful coexistence" was about all that was needed. After all, why risk war? "War between countries," they argued, "is not needed for this victory." The Chinese became increasingly impatient with Khrushchev's excessive caution when all the historical forces were so clearly in his favor. It was not time, they opined in 1960, to "relax" or to be "tranquil"; it was time to push ahead vigorously and to prepare for a "just war to end the imperialist unjust war when and if the imperialists should unleash it."[36] That was not the sort of talk Khrushchev—or the Americans—liked to hear.

Crisis and Bluster

If seduction and example were Khrushchev's preferred methods for exploiting opportunities in the third world as colonialism declined, his policy toward the capitalist states themselves was to seek to manipulate the various antagonisms or "contradictions" among them that Leninist theory had long held to be natural and inevitable conditions of the capitalist state of being.

Stalin had been familiar with this tactic, and Khrushchev claimed in 1960 that it was related to Soviet victory in World War II: "We smashed the aggressors, and in so doing we made use also of the contradictions between the imperialist states."[37] Although postwar developments in the capitalist world had not been as invigoratingly contradictory as an ardent Leninist might desire, all was far from well in the West, and it gave the Soviets great pleasure in 1960 to announce that, what with the "mounting disintegration of the colonial system" and all, "a new stage has begun in the development of the general crisis of capitalism." The Soviets had also apparently noticed that the Americans didn't even seem to know what their national purpose was: "A profound crisis in bourgeois politics and ideology" is going on over there, they delightedly observed.[38] Moreover, when Khrushchev met various Western leaders, he discovered that they didn't present a united front. Instead, they spoke to him in many tongues (some of them forked), and from time to time they even contradicted each other—proof that Lenin had been right all along.

Khrushchev's idea, then, was to see what he could do within the peaceful coexistence struggle to make these shades of disagreement work to the Soviet benefit. At one point he reportedly explained the strategy to Arkady Shevchenko, a Soviet UN official who later defected to the West. Khrushchev intended to exploit "intra-imperialistic contradictions," as he called them, pitting the Western countries against each other and seeking out opportunities for "kindling distrust" of the United States in Europe.[39]

To accomplish this, Khrushchev blustered and sometimes built tensions to crisis levels through threats and displays of force. He employed the technique first at the time of the Suez episode and seems to have concluded that it worked quite well there: it was his "stern warning" that "stopped the war," he publicly claimed later.[40]*

*In his memoirs he argues that Eisenhower's opposition to the invasion was just a "gesture," and that "when we delivered our stern warning to the three aggressors . . . they took us very seriously. I've been told that when [France's] Guy Mollet received our note, he ran to the telephone in his

But it was Sputnik, the accomplishments it symbolized, and the supreme confidence it inspired that really set him off. Soon he was indelicately pointing out that the technology capable of boosting heavy satellites into orbit could also be used to develop sophisticated intercontinental ballistic missiles, that the Soviet Union was doing so, and that they were planning to build hundreds of these instruments of mass destruction. In 1959 he declared that the Soviets could now "wipe all our potential enemies off the face of the earth." Calculations in the West determined that if Khrushchev indeed built to capacity, the USSR would have two or three times as many ICBMs as the United States by the early or middle 1960s—a phenomenon known as the missile gap.[41]

Crises over the Taiwan Straits.

An opportunity for rocket-rattling bluster in the Sputnik era presented itself in September 1958. The Chinese Communists were especially irritated by the fact that the Nationalist Chinese on Taiwan still controlled several small islands close to the mainland. In 1954 and 1955 they had pushed the Nationalists out of some of these and made menacing noises about several others. The United States had helped the Nationalists to shore up their military positions in the area and had made various veiled and conditional military threats, including some atomic ones, and the Chinese never forced the issue.[42]

Now, four years later, Khrushchev's Chinese allies were up in arms again, shelling and blockading the offshore islands and threatening to invade them. Increased efforts by the Nationalists and the Americans to break the siege were beginning to be successful, and the Chinese offered to negotiate. During the crisis the Soviets issued suggestions that it might become involved, should the Americans threaten the "Chinese Communist regime," but as the Chinese bitterly pointed out later, Khrushchev's threats became specific ("an attack on the People's Republic of China . . . is an attack on the Soviet Union," and "if China falls victim to an atomic attack, the aggressor will at once get a rebuff by the same means") only after the crisis had eased and there was little or no danger of nuclear war.[43]

Crises over Berlin.

Far more central to Khrushchev's concerns was the peculiar status of West Berlin, a city tied to the West even though it was situated in the middle of

---

pajamas and called [Britain's] Eden. I don't know if this story is true, but whether or not he had his trousers on doesn't change the fact that twenty-two hours after the delivery of our note the aggression was halted. We only had to issue our warning once. . . . It was a great victory for us" (1970, p. 436).

Soviet-controlled East Germany. There was a specific practical problem with this anomaly for Khrushchev: East Germans could easily escape the paradise being created for them by going to West Berlin, and by 1958, 10,000 a month were using this route to flee to the decadent capitalist world.[44] Khrushchev declared West Berlin to be "a bone in my throat."

Khrushchev directed a large percentage of his strutting and fretting toward this situation and, more generally, toward the threatening development of West German rearmament. In the process he created two crises that precipitated considerable disagreement over tactics in the West and that had both sides nervously rattling their rockets for a while.

In November 1958 he declared that in six months he would hand over control of the Berlin access routes to East Germany and that any effort by the West to reestablish these rights by force would be regarded as an attack on the Soviet Union. The United States responded that it could not tolerate such unilateral moves and issued various warlike noises of its own. For several months there was serious talk, in Washington at least, that the crisis could lead to "general war" or "all-out war." The United States asserted that it would do whatever was necessary to maintain its rights in Berlin and that nuclear war was not "a complete impossibility." For his part, Khrushchev observed that "if you send in tanks, they will burn and make no mistake about it"; and if that happened, Soviet missiles would "fly automatically." Soviet fighters also buzzed American planes flying the air corridor to Berlin.[45] Eventually, the crisis abated as Khrushchev backed off from his ultimatum deadline and agreed to hold talks on the Berlin issue.

Berlin remained an unsolved issue in September 1959 when Khrushchev toured the United States, meeting with Eisenhower and mixing noises about peaceful competition with cheery predictions about the eventual collapse of his host's political and economic system. In May 1960 there was to have been a summit meeting about Berlin in Paris, but Khrushchev threw a tantrum and walked out of the conference because the United States had been violating Soviet airspace with U-2 spy planes. His defense minister threatened to "deal a crushing blow to the bases from which they take off" should there be more overflights.[46]

The Berlin issue was a major concern during 1961, John Kennedy's first year as president. Khrushchev again created a crisis by threatening to give control of West Berlin access routes to East Germany, and the United States again responded that this was not acceptable. For several months in the late summer and fall the air was filled with the sound of bluster. Khrushchev called the idea that the West would fight for the 2 million people of West Berlin a "fairy tale"; in a war over the enclave "hundreds of millions might perish," he pointed out.[47] A clash in the area would rapidly escalate, Khrushchev claimed, as he reminded "those who are thinking of war" that "distances will not save them." He could also see that the West did not respond to his challenges with a unified voice, and sought to exacerbate these disagreements, sometimes by peaceful gestures and sometimes through warlike rhetoric, as when explaining to the British ambassador that six Soviet bombs "would be quite enough to annihilate the British Isles" while "nine would take care of France."[48]

In the midst of the crisis period Khrushchev spectacularly shattered a two-year-old voluntary nuclear test moratorium by exploding the biggest thermonuclear bombs ever detonated—one as large as fifty-eight megatons. And in 1961 the Soviets with great fanfare lofted the first and second men into space, while Khrushchev, noting untruthfully that he now had 100-megaton bombs, pointed out that his cosmonauts could be replaced "with other loads that can be directed to any place on earth."[49]

Meanwhile, the United States tallied up its own nuclear arsenal and announced that it could "conduct nuclear actions from the level of large-scale destruction down to mere demolition work," and it scurried to catch up in the testing race. Both sides expanded their military readiness during the crisis and instituted various troop maneuvers.[50] In October there was even a dramatic foray in which Soviet and American tanks pointed their guns at each other in Berlin. By that time, however, Khrushchev had unilaterally solved his major Berlin problem: he had a wall constructed around West Berlin, stifling the enervating exodus from East Germany—a move that caught Western leaders utterly unprepared, sent them into confusion and disarray, and about which they did nothing.[51] Accordingly Khrushchev lifted his deadline, and the crisis gradually dissolved.

Crisis over Cuba.

Khrushchev's thrusts and parries reached their zenith the next year, and, as Richard Betts and many others have observed, in the process they probably nudged the United States and the Soviet Union as close as they have ever managed to get to the "nuclear brink."[52]

As it turns out, Khrushchev's stratospheric claim about how many ICBMs his factories were producing was at best a bluff, at worst a lie. Meanwhile, however, the United States had desperately built up its own arsenal. By 1962 a missile gap had materialized—but the opposite of what had been predicted: the United States had two to four times more than the Soviets. But the Soviets did have quite a few shorter-range missiles and bombers to help redress the imbalance—if they could be implanted someplace close to the United States. Cuba was a choice spot, and Castro indicated that he would be glad to have some missiles on his turf in order to help deter the Americans from supporting another invasion of Cuba like the abortive Bay of Pigs attempt the year before.[53]

The Kennedy administration repeatedly pointed out that if a "significant offensive capability" were found on Cuba, "the gravest issues would arise."[54] Khrushchev heard the message, assured the United States that no offensive weapons would be installed in Cuba, and then continued to put them in. Apparently he hoped that he would be able to sneak them by, presenting Kennedy with a *fait accompli* like the one over the Berlin Wall that would leave the president and other Western leaders contradictorily sputtering in impotent disbelief—the tactic of "displaying a bold initiative and throwing his enemy into confusion," as Shevchenko has expressed it.[55] He may also have believed it when he told a visiting American poet that "Kennedy is too liberal to fight," fondly recalling perhaps the young president's ineptness on the Bay of Pigs, backdown in Laos, ineffectiveness on the Berlin Wall, and waffling on Cuba.[56]

It all proved to be a substantial miscalculation on Khrushchev's part. The United States discovered the missiles while they were still being assembled in Cuba, instituted a naval blockade of the island, went on military alert, and poised itself to take out the missiles with air strikes or an invasion. Khrushchev mulled things over for several days, labelling Kennedy's action "outright banditry" and "the folly of degenerate imperialism." As he saw it, the degenerate American bandits were pushing "to the abyss" of a world war, and he threatened that if Soviet ships were interfered with, they would be forced to take measures "necessary and adequate in order to protect our rights." Eventually, however, Khrushchev gave in and had the offending missiles removed in exchange for a conditional pledge from the Americans that they would not invade Cuba as well as some informal assurances that American missiles in Italy and Turkey would be removed.[57]

Crisis and the Nearness of War

While there have been many notably unpleasant periods of alarm and war fear during the Cold War, in retrospect it seems clear, as Betts has concluded, that the only time the United States and the Soviet Union ever got "close to war" was during the crisis over missiles in Cuba. Betts calls it the "epochal military confrontation" of the era, and Graham Allison considers it a "seminal event" during which the world "paused at the nuclear precipice. Never before had there been such a high probability that so many lives would end suddenly."[58]

That may be, but it is worth considering how high that probability was. At the time, of course, war seemed uncomfortably close to participants and nonparticipants alike as they attempted to peer into the uncertain future—as it had also during the less directly confrontational crises over Berlin. According to one of Kennedy's advisers, "War loomed large on the horizon." Secretary of State Dean Rusk contemplated that the situation could well lead to general war, and at one point the president joked to his colleagues, "I hope you realize that there's not enough room for everybody in the White House bomb shelter." A presidential aide, Theodore Sorensen, has reported Kennedy's own probability estimate: "The odds that the Soviets would go all the way to war, he later said, seemed to him then 'somewhere between one out of three and even.' "[59]

Judging from Soviet actions in the crisis and from later accounts, Kennedy's crisis-induced estimate of what the Soviets were likely to do was wildly high. In response to American demands and mobilization, the Soviets, thoroughly outclassed and outmaneuvered, never even went on a demonstration alert. In his memoirs, Khrushchev admits that the Soviet "anxiety" level was "intense"— although he (accurately) surmised that the Americans "were no less scared than we were of atomic war." He had adopted a policy that had led to a hopelessly overextended position; but in his Cuban ploy he "had no desire to start a war," he says, and he was "well aware that a war that started over Cuba would quickly expand into a world war."[60] His concern about escalation, and its near automaticity, was also expressed in a long, emotional letter he wrote to Kennedy at the height of the crisis in which he argued that the two leaders were pulling on a rope "in which you have tied the knot of war" and suggested they seek to "relax the forces pulling on the ends of the rope" rather than to tighten the knot "and thereby to doom the world to the catastrophe of thermonuclear war."[61]

Clearly, from the start he saw the horrors of potential nuclear war before him and had no intention of working his way closer toward that calamity. As Shevchenko observes, the Soviets were not on the "brink": "At no moment did Khrushchev or anyone else in Moscow intend to use nuclear weapons against the United States. When the crisis broke, our leaders were preoccupied almost exclusively with how to extricate themselves from the situation with a minimum loss of face and prestige." A report from a "reliable, well-placed" Soviet source says that the leadership issued a formalized secret directive that it had decided not to go to war even if the United States invaded Cuba.[62]

For their part, the Americans were also intensely concerned about escalation. Kennedy had been greatly impressed by Barbara Tuchman's *The Guns of August* and concluded that in 1914 the Europeans "somehow seemed to tumble into war . . . through stupidity, individual idiosyncracies, misunderstandings, and personal complexes of inferiority and grandeur." He had no intention of becoming a central character in a "comparable book about this time, *The Missiles of October.* " Secretary of Defense Robert McNamara recalls being "preoccupied" by the possibility of "blundering into disaster," of somehow managing to "stumble into a nuclear war." To keep things under control, the Americans carefully limited their goals to the removal of the offending arms from Cuba; as Kennedy put it, "I am not going to push the Russians an inch beyond what is necessary."[63]

Although it was certainly possible to imagine an escalation sequence that would lead to major war, the United States had many lower rungs to climb first—tightening the blockade, bombing the sites, invading Cuba, fighting limited battles at sea—before getting there. A minimal escalatory step, an air strike against missile sites in Cuba, was scheduled; but one of the American decision-makers, George Ball, says he "doubted if that schedule would be kept, in view of the President's manifest desire to avoid any irrevocable act." Moreover, the President was apparently quite willing to consider removing the Turkish missiles if that is what it took to get the Cuban missiles out without further escalation. McNamara recalled Kennedy saying, "I am not going to war over worthless missiles in Turkey. I don't want to go to war anyhow, but I am certainly not going to war over worthless missiles in Turkey." Transcripts of some of the climactic meetings at the White House tend to corroborate this view, as does the remarkable disclosure by Rusk twenty-five years after the event that Kennedy had actually established mechanisms for arranging the missile trade should it come to that.[64]

Twenty-five years after the crisis some of the Americans who participated in the 1962 decisions were inclined to estimate in retrospect that the probability of an escalation to a nuclear exchange was more like one in fifty—still far too high, they would argue, and few would disagree. But even this figure may well be exaggerated. As two analysts who have worked with the transcripts of the American meetings have observed, even if the Soviets had held out for a deal that was substantially embarrassing to the United States, the odds that the Americans would have gone to war "were next to zero."[65] And the testimony of Khrushchev's memoirs and other evidence certainly suggest that the only serious Soviet desire from the beginning of the crisis was to avoid war while trying to get the best possible deal in a difficult situation.*

*One ploy open to the Soviet Union was simply to deny that they were putting any nuclear arms in Cuba at all and see if they could bluff their way out (bluff was certainly in Khrushchev's repertoire) while quietly dismantling the missiles. The only reason the American leaders believed missiles were going in was because they trusted the CIA experts who told them so: in looking over the CIA photographs, Robert Kennedy said that "what I saw appeared to be no more than the clearing of field for a farm or the basement of a house. I was relieved to hear later that this was the same reaction of virtually everyone at the meeting, including President Kennedy. Even a few days later, when more work had taken place on the site, he remarked that it looked like a football field" (1971, p. 2). The Bay of Pigs fiasco had taken place only a year and a half earlier, and the CIA's credibility was not exactly at peak levels. Accordingly, in some quarters there was a strong tendency to believe that Kennedy was lying or had been deceived. As the London *Tribune* editorialized, "No British prime

Furthermore, as Brodie has observed, the episode never really had the ring of the kinds of crises that have led to war in the past:

> From beginning to end the confrontation we call the Cuban missile crisis—the most acute crisis of any we have had since World War II—shows a remarkably different quality from any previous one in history. There is an unprecedented candor, direct personal contact, and at the same time mutual respect between the chief actors. Normal diplomatic formalities of language and circumlocution are disregarded. Both sides at once agreed that their quarrel *could* lead to nuclear war, which is impossible to contemplate and which would leave no winner. In effect they are asking each other: How do we get out of this with the absolute minimum of damage to each other including each other's prestige?

It's very difficult to have a war when no one has the slightest desire to get into one. Moreover, as Robert Jervis has suggested, "a major cause of past wars was the belief that armed conflict could not be avoided." Although the fear of war was high in 1962, the fatalistic belief that it was unavoidable, which obsessed decision makers in 1914 and which, Jervis argues, is "probably a necessary condition for war" today, never dominated the thinking processes of the decision makers even at their gloomiest. Instead, they sought from the beginning to find a way to clamber out of their self-dug pit.[66]

The Irrelevance of Nuclear Weapons (continued)

It is not at all clear that Khrushchev would have been much less anxious if all he had had to worry about was escalation to a war of the kind he had already experienced: "I have participated in two world wars," he wrote Kennedy at the height of this nuclear crisis, "and know that war ends only when it has carved

---

minister, we trust, . . . would order the turning out of the Palace Guard on evidence from so unreliable a source as the CIA. . . . If [missiles] are being installed . . . it may be assumed that Khrushchev has taken leave of his senses and has completely abandoned [his] military policies" (Reporter 1963, p. 90). The Soviets may have considered this a denial. They refused for days to confirm Kennedy's assertion, and reportedly their UN ambassador had instructions to deny the presence of Soviet missiles in Cuba (Garthoff 1987, p. 50n). He tried it at one point in the crisis (Larson 1963, pp. 136–37), but, perhaps because it didn't seem to generate a significant number of believers, the tactic was not pursued.

its way across cities and villages, bringing death and destruction in its wake." And in a speech to Soviet textile workers a year after the crisis Khrushchev recalled the loss of his son in World War II and the millions of other deaths suffered by the Russians, and then he lambasted the Chinese: "Some comrades abroad claim that Khrushchev is making a mess of things, and is afraid of war. Let me say once again that I should like to see the kind of bloody fool who is genuinely not afraid of war." The Soviet press reported that it was this statement that was cheered more loudly and wholeheartedly than any other by his audience.[67]

George Ball has reportedly concluded that the caution shown in the crisis "would not have been present to the same degree if only conventional forces had been involved."[68] But as usual, the issue is not whether nuclear war is more caution-inspiring than a conventional major war, but whether major conventional war is not already traumatizingly horrible enough to inspire sufficient caution. Khrushchev's statements strongly suggest that for him in this crisis, it was; and, as noted, the American president was intensely nervous about repeating the conventional war experience of 1914. The notion that these leaders would have glibly allowed the crisis to escalate if all they had to worry about was a repetition of World War I or II is singularly unconvincing.

The End of Crisis and the Beginning of Detente

If the Cuban missile crisis never ventured very far up the escalatory ladder, something else that didn't occur is also of interest: the Soviets never reacted by creating trouble somewhere closer to home like Berlin or Turkey. In 1962 American decision makers were very concerned about this possibility, particularly about retaliation against Berlin. In the speech that opened the public phase of the crisis, Kennedy specifically warned the Soviets about such a move, and at the end of the crisis McNamara urgently argued that plans were needed "for how to respond to the Soviet Union in Europe, because sure as hell they're going to do something there."[69] Conditioned by five or six years of Khrushchevian bluster and swagger, and by two Soviet-instituted crises over Berlin, the Americans poised themselves in the wake of the missile crisis for the next challenge.

But, quite amazingly, it never came: Cuba proved to be the last crisis. Not only were there no immediate or delayed countermoves in Berlin or elsewhere, but

Khrushchev, probably because he had now vividly seen what crisis and bluster could lead to, largely abandoned the whole tactic. The change has been essentially permanent. Since 1962 there have been no serious confrontational crises between the United States and the USSR, and Soviet use of rocket-rattling bluster has been extremely limited.[70]*

McGeorge Bundy, one of the participants in the Cuban crisis deliberations, has observed that, because "there has been no open nuclear threat by any government" since 1962, "I think it is not too much to say that this particular type of atomic diplomacy has been permanently discredited." Khrushchev and his successors over the next decades did not give up the idea that the "struggle" against capitalist evil should be pursued. They continued ideologically to support—and, where it seemed prudent, materially to assist—wars of national liberation, including an important one brewing in Vietnam. They were also ready at a moment's notice to dip into their repertoire of seductive techniques when a third world country seemed to be in a receptive mood. And they still tried to promote themselves as the exemplary wave of the future—although some of the luster was gone by the mid-1960s as Western economies surged, the United States came to dominate the space race, and the failure of various highly-touted agricultural schemes forced the Soviets ignominiously to buy Western wheat. But Khrushchev-style mechanisms to exploit contradictions among the capitalist states simply proved too dangerous, and they have been abandoned in favor of diplomatic efforts to mellow tensions and to control conflicts that could lead to major war. Thus, Khrushchev led the Soviet Union out of what might be called the classic Cold War period into an era that was later to be dubbed "detente."[71]

At first this was primarily a matter of tone: as Brodie has observed, "Khrushchev's communications became immediately sober and polite, where they had often previously been violent and rude." And soon there were substantive improvements. In December 1962, Khrushchev politely made some major concessions with respect to obtaining an agreement about banning atomic tests and was even willing for a while to consider on-site inspection within the borders of the Soviet Union as part of the verification apparatus.[72] In the summer of 1963 a treaty banning all above-ground tests was signed. It was a major step—the first significant arms control agreement between the two nuclear powers, and one negotiated in an atmosphere that was nonpropagandistic, businesslike, and constructive. The treaty by no means ended the nuclear arms buildup, nor did it resolve central ideological differences between the two sides. But it set in motion

*The U.S.–USSR confrontation during the Arab-Israeli war of 1973 is discussed on p. 162, and the chief revival of bluster, over NATO's effort to deploy new missiles in the early 1980s, is discussed on pp. 202–5.

a process that decoupled nuclear and major war issues from the rest of the Cold War.

Most analysts have trouble seeing how a major war could come about unless an episode of crisis or at least of heightened tension and threat were to precede it.[73] Since 1962 the United States and the Soviet Union have largely abandoned crisis, tension, and threat as devices for dealing directly with each other. To that degree they have spent decades forgetting how to get into a major war.

8

Vietnam: China Abandons the Cold War

ALTHOUGH international Communism may have abandoned the crisis technique after 1963, it retained its deep affection for wars of national liberation. A degree of disagreement on this tactic persisted, however: the Chinese continued to regard such wars with infinite enthusiasm; and the Soviets, while finding the wars in principle to be desirable, virtuous, and inevitable, were concerned about their escalatory potential. Strains continued to develop over this issue and even more over Chinese outrage at the way the Soviets began to cuddle up with the West after the Cuban missile crisis. Eventually this disagreement led to a deep split in the international movement, and increasingly China began to present a shrill, independent Cold War challenge to the United States and then a direct military threat—as well as an ideological one—to the Soviets themselves.

The issues of Chinese belligerence and of wars of national liberation became focused on an ongoing war in a distant corner of the world, Vietnam. After a great deal of careful and agonized thought, a wide consensus was reached in Washington that Vietnam was a crucial, prototypical Cold War contest. Although both the Soviets and the Chinese supported the Communist side in Vietnam, the American venture there was directed primarily at the challenge and threat China presented in the area, and it is at least possible that American actions did in fact prevent a larger, more direct contest with China later. But events outside Vietnam in Indonesia and China very quickly reduced the war's significance in this regard, and it became something of a Cold War anachronism. By then, however, the war had taken on its own grim momentum and it lingered on—a costly, wrenching, and exasperating contest of will against the tenacious North Vietnamese Communists, enemies who turned out to be virtually unique in the history of modern warfare in their willingness to accept punishment.

Then, astoundingly, the Chinese abruptly changed course. While continuing to be antagonistic to the Soviet Union, they assiduously sought to improve relations with the United States and eventually began to drop out of the Cold War entirely.

The 1963–1974 period is notable, then, for three major Cold War developments: (1) the rise on one level of detente between West and East; (2) the thrashing out (although not the final resolution) of the war-of-national-liberation issue in Vietnam; and (3) the amazing conversion of China from belligerent, dynamic, ideological purism to placid, nonideological accommodation. When the chaos and trauma ended, West and East were even farther away from war with each other than they had been at the beginning.

Forgetting about the Unthinkable: Detente, Arms Control, and Europe

A remarkable decline in concern about war between the United States and the USSR occurred after the Cuban missile crisis and after the signing of the partial test ban treaty in 1963. It seems clear in hindsight that the world was never remotely close to major war during Khrushchev's era, but largely because of his tactics, it often *sounded* like war was around the corner. Even in hindsight one can hardly fault people for being deeply concerned, even panicked, about it at the time. In the West, where such things are allowed, there were frequent peace marches and noisy convocations urgently demanding peace and disarmament. Philosopher Bertrand Russell, previously an advocate of preventive war, was a major spokesman for the movement, and at times of highest tension, such as during the Cuban missile crisis, he was given to putting out cheerless pamphlets entitled "You Are To Die."[1] In England he helped to organize the Campaign for Nuclear Disarmament (CND), which invented the peace symbol—a circle around a configuration that looks like a missile but is supposed to represent both a broken cross and an overlapping of the semaphore N and the semaphore D. The symbol lingered on—indeed it eventually became quite a trendy decoration—but the movement itself lapsed when tensions slackened in 1963.[2]

A similar development occurred in the United States where there had also been an active ban-the-bomb movement. Much of its energies had been focused on protesting Kennedy's arms buildup measures of 1961, particularly his ill-fated proposals for developing a fallout-shelter program to protect some of the citizenry in the event of nuclear attack or accident. Reflecting such interest, over 400 articles per year on nuclear-related topics are listed in the *Reader's Guide to Periodical Literature* for 1961, 1962, and 1963. Output dropped to less than 200 in 1964 and to about 120 in 1967.[3] Rob Paarlberg has aptly called the phenomenon "forgetting about the unthinkable."

The experience suggests once again the irrelevance of nuclear weapons and the nuclear arms "race" to fundamental issues and perceptions of war and peace. For at the same time that concern over major war was mellowing, the United States and especially the USSR were busily expanding and improving their nuclear weapons arsenals. Each year they became more capable of pulverizing each other's society—the partial test ban treaty of 1963 didn't cramp their style in the slightest. In that sense the world became increasingly dangerous, but at the same time it began to *sound* safer; and as usual, it was tone, not content, that mattered.

Nikita Khrushchev, the principal architect of all this, was ousted—for "harebrained scheming," his topplers explained—in October 1964, but his basic foreign policies were continued. East-West exchange remained comparatively civil and businesslike in tone, and neither side showed any interest in crisis as methodology or—except for some curious and essentially anachronistic flurries in the early 1980s (see chapter 9)—in belligerence and dramatic posturing. Mutually beneficial arms control measures have been pursued, and in the decade after Khrushchev's ouster, two major agreements were worked out: one in 1968 restraining the proliferation of nuclear weapons to countries that did not yet have them, and one in 1972 banning certain antimissile defenses and putting crude but utterly unprecedented ceilings on nuclear weapons delivery systems.

In Europe, Berlin and Germany remained divided, but both Cold War contestants became increasingly able to live with the situation. However, relations there did sour for a while in 1968 when the Soviet Union, fearing that a satellite was escaping its designated orbit, found it prudent to invade Czechoslovakia and occupy it more completely. In the long run, patience and calm about the German and Berlin issues worked better than crisis and bluster for the Soviets: by the end of the 1960s, a new leader, Willy Brandt, came to authority in West Germany, and he actively improved relations with the Soviet Union and its East European colonies.

American-Soviet trade increased, particularly in the early 1970s, and Western bankers began to make substantial loans to the Soviet Union and its East European colonies so that those countries, devoted to the ultimate downfall of capitalism, might more quickly develop toward the inevitable state of Communist bliss that Marx had envisioned so very long ago.

This all reached a sort of peak in 1975 when officials representing thirty-five countries on both sides of Stalin's Iron Curtain signed a set of somewhat airy accords in Helsinki, Finland. Mutual respect was pledged, some limited arms control measures regarding troop movements in Europe were created, and civil liberties were theoretically accepted. All proclaimed current national frontiers to be "inviolable"—thereby essentially accepting the Soviet-designed status quo in East Europe—and, twelve years after Khrushchev had accepted the notion, all pledged to employ neither force nor the threat of force in dealing with each other.

Meanwhile, signs appeared that the United States and the Soviet Union might be able to work together to keep what Khrushchev once called "local wars" under some degree of mutually beneficial control. When India and Pakistan got into a brief war in the fall of 1965, the Americans and the Soviets cooperated to bring mediation and moderation to the conflict. And although aligned on opposite sides, they kept their mutual—and mutually wary—distance from the brief Arab-Israeli War of 1967 and the lengthy crisis that led up to it. During the war they even used the new "hot-line" communication link to assure each other of their lack of direct complicity in the conflict and of their mutual desire to bring hostilities to an end as soon as possible.[4] Their desire to keep their relations essentially unscathed by the India-Pakistan-Bangladesh war of 1971 also seems clear.

Curiously, the one instance in the post-Khrushchev era in which the United States and the Soviet Union most nearly slumped into crisis stems from disagreement over how best to mediate or manage a local conflict. Syria and Egypt, using military gear mostly supplied by the Soviet Union, attacked American-supplied Israel in 1973. Israel soon turned the attack around and began pushing the Arabs back into their prewar territory. After a ceasefire collapsed, the Soviets proposed that they and the Americans jointly intervene to police it, and they further suggested that they might "be faced with the necessity urgently to consider" taking action on their own if the United States refused to join in. The Americans took substantial umbrage at the thought of unilateral Soviet intervention in the war and sent a warning note to that effect, pointedly putting their forces—primarily conventional ones—on an advanced state of alert. The Soviets dismissed the American alert as "a false alarm," and the whole exercise was made academic by the Arabs, who, before they had even heard of the American alert, withdrew the invitation for Soviet intervention.[5] Thus ended the big "crisis" of the post-Khrushchev era.*

*Richard Betts concludes, "The circumstantial evidence for inferring efficacy in the U.S. threat is weak, and much points in the direction of concluding that it was beside the point. If the alert was

The Sino-Soviet Split

The dispute between the Soviets and the Chinese continued to heat up in the early 1960s, but it was by no means obvious at the time that the disagreements between the two large Communist countries would lead to an outright break. For one thing there were strong economic ties: the Chinese were substantially dependent on the Soviet Union and there was a brisk trade between the two countries of some $2 billion per year. As a team of analysts of the conflict pointed out in 1961, "The consequences of a lasting rift between the two chief Communist powers would be serious to both; for China it would amount to a setback from which to recover it might take her the better part of a decade. However serious her dissent from Soviet Russia's political concepts, economic considerations would seem unlikely to allow friction to endanger monolithic solidarity within the bloc."[6]

Moreover, important military links existed. The Chinese may have been unhappy because Khrushchev's verbal aid in the Taiwan Straits crisis of 1958 came so late, but he *did* eventually reaffirm that the Soviets would consider an attack on China to be an attack on themselves (see p. 149). Since Chinese-American relations remained intensely hostile, China would step out from under the Soviet nuclear umbrella only at considerable risk. And although ideological disagreement between the two big Communist countries clearly existed, they had, as Donald Zagoria pointed out in 1962, "much more in common with each other than with the Western world, which both view as a decaying social order doomed to the dustbin of history." Whatever their differences, he concluded, their "overriding common aims," their "joint commitment to an international revolutionary process which they believe is historically inevitable and which they believe it is their duty to aid," and their "shared determination to establish Communism throughout the world, sets limits on conflict between the two." Given these ideological ties as well as their web of economic, political, military, and other relations, Zagoria reasonably argued that a "total break of diplomatic, economic, and military relations is a possibility that seems remote."[7]

Yet it happened, and the driving force seems to have been differences over how to manage and carry forward the international Communist impetus. The Chinese greeted Khrushchev's Cuban fiasco of 1962 with scathing derision, and for weeks

---

influential, it is also hard to argue against the proposition that the conventional force elements in it were sufficient, the nuclear component superfluous" (1987, p. 129).

they accused him of "adventurism" for trying the ploy in the first place and of "capitulationism" for pulling out in the second.

In the first half of 1963 the Soviets made some efforts to patch up the differences, but by the summer they apparently decided to split the alliance. By signing the partial test ban treaty, they deliberately turned away from China, whose leaders had been screaming for years that any such deals with the capitalist world were at best foolish and at worst treasonable. But the experience of the Cuban crisis seems to have convinced Khrushchev that efforts to keep the danger of major war under control were more important than maintaining the disintegrating alliance with China: the "paper tiger," he told the Chinese, has "nuclear teeth." The treaty propelled the Chinese into a new torrent of invective: it was a "dirty fraud," they screamed, and they accused the Soviets of following "a policy of uniting with the forces of war against the forces of peace, uniting with imperialism for the struggle against socialism, uniting with the USA for the struggle against China, uniting with the reactionary forces of different countries for the struggle against the peoples of the whole world."[8] The Chinese, in short, were not happy.

Some of the antagonism between Mao and Khrushchev was clearly personal. The Soviets declared Mao "a megalomaniac warmonger" and "an irresponsible scribbler" who "chatters about war and does not understand what he is chattering about," and the Chinese called Khrushchev "a Bible-reading and psalm-singing buffoon."[9] But after Khrushchev was deposed in October 1964, the antagonism continued to prosper. As far as the Chinese could see, Khrushchev's successors simply continued his policy of wary, but businesslike, accommodation with the capitalist world: "Khrushchevism without Khrushchev," they characterized it, rather accurately.

Sino-Soviet relations disintegrated. By 1965 trade between them was down to 25 percent of 1960 levels, and by 1970 it was down to 3 percent. The two former military allies began to edge toward war with each other as both sides built up military forces along their lengthy joint boundary. By 1969 some shooting had taken place, and the Chinese were claiming that "Soviet revisionism" and "U.S. imperialism," "working hand in glove" to do "foul and evil things," might soon band together to launch "a large-scale war of aggression" against China. In 1964 the Chinese had exploded their first nuclear weapon, and apparently the Soviets in 1969 were at least toying with the idea of launching a preemptive strike against Chinese nuclear assets. Such evidence caused *New York Times* reporter Harrison Salisbury to conclude at the time that the two countries were "headed toward a collision course and war" and that such a war *"will be nuclear.* No ifs, ands, or buts."[10]

No war ever took place, in part, suggests one report, because the Americans, far from "working hand in glove" with the Soviets, let it be known that they would view such a war with perceptible dismay. Actually, however, the prospects were not all that favorable for the Soviet Union even if the Americans had said they would support a Soviet attack and even if the Chinese were unable to retaliate with their own primitive nuclear force. A massive nuclear attack on China would have caused radioactive fallout to threaten Soviet citizens as well as those of other neighboring countries, while a small "surgical" nuclear strike against China's nuclear facilities could not have eliminated its ability to wage a vast, endless conventional and guerrilla war.[11] Once again it is not at all clear that nuclear weapons made an important difference. The prospect of a World War II–type conflict was impressively sobering in itself: the threat of a large conventional conflict sufficiently deterred the Soviet Union.

The Contest in the Third World

The Sino-Soviet split considerably complicated the Cold War. In continuing to apply its policy of containment, the United States now found there were two quite separate Communist movements afoot in much of the third world.

In some respects Moscow was the more important antagonist, because it could probe more widely, had more money, was more firmly ensconced in most areas, and possessed a huge military arsenal. But the Soviets were proving to be pragmatic in their third world activities, and they showed considerable caution about letting Cold War contests escalate. The Chinese, on the other hand, seemed to be becoming ever more romantic, fanatical, and hysterical about the contest, and they appeared to be remarkably casual about escalation and major war. Indeed, the calamities they were inflicting on themselves often were of warlike proportions: in its Great Leap Forward of the late 1950s China sought to push toward utopian socialism in a hurry, and a famine resulted that claimed 30 million lives, the largest such loss in history.[12]

The Chinese seemed to bring a similar destructive romanticism to issues of international politics. According to a major Chinese figure, Lin Biao, in 1965, North America and Western Europe could be called "the cities of the world," whereas Asia, Africa, and Latin American constituted "the rural areas of the world." As he figured it, "The contemporary world revolution" can be characterized as "the encirclement of cities by the rural areas." Although it can be accomplished "only through long and tortuous struggles," the "colossus of U.S.

imperialism" can be "split up and defeated" as "the peoples of Asia, Africa, Latin America and other regions . . . destroy it piece by piece, some striking at its head and others at its feet." And he repeated the usual Maoist notion that the Chinese could cope with a "U.S. imperialist war of aggression": "The vast ocean of several hundred million Chinese people in arms will be more than enough to submerge your few million aggressor troops."[13]

Thus, Chinese rhetoric remained shrill and fantastic while Soviet rhetoric mellowed, and Americans were led to conclude from this that, as John Kennedy expressed it two months after the Cuban missile crisis, the United States is "better off with the Khrushchev view" of the world situation "than we are with the Chinese Communist view." The public concurred. Four times between 1961 and 1964 the polls asked, "Looking ahead to 1970, which country do you think will be the greater threat to world peace—Russia or Communist China?" The proportion choosing Russia dropped from 49 to 20 percent, and the proportion choosing China rose from 32 to 59 percent.[14]

Nevertheless, in most areas of the third world, particularly those outside East and Southeast Asia, the most active and effective opponent was the somewhat subdued but methodically persistent Soviet Union. As good Leninists, the Soviets continually reviewed their tactics, and by 1967 or so they were coming to realize that one of Khrushchev's favorite devices, the attempted seduction of non-Communist third world leaders, was not working so well. Castro had quite willingly led his country into the Soviet camp, but other leaders were less easily wooed. Soviet commentators observed that successes around the time of Sputnik had caused them to conclude that most of "the developing countries would opt for the noncapitalist way without much delay." However, "sober" and "realistic" analysis now suggested that while the "national bourgeoisie" often led the "struggle against colonial regimes," it "already has demonstrated its inability to continue playing such a role."[15]

Such analyses were doubtless impelled in large part by a pair of major setbacks for Soviet policy in Africa, where promising seductees were replaced by less "progressive" regimes. In 1965, Ahmed Ben Bella was toppled in Algeria, and in 1966, Kwame Nkrumah, after parlaying the half billion dollars of foreign reserves left by the British decolonizers into a $1 billion debt, was pointedly requested by the military not to return to Ghana after a foreign tour. More of the same came in 1968 when Soviet-approved Mobido Keita was ousted in Mali. Even where Soviet favorites remained in power, they often proved to be distressingly unmalleable. Signs of this could be seen as early as 1962 when the radical leader Seko Toure of Guinea expelled the Soviet ambassador for meddling in internal affairs.

Worst of all was the situation in Egypt. By 1970 the Soviets had ladled out over a billion dollars of aid, and they had faithfully cheered the Egyptians on in their repeated conflicts with Israel, sending over aircraft, armor, guns, and thousands of Soviet advisers to seal the bargain. They had also actively supported Nasser in his various pan-Arab efforts, including a bizarre, costly, and largely unproductive war he tinkered with in Yemen during the 1960s. Yet under Nasser's successor, Anwar Sadat, Soviet "influence" in Egypt disintegrated. In 1972, Sadat expelled Soviet troops and advisers and took over several airfields the Soviets were operating in Egypt because, he said, the Soviet Union "had begun to feel it enjoyed a privileged position in Egypt" and, most interestingly, because it seemed to be trying to restrain him from launching his 1973 war against Israel. Relations continued to be strained, and in 1976, Sadat broke off almost entirely from the Soviets, arguing that the "Russians no longer had anything to offer" in solving the problems of the Middle East.[16]

Because of such unpleasantries, the Soviets began to turn more toward reliance on standard Marxist parties in the third world as well as toward the support of various promising guerrilla and national-liberation movements—it found a dozen of these in the Middle East and Africa alone.[17]

Opportunities also presented themselves in Latin America. Castro, now firmly in power and possessed by a messianic self-image, was an eager conduit of aid and comfort to various armed revolutionary movements around the area, particularly to Castro-style insurgencies in Venezuela, Colombia, and Guatemala. He could get quite romantic about such uprisings, which he saw as "inevitable" and progressive, whereas the Soviets approached them with more wariness, often preferring the quiet, insidious opportunism of old-line Communist parties. A potentially favorable regime in Brazil was toppled by a military coup in 1964, but by the end of the 1960s the Soviet Union optimistically claimed to see the "revolutionary process" at work under leftist military regimes in Peru, Panama, and Bolivia.[18]

Communist incursions in Latin American, whether real or potential, really set the Americans' teeth on edge. Kennedy had created an expanded aid program, called the Alliance for Progress, which was intended to make Latin American regimes more productive and responsive, and therefore, he hoped, less susceptible to Communist designs and appeals. His successor, Lyndon Johnson, became highly alarmed in 1965 that a chaotic, civil warlike situation in the Dominican Republic might bring about "another Cuba," and he sent 22,000 U.S. troops to police and stabilize the situation. As with Eisenhower's similar venture in Lebanon in 1958, the intervention generally worked out in the Americans' favor, and no substantial combat ensued.

The election of a Marxist, Salvador Allende, to the presidency of Chile in 1970 was welcomed by the Soviets as "second only to the victory of the Cuban revolution . . . as a revolutionary blow to the imperialist system in Latin America." Such cheerleading, however, did not come accompanied by the economic aid Allende desperately needed as he mismanaged the economy, as the Americans cut aid and put on economic pressure, and as the price of Chile's chief export, copper, fell. It appears the Soviets were reluctant to take on another costly economic burden in Latin America like Cuba, and they watched helplessly and from afar as a military coup toppled the Allende regime in 1973.[19]

The Cold War Stakes in Vietnam

While detente continued on such issues as nuclear arms, major war, and the fate of Europe, and while the United States and the two Communist giants gingerly thrusted and parried in various parts of the third world, it was in Vietnam that the Cold War underwent its most important, and bloodiest, development.

After the French withdrew from Indochina in 1954, the United States sought to waft its containment umbrella over the three non-Communist states that emerged from the four-way partition of the former French colony. One of these, Cambodia, largely pursued a neutralist course, but both Laos and South Vietnam accepted American aid against domestic Communist insurgencies that were being encouraged and aided by Communist North Vietnam. As noted in the previous chapter, an early decision of the Kennedy administration in 1961 was essentially to abandon its overextended position in Laos, retreating to South Vietnam, where the prospects for victory against the insurgency seemed far greater: aid was increased, and the number of U.S. advisers stationed there jumped from around 900 to over 16,000.[20]*

The anti-Communist position in South Vietnam gradually deteriorated, however, and by 1965 a difficult dilemma confronted the Johnson administration: the Hanoi-backed Communist insurgents appeared to be on the verge of victory in South Vietnam, and it seemed that the only way to rescue the situation was to send American troops.

The United States had faced situations like this before. In China in the late 1940s, in Indochina in 1954, and in Laos in 1961 it reacted by declining to send troops to bolster the anti-Communist side, which then proceeded to collapse. In

---

*In 1963 the American commitment became substantially deeper when the United States approved a successful coup against the chief leaders in South Vietnam in part because they were trying to work out a separate deal with the North Vietnamese (Hilsman 1967, p. 498).

Korea in 1950 it sent troops and fought a costly war. In Lebanon in 1958 and in the Dominican Republic in 1965 (at the same time as the Vietnam decisions) it sent policing troops into deteriorating situations, but it never had to do much fighting—something that was far from certain when the troops were sent. The United States had also aided quite a few other regimes facing Communist insurgencies—among them, Greece in the late 1940s, the Philippines between 1945 and 1954, and Venezuela in the 1960s—but in these cases the incumbents won without making it necessary to consider sending American troops. Both the logic and the reality of containment suggest that such decisions have to be made from time to time.

The 1965 decisions of the Johnson administration to send troops to Vietnam have been regularly criticized as inept and "wooden-headed."[21] For the most part, however, the extensive documentation available on the era suggests that the process was something of a model of what good decision making is supposed to be: extensive information was gathered, a wide range of alternatives was surveyed, objectives were reevaluated, risks were realistically assessed, and potential problems were appraised.[22]

A consensus existed both within and outside the administration that it was very important to keep South Vietnam out of Communist hands. In 1972 reporter David Halberstam published a best-selling book, *The Best and the Brightest*, in which he tried to figure out how all those smart Kennedy and Johnson people in the White House could have become the "architects of a war which I and many others thought the worst tragedy to befall this country since the Civil War." After all, Halberstam pointed out, "they were intelligent men, rational men, and seemingly intelligent, rational men would have known the obvious, how unlikely bombing was to work, and how dangerous it was to send combat troops, and that if we sent American units we would be following the French."[23] One reason, as it happens, is that almost all of the bright people in the White House agreed with the views Halberstam had expressed in 1965 about Vietnam: A "strategic country in a key area, it is perhaps one of only five or six nations in the world that is truly vital to U.S. interests." The "seemingly intelligent, rational men" in the White House had in fact evaluated the various alternatives to sending in American combat troops. Far from closing out unpleasant alternatives, they listened carefully—none more attentively than Johnson himself—to a carefully argued proposal from Undersecretary of State George Ball for a judicious loss-cutting withdrawal, a proposal far more radical than almost anything heard at the time outside the government. They rejected Ball's proposal because they agreed with Halberstam's assessment that Vietnam was "truly vital" to American interests and because they found the same drawbacks as Halberstam to withdrawal: it might bring a bloodbath ("those Vietnamese who committed themselves fully to the United States will suffer the most"), it would hamper American clout ("the United States' prestige will be lowered throughout the world"), and it would have a domino effect ("the pressure of Communism on the rest of Southeast Asia will intensify" and "throughout the world the enemies of the West will be encouraged to try insurgencies like the one in Vietnam").[24]

The Cold War stakes in Vietnam were both methodological and geopolitical.

Methodologically, Vietnam was seen to be an important testing ground of the efficacy of wars of national liberation. Throughout the world, Defense Secretary Robert McNamara observed, the conflict was regarded as "a test case of U.S. capacity to help a nation meet a Communist 'war of liberation' "; North Vietnamese leaders agreed: "South Vietnam is the model of the national liberation movement of our time. If the special warfare that the United States imperialists are testing in South Vietnam is overcome, then it can be defeated anywhere in the world." Since the Chinese were hysterically arguing that "the whole cause of world revolution hinges" on such "revolutionary struggles" of the third world, it followed that a highly visible defeat for the skilled revolutionary strugglers in Vietnam would help to gum the hinge up, discouraging similar applications of the method throughout the world, even as an American collapse in South Vietnam would, as Halberstam so brightly observed, encourage them. Moreover, an American success in Vietnam might be particularly discouraging to the Soviet Union, which had from time to time expressed misgivings about wars of national liberation anyway (see p. 141). As reporter Neil Sheehan, another future critic of American policy in Vietnam, put it in 1964, "If the United States wishes to influence world Communism along less militant lines, it could strengthen the Soviet Union's position in the Chinese-Soviet dispute by demonstrating that China's new strategy for Communist conquest will be as unsuccessful as the previous Communist attempts in Western Europe and Korea."[25]

Geopolitically, Vietnam was held to be vital because of the wide threat China seemed to present in East, South, and Southeast Asia in the early and middle 1960s. Since 1949 China had proclaimed itself leader of national-liberation wars in Asia (and, for that matter, the world),[26] and in the 1960s it continued to cheer them on and to assure them it felt "duty bound to support and aid" them.* But it was also using two other methods to spread its influence or, as some saw it, to seek hegemony, in the area.

One of these was direct warfare: in 1959 it had invaded and occupied semiautonomous Tibet, and in 1962 it had invaded India in a border dispute. The war with India only lasted a month and caused only about 1,000 battle deaths,

---

*In saying this, however, Lin Biao stressed that "foreign aid can only play a supplementary role. . . . To fight a people's war and be victorious, it is imperative to adhere to the policy of self-reliance . . . and be prepared to carry on the fight independently even when all material aid from outside is cut off" (1972, p. 390).

but it clearly suggested that the Chinese were prepared for such a conflict if the opportunity arose. An ominous new element was added when China exploded its first atomic bomb in October 1964, and in 1965 there were fears China might attack India again, possibly leading to a "breakdown of the Indian Republic," as columnist Walter Lippman put it at the time.[27]

The other method related to China's increasingly close ties to the huge island republic of Indonesia on the other side of Vietnam. Led by its mercurial president-for-life, Sukarno, Indonesia had embarked on a clamorous policy of hostility toward the West and toward its Western-oriented neighbors. Since 1962 Sukarno had adopted a "confrontation policy" in Southeast Asia and had nestled increasingly closer to China and to the leaders of the Indonesian Communist Party, which, with two million members, was the third largest in the world. Through threat and tantrum he managed to wrest the western half of New Guinea from its Dutch overseers in 1962, and in 1963, apparently as much on impulse as anything else, he launched a "crush Malaysia" campaign which led in 1964 to a noisy, if ill-fated, guerrilla attack upon his newly decolonized neighbor.[28]

By early 1965, as the Americans were making their crucial decisions about Vietnam, Sukarno had piloted his country into an informal alliance with Mao's China, and shortly after a visit from the Chinese foreign minister, he had come up with a snappy new slogan: "Crush America." Then, in what Mao called a "bold revolutionary move," Sukarno dramatically withdrew Indonesia from the United Nations and set up a rival organization he called the Conference of the New Emerging Forces. The Chinese suggested that they'd join, helped Sukarno to begin building an appropriately grandiose complex to house the new organization, and, some evidence suggests, toyed with the idea of testing an atomic bomb in Indonesia and letting Sukarno take the credit for it.[29]

Geopolitically, then, South Vietnam seemed to be wedged strategically—and vulnerably—between the glowering Chinese threat from the north and the clamorous Indonesian threat from the south: the "Peking-Djakarta axis," it was often called at the time. Johnson saw an even wider connection: he called it the "Djakarta-Hanoi-Peking-Pyongyang axis." Never one to be outdone on the rhetoric front, Sukarno in mid-1965 proclaimed the existence of a "Djakarta-Phnom Penh-Hanoi-Peking-Pyongyang axis." Somewhat later he explained the strategy for defeating imperialism: Communist China would "strike a blow against the American troops in Vietnam from the north while Indonesia would strike from the south."[30] In his autobiography, Johnson reprints that statement and supplies a map of Southeast Asia with ominous black arrows projecting downward from China and North Vietnam and upward from Indonesia (see figure 8.1). He describes the phenomenon as "Communist pincers." For New York Times editorial columnist C. L. Sulzberger the situation resembled a "vast nutcracker."[31]

Whatever the metaphor, American officials were not alone in viewing military

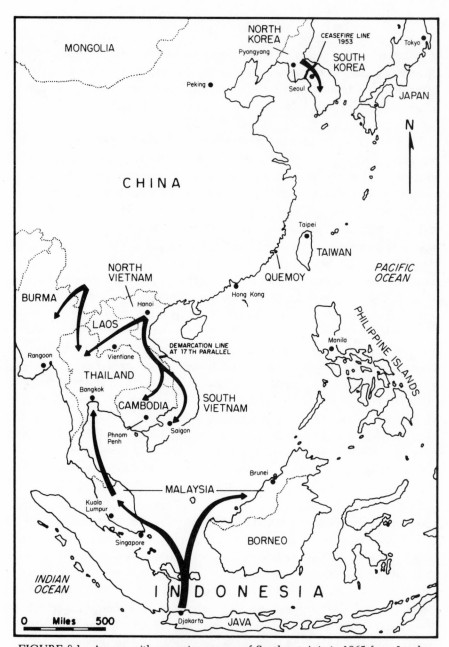

FIGURE 8.1   A map, with menacing arrows, of Southeast Asia in 1965 from Lyndon Johnson's autobiography. The map is accompanied by this caption: "The Communist pincers—Djakarta-Hanoi-Peking-Pyongyang axis on the move: Hanoi into Laos, Cambodia, and South Vietnam; Djakarta into Malaysia and Borneo; Malaysian Communists and Hanoi-trained guerrillas into Thailand; Peking-trained guerrillas into Thailand and Burma; Pyongyang sends guerrillas into South Korea (*black arrows*)."

SOURCE: Lyndon Baines Johnson, *The Vantage Point: Perspectives of the Presidency, 1963–1969* (New York: Holt, Rinehart & Winston, 1971), p. 606. Copyright © by HEC Public Affairs Foundation, by permission of Henry Holt and Company, Inc.

and political conditions in the area with alarm. So did the dominoes. Cambodia's Prince Norodom Sihanouk, a proclaimed neutralist, observed in 1964 that if the United States lost in Vietnam, he would be greeted on his next visit to Peking with the command, "Sihanouk, on your knees." The prime minister of Malaysia declared in 1965 that "it is imperative that the United States does not retire from the scene"; and the leaders of Thailand, Australia, South Korea, New Zealand, Singapore, and the Philippines made similar statements. A neutralist leader in Laos urged the United States to bomb China, and Indian leader Indira Gandhi privately told Vice President Hubert Humphrey that the American presence in Vietnam was important to India, although she helpfully explained that because of domestic pressures she would have to be critical in public. Humphrey observes that, with the exception of those in Pakistan, "every Asian leader who was publicly critical of us was privately encouraging us to remain in Vietnam."[32]

With such evidence, most American decision makers came to agree with future war critic Sheehan's cosmic conclusion: "The fall of Southeast Asia to China or its denial to the West over the next decade because of the repercussions from an American defeat in Vietnam would amount to a strategic disaster of the first magnitude." Only the United States, he argued, could meet "the Chinese Communist challenge for hegemony in Asia." Interestingly enough, support for the notion that China was seeking hegemony in Asia is supplied by Nikita Khrushchev in his memoirs: "At least when I knew him," Khrushchev relates, Mao "was bursting with an impatient desire to rule the world. His plan was to rule first China, then Asia, then . . . what?"[33]

American Strategy in Vietnam: The Search for the "Breaking Point"

Deciding to meet a "hegemonic challenge" is one thing; figuring out how to do it is another. The strategy chosen for preventing a Communist victory in South Vietnam was attrition.

The basic idea was to send over large numbers of American troops to "seize the initiative" and to carry the war to the enemy through relentless "search and destroy" operations. It was assumed that the enemy would eventually reach its breaking point: it would become "convinced that military victory was impossible and then would not be willing to endure further punishment," as the general in charge, William Westmoreland, put it at the time.[34]

Reflecting on these decisions six years later, Secretary of State Dean Rusk recalled that he thought "that when we had established a position in Vietnam which would be clearly impossible for them to overrun militarily that then the chances were very high that they would pull back—maybe only for a time—but pull back or take part in some serious negotiations." In part, such thinking was based on the observation that American goals in Vietnam were rather limited: the United States was seeking not to overthrow the Communist regime in the north but only to prevent the extension of its control to the non-Communist south. In this view, the North Vietnamese were not fighting for the survival of their state the way the Germans and Japanese had been in World War II. They merely had to give up the fight in the south, and they would be graciously permitted to retreat to an independent existence in the north. If they did so, Johnson publicly promised, he might very well send them lots of development aid.[35]

There were at least three ways the American strategy might have been successful. All had encouraging historical precedents.

One of these was the "fade away" thesis. As the State Department's Walt Rostow put it at the time, if the Communists failed to win, then they might "finally give up in discouragement" as they had in Greece, Malaya, and the Philippines. Even if they constantly rebuilt their battered units, Westmoreland anticipated, they would do so "each time with manpower less adequately trained." So weakened, McNamara hoped, they "would choose to reduce their efforts in the South and try to salvage their resources for another day."[36]

Another possible path to success would have been through a deft combination of military effectiveness and diplomatic maneuver. Denied military victory, the Communists might have tried to cut a deal. After all, when their military efforts in Korea were stalemated, the Communists had negotiated an agreement to return to prewar boundaries. Moreover, the Vietnamese Communists in Indochina in 1954 and in Laos in 1961 had been willing to accept compromise settlements rather than continue the war. To be sure, the Indochina agreements were basically face-saving devices for Western countries to withdraw, but they did show the willingness of the Communists to accept partitions and at least temporary cease-fires rather than continue to pursue a costly war.

A third possibility was that the Soviet Union, an important North Vietnamese ally and supplier, might become discouraged. Wooed by the benefits of detente and wary of the costs and escalatory dangers of wars of national liberation, the Soviets might be able to pressure their little client into a more accommodating stance. Anticipations in the White House were that Moscow's influence in Hanoi would rise and its willingness to back the war would decline as the American threat to North Vietnam increased. As presidential aide Bill Moyers recalled, "The President—well, most of us shared this at the White House—we felt that he could reason with the Russians and they would deliver."[37]

American policymakers, then, did have some plans for success in the war. The idea was to push the North Vietnamese Communists until they broke; as Leslie Gelb and Richard Betts characterize the thinking of the time, "How could a tiny, backward Asian country *not* have a breaking point?"[38]

Expectations varied about where that breaking point might be. Some in the administration were fairly confident of early victory once American might and "can do" inventiveness were properly applied against what Johnson called "a raggedy-ass little fourth-rate country." Moyers says, "There was a confidence—it was never bragged about, it was just there—a residue perhaps of the confrontation of missiles over Cuba—that when the chips were really down, the other people would fold." An atmosphere of self-confidence—even of omnipotence—was also created by Johnson's spectacular reelection triumph of 1964.[39] Others feared a long war with no early guarantee of success. Specific predictions included General Westmoreland's timetable, which seemed to suggest a reasonable hope for the defeat and destruction of enemy forces by the end of 1967, and conclusions by top Defense Department officials of a fifty-fifty chance of success by 1967 or 1968.[40] Despite assertions that intelligence reports of the time were "invariably pessimistic," these projections were based on Central Intelligence Agency assessments that, under the right conditions, "Hanoi probably would, at least for a time, alter its basic strategy and course of action in South Vietnam." Given the uncertainties of the time, these estimates seem quite reasonable even in retrospect. Potential costs were also soberly assessed, and calculations about probable American casualties proved to be quite accurate.[41]

Thus, the United States went into the Vietnam War in 1965 only after careful reevaluations of basic policies and after remarkably sober and realistic assessments of probable outcomes, costs, and benefits. It is doubtful that American decision making upon entering World War II showed such careful, fully rounded consideration of essential values and probable costs and consequences (see p. 230).*

In their calculations, American decision makers made one crucial mistake: As Rusk observed in 1971, they "underestimated the resistance and determination

---

*Latter-day critics of the decision, like Halberstam, have argued that the "seemingly intelligent, rational men" ignored the "obvious"—that if American units were sent over, "we would be following the French" (1972, p. 810–11; also Tuchman 1984, p. 376). But the relevance of the French experience was hardly "obvious": their military history over the previous half century had been fraught with inept leadership, precipitous collapse, and mutiny. Even so, they had been able to control the area for decades against local resistance and in 1954 had been able to get the Communists in Indochina to accept partition, a reasonable half loaf, after inflicting casualties vastly lower than those delivered by the Americans a decade later. Moreover, as noted, Communist insurgencies in Southeast Asia had previously been successfully put down in Malaysia and the Philippines.

of the North Vietnamese." But experience suggests that this misestimation, however unfortunate, was quite reasonable. As it happens, the willingness of the North Vietnamese Communists and their southern allies, the Vietcong, to accept punishment in Vietnam was virtually unprecedented in the history of modern warfare. If the battle death rate as a percentage of the prewar population is calculated for each of the hundreds of countries that have participated in international and colonial wars since 1816, it is apparent that Vietnam was an extreme case. Even discounting heavily for exaggerations in the "body count," the Communist side was willing to accept battle death rates that were about twice as high as those accepted by the fanatical, often suicidal, Japanese in World War II. Furthermore, the few combatants who did take losses as high as the Vietnamese Communists were mainly those like the Germans and Soviets in World War II who were fighting to the death for their national existence—not merely for expansion, like North Vietnam.[42]

This extraordinary Communist tenacity could not have been confidently anticipated. Evidence from the French Indochina War certainly was of little help: in their major battles in the war against the Americans and South Vietnamese the Communists suffered tens of thousands of battle deaths, while in the massed battle against the French at Dien Bien Phu in 1954 they had lost about 7,900 men—and apparently had been pushed to the limits of collapse as a result.[43]

The failure of American decision makers to appreciate the fanaticism of the enemy may be regrettable, but it can hardly be judged unreasonable. In Vietnam, it seems, the United States was up against an incredibly well functioning organization—firmly disciplined, tenaciously led, and largely free from corruption or enervating self-indulgence. To a degree that was virtually unprecedented, the organization was able to enforce upon itself an almost religious devotion to duty, sacrifice, loyalty, and fatalistic patience. Although the Communists often experienced massive military setbacks and periods of stress and exhaustion, they were always able to refit themselves, rearm, and come back for more. It may well be that, as one American general put it, "they were in fact the best enemy we have faced in our history."[44]

The decisions to question, therefore, are not so much those of the Americans, but rather those of the Vietnamese Communists who continued to send thousands upon thousands of young men to the south to be ground up by the American war machine and who willingly accepted virtually unprecedented losses for a goal that was far from central to their survival as a nation and that could have been pursued in far less costly ways.

The Cold War Devitalization of Vietnam

When the American decisions of 1965 to send troops to Vietnam were taken, a consensus existed in the United States about their necessity and wisdom. In both the administration and Congress there were, as Gelb and Betts note, "ambivalent or uncertain doves" but very few "whose negative views on escalation overrode their willingness to support it." Even those who opposed American military escalation at the time, like senators William Fulbright and Wayne Morse, did not advocate withdrawal. As Fulbright put it, a withdrawal would "betray our obligation," "weaken or destroy the credibility of American guarantees," and encourage the view "that guerrilla wars supported from outside are a relatively safe and inexpensive way of expanding Communist power." Instead, the senators advocated negotiations or the use of the United Nations—methods, the administration argued (and later events were to confirm), that were of little interest to the Communists: as the North Vietnamese repeatedly pointed out, they were in the war to win, and therefore there was essentially nothing to negotiate about.[45]

Although Johnson has sometimes been accused of lying to the American people about what he was leading them into, his July speech announcing the troop commitment left no doubt that an open-ended Korea-size war was likely. Between 75,000 and 125,000 men would be sent almost immediately, he announced; furthermore, "additional forces will be needed later, and they will be sent as requested." The public responded favorably, and polls registered substantially increased support for the war.[46]

Within a year, however, support for the war both among the elite and among the public had begun to decline. Johnson saw the defections and began to feel betrayed: "When the going got hard, when the road got longer and dustier, when the casualties starting coming in—why, certain folks started looking for the cellar."[47] But while the going was certainly getting harder, the benefits of making the trip at all were also becoming less clear. The consensus on Vietnam faded not only because the *costs* of keeping South Vietnam out of Communist hands were increasing, but because the Cold War *value* of doing so was declining at the same time. Using consistent Cold War standards, Vietnam ceased being clearly vital to American interests within a year after the decisions to send troops were made. Two key developments were responsible for this change.

Sukarno had proclaimed 1965 to be "The Year of Living Dangerously," and in the fall of that year the Communists in Indonesia, apparently with his blessing and with Chinese encouragement, launched a clandestine effort to eliminate major anti-Communist leaders in the army. The maneuver failed spectacularly: there was a violent counterreaction in which hundreds of thousands of people, including the party's leaders, were killed. Within weeks the party had been destroyed, Sukarno had been reduced to a figurehead, and the nation's foreign policy had been redirected toward neutrality and the West.[48] The Indonesian threat to American interests—the southern black arrows on Johnson's map—evaporated almost overnight.

Following close upon this foreign policy catastrophe and perhaps partly stemming from it (as well as from some contemporaneous setbacks in South Asia and Africa), the Chinese embarked on a bizarre ritual of romantic self-purification known as the Great Proletarian Cultural Revolution.[49] Although still verbally belligerent toward the United States, the Chinese mostly turned their energies inward—except for those focused northward at the Soviet Union as confrontations increased along the frontier. The Chinese challenge to American foreign policy in Southeast Asia diminished: the northern arrows on Johnson's map faded considerably.

But by the time these remarkable and utterly unpredictable events in Indonesia and China had taken place, the United States had made its massive commitment of troops to Vietnam. The United States became thoroughly enmeshed in a war that soon became something of a Cold War anachronism. As McGeorge Bundy, a central figure in the decisions of 1964 and 1965 later observed, while Vietnam seemed "vital" when the big troop buildup began, "at least from the time of the anti-Communist revolution in Indonesia, later in 1965, that adjective was excessive, and so also was our effort." Someone who was quick to see the change was George Kennan. In testimony in February 1966 he termed the Indonesian events "an enormous reverse" for China and concluded that in light of what had happened there and elsewhere, the "danger of the so-called domino effect" was "considerably less than it was when the main decisions were taken that have led to our present involvement." In fact, he speculated, the United States might not choose military involvement "if the choice were ours to make all over again today."[50]

During 1966 and 1967, American policy in Vietnam was increasingly questioned and the administration was repeatedly challenged to explain why Vietnam was so important. The war could still be justified as a test case against wars of national liberation; and Cold War rhetoric, including the lessons of Munich, continued to be pronounced relevant, although with ever-decreasing resonance. A common argument was of the unsatisfying, question-begging "We are there because we are there" sort: We must fight because American prestige, honor, and credibility are at stake. As Henry Kissinger put it at the time, "What is involved now is confidence in American promises"; the "commitment of 500,000 Americans has settled the issue of the importance of Vietnam."[51] Other arguments stressed that the "loss" of Vietnam or of Indochina or of Southeast Asia would cause political chaos within the United States like the McCarthyism that sprang up after the "fall" of China to Communism in 1949 (a highly imperfect analogy since the foreign impetus to McCarthyism was not China's "fall" but rather the Korean War a year later). Also, there was the notion that we, unlike the French, are not in the habit of losing wars and would not like to blemish a perfect record.

The bloodbath argument remained relevant: American withdrawal, it asserted, would deliver into the hands of a merciless enemy the people who had trusted the United States and placed their fate in its hands. This argument, at once moral and expedient, was quite effective with some potential war opponents; and the brutality the Communists visited on tens of thousands who opposed them after the takeover in North Vietnam in 1954 gave it cogency, as did, later, the systematic massacres of thousands by the Communists when they briefly held the city of Hue during the Tet offensive of 1968.[52] As the war continued, however, the bloodbath argument gradually diminished in effectiveness: it is difficult to justify war—an activity based on the deliberate taking of lives—in order to save lives. Moreover, many came to feel that once the United States had lost tens of thousands of lives and paid tens of billions of dollars in an effort to save the South Vietnamese from this fate, it was time for the South Vietnamese to take charge of their own destiny.

By 1967 considerations like these were leading more and more people to question American policy in Vietnam. For many questioners in the administration the devitalization of Vietnam was an important consideration. McNamara was becoming increasingly disillusioned, and in 1967, the year he resigned, he observed that the dominoes were holding firm: "Witness Indonesia and the Chinese confusion," he urged. "The fact is that the trends in Asia today are running mostly for, not against, our interests." The point was brought home to McNamara's successor, Clark Clifford, when he made a goodwill tour of some of the domino countries at the end of 1967. The leaders who in 1965 had urged U.S. persistence in Vietnam were now remarkably relaxed about the war they once said was so important to them. "It was strikingly apparent to me," Clifford recalls, that these countries *"no longer* shared our degree of concern about the war. . . . Was it possible that our assessment of the danger to the stability of Southeast Asia and the Western Pacific was exaggerated? . . . Was it possible that we were continuing to be guided by judgments that might once have had validity but were now obsolete?"[53]

It was entirely possible. After the Tet offensive of 1968, in which the Communists seemed to demonstrate that the end of the war was likely to be a long way off, the Johnson administration had to reevaluate its strategy. As a result of this exercise, it essentially decided to cease the American escalation and to begin to turn the war over to the South Vietnamese.[54] The war's popularity had been declining for years—although the war never became more unpopular than the Korean War during the periods in which casualties were comparable, a fact which suggests that neither the later war's television coverage nor its active antiwar movement was especially influential in reducing its appeal.* However, the protest movement probably had some impact on the 1968 presidential election. By continually trashing the campaign of Democrat Hubert Humphrey, the protesters helped assure the narrow success of the most hawkish of all viable candidates, Richard Nixon.[55]†

Once in office, Nixon continued Johnson's policy of Vietnamization and of reducing the American casualty rate by decreasing American combat activity. He tried to keep the military pressure on, especially by bombing, and he continued to hope that the Communists could be made to cave in.[56] Reluctantly and under substantial pressure (from, among others, ex-presidential candidate Humphrey) Nixon also eventually began to withdraw American troops even as peace talks with the enemy, started in Johnson's final year, dragged on.

By the 1970s the United States still continued its association with the war in large measure because the North Vietnamese held some American prisoners. Although it may not make a great deal of sense to continue a war costing thousands of lives in order to gain the return of a few hundred prisoners, it is difficult to exaggerate the potency of the prisoner of war issue. In May 1971, 68 percent of those surveyed on a public opinion poll agreed that all U.S. troops should be brought home from Vietnam by the end of the year. However, when asked if they would favor withdrawal "if it threatened [not *cost*] the lives and

---

*Particularly through 1968, antiwar protesters generated negative ratings among the public to an all but unprecedented degree, and this probably helps explain their ineffectiveness; the war might have been less popular if no protest movement had existed (see Mueller 1973, pp. 164–65; 1984a, p. 152; Tuchman 1984, p. 327). Moreover, contrary to still-accepted lore, the war was disproportionately supported by young people and the well-educated. The continually repeated notion that television was vital in shaping attitudes on the war essentially relies on the naive and patronizing assumption that people will know how they feel about such an event only if they regularly see it pictured on their television screens.

†Some of the more creative members of the antiwar movement had been able to convince themselves that Nixon had been converted from a virulent anti-Communist to a crypto-liberal: the "new Nixon" (see Mailer 1968). For his part, Nixon let it be known during the 1968 campaign that he had a "secret plan" to end the war. Insofar as that was true, however, his "plan," inspired by what he took to be Eisenhower's success in ending the Korean War, was to threaten the North Vietnamese with nuclear annihilation, a bluff he once opined would have them "in two days begging for peace" (Karnow 1983, p. 582). Eventually he did try making some threats, but with no success (Herring 1986, pp. 224–26; Bundy 1988, pp. 538–40).

safety of United States POWs held by North Vietnam," support dropped to 11 percent. Henry Kissinger, the chief American representative at the Vietnam peace talks, was well aware of the political imperative. In reviewing American options, he concluded that unilateral withdrawal and Vietnamization would not "do the trick" because they "would not return our prisoners."[57] Apparently, the option of ending the war without the return of the prisoners was not even a hypothetical consideration.

Finally in January 1973, Nixon and Kissinger were able to cut a deal with the Communists: the United States withdrew its substantially reduced direct military participation in the war, Communist troops were allowed to remain poised for action in the south under a cease-fire arrangement, and the Americans got their prisoners back. Nixon, echoing Neville Chamberlain's unfortunate slogan of 1938, perhaps unconsciously, called the deal "peace with honor," and Kissinger received the Nobel Peace Prize for his efforts. As virtually everyone else expected, furious war eventually broke again—in 1975. The South Vietnamese lost ignominiously, an event to be discussed more fully in the next chapter.

Did Vietnam Prevent World War III?

Probably not; but let us speculate. *New Yorker* correspondent Robert Shaplen, one of the most careful and astute observers of Southeast Asia, has suggested that the spectacular Communist failure in Indonesia in 1965 was caused in part by faulty timing brought by the American involvement in Vietnam: "Had it not been for the American buildup in South Vietnam in the spring and summer of 1965, which averted a probable Vietcong victory and posed a threat of new American power in Southeast Asia, the astonishing Communist coup attempt might not have taken place so soon, and consequently might not have failed." Jay Taylor largely concurs. The Indonesian Communists apparently had a "longer-range program" envisioning a takeover by 1970 or so. But they and their Chinese allies—and possibly Sukarno as well—became anxious in 1965 to push the Indonesian revolution forward: "Mao in particular was eager for the victorious consummation of the Peking-Jakarta axis as a blow to both the United States and the Soviet Union." The American intervention in Vietnam, Taylor concludes, had a "major" effect on Indonesian events by building them up to a "crisis pitch." Had the Communists waited, says Taylor, "the final leap forward was much more likely to have succeeded."[58]

If the United States had decided in 1965 to draw back and watch South Vietnam be taken over by the Communists, and if Communist machinations in Indonesia, unhampered by hasty planning and buoyed by compatriot success in Vietnam, had succeeded, the result would have been twofold: (1) a catastrophe for American foreign policy as the Communists suddenly emerged victorious in two key areas, and (2) a supreme emboldening of confidence and self-satisfaction among Communists throughout the world. The Soviets might have concluded that the future was close at hand after all, and the Chinese would surely have seen the events as cosmic fulfillment of their oft-intoned prophecies about the visceral decadence and paper-tigerhood of the American capitalists. Instead of turning their energies inward, the Chinese might well have decided to probe aggressively outward in the area, meeting panicky resistance from U.S. leaders whose vision of Mao as a latter-day Hitler would seem confirmed. A major conflict between the United States and China could easily have ensued.

A few years after leaving office, Dean Rusk, still remembering the lessons of Munich, defended his Vietnam policy with the rhetorical question, "How much is it worth to prevent World War III?"[59] Rusk's defense, like the considerations arrayed here, is based on reasoning that is highly speculative. Moreover, even if one agrees with all the speculations, it still does not follow that a U.S.– Communist conflict in the wake of Communist successes in Vietnam and Indonesia would have escalated all the way to world war. Nevertheless, Rusk's musings should not be casually dismissed.

Could the War Have Been Won?

In Senate testimony in 1969, Westmoreland was asked if he thought the war could be won. "Absolutely," he replied. If the United States had bombed extensively after the Communist defeat in the Tet offensive of 1968, "the war would be over at this time—or would be nearly over." Other military figures point to the failed Communist offensive of 1972 and argue that the Communists would have collapsed if they had been aggressively pushed in the wake of that event.[60]

Some analysts take a longer-term view. Guenter Lewy suggests that had the war been fought differently from the beginning—using "surprise and massed strength" at "decisive points," applying careful programs of population security and Vietnamization—the outcome of the war might have been different. Gelb and Betts somewhat ironically suggest that victory might have been achieved through "some combination" of "using nuclear weapons, dispatching a million men to fight, removing all sanctuaries and bombing restrictions, running a nearly perfect pacification program, . . . and demanding and receiving . . . fundamental political reforms." Some second-guessers in the military have seen possible success in an invasion of North Vietnam, in an invasion of Laos to seal the border between North and South Vietnam, or in various kinds of enclave strategies.[61]

To be convincing, however, these strategists need evidence that the North Vietnamese "breaking point" had been, or could have been, reached. The Communists in Vietnam have been virtually unique in modern history in their willingness to tolerate casualties, and their remarkable tenacity and resiliency after major setbacks suggests that their breaking point might have been very high, possibly even near extermination levels. Therefore, their claims that they were ready to fight for ten, twenty, or fifty years should be taken seriously—even after winning their thirty-year war in Vietnam, they waged another long war in Cambodia. As Konrad Kellen puts it, "Short of . . . being physically destroyed, collapse, surrender, or disintegration was—to put it bizarrely—simply not within their capabilities."[62]

Thus, while it seems clear they could not be beaten at a cost the United States was willing to pay, it is also possible that they would not have given up no matter how far the United States and the South Vietnamese escalated the war, no matter how clever and efficient the counterinsurgency strategy. Even using nuclear weapons on North Vietnam and the infiltration trails might not have worked unless they had been dropped at near-annihilation levels; and exactly how they could have been used effectively in the internal war in the south, which is where the war ultimately had to be won, is difficult to imagine. An invasion of North Vietnam might have led to a major response by the Chinese or the Soviets, and the war against North Vietnam might have been "won" in the same sense that the invasion of North Korea in 1950 "won" the war against that country. But even without such an escalation by North Vietnam's allies, the United States might well have found itself bogged down in a lengthy, costly, agonizing guerrilla war conducted throughout Indochina—a war rather like the one the French fought, and lost, in 1954.

As noted in the discussion of the Japanese surrender in 1945 (pp. 87–89), a war's end is determined more by the losing side than by the winning one. Wars are not fought to annihilation but rather until one side decides it has had enough and breaks. In Vietnam, after a long, costly struggle, it was American will that broke. And so, although the war did not come out the way American strategists had planned, it does represent a triumph for the strategy of attrition.

China Abandons the Cold War

While the Americans and the Communists were seeking to push each other to the military limit in Vietnam, an astounding change began to take place in the diplomatic relations between the United States and the country it had chiefly gone to war to contain, China.

American policymakers are often accused of having treated the Communist world as a monolith centered in Moscow. However, from the beginning Washington has shown a fair amount of discernment and flexibility about real or potential schisms in the bloc. Yugoslavia's defection at the end of the 1940s was seized upon quite readily, and later a careful eye was kept on the developing Sino-Soviet dispute to see if it presented opportunities for American policy.[63] Although, as noted, there was no reason in the early 1960s to assume that Sino-Soviet disagreements would necessarily lead to an outright break, policymakers were sensitive to issues in the debate. Vietnam, in fact, was principally designed to contain a burgeoning Chinese threat, not a Soviet one, and to encourage Soviet misgivings about wars of national liberation in their debate with the Chinese.

Despite deepening enmity over Vietnam and other issues, a number of efforts were made to open up a separate dialogue with the Chinese as the Sino-Soviet disagreement heated up. As the State Department's Roger Hilsman observed in 1963, the United States sought for years to arrange an exchange of journalists, but China was unwilling even to discuss this modest proposal unless the United States made a major concession first: abandon its alliance with the regime on Taiwan. Similarly, the United States tried to show flexibility in 1966 by proclaiming that its policy toward China was one of "containment without isolation," but this probe brought no positive response from China, nor did an offer to have Chinese newsmen cover the elections of 1968. Under an agreement in the mid-1950s, regular meetings between representatives of the two countries were held in Warsaw; by the end of the 1960s, 134 of these encounters had been held—all of them unproductive.[64]

In the context of the 1969 Sino-Soviet border clashes, however, things began to change profoundly. The new Nixon administration had let it be known that it favored improvement of relations, a policy that did not, as Kissinger has acknowledged, "differ substantially" from that of previous administrations. But unlike its predecessors, the Nixon administration found glimmers of responsiveness from China. Further glimmers were eagerly encouraged in large part because the administration hoped that a friendlier China might be able to help with the ongoing Vietnam problem. From a tentative beginning, relations improved with impressive speed. By 1972 the Chinese had allowed the Taiwan issue to be finessed—using a State Department formula devised in the 1950s—and Nixon had made a capping visit to China.[65]

American leaders have extensively congratulated themselves for this remarkable development. It took "two years of complex, subtle, and determined signals and negotiations," recalls Nixon, during which the Americans maintained an "almost miraculous secrecy." "We were on a tightrope; we had to be careful . . . or we might drop into the abyss," Kissinger intones dramatically; but when it was all over, "in one giant step we had transformed our diplomacy."[66]* But the true transformer on the tightrope was clearly China's Premier Zhou Enlai, who was jockeying for position with Mao's heir-designate, the fanatical Lin Biao. In the fall of 1971, after various internal altercations, Lin ceased to exist—he died in a plane crash while trying to flee the country, they said—and Chinese foreign policy continued its amazing shifts.

The core of the foreign policy conflict between Zhou and Lin seems to have been over two issues. One concerned the designation of the country of greatest threat: the United States (Lin) or the Soviet Union (Zhou).[67] With the triumph of Zhou's approach, and with Mao's assent, China continued to improve relations with the United States.

The other issue concerned China's relations with the progress of international revolution. Lin was the chief spokesman for the belligerent notion that China must aid and encourage wars of national liberation since the progress of world revolution hinged on them. Zhou favored a selective approach: In countries that recognized its world role, China would stress accommodating diplomacy and would distance itself from local Communist revolutionaries.[68] Thus, under Zhou, China began to show a decreasing interest in the distant insurgencies that had been such an all-consuming passion just a few years earlier.

Under Zhou's protégé and successor, Deng Xiaoping, China continued to improve its relations with the United States as well as with the dominoes of Southeast Asia. For a while the Chinese still acknowledged a lingering sense of fraternal duty to fellow Communists in the region, but by early 1981 even this was mellowed: "Now we have only ideological and moral relations" with those parties, China's premier said, and "we sincerely wish" that countries in the area "will be united from within and enjoy stability and prosperity."[69]

The extraordinary changes in the Chinese worldview began during the domes-

---

*It has often been argued that only a conservative Republican like Nixon could have led Americans to accept this rapprochement with China. But a poll conducted during the Johnson administration in 1964 certainly suggests the public was quite flexible on this issue. Although opinion toward Communist China was highly unfavorable at the time, 60 percent of those with opinions said they would favor exchanging ambassadors if the president decided that "it was in our best interests" (Patchen 1966, p. 281; Mueller 1973, p. 74).

tic fulminations of the Cultural Revolution. A degree of internal reform was to come later; but, as with Yugoslavia twenty years earlier, the United States showed itself entirely willing to improve relations while overlooking a domestic system that by American standards was as reprehensible as ever. As Reagan adviser Richard Pipes observed in 1985, "China has turned inward and ceased being aggressive, and so we are friendly toward China, just as we are toward Yugoslavia. We may deplore their Communist regimes, but these countries are not trying to export their systems and therefore they do not represent a threat to our national security."[70]

American entry into the war in Vietnam was chiefly directed toward confronting the ideological, methodological, and geopolitical threat that China presented in Asia. In a few years this threat had unexpectedly evaporated, and China had essentially dropped out of the Cold War. American participation in the containment war in Vietnam may have helped to encourage this highly favorable development; but if so, its impact was probably peripheral and indirect.

9

Soviet Overreach and the Demise of the Cold War

FOR THE MOST PART, detente continued to prevail between the United States and the Soviet Union in the 1970s. In 1972 the two countries worked out an important arms control agreement, and in 1979 they signed another. But as the Chinese were on the way to abandoning their romantic affection for revolution and wars of national liberation, the Soviets, although cautious about direct confrontation with the United States, remained loyal to that part of the faith. And for a while, from 1975 to 1979 or so, they had reason to believe progress was again rolling in their direction.

It began in Indochina in 1975. With his usual deft instinct for the hyperbolic, Richard Nixon had declared that "peace with honor" descended upon Vietnam in 1973, but peace itself, as it happens, took a bit longer. It came to that war-torn country only in 1975 when North Vietnam launched an offensive that in fifty-five days toppled the South Vietnamese regime that the United States had been supporting with so much blood and treasure for two decades.

The United States spent the next few years in a sort of containment funk. For the most part it stood idly by while the Soviet Union, in what seems in retrospect to have been remarkably like a fit of absent mindedness, opportunistically collected an overseas empire of nine or ten unimportant countries, all of which reacted by almost instantly becoming economic and political basket cases and by turning expectantly to the Soviet Union for maternal warmth and sustenance.

Under the glum and uninspired leadership of Leonid Brezhnev, the Soviets also substantially built up their nuclear weapons inventory. When they began to put a new set of missiles in Eastern Europe, NATO noticed and reactively began a similar program. Hoping to capitalize on popular protests in Western Europe against these developments, the Soviets turned to Khrushchevian bluster for a while, and the new American president, Ronald Reagan, proved their equal in such windy matters. The result was a noisy flap in the early 1980s. Although war between the two alliances was as wildly improbable as ever, quite a few people began once again to worry about the unthinkable, and that caused them to agitate in great numbers.

When this all subsided in the mid-1980s, the Soviets found themselves saddled with a stagnant economy, a dependent and near-useless empire, an expensive and unproductive military, and a costly and enervating Vietnam-style war in neighboring Afghanistan. Overarmed, overextended, and underproductive, the Soviets could only wave at the future as it streaked by. Increasingly the future seemed to be over there in the greedy, hyperproductive, high-living democratic capitalist world whose chief exemplar was now an economically resurgent, if unarmed, Japan.

In some important respects it was the stuff of comic opera. When the Americans allowed containment to lapse somewhat, the Soviets took advantage of the opportunity and eventually came to the realization that they would have been better off contained. The Soviet Union's new leader, Mikhail Gorbachev, was not, however, amused. The Soviets began to think about giving up on just about everything Lenin preached for, Stalin murdered for, Khrushchev finagled for, and Brezhnev spent for: they began to consider abandoning their love affair with unproductive expansion, with the dream of worldwide revolution, with a huge military, and, essentially, with ideology. Logically, those steps would lead to the termination of what remained of the Cold War. The path had been blazed earlier by the Yugoslavs and the Chinese. If the Soviets followed it, the last vestigial reason for major war would vanish from the face of the earth—at least until someone invented a new one.

Collapse in Indochina

Although the Americans withdrew from Indochina in early 1973, they continued to supply their erstwhile allies, and Nixon promised them forceful action should the North Vietnamese violate the 1973 accords in a major way. By 1975, however, Congress had cut off all funds for American military activities in the area, had put severe legal restrictions on the president's authority to deploy American military forces, and had cut back on aid to South Vietnam. Meanwhile, the Soviets, despite detente and persistent American hopes, continued to supply the North Vietnamese.[1]

In launching their offensive of 1975, the North Vietnamese had expected to secure a position for a final push in 1976.[2] They failed, however, to appreciate fully the South Vietnamese government, which reacted to the attack with an incompetence that can only be called spectacular: demoralized retreat resulted when political leaders spewed out harebrained orders and military leaders abandoned their troops. Disintegration was general in Indochina: as South Vietnam was succumbing to the Communists, similar collapses were taking place in Cambodia and Laos in a relationship that generally was independent and coincidental, like falling stars, rather than sequential and causal, like falling dominoes.

Nixon had been removed from the scene a year earlier by the Watergate scandal, and his successor, Gerald Ford, was unable to muster sentiment in Washington for an American military response. Some have argued that if Nixon, unburdened by scandal, had still been in power, he would have been able to get the United States to react militarily or to credibly threaten American retaliation, which would have deterred the offensive in the first place.[3] But the Communists had launched plenty of offensives even when the Americans were there in full strength, and if the South Vietnamese had fought with some degree of intestinal fortitude and had held on to significant areas, even Ford might have been able to engineer military aid. As it was, the American reaction was largely restricted to impotent hand wringing at a distance and hasty evacuation on the scene.

American impatience with—even contempt for—the South Vietnamese had always been high.[4] With the stunning collapse in South Vietnam these prejudices and perspectives seemed to receive grand confirmation, and Americans accepted their tumultuous foreign policy debacle with remarkable equanimity. In part, this was because by 1975 the war had become substantially decoupled from American sensibilities. The settlement of 1973 had supplied a clear and dramatic end to American participation in the war; and although there were no welcoming parades for masses of returning veterans like those that had taken place after World War II, there was a sort of emotional substitute as hundreds of American prisoners of war came home from North Vietnam and were greeted as heroes. Therefore, although the events of 1975 in Vietnam are usually characterized as an "American defeat," they were separated by a full two years—a "decent interval," it has been called—from direct American military participation in the war. Thus, it was easy, and fairly reasonable, to credit the perpetually inept South Vietnamese with the loss.

Acceptance of collapse was also facilitated by an ancillary, if essentially insignificant, event. During the final battles Cambodian Communists captured an American ship, the *Mayaguez*. U.S. troops quickly recaptured it; and although it cost thirty-eight American lives to rescue the thirty-nine sailors aboard the ship, the drama and macho derring-do of the adventure made it attractive to believe that although Communists could defeat American allies in Southeast Asia, they were no match for true American might.[5]

At any rate, far from engendering a debate over "who lost Vietnam," the debacle in Indochina, amazingly enough, was actually used by the man who presided over it, Gerald Ford, as a point in his *favor* in his reelection campaign of 1976. When he came into office, he observed, "We were still deeply involved in the problems of Vietnam"; but now "we are at peace. Not a single young American is fighting or dying on any foreign soil."[6] His challenger, Jimmy Carter, seems to have concluded that it was politically disadvantageous to point out the essential absurdity of Ford's remarkable argument.

In general, in fact, foreign policy was the great nonissue of the 1976 campaign—the first since World War II in which there was no sense of international urgency, much less of crisis. In 1948 the election had occurred in the wake of various alarming developments in Europe and during the Berlin blockade; in 1952 there was the Korean War; in 1956 there were simultaneous crises in Suez and Hungary; in 1960 the choice was over who could best handle Khrushchev on issues like Cuba, Berlin, Laos, and the Congo; in 1964, 1968, and 1972, Vietnam policy was in various ways a central concern. The 1976 campaign, by contrast, was fully dominated by domestic—particularly economic—considerations. Asked what was the most important problem facing the country in October 1976, less than 5 percent mentioned a foreign policy issue (up from 3 percent in 1975 and 2 percent in 1974).[7]

Indochina became a particular recipient of this virtuosic inattention. At the time of the collapse, the *New York Times* hopefully headlined an article, "Indochina Without Americans / For Most, A Better Life," and Americans began to forget about events there with a considerable sense of relief. Few were even interested in finding out if the bloodbath theorists were going to be correct. As it happened, they were. After taking control of South Vietnam, the Communists executed at least 65,000 people and systematically destroyed the economy. For the first time in Vietnam's troubled history, masses of people sought to flee, and tens, or possibly hundreds, of thousands died in the process. In neighboring Cambodia control fell to a shadowy group of Communist theorists whose principles apparently required them to cause some 2 million of Cambodia's 8 million people to die by execution, starvation, or disease—in proportion, probably the most savage genocide in history.[8]

By and large, Americans chose to remain blissfully aloof from all this. From the collapse in Cambodia in April 1975 until the end of 1977 the three evening news telecasts devoted a total of twenty-nine minutes to the cataclysm taking place there. In July 1975 the *New York Times* ringingly editorialized that the silence about the genocide in Cambodia "must be broken" and then ignored the issue in its editorial column for over three years.[9]

Some of the inattention may have stemmed from a deep desire in America *not* to know what was going on in Southeast Asia, because if the horrors there were fully appreciated, a logical proposal might have been to send American troops back to try to halt the holocaust. (When just such a proposal was made in 1978 by former peace candidate George McGovern, NBC television gave the story twenty seconds of coverage.) In the aftermath of collapse in Indochina, there was a strong feeling of exhaustion with that sort of war: "No more Vietnams," as the slogan went. Much of this approach, actually, had been set in motion quite a bit earlier—in the Nixon Doctrine of 1969, which essentially put a no-more-Vietnams lid on the Truman Doctrine. The president warned potential dominoes that although the United States would provide them with economic and military assistance against insurgencies, they should not count on direct American participation in their wars.[10]

The situation in Asia was therefore left for Asians to correct—or make worse. In 1979, after a number of border clashes, the Vietnamese became engaged in yet another war by invading Cambodia and toppling the even more brutal Communist government there. With Soviet aid, they continued their occupation despite lingering guerrilla opposition—"Vietnam's Vietnam," some called it— and despite a punitive attack across their northern border by the Chinese, who were angered at what they took to be Vietnamese imperialism in Cambodia.

By 1980, then, the Soviet Union found itself supporting economically feeble dependencies in Vietnam and Laos as well as yet another war perpetrated by scrappy Vietnam—this, one of occupation in Cambodia. All this increased Soviet frictions with China and encouraged the Chinese to seek ever-closer ties with the Americans and the capitalist world—hardly the legacy of an Indochina collapse that the containment theorists in Washington had envisioned a mere fifteen years earlier.

The Rise of the Soviet Overseas Empire

Between 1975 and 1979, the Soviet Union doubled and redoubled its Southeast Asian gains in Africa, the Middle East, Central Asia, and Latin America. But with gains like these, many Soviets were soon led to ask, who needs losses?

For twenty years the only accretions to the Soviet camp had been Cuba and portions of a divided Laos. Beginning with the Indochina additions of 1975, however, a set of tempting opportunities arose for the Soviets in various corners of the third world, and they reacted like assertive, but cautious, opportunists: the "correlation of forces," they came happily to believe, had magically and decisively shifted in their direction.[11]

In the wake of Communist successes in Southeast Asia in the spring of 1975, opportunity first presented itself in Angola. The Portuguese were in the process of decolonizing, and three groups were battling for control: one mainly backed by Cuba, the Soviets, and Portuguese radicals; one mainly backed by China and South Africa; and one mainly backed by China, the United States, and neighboring Zaire. In late 1975 and early 1976, Cuba and the Soviets greatly increased their aid, including (apparently at the avid suggestion of Cuba) the introduction of thousands of Cuban troops, which were soon doing most of the fighting. At the same time, China, uncomfortable at being on the same side as South Africa, withdrew its support. Next, the U.S. Congress, wallowing in a no-more-Vietnams syndrome and ignoring the fervent pleas of President Ford and Secretary of State Kissinger, voted to cut off aid, and the South Africans then also disengaged. As a result, the Soviet-Cuban faction won and took control of the country.[12]

After that triumph, it was necessary for Cuban troops and Soviet advisers to stay on to deal with the occasional coup attempt; to continue fighting a counterguerrilla war against persistent rebels; and to protect the greedy capitalists of the Chevron Corporation, whose royalty payments for sales of Angolan offshore oil became, along with Soviet aid, the country's chief prop against total economic collapse. The Cubans and Soviets also used Angola as a base for supporting various other liberation movements in southern Africa, especially ones aimed at Zaire and at South Africa–controlled Namibia.[13]

Meanwhile, something similar was happening in another former Portuguese colony in Africa, Mozambique. Without the benefit of much international attention (or of any Cuban troops), a Marxist group came to control there, and in 1977 it signed a friendship pact with the Soviet Union and cheerfully accepted its aid and advice. Like Angola, it soon became an economic shambles, in large part because of a continuing civil war against rebels assisted by South Africa.

Through a series of coups and reshufflings, the government of Ethiopia was also moving in a radical direction. A coup in February 1977 brought in some Marxists whom the Soviets and Cubans found especially to their liking, and they supported the new government's efforts to subdue a secessionist rebellion in the north and to fight a border dispute with neighboring Somalia. With that, Somalia, formerly quite friendly to the Soviet Union and Cuba, broke relations; and the Soviets found themselves gamely seeking to prop up Ethiopia as it descended into a period of massive famine brought about by drought, the continuing wars, and the regime's spectacular, ideology-inspired mismanagement of its economy.[14]

Opportunity also presented itself nearby in South Yemen, where a radical pro-Soviet faction seized control in 1978 and brought the country into the Soviet camp. There has been intermittent chaos since—a brief border war with North Yemen in 1979, a coup in 1980, and a coup plus something of a civil war in 1985. The Soviets continued to play the role of beleaguered protector and spiritual godfather.

In 1978, Afghanistan also moved into the Soviet embrace. A military coup brought in a Marxist government, and the Brezhnev regime delightedly welcomed it with aid and 7,000 advisers. However, an anti-Communist rebellion soon developed when the new government vigorously instituted political, economic, and antireligious reforms. The rebellion grew stronger as the Communist leaders fought among themselves, and the Soviets could soon visualize a rebel victory that would set up an intensely hostile regime in this large, neighboring state. Accordingly, they invaded Afghanistan in December 1979, murdered the ruling Communist leader, placed a right-thinker of their own choosing in charge, and took over the war themselves.

They went in with a large contingent of troops, apparently planning to nip the rebellion in the bud, thus avoiding a long, enervating war like the Americans had suffered in Vietnam. Instead, they soon found themselves bogged down in exactly that sort of war, because, as usual, the length of the war was determined not by the enemy's resources but by its willingness to persist. In this case the Soviets were up against several groups that regarded it as their holy duty to fight the foreign intervention even if the war took decades. The rebels obtained sanctuary in neighboring Pakistan, and they were granted various forms of aid, including increasingly sophisticated weapons, from China, the United States, and elsewhere. Their Afghan adventure developed sizable political costs for the Soviets as well. It severely undercut the credibility and respect they had sought for decades to develop in the third world, particularly in Moslem areas, and the United States under the Carter administration reacted as if it had been traitorously jilted by a false-hearted lover. The unprecedented invasion of a third world state by the Soviets caused Carter to announce that his "opinion of what the Soviets' ultimate goals are" had undergone a "dramatic change."[15]

Cold War patterns can be neatly traced in some public opinion data. In the 1950s American evaluations of the Soviets had been overwhelmingly unfavorable (see figure 9.1), but by the mid-1960s, as Cold War tensions relaxed, it became markedly less unfavorable. Despite Soviet support for the Communist side in Vietnam, American opinion mellowed during the war, reacting favorably to such pleasant ventures as the Nixon visit to Moscow and the arms control agreement of 1972. In the wake of the Soviet-Cuban adventure in Angola in late 1975, the public became sharply more unfavorable, but progress toward a new strategic arms treaty, signed in June 1979, brought with it renewed mellowing. Then the Afghan intervention at the end of 1979 sent the Soviets' unfavorable rating soaring once again.

The new treaty had developed ratification troubles in the U.S. Senate, in part because the Soviets seemed so anxious to have it approved. Carter argued that

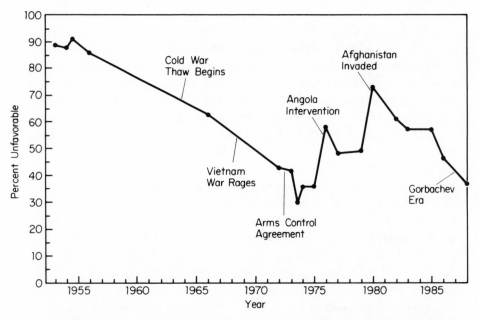

FIGURE 9.1   Attitude Toward the Soviet Union. Responses to the question: "You will notice the boxes on this card go from the highest position of 'plus 5' for a country which you *like* very much, to a position of 'minus 5' for a country you *dislike* very much. How far up the scale or how far down the scale would you rate the following countries?" ("No opinion" excluded from percentage base. "Unfavorable": ratings of −3, −4, −5.)

SOURCE: Richard G. Niemi, John Mueller, and Tom W. Smith, *Trends in Public Opinion: A Compendium* (Greenwood, CT: Greenwood, 1990).

the treaty was not a seal of approval for the Soviet system but a hard-nosed agreement that was in everybody's best interests. When the Soviets invaded Afghanistan, however, he acted as if the treaty was a certificate of good behavior after all and had it shelved.[16] He also imposed economic sanctions and, together with fifty-four other nations, withdrew his country's team from the summer Olympics held in Moscow in 1980.

At the same time, the administration and the American press had been launched into a state of splendid hysteria because a fanatical new regime in Iran had taken a few dozen American officials hostage. From this the Americans had characteristically managed to conclude with exquisitely masochistic logic that the whole country was bound into some sort of thralldom: "America held hostage," as the television sloganeers dramatically put it. Over the course of the hostage episode—which, in the exacting count of the time, lasted 444 days—Carter repeatedly wrung his hands in public and the press set about trying to interview and reinterview every friend, relative, acquaintance, and grade-school teacher of each hostage.[17] Along with an inflation substantially caused by major petroleum price increases engineered in the 1970s by a cartel of oil producers, the issue preoccupied Carter's unsuccessful reelection campaign of 1980.

Alarmed that the Soviet probe into Afghanistan might merely be a prologue to further adventures in the oil-rich Persian Gulf area, the president issued the Carter Doctrine of January 23, 1980, in which he sternly threatened to use "any means necessary" to defeat a Soviet military move in the area. His replacement, Ronald Reagan, basically reiterated the threat the next year.[18]

With these proclamations, the United States let it be known with some sense of firmness that it didn't like the way the Soviet overseas empire was expanding. In the early 1960s, it had worked assiduously to prevent a Soviet "foothold" in Africa in the Congo troubles of those days; but in the late 1970s, in the semi-isolationist post-Vietnam era of the Nixon Doctrine, it had done little to stop the Soviets from making major imprints in Angola, Mozambique, Ethiopia, South Yemen, and Afghanistan.* Now it groped for a method of dealing with the expansion.

There was another area of growing concern: Latin America. In 1979, in the tiny Caribbean island state of Grenada, a handful of Marxists, reportedly armed with "twenty-five guns, a small truck, and two cars, one of which was rented," seized power—or whatever it is one seizes in a place that small. Cuba and the Soviets quickly moved to aid and advise the congenial new regime.[19]

Meanwhile, a more important change was taking place in a somewhat larger

*As Bruce Porter has put it, "What the USSR achieved in the third world between 1973 and 1980 would have been totally unacceptable to the United States only a few years earlier; two decades earlier it might have led to war" (1984, p. 242).

Latin American country. In January 1978 a prominent Nicaraguan newspaper editor who opposed the long-running dictatorship of Anastasio Somoza was assassinated. Although Somoza probably had nothing to do with the murder, the event triggered a widespread uprising against him.[20] Various rebel factions received aid and encouragement from Costa Rica, Panama, Venezuela, and Cuba. The United States did not aid the rebels, but it put considerable pressure on Somoza to step down; and, as it had in China in the late 1940s, in Indochina in 1954, in Cuba in 1958, in Laos in 1961, and in Indochina again in 1975, it critically reduced its aid to the incumbent regime. After a war in which perhaps 10,000 died, at least 90 percent of them civilians, a new group took over in mid-1979. Revolutionary Marxists were prominent in this group, but the Carter administration decided to support the regime in hopes of influencing it in a favorable direction. Although the United States was its major aid donor for its first two years of existence, the new regime swiftly moved in a Castroesque direction, confiscating land and property, courting and being courted by the Cubans and Soviets, propagandizing against capitalism and the chief hand that was feeding it, scaring away foreign and local capital, performing its "internationalist" duty by aiding like-minded revolutionaries in El Salvador, and eventually closing down the anti-Somoza newspaper, the murder of whose editor had triggered the rebellion in the first place.

Fed up, the new Reagan administration in 1981 cut off aid, instituted economic pressure, and soon started aiding armed rebels seeking to overthrow the new regime. As American pressures took effect and as the counterrevolutionary war gained steam, the Nicaraguan regime was forced back on its own meager, mostly incantatory, resources. It also looked expectantly to the Soviet Union for help.

Rollback Wars and the Rising Costs of Empire

By this time, however, some Soviets were beginning to tally up what all this revolutionary progress was doing for—or to—number one. Ideologically, some saw it all as quite a lark: "The feat accomplished in Nicaragua," enthused a Soviet spokesman in 1979, "reflected the intensification of revolutionary processes on the Latin American continent and the steadfast striving of its peoples for genuine independence." The Nicaraguan events, he concluded, "doubtless will be an inspirational stimulus in the struggle . . . against imperialism and its henchmen."[21]

But progress could have its downside as well. Not only did it alarm the West in ways that were sometimes costly and unpleasant, but the economic bill to the Soviet Union for maintaining its growing collection of dependencies around the world was rising dramatically. The expenses took the shape of implicit trade subsidies, export credits, military and economic aid, incremental costs of Soviet military operations (mainly in Afghanistan), and associated maintenance costs. Not including any special expenses for maintaining its military presence in East Europe, the costs of the Soviet Union's old and new empire rose between 1971 and 1980 from around 1 percent of the Soviet gross national product to nearly 3 percent when measured in dollars, and from under 2 percent to about 7 percent when measured in rubles. (By contrast, insofar as the United States can be said to have a comparable empire, the costs are less than .5 percent of its GNP.)[22]

By the early 1980s a debate had broken out in the Soviet Union over the wisdom of the imperial impetus. One school of thought remained loyal to cherished ideology. Another found third world nations to be independent and often ungrateful, and advocated a policy based on pragmatism rather than on ideology. Yet another contended that Soviet ventures in the third world were simply not useful and tended to threaten international peace.[23]

Moreover, once the Soviet Union had collected a shaky dependency, there was often the new problem of what in containment terms might be called the rollback war. When the United States declined to do much of anything about the forceful Soviet reoccupation of Hungary in 1956, it tacitly acknowledged that it would not use force to alter the status quo in the Soviet empire in Central and Eastern Europe—a proposition made explicit in the Helsinki Accords of 1975. With the fiasco of the Bay of Pigs and the semiagreement after the crisis of 1962, the United States also essentially accepted the status quo in Cuba. But after 1975 the United States discovered an interesting new opportunity, because most of the states the Soviet Union had newly gathered into its embrace were opposed by armed domestic insurgencies, most notably Cambodia (under Vietnamese control), Angola, Mozambique, Ethiopia, Afghanistan, and Nicaragua. The tables were thus turned, and the United States now found itself with a set of indigenous anti-Communist "wars of national liberation" of its own which it could aid and support as it struck its fancy, substantially increasing Soviet imperial costs.

Furthermore, the process brought up the prospect that one or another of these new chicks could fall out of the nest, thereby causing a weakening of a link in the "worldwide socialist system," which the Soviets had proclaimed to be unacceptable in the Brezhnev Doctrine of 1968 when they sought to justify their forceful reassertion of control over wavering Czechoslovakia. To be sure, the Soviets had suffered setbacks before in the third world. Several countries that had been moving in a most pleasantly progressive course had engaged in backsliding—among the more important were Algeria, Sudan, Egypt, Somalia, Ghana, and Indonesia. But these countries had never been as thoroughly dominated by pro-Soviet Marxists as most of the new dependencies of the late 1970s. Although the Soviets consider only Cuba and the Indochina states to be true members of their "socialist community," they have a strong ideological identification with most of their other acquisitions, the "revolutionary democracies," as they call them.[24]

By the mid-1980s Reagan had advanced his own doctrine. He did not propose throwing the Soviets out of Eastern Europe and Cuba, but he did thoroughly reject the proposition that there was anything irreversible about Communist progress. He actively sought to support anti-Communist insurgencies around the world, particularly those in Nicaragua (controversially) and in Afghanistan (uncontroversially); and in 1983, after a coup had brought a new crew of Marxists to power in Grenada, American troops invaded the island and installed a non-Communist government there.[25] In his triumphal reelection campaign of 1984, Reagan liked to recall that "country after country fell under the Soviet yoke" in the "four years before we took office" but that "not one inch of soil has fallen to the Communists" under his administration; in fact, one (admittedly small) country had been induced to topple in the opposite direction.[26]

At the same time, however, the Reagan administration retained the Nixon Doctrine's skittishness about repeating the Vietnam experience. In 1984, a year after Grenada, Secretary of Defense Casper Weinberger tried to make this clear by proclaiming "six major tests" that should be passed before U.S. combat troops are sent abroad: (1) The engagement should be "deemed vital" to the national interest; (2) it should be done "wholeheartedly and with the clear intention of winning"; (3) there should be "clearly defined political and military objectives" and a precise knowledge of how they can be accomplished; (4) the relationship between objectives and forces must be "continually reassessed"; (5) Congress and public opinion must support the action; and (6) combat should be a last resort.[27]

Except for the impossible demand that it be known precisely how the objective is going to be accomplished, the 1965 Vietnam decisions would, with only minor quibbles, pass all of Weinberger's tests, whereas the Grenada caper would fail most of them. However, the subtext of Weinberger's remarks—that the United States plans only to get into wars it thinks it can win cheaply—came through loud and clear. William Safire of the *New York Times* labelled it the "doctrine of only-fun-wars."*

*Or: "If we can't win in a week by pulverizing the place, it's not worth jeopardizing our men's lives or all the expensive equipment" (1984). It should not be assumed, however, that the Grenada

The fulmination and bravado coming out of Washington in the 1980s were mainly opportunistic exploitations of an exquisite irony that had developed in the late 1970s. Following the Vietnam collapse, the United States in effect had allowed containment to lapse in the third world, and partly because of that the Soviets felt free to gobble up several targets of opportunity, thereby confirming in part the assumption of containment theory that the USSR possessed a natural propensity to expand.[28] But containment theory also assumed alarmingly that successful expansion would serve to whet an aggressor's desire for more territory. Instead, Soviet successes tended not only to satiate its appetite for expansion, but, given the peculiar properties of the morsels it happened to consume, the process served to give the expanders a troubling case of indigestion.

Revolution, Subversion, and Bluster in the Capitalist World

It could be argued that from the Soviet perspective something like progress took place at the end of the 1970s in the third world. In the first world, however, things were not so good. The prospects in the West for a classic proletarian revolution (à la Marx) or for a Communist-led revolt of the masses (à la Lenin) or for a manipulative Communist takeover (à la Czechoslovakia) were pretty dismal and getting worse.

Confronted with diminishing electoral support caused in part by a decline in the size of the working-class population, the Communist parties in the West had two choices. One was to cling comfortably to familiar ideology and to Moscow as in days of yore. Where this was the pattern, as in France, the party gradually began to seem more like an outdated religious sect than a viable political organization. Moreover, association with the Soviet Union could become a substantial

---

adventure was a sure thing. Safire characterizes the operation as "the quick crushing of a lightly armed gang of thugs by a huge task force," but it was by no means clear that the American costs would necessarily be low. The Soviets and Cubans had armed the "thugs" with enough firepower to equip a 10,000-man army. Moreover, there were over 700 Cubans on the island, some 150 to 200 of them seasoned soldiers (Valenta 1984, pp. 14, 22), who were ordered by Castro not to surrender to American forces (Gonzalez and Ronfeldt 1986, p. 6). Had they launched a persistent guerrilla defense and generated a certain amount of popular support, they could have inflicted substantial casualties on the clumsy invaders, who, far from having "precise" plans for carrying out their objectives, didn't even have adequate maps of the island.

liability as post-Helsinki civil rights concerns (particularly over Soviet strictures on Jewish emigration) became prominent, as dissident propaganda about crimes against the Soviet people (especially that promulgated by the exiled Aleksandr Solzhenitsyn) gained a respectful hearing, and as the clumsy Afghan venture stirred outrage and contempt.[29] The Moscow-oriented Communist party in the United States had never been large, but in the first decade of the Cold War it had inspired a great deal of comment and concern because of its perceived links to the Soviet enemy and because of its espousal of a threateningly subversive ideology. Concern continued into the 1960s, but by the 1970s American Communism had become one of the great nonissues of American politics (see figure 9.2).[30]

To avoid the Moscow albatross, a Communist party in the West could pursue a second approach, that of "Eurocommunism," in which it pledged to work within the parliamentary system, to democratize its internal processes, and to distance itself from the Soviets. Even the French Communists tried that for a while, but they soon regressed. The Italian Communists, however, stuck with it and as a result maintained their vote percentage—but at the cost, essentially, of ceasing to be a Communist party. In Italy, in fact, they started calling it "Euroleft."[31]

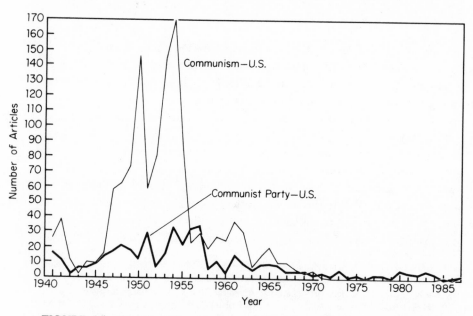

FIGURE 9.2 Concern About Domestic Communism. Number of articles on U.S. Communism and the U.S. Communist party cited in *Reader's Guide to Periodical Literature,* by year.

Portugal and Spain.

Although Communism, once a vibrant, popular, and threatening ideology, was waning—sometimes to the point of extinguishment—in the major Western countries, it sprouted for a while as a potentially potent force in two of the poorer countries in Europe. In the mid-1970s, dictatorships in Portugal and Spain were dismembered, and in both places radicals and Moscow-oriented Communists came into positions of influence and authority.

The situation in Portugal, a NATO member, was of greatest concern to Western leaders. In the year after radicals seized control in a coup, Communist party membership increased from 4,000 to 100,000, and the Soviets pumped some $10 million per month into the local party coffers.[32] NATO leaders began to worry about the country's role in the alliance. Suppose Communists came to dominate the government, President Ford mused. "How could the West share military secrets with them? What would happen if the Soviets won access to Portuguese airfields or naval bases? Would we have to strip Portugal of its NATO membership?" It is an indication of how much the Cold War had changed that the possibility of having a Communist government in an anti-Communist military alliance could even be seriously contemplated: when the alliance was founded, it was assumed, of course, that American obligations would cease automatically if a signatory government became Communist. Fortunately for Ford, he never had to work out his remarkable puzzle, because the Portuguese held open elections in 1975—the first in forty-nine years—and overwhelmingly elected non-Communists to office.[33]

Democracy also won out in Spain. There the resurgent, newly legalized Communists tried various strategies including Eurocommunism, but they soon succumbed to factional discord and by 1982 were garnering less than 4 percent of the vote.[34]

In a remarkably short period of time, then, both Portugal and Spain were able to move from entrenched, antiquated dictatorships to flexible, modernizing democracies despite the existence of strong antidemocratic forces on both ends of the political spectrum. Equally remarkable, these historic changes were made almost entirely without violence. In Portugal's revolutionary year from 1974 to 1975 less than a dozen civilians were killed in political violence. And, although there has been violent secessionist activity in some areas of Spain both before and after the rise of democracy there, the political transformation itself was made peacefully. Even forty years later, Spaniards still remembered the horrors of civil war: as Spain's prime minister observed, they had "suffered too much historically to forget the constant fighting that was caused by the family demons among us."[35]

Bluster Makes a Comeback: The Debate over Missiles in Europe.

In one of the more remarkable developments in recent history, thermonuclear war became all the rage again for a few years in the early 1980s. The unthinkable, all but banished from public discourse after 1963 (see pp. 160–61), exploded back into popular consciousness; and, as before, people didn't like what they found themselves thinking about. Accordingly, they launched protests, signed petitions, and organized marches. Between 1972 and 1978 the number of items on nuclear and disarmament issues in the *Reader's Guide to Periodical Literature* had averaged 71 per year; in 1981 it jumped to 318, and in 1983 it hit 665.[36]

Some of this consciousness raising, one might think, could be attributed to the vast increases in strategic nuclear arsenals that occurred after the test ban treaty of 1963. Both sides built up their intercontinental ballistic missile forces until each had more than 1,000, and both also vastly increased their stock of submarine missiles.[37] More menacingly, major improvements in missile accuracy were being made, and it had become technologically feasible to put more than one warhead on a single missile; together, these developments raised the ominous possibility that one side, or both, could achieve a "first-strike capability," at least against the other's land-based missiles. If it takes, say, two bombs to destroy a missile, a target country is reasonably safe when all missiles carry only one warhead, because an attacker could count on destroying only half of a defender's retaliatory capability with a first strike. But if each missile has three warheads, an aggressor would need to use only two-thirds of its missile warheads to destroy the other side's entire force. Scary.

But these developments don't really explain the rise of nuclear consciousness of the early 1980s. The new, vastly expanded arsenals had been in place for a decade at least, and the peculiar dilemma posed by the existence of accurate multiple-warhead missiles was neither new nor well appreciated by the protesters. Rather it was, as usual, rhetoric and bluster that caused concerns about thermonuclear war to escalate, and it was a relatively minor weapons development—the proposed implantation of a few hundred shorter-range missiles in Europe—that triggered much of the rhetoric. Political opportunism, both in the West and East, played its part, too.

As part of its expensive nuclear arms buildup in the 1970s, Brezhnev's Soviet Union began adding sophisticated new intermediate-range (3,000 miles) triple-warhead missiles to its arsenal in Europe. NATO became alarmed because it had nothing comparable and in 1979 scheduled the deployment of similar counter-vailing weapons unless the Soviets could be prevailed upon to limit their missiles.[38]

While talks on the issue ambled on unproductively, Ronald Reagan was elected president, and almost instantly he began to strike a lot of people as a fire-breathing warmonger. He announced that he would substantially build up U.S. military forces (expanding Carter's policy) and would seek to develop a strategy so that the United States might manage to come out ahead, or "prevail," in a nuclear war (basically continuing a policy developed by Kennedy, elaborated by Nixon, and accepted by Carter). Reagan also explained that he "could see where you could have an exchange of tactical weapons [in, for example, Europe] . . . without it bringing either one of the major powers to pushing the button"—one of those small, self-evident truths, largely enshrined in NATO doctrine, that no previous president had so foolishly and so baldly expressed in public before, having preferred the politic, but patently absurd, suggestion that any sizable Soviet attack would necessarily escalate to strategic nuclear war. At about the same time, Reagan's secretary of state, Alexander Haig, came up with the well-seasoned observation that in response to a conventional attack by the Soviets in Europe the United States might seek "to maintain violence at the lowest possible level" by lobbing a nuclear bomb or two in their direction "for demonstrative purposes."[39]

A lot of Europeans were appalled, and soon they had convinced themselves that Reagan was going to drag them into a war and then watch calmly from the sidelines as the war was fought out to the last radiated European: "Euroshima," one creative pamphleteer called it. By the end of Reagan's first year in office, mass demonstrations aimed at preventing the installation of the new NATO missiles were regularly being staged in several European countries. The protests were particularly extensive in Germany, Britain, and the Netherlands, where they were led by Socialist parties that saw the movement as a useful device to advance their cause against conservative parties. Where the Socialists remained quiet, as in France and Italy, the movement never took flight.[40]

The antinuclear frenzy also caught on in the United States. As in Europe, some of this might have related to partisan politics, because Reagan's inexperience in foreign and defense policy, embellished by an apparent hostility to arms control measures, seemed to be his area of vulnerability.* His domestic policy was substantially unattackable because his accession to the presidency had coincided

---

*In the vanguard of the movement was the intellectual (nonunion) left, a group that seems to be able to deal with only one issue at a time. Its preoccupations have shifted about every three to five years: anti-McCarthyism in the late 1950s; ban-the-bomb, arms control, and fallout-shelter issues in the early 1960s; civil rights for blacks in the mid-1960s; Vietnam in the late 1960s; the environment in the early 1970s; feminism in the late 1970s; nuclear and Freeze issues in the early 1980s; Central American, African famine, and South African issues thereafter. (For further discussion, see Mueller 1973, pp. 157–59.) However, the antinuclear movement of the early 1980s seems to have had a broader political base than its precursor of the early 1960s.

with a remarkable plunge in the American inflation rate and a not-unrelated surge in the economy in general. These were due in part to a drop in international oil prices previously artificially inflated by the petroleum cartel.

At any rate, wide nuclear alarm broke out with Jonathan Schell's book and *New Yorker* essay, both entitled "The Fate of the Earth" as its focal points. Fortuitously published in 1982, the article passionately, if repetitively, argued the not entirely novel proposition that nuclear war would be terrible.* By early 1983 even the Catholic bishops had gotten into the act with an airy pastoral letter declaring that it may be okay to threaten mass destruction but only if you didn't plan to do it. At Brown University protesters demanded that the student health service stock suicide pills for mass use in the event of nuclear attack. On a more positive note, American protesters coalesced around a proposal that the United States and USSR should freeze their nuclear weapons programs at present levels, and by early 1983 they had gotten the House of Representatives to vote 278 to 149 in favor of a Freeze resolution.[41]

Meanwhile, the Soviets reasoned that the antimissile protest was not exactly to their disadvantage. NATO was offering to refrain from putting in its new missiles if the Soviets would take theirs out; but if the protesters had their way, NATO's missiles could never go in anyway, and thus the Soviets would get something for nothing. Like a bunch of greedy capitalists with a bargain in sight, the Soviets sought to help the protest along. They encouraged European Communist parties to support the protests, and they also trotted out a version of the Khrushchevian technique of thermonuclear bluster that had been mostly dormant for two decades. They launched a noisy "peace offensive" with an accelerating barrage of dire pronouncements about how, if threatened, they would launch their enormous thermonuclear destructive forces at the first warning, and about how the unfortunate first targets of these hasty launches would necessarily be the proposed missiles to be implanted in Western Europe.[42]

Poll data suggest that Europeans were rather unsettled by Reagan's loose talk about nuclear war.[43] But the protest and bluster neither changed the 1979 NATO decision nor Reagan's determination to implement it.[44] Things came to something of a head in March 1983 when the West Germans voted to give parliamentary control to the party that supported deployment. When the parliament voted later in the year to accept the new missiles, the Soviets stormed out of negotiations on the issue.

Reagan, of course, was perfectly capable of escalating his rhetoric as well; and in 1983, at a meeting (appropriately enough) of the National Association of Evangelicals, he called the Soviets "the focus of evil in the modern world" and

---

*Schell was not alone. The *Cumulative Book Index* indicates that whereas fewer than 16 books on nuclear issues were published in the four-year period from 1977 to 1980, there were 25 in 1981, 54 in 1982, and 80 in 1983 (McGlen 1986).

an "evil empire" and implied similarities between the Soviet regime and that of Adolf Hitler.[45] It was hardly a fair comparison, because Hitler had started a major war where the Soviets had not, and because Hitler might well have murdered even more people than Stalin if he had managed to stay in office as long. The evangelicals in the Soviet Union had been calling the United States the center of evil, or worse, with substantial regularity for a good sixty-six years, and they had been comparing it to Nazi Germany off and on for fifty; but Reagan's remarks were generally taken to mark a new low in invective in an international era that had once been hopefully labelled "detente."

At about the same time, Reagan devised and promptly fell in love with a new gimmick that scared the Soviets even more than his unpleasant words. At his suggestion, various defense researchers had been looking hard at the possibilities for building an effective defense against a missile attack. Relying heavily on the potential for zapping incoming missiles with laser beams, it seemed possible to build a defense that would work. Rather than merely freezing nuclear weapons at present levels, as his noisy opponents were urging, Reagan delightedly proposed to build a defense that would make the weapons (and perhaps his opponents as well) "impotent and obsolete."[46]

The Soviets were deeply alarmed at this idea (which is one reason Congress went along with Reagan's proposal to work on it), in part because they saw its offensive potential—either to destroy Soviet missiles on the ground or to neutralize a Soviet retaliatory strike. And it also promised a new, extremely expensive arms race in an area of highly sophisticated technology.

The Soviets had always been in awe of Western technological prowess—as Khrushchev puts it in his memoirs, "these 'rotten' capitalists keep coming up with things that make our jaws drop in surprise."[47] By the mid-1980s they were becoming distinctly aware that they were in deep trouble in many areas, but particularly in sophisticated technology. The economic, military, and ideological excesses of the Brezhnev era were catching up with them.

The Multiple Dilemmas of the Soviet Union in the Late 1980s

As it happens, Brezhnev was not there to notice. After a long series of illnesses that were debilitating, but that did not cause him to resign from office (he outlived himself, as some have put it), Brezhnev died in November 1982. He was succeeded in the top office by the sixty-eight-year-old Yuri Andropov, who star-tlingly shattered tradition by complaining pointedly and in public about danger-ous problems in the Soviet system. He even went so far as to suggest that some of these could not credibly be blamed on the treacheries of the surrounding capitalist world.[48] When Andropov died, only fifteen months after taking office, he was replaced by the aged old-liner, Konstantin Chernenko, who died a year later.

Within five hours of Chernenko's death in March 1985 the reins of the Soviet Union were given over to a healthy fifty-four-year-old, Mikhail Gorbachev, who was an Andropov protégé. He found plenty to be concerned about. To begin with, the manifest and manifold economic, political, and social problems of the domestic system loomed large. Among those were slackening economic growth rates, persistent agricultural inadequacies, industrial stagnation, energy shortages, severe technological deficiencies, declining life expectancy, rising infant mortality rates, rampant alcoholism, and potential problems from bottled-up ethnic nation-alism and from demographic shifts favoring the religious, technologically back-ward, non-Slavic sections of the country.[49]

Moreover, these distressing phenomena were presided over, and in many important respects caused by, an entrenched elite of bureaucrats and party hacks who compensated for any administrative and intellectual failings with a truly virtuosic flair for bureaucratic infighting that allowed them to hang on to their privileges. Furthermore, many of the problems originated in the very ideology of the system itself. The ideology seems to require a stifling centralism that discour-ages imagination and innovation, and it fairly wallows in a suspicious secretiveness permeated by a mortal dread of the potentially subversive effects of such modern-izing necessities and pleasures as personal computers, videotape recorders, photo-copy machines, and telephone books. In many important respects, then, the system was, not to put too fine a point on it, rotten to the core. Or, as one observer has suggested a bit more mildly, "The Soviet Union needs its inefficiencies to remain Soviet."[50]

Adding to all this was the overbearing burden of defense expenditures, which took up at least twice the percentage of gross national product as for the United States, and which tended to exacerbate the shortage of skilled manpower by pulling a large share of the most sophisticated people out of the general economy. The economic prognosis was also clouded by two unpleasant developments in world trade: declining prices for the Soviet Union's largest export, oil, and increased competition in the third world for its second largest, arms.[51]

By the mid-1980s, the Soviet Union served as a model only for the myopic. The notion that it could ever have been considered the "wave of the future" seemed so incomprehensible that commentators had to go out of their way to explain that it had ever generated appeal. As Seweryn Bialer wrote in 1986, "The initial attraction of the Marxist-Leninist credo and the enthusiasm for the Soviet model of development is perhaps difficult to understand today. . . ." The confident, highfalutin visions of the Khrushchev era concerning future Communist progress—some of them fearfully accepted in the West—proved ludicrous. The "main content" of "our epoch," the Soviet Party Program of 1961 had proclaimed, was "the transition of more and more peoples to the socialist path." At that time, an important Soviet theorist projected that the proportion of the world population in his camp, then 35 percent, would rise to 54 percent by 1980, and its 33 percent of world industrial production would rise to 60 percent. With the defection of China, these predictions proved theoretical indeed: the size of the camp shrank to 14 percent by 1980, and its share of global industrial production declined to 30 percent.[52]

The colonies in Eastern Europe were also stagnating. Some of them, especially Poland, had staved off an economic reckoning in the 1970s by borrowing heaps of money from Western banks. In 1980, at the insistence of its Western creditors, the Polish government, whose debt to the West had risen to $22 billion from $1 billion in 1970, began to make some economic reforms, especially price increases; and this set off a mass uprising that may well be, as Valerie Bunce has observed, the first genuine proletarian revolution in history. All of this induced painfully negative economic growth in Poland and almost led to a Soviet troop intervention. By the mid-1980s the comparatively well off countries of Eastern Europe had become a considerable burden on the Soviet Union and on its long-suffering and often-resentful citizenry.[53]

If the Soviet Union and the Communist states of Eastern Europe had lost their appeal as examples, the overseas colonies the Soviets had ardently been collecting hardly served as models for emulation either: in varying degrees all were fraught with misery. Characteristic were economic backwardness or outright collapse; persistent civil, and in some cases, international warfare; systematic brutality; and mind-boggling administrative incompetence. At best they had simply traded an economic dependency on the West for one on the far less wealthy Soviet Union—to the tune, for example, of some $2 billion a year for Vietnam, and $3 to $5 billion a year for Cuba. Thus, the new Soviet colonies formed, if anything, a negative example for the third world. For instance, the flood of refugees into Thailand from Laos and Cambodia after 1975 helped Thai counterinsurgency efforts; one Thai general recalled that he used to "tell the people what Communism would bring." But after the refugees came, he observed, "the people would tell *me* about the Communists. They had learned." In the third world, observed Allen Whiting in 1985, "the Communist lamp is out."[54]

For role models, the logical place for third world countries to look if they strove for prosperity was the rapidly growing, Western-oriented, capitalist, and at least semidemocratic states of East Asia: Japan above all, and also South Korea, Taiwan, and Singapore.

Gorbachev's Counterrevolution

In the decade after Vietnam, then, it became evident that the Soviet model retained little seductive appeal. Furthermore, insofar as countries joined the Soviet system anyway, their comradeship generally proved costly and unrewarding to the Soviet Union notwithstanding occasional gains like the military base at Camranh Bay in Vietnam.[55]

Faced with these realities as well as with his massive domestic problems, Gorbachev launched major changes in both domestic and foreign policy. Domestically, the Soviet Union sought to restructure and reform its internal system to make it productive. Internationally, it began to act like an old-fashioned, self-interested participant in the world community, rather than like a revolutionary, system-shattering one. And, like other such countries in the post-1945 era, it began to appreciate the virtues of decolonization. The domestic reorderings were designed to reverse the Soviet trend toward economic and social backwardness and uncompetitiveness. The international changes were principally designed to help service these overriding domestic requirements, but if carried through to their logical conclusion, they would have the effect of bringing about an end to what was left of the Cold War.

Gorbachev's domestic reforms were to be carried out under the slogan of *perestroika*—restructuring—and were designed, as he put it in a 1987 book, as a "policy of accelerating the country's social and economic progress and renewing all spheres of life." By 1988, however, he seems to have determined that the word *accelerating* was a bit of a euphemism. What had been passing for Soviet economic growth, he candidly pointed out, was an artificial concoction of unusually high oil prices and extensive vodka sales. If those two factors are discounted, noted Gorbachev, there had been "no increase in the absolute growth of the national income" for twenty years and "at the beginning of the 1980s, it had even begun to fall. That is the real picture, comrades!"[56] There were also signs that the real picture might get grimmer before it got better, because international oil prices were soft, and because Gorbachev had launched a major campaign against the debilitating and productivity-hampering effects of alcoholism by restricting vodka sales, taxes on which had represented 12 percent of the country's revenues. (By encouraging home-brewing, the reductions would also increase the country's death rate from alcohol poisoning, which had already reached 51,000 per year in 1978.)[57] At any rate, what was required was a major shake-up of the system, not simply a restructuring of it; and Gorbachev set about trying to initiate some semblance of productive reform among the smug, corrupt, nepotistic, inbred, self-serving elite that dominates the theoretically classless Soviet society.

Whatever Gorbachev's success with domestic reform, its imperatives suggested the need for at least three important changes in Soviet relations with the outside world. First, it was prudent to reduce the Soviet Union's colossal defense budget, which probably ran at 12 to 14 percent of the GNP in 1970 and rose to 17 percent or more in 1982.[58] Accordingly, although the Soviets had walked out in 1983 on the negotiations for limiting intermediate-range missiles in Europe, under Gorbachev they came bounding back, made all sorts of concessions, and in December 1987 signed a treaty eliminating the weapons along the lines that had been proposed by NATO eight years earlier. Gorbachev expressed hopes for similar agreements designed to bring about reductions in far costlier strategic and conventional weapons and to curtail a punishingly complicated arms competition in connection with technologically sophisticated space weapons. Aiding in his quest were Soviet military leaders who had apparently become convinced that the country could never be truly effective militarily with an enfeebled economy and thus found a degree of self-interest in reforms, controls, and at least temporary reductions.[59]

Second, to achieve his domestic goals, Gorbachev saw the need for, as he put it in 1985, "not only a reliable peace, but also a quiet, normal international situation." Thus, he came to find it in the Soviet interest to be unprovocative and to establish and strengthen calm, businesslike relations with the West, curiously no longer so decadent. Perhaps recalling the 1961 party program that ringingly declared "our epoch" to be one "of struggle between the two opposing social systems," an important Soviet official observed in 1987, "Previously we reasoned: the worse for the adversary, the better for us. . . . But today this is no longer true. . . . The better things are going in the European world economy, the higher the stability and the better the prospects for our development."[60] With that, the Soviet Marxists began to seek entry into such quintessentially capitalist institutions as the International Monetary Fund, the General Agreement on Trade and Tariffs, and the World Bank. It's certainly a revolution, but not the kind Lenin had anticipated.

Finally, it was likely that Soviet dealings with the third world were to be changed. Not only had its revolutionary activities there proved costly, but they had unduly upset the West, particularly the United States, and thus had hampered the creation of the "quiet, normal international situation" that Gorbachev felt was necessary for Soviet reform. Brezhnev used to take delight in tallying up the growing number of countries with a "socialist orientation," and he used to like to pledge economic and military support for them. But as early as 1983 under Andropov, third-world clients were being told that their "economic development" and "social progress" could "of course" only be "the result of the work of their peoples and of a correct policy of their leadership." And Gorbachev tended to ignore them altogether in important speeches while reducing the Soviet assistance pledge to "profound sympathy."[61] By the Gorbachev era, the Soviet Union had at least temporarily lost interest in expanding its empire of overseas dependencies,* and grew uneasy about its financial commitment to some of the radical states it had collected over the years. In a notable policy shift, the Soviets under Gorbachev tried to expand trade and perhaps to seek influence with some of the major non-Western countries—Mexico, Brazil, Japan, Argentina, India, Kuwait, even Israel—and they did so without much reference to ideology. Gorbachev also began to extract the Soviets from their enervating Afghanistan quagmire, which he characterized as a "running sore," and watched quietly and without perceptible lament as impoverished Mozambique slipped out of the Soviet sphere. There were also moves to reduce Soviet involvement in Cambodia and Angola.[62]

Of course, the Soviets' reduced interest in third-world revolution may eventually prove to be a tactical consideration, and they might return to international revolutionary evangelism once they feel more comfortable domestically. But given their costly and often frustrating colonial experiences over the last decades, the change may prove to be strategic and lasting: they may eventually decide permanently to sit back and let what their ideology tells them are inevitable historical developments take place unaided and at history's own leisurely pace.

By the mid-1980s Soviet theorists were already finessing the ideological issue by stressing the "long-term character" of revolutionary developments and arguing that revolution can best be aided by "the acceleration of socioeconomic development and the perfection of socialism in the Soviet Union." With the passing of such influential old-line ideologues as Mikhail Suslov (in 1982), ideology, which has long been heavily flavored by a cynical opportunism anyway, may be losing whatever hold it has had.[63] Francis Fukuyama has observed that "the role of ideology in defining Soviet foreign policy objectives and in providing political instruments for expansion has been steadily declining in the postwar period." Gorbachev's changes, he concludes, "have further accelerated that decline." By

---

*When leaders of the tiny and impoverished African country of Benin, now under control of the People's Revolutionary Party, made a pilgrimage to Moscow in 1986, they signed a "Declaration of Friendship and Cooperation," not a treaty, with the Soviets. Notably, the declaration did not include a provision familiar in earlier Soviet agreements with such countries for consultations in the case of a security threat (Fukuyama 1987, p. 11).

the mid-1980s, observes Jack Snyder, Suslov-style ideologues were sometimes being derided by the reformers as "Old Believers" whose dogma "smacks of romanticism." Since most of the costs would be purely theological, those less steeped in theory might begin to see third-world cutbacks—even outright decolonization—as a thing of beauty: a reform that pumps more money into the system without threatening entrenched privilege.[64]

The Demise of the Cold War

Since 1945 the Soviet Union and its various far-flung co-conspirators have been, because of their ideological commitment to world revolution, the chief proponents of substantial instability in the world status quo. And it is this propensity that has been most likely, one way or another, to bring about major war in the post-1945 world. But over the years the arsenal for furthering Communist internationalism, as catalogued in chapter 7, has been rendered ineffective or has proved to be inadequate: Major war never made any tactical sense; Korea undercut the perceived viability, if any, of direct military probes; crisis and bluster mostly went out with Khrushchev; revolution and subversion in the capitalist world soon lost whatever potential they ever had; revolution and war in the third world proved costly and inconclusive; and progress by example and seduction became, by the 1980s, something of a joke. Frustrated in this endeavor and preoccupied by internal problems, Gorbachev seems to be leading the Soviet Union toward abandoning its revolutionary commitment to worldwide revolution—or at least toward reducing that commitment to warm smiles and lip service.[65] In this he is following the path, essentially, of such other former ideological hard-liners as Yugoslavia and China.

If that change comes about and proves to be lasting, the whole premise upon which containment policy rests will have been shattered, and the Cold War would logically come to an end. And the United States is likely to comprehend that logic. When the perceived threat from international Communism waned in the past, the United States was generally quick to respond favorably. As Reagan's secretary of state, George Shultz, observed in 1985, the United States soon became accommodating when Yugoslavia and China quietly reduced or abandoned their commitment to the world revolution, even though their internal systems remained at the time as objectionable as ever.[66]*

*In the 1950s hard-line anti-Communist John Foster Dulles had put it this way: "The basic change we need to look forward to isn't necessarily a change from Communism to another form of govern-

The United States has opposed the Soviets' "evil empire" (and Hitler's too) not because it has been evil, but because its expansionary, imperial designs have seemed threatening. (Although the Nazi regime was widely considered to be bad—even monstrous—the United States went into forceful opposition only when the threat became directly pertinent through a surprise attack by a Nazi ally and then by a declaration of war by the Germans.) There might still be bloody Marxist revolutions around the world, but if they have no threatening external referent, these revolutions would have little consequence for American security; even in Reagan's 1980s little concern was shown about the Maoist rebellion in Peru, in large part because those rebels did not relate to more significant bastions of international Communism (a Maoist motherland no longer existed).

Indeed, the experience during the post-Vietnam decade had already eroded much of the rationale for containment. Although Soviet-inspired international Communism may not have become tame or benevolent, it was clear by the mid-1980s that the movement lacked the effective, infectious dynamism presumed by the domino theory. By the logic of containment, if the collapse of a distant country to Communism does not lead to similar developments in more important, closer countries, then that collapse is of no great consequence to American security. In contrast to the view of the 1950s that everywhere is important, it began to seem that almost nowhere was important.* Areas that still seemed vital to American security included North America, Japan, and Western Europe; and, for reasons more of sentiment than of security, South Korea and Israel.[67] The perceived importance of the Persian Gulf area was tied to the varying need for oil. Much of the rest of the world had begun to fall beyond the pale of containment. Indeed, the Reagan administration discovered that getting support for even rather inexpensive anti-Communist ventures in Central America, an area close to home, could be very difficult, and the president was given to arguing that Communist gains there were undesirable in part because they would "send millions of refugees north," hardly the sort of contagion feared by containment theorists.[68]

But if containment ceases to make much sense as a basis for American foreign policy, this will be in part because the policy itself was successful. In 1945 the West was confronted with a well-armed opponent committed to a dynamic,

---

ment. The question is whether you can have Communism in one country or whether it has to be for the world. If the Soviets had national Communism we could do business with their government" (Gaddis 1982, p. 143). Figure 9.1 documents mellowed public hostility toward the Soviet Union in periods of diminished perceived threat: the early 1970s and the Gorbachev era.

*See, for example, Ernst B. Haas: "Why commit ourselves to maintaining American influence in the Third World? . . . Marxist victories do not necessarily threaten our way of life. Crudely put, my argument says: who cares what happens to Ethiopia, Laos, or El Salvador?" (1983, pp. 113–14).

expansionary, even messianic ideology that was explicitly contemptuous of Western values and security and seemed viscerally to threaten them. Containment proposed holding the ideologues in place until, frustrated, they changed and ceased to be threatening. It took much longer than the original containment theorists probably hoped, but change seems finally to be coming about—and has been in the works in some respects for twenty or thirty years.

Of course, containment alone did not cause the Soviet dilemma. The American military threat may have partly impelled the Soviets to overbuild in defense, but they might well have done that anyway given Soviet—or even historic Russian—suspicion of the outside world. And of course, containment did not cause them to adopt their stifling economic and bureaucratic system, to get involved in a costly and demoralizing war in Afghanistan, or to take on their pathetic array of dependencies in Africa, Latin American, Southeast Asia, and Eastern Europe. But containment did assume that the threatening Soviet dynamic would eventually self-destruct in one way or another, and to a considerable degree it does seem that the essential contradictions of the Soviet system and ideology have finally caught up with it.

The Cold War and World War III

As expressed in the Truman Doctrine, containment was also built on the fear that if the expansionary forces of international Communism were allowed free rein, a major war could result—rather in the manner of the 1930s. In retrospect it seems clear that this fear underestimated both the uniqueness of Hitler and the anachronistic nature of imperial Japan, and that it overestimated the willingness of international Communism to take risks and to use war as a tactic to secure its ends. But seen in historic context, the fears of the containment advocates were not at all unreasonable at the time. Designed essentially to prevent a wider war, the containment war in Korea probably did dampen Stalinist interest in military probes (a burden of chapter 6), and the one in Vietnam probably did help to frustrate Maoist ardor for wars of national liberation (see chapter 8). Thus, these costly, if limited, wars may have hastened the end of the Cold War and the eventual success of containment. But it is by no means obvious that they were crucial or even necessary to the process.

Overall, there is little in the history of the Cold War to suggest that a direct war among its major participants was ever very likely, and thus even if the

Soviets revert to their former ideological evangelism the prospects of major war are unlikely to rise severely. The experience of the two world wars had thoroughly discredited major war as a methodology, and the existence of nuclear weapons helped to dramatize, probably unnecessarily, this elemental and well-comprehended fact. Moreover, as far as the threat of major war has been concerned, the Cold War has gradually mellowed. It has been in remission at least since 1963 with respect to the Soviets and since the early 1970s with respect to the Chinese.

Nevertheless, the deep ideological conflict and the visceral clash of interests between the two sides were very real; and that, of course, is the kind of thing that has led to war in the past and did, in fact, lead to various smaller armed conflicts, as well as to a number of quite unpleasant crises, during the Cold War era. Therefore, if the Cold War evaporates as the Soviet Union begins to act like an ordinary Great (or semi-Great) Power rather than as the carrier of a messianic universal ideology, one of the few remaining potential causes of major war will no longer be around. It will be the end of the world as we know it.[69]

III

CONCLUSIONS

10

The Obsolescence of War in the Developed World

THE ARGUMENT to this point can be summarized as follows. For a few centuries now, it appears, the notion has been gaining acceptance in the developed world that war there is both abhorrent—repulsive, immoral, and uncivilized—and methodologically ineffective—futile. At first only a minority, and perhaps the governing elites of a few small nations like Holland, found this notion compelling. The rulers of Great Powers and their peoples generally continued to find war to be, at best, admirable and invigorating—a true test of greatness—and, at worst, an unpleasant occasional necessity.

World War I—the "Great War"—changed that rather substantially. The grotesqueries and staggering physical costs of that catastrophic exercise made peace advocates into a decided, if not always a deciding, majority in the developed world. The most common lessons drawn from the Great War were that all efforts must be made to prevent a recurrence and that no sane person could conceivably want to risk a repetition.

Unfortunately for those with that perspective, there remained in Europe at least one man, Adolf Hitler, who was both sane (at least in the sense of being capable of coherent, self-interested calculation) and highly risk-acceptant. Combining these qualities with luck and ruthlessness and with a manipulative talent of genius proportions, Hitler was able to lead his country into a series of sequential, separate wars that culminated in another cataclysmic world war. Joining in the fray was Japan, a strong but less advanced country that still clung to old-fashioned romantic notions about war.

The world wars can be seen, then, as horrific learning experiences. Most people in the developed world had gotten the point by 1918. The rest, the Japanese in particular, got it by 1945. The developed world became Hollandized. There have been profound ideological differences since 1945, centered on the lingering romantic affection of Communist states for revolution and on their visceral desire to alter the status quo in a direction they have devoutly believed to be desirable and inevitable. But, unlike Hitler, the Communists have not regarded direct warfare as a sensible method for advancing their ideology. Conceivably they might have been tempted to toy with war as a methodology; but their opponents, unlike those of Hitler and Japan in the 1930s, have devised credible policies and alignments to threaten that even small armed incursions could very well dangerously expand into a mutually punishing, counterproductive general war like the two world wars. That is, to array the three central buzzwords of the Cold War era in a single sentence, *containment* has sought to *deter* war through its threat of *escalation*. A somewhat similar phenomenon has kept the anti-Communist countries of the West from seriously contemplating the use of war to alter territorial divisions and occupations in Europe that they consider illegitimate and undesirable.

Fearing escalation to a general war, then, the developed countries have been content to keep their disagreements under control. There have been crises and even bloody surrogate wars outside the developed world, but these have been carefully delimited. Although a few of these sometimes seemed at the time to be inching dangerously close to the brink of major war, in retrospect and with fuller information, their escalatory potential seems to have been greatly exaggerated. Given the cautious, war-wary approach of the chief contenders, major war between them has never been remotely likely.

Hovering over all this has been the spectre of nuclear weapons carrying with them the promise that World War III would be even more destructive than World War II. Their existence and their destructive potential certainly form dramatic reminders of what escalation could lead to; but it seems highly unlikely that the leaders of the essentially content, risk-averse, and escalation-anticipating major states of the developed world have been so unimaginative as to need such reminding. It is *conceivable*, of course, that the leadership of a major country could be seized by a lucky, clever, risk-acceptant, aggressive fanatic like Hitler, or that an unprecedentedly monumental crisis could break out in an area, like Central Europe, that is of vital importance to both sides, or that a major country could be compelled toward war because it is consumed by desperate fears that it is on the verge of catastrophically losing the arms race. It is not obvious that any of these circumstances would necessarily escalate to a major war, but the existence of nuclear weapons probably does make such an escalation less likely.

Thus there are imaginable circumstances under which it might be useful to have nuclear weapons around. In the world we've actually inhabited, however, those extreme conditions haven't come about, and they haven't ever really even been in the cards. This enhancement of stability is, therefore, purely theoretical—extra insurance against unlikely calamity.

Finally, in the 1980s it appears that after a long record of failure a major source of conflict in the developed world—Communist ideology—may be beginning to mellow decisively. As an international force for action, it has been waning for decades as Communist states like Yugoslavia and especially China abandoned ideological purism for a more pragmatic approach. And it may be that the papal center of the world movement, Moscow, is now in the process of following the same path. Surrogate wars and contests of will in impoverished corners of the world seem more and more irrelevant to pressing concerns, and crisis has been abandoned as a methodology for over a quarter century. There is no reason to assume that the major developed countries have forgotten how to get into a war with each other, but they're working on it.

From a rational perspective, then, war among developed states seems to have become unthinkable—rejected because it's unwise, a thoroughly bad and repulsive idea. This chapter investigates the prospects that the present state of affairs will linger for a while and that the chances of major war will continue to diminish. The prospects look rather good for the foreseeable future not only because war has lost its evident appeal but also because substantial agreement has risen around the twin propositions that prosperity and economic growth should be central national goals and that war is a particularly counterproductive device for achieving these goals. Associated with this are changes in perspectives about how a country achieves status and "power" in the modern world. Increasingly, economic strength is being used as the crucial measure, replacing military prowess and success in war.

The chapter then examines some of the methods by which war in the developed world might still erupt. In part, it seems, the long peace has been based on the assumption that escalation would be easy and perhaps even automatic—an assumption that in many ways is dubious, perhaps even a myth. The chapter concludes with an assessment of the possibility that, myth or no myth, war in the developed world is in the process of becoming, like dueling and slavery, subrationally unthinkable and therefore obsolescent.

War Becomes Rationally Unthinkable

In many respects, the warless condition of the developed world is firmly entrenched. Not only is this condition the result of a long historical trend, as suggested in parts 1 and 2, but it seems to have become deeply ingrained in world perspectives: war has lost the romantic appeal it once had, and it has been discredited as a method for obtaining desirable goals.

War as Romance.

By ceasing to be regarded as romantic, war no longer retains much appeal as a desirable activity in and of itself. In the nineteenth century the idea that war was an outrageously repulsive exercise began to gain truly widespread acceptance for the first time in the history of Western civilization. Like most people with an exciting idea, peace advocates of that era had a way of talking mainly to other people who had the same idea; partly because of this, they tended to overlook the existence of a lingering war romanticism. World War I substantially destroyed the notion that war was admirable and desirable, and eventually war romanticism died out in the developed world.

Of course, war can still be fascinating, and it continues to inspire novels, histories, movies, and, most appropriately perhaps, comic books. In pacifist William James's phrase, it probably still remains "supremely thrilling excitement" and "the supreme theater of human strenuousness" for many.[1] But this fascination need not necessarily inspire emulation. In George Bernard Shaw's 1905 play, *Major Barbara,* a Latin teacher asks an arms manufacturer, "Well, the more destructive war becomes, the sooner it will be abolished, eh?" "Not at all," Shaw has the arms maker reply. "The more destructive war becomes the more fascinating we find it."[2] Shaw's snappy repartee contains a non sequitur, as the experience with civil war in the United States suggests. For well over a century the war has haunted American perspectives and has become probably the most fascinating and memorable event in American history—libraries full of books have been written about it, remembrance clubs persist, and it is still a popular summertime activity for young men to dress up in Civil War garb and reenact the battles (except for the bloodshed). The Civil War retains its extraordinary fascination in America, but no one has seriously suggested that it be tried again. Popular fascination with war, genocide, dueling, gunfights, or chainsaw massacres does not mean that any of these subjects is therefore embraced as desirable or admirable.

War as Method.

In addition to losing its romantic appeal, war has been substantially discredited as an effective method. Some wars have been fought, in part at least, for thrills and excitement; but most are waged for a purpose extrinsic to the method itself—to gain territory, establish dominance, expand trade, coerce an opponent, prevent secession, advance prosperity, prove superiority, settle scores, stave off attack, resolve disagreements, adjust borders, encourage revolution, institute hegemony, fend off encroachments, create independent nations, determine status, replace a leadership regime, or promote an ideology or religion.[3]

Developed countries continue to subscribe to some of those goals, and they have sometimes made use of warfare or warlike procedures as a potentially productive method for advancing their objectives outside the developed world. With the experience of the world wars behind them, however, major war has simply not seemed sensible as a method, as discussed in part 2. The psychic and physical costs of major war (with or without nuclear weapons) have unambiguously become prohibitively high—so high, in fact, that even belligerent methods short of war, such as crisis and military maneuver, have been applied only sparingly (and with declining enthusiasm) in large part because of fear they might escalate to war. Moreover, most developed countries, particularly the United States and the Soviet Union, have been essentially content with the status quo, having emerged from the last major war comfortably predominate in their respective spheres. Thus, peace, by and large, has been far preferable to war; and insofar as it seemed desirable to attempt to change the status quo, methods short of major war—like diplomacy, subversion, surrogate war, or carping and whining—have been applied. When those methods have failed, the malcontent has preferred failure to escalation.

The Quest for Prosperity.

In addition to these developments, an important shift of values seems to have taken, or to be taking, place: Throughout the developed world countries are coming to the conclusion that the most desirable thing to have, after such basic concerns as life and security are taken care of, is prosperity. That is, just about everybody would rather be rich than just about anything else.

It was not always so (and as discussed later, it will not necessarily always be so in the future). At one time goals like religious purity or territorial expansion or military dominance were considered to be far more important than economic growth, and many people disparaged the quest for wealth as gross and "materialistic": as Homer Lea put it in 1909, "commercialism" is a "debased" form of "strife" because it lacks "honor" and "heroism."[4] In our own era, Communist ideologues have held revolutionary progress to be far more important than the quest for prosperity: Mao Zedong's widow is credited with the slogan "It is better to eat Communist weeds than capitalist grain" (although Communists would argue, of course, that true prosperity is possible only after revolution dismembers capitalism). But as chapter 9 documented, the notion that the worldwide quest for prosperity should be a primary, not a secondary, goal has gained acceptance even in such classical bastions of Communist ideology as Beijing and Moscow. In a 1987 speech Mikhail Gorbachev neatly blended the quest for wealth with more typical status words when he proclaimed it his goal to bring the USSR into the twenty-first century as a "mighty, prospering power."[5]

This development is important because the conviction has also become widespread that whatever value war might conceivably still have for obtaining some goals, it is particularly counterproductive in the quest for prosperity.

It is possible, of course, to hold that war—particularly a war of expansion, confiscation, or empire—can be economically beneficial. This belief has existed, and wars to increase empire and to settle imperial and economic issues have been fought. But in general these wars have been importantly motivated by noneconomic issues as well—they were fought to advance religion or achieve dominance or hegemony, to secure a place in the sun, to gain "influence."

Overall, economic motives, contrary to Leninist dogma, seem to have become decreasingly significant as motivations for war over the last centuries. Luard concludes that economic objectives were sometimes important in the wars of the sixteenth century—although usually they were not a major consideration even then. Since that time economic motivations have become increasingly rare, particularly in the developed world. After 1789, he observes, "wars were not fought between European states to win better trading terms, reduction of tariffs, or even access to the colonies of others," concerns which were "perhaps the most contentious economic issues of the time." Since 1917 there have been wars of ideology and of territorial expansion, and economic objectives "played some part in motivating Japanese attacks in the Pacific in 1941," but "it is difficult to point to any other war in which they have had any significant role." Even severe pressure on resources, "though of acute importance to many states, especially in the case of oil," seems not to have "played any part in stimulating war."[6]

This may overstate the case somewhat, but the idea has been gaining acceptance for at least two centuries now that, from a purely economic standpoint, war is a singularly dubious enterprise. As discussed in chapter 1, this notion gained considerable credence in Europe in the nineteenth century, was central to the antiwar pamphleteering of Norman Angell, and is summarized nicely in historian G. P. Gooch's 1911 pronouncement: "Even a successful conflict between states can bring no material gain."[7]

There were those in 1911 who disagreed about the economic value of war, but not too many; and the world wars certainly hammered home the validity of Gooch's proposition, at least as it pertained to major war.* But even very small, successful wars fought by rich countries can be unprofitable—from an economic standpoint, neither the American conquest of Grenada in 1983 nor the British combat with Argentina over the Falklands in 1982 made much sense. Conceivably, a quick, decisive war of conquest against a well-endowed target of opportunity could bring economic gain—Hitler's occupation of France may have netted him a profit (see p. 91). But clinging even to valuable possessions can be economically unproductive in the long run. Colonial countries in the postwar era have found imperial divestment economically beneficial, especially when the price of occupation includes war or even disruptive discontent, a lesson the Soviet Union seems now to be appreciating in Eastern Europe and perhaps even in Central Asia.[8]

As long as human beings control their own destiny, there will be no war when they hold prosperity to be their overriding goal and when they are convinced as well that war is economically unprofitable. The notion that war, particularly in the developed world, is economically counterproductive has been widely, perhaps universally, accepted. Therefore, as long as that view doesn't change, the prospects for major war will diminish to the degree that countries pursue prosperity above all—whether they make much progress toward achieving it or not.[9]†

Status and Power: The Curious Case of Japan.

More broadly, the quests for economic growth and prosperity in the developed (and not-so-developed) world have begun to complicate severely the still-lingering issue of power (remember power?). The word has been scarcely used at all in this book except when capitalized in the appellation "Great Power" and when quoting others. The time has come, however, to give this generally overused and semimeaningless word some direct consideration.

The complications can be best illustrated by considering the remarkable economic resurgence of Japan, a country that seems to have all sorts of power, but then again, on the other hand, well, doesn't. Without benefit of missile or bazooka it has obtained status, influence, respect, and admiration; and it inspires emulation, envy, and genuflection. If that's not power, who needs it?

*It could be argued, however, that in strict economic terms the United States grew richer because of World War II—the only country to do so (see Kennedy 1987, p. 358).

†Of course, prosperity is not the only goal that implies peace. The leaders of a few countries, like Albania, Burma, Rumania, and pre-1974 Portugal, have found great emotional comfort in ethnocentric isolationism and have sought to withdraw their countries from the outside world. In the past, China and Japan have spent centuries on end following a similar policy. Such countries may sacrifice economic and intellectual growth, but they do not present a threat to others.

The century's resident guru in matters of international power theory has no doubt been Hans J. Morgenthau. He opened his widely hailed textbook of 1948 with the proclamation that "international politics, like all politics, is a struggle for power," and he then defined *power* as "man's control over the minds and actions of others." Power, he maintained, is sometimes an end in itself, but primarily it is a means to get other things a country might value—like prosperity, for example. A nation's power, Morgenthau determined, is derived in part from its geography, natural resources, industrial capacity, population size, national character, national morale, and the quality of its diplomacy. But a crucial component in all this is the ability to blow other people up: "The dependence of national power upon military preparedness is too obvious to need much elaboration," said Morgenthau without much elaboration, and "military preparedness requires a military establishment capable of supporting the foreign policies pursued."[10]

Pity the Japanese, then. Geographically ill-placed and resource poor, they have had to try to make do with their industrial capacity, population size, character, morale, and diplomacy because they have been, to say the least, singularly unprepared militarily. Morgenthau conceded that a country which is comparatively weak militarily can sometimes partially compensate for this defect if it has terrific diplomats. But the names of few hyper-deft postwar Japanese diplomats spring readily to mind, and the Japanese clearly exercise so much "control over the minds and actions of others" (if that's what it is) because of their economic strength. Power did not bring prosperity: although it is not clear that the Japanese have "struggled" to get power, it came along when they pursued, and achieved, their remarkable prosperity. That is, prosperity brought power; and using Kenneth Waltz's characterization of a Great Power, Japan is one of those countries that "set the scene and action for others as well as for themselves."[11]

The phenomenon is not entirely new. Small European countries like Holland and Switzerland have followed a Japan-like approach. If they control minds and actions of others, and if they set scenes, it is because of their business clout and their attractive economic prosperity, not because of their military preparedness or their diplomatic wheeling and dealing; but since they are small, no one has been tempted to call them Great Powers. In 1880 the United States was far more advanced economically than any Great Power except Britain; and in 1914 its national income was greater than that of Britain, France, Germany, and Russia combined. Yet its armed forces, which were mostly engaged in chasing Indians, were far smaller than Italy's. The United States was sometimes considered to be Great in the late nineteenth century (and later, of course, it was to enter the club with a vengeance). But because of its distant location, its substantially autarkic economy, and its even more substantial lack of interest in playing the Great Power game, it did not command much influence in the machinations of the Great and mighty.[12]

Contemporary Japan, by contrast, is a large country and is heavily involved in international affairs, and its enormous economy automatically causes it to have an impact on the minds and actions of others. Therefore, by the definitions of Morgenthau and Waltz, Japan is powerful.[13]*

In 1988 Paul Kennedy's *The Rise and Fall of the Great Powers* became a best-seller. Like Morgenthau, Kennedy is centrally interested in the issue of power, but he sees economic strength as a far more vital component: "Wealth is usually needed to underpin military power," he argues, "and military power is usually needed to acquire and protect wealth." Great Powers decline, says Kennedy, because they tend to overextend their economies through conquest, overmilitarization, and war. Modern Japan is a central concern in Kennedy's narrative, and he is often uncertain about how to characterize it. He defines a Great Power classically: "a state capable of holding its own against any other nation." However, he then treats Japan as a Great Power, or at least as a "major" one, even though Japan, despite its self-defense forces, would presumably have difficulty "holding its own" against pretty much anybody.[14]

This curiosity suggests that in the developed world, at least, a remarkable change in the gauging of status has occurred. Recall the observation made by Leo Tolstoy in *War and Peace* in 1869: "All historians agree that the external activity of states and nations in their conflicts with one another is expressed in wars, and that as a direct result of greater or less success in war the political strength of states and nations increases or decreases."[15] A century later countries were becoming aware that Greatness, or at least majordom, and the status those words imply, can be achieved in the Japanese manner, purely through economic means: prosperity is power is status. In many ways the Japanese experience finds a parallel in West Germany as well.

Thus, status and political strength are increasingly being expressed in the dreary but bloodless medium of economic statistics. Consider in this regard *il sorpasso*, the exuberant boast of Italy in 1987 that its gross domestic product was now greater than Britain's. From this the Italians jubilantly concluded that they deserved admission into the rich-nations club, the Group of Five, supplanting the British. (Members of this club get to stay for dinner at meetings of the Big People, while lesser entities are required to retire quietly after coffee.) The fact that they could brandish a larger economic figure than the British gave the Italian people a lot of pride, and they celebrated as if they had just won a great battle.[16]

Equally interesting is the way the unamused British chose to reply to this Latin

---

*It could be argued, of course, that Japan does in effect have a large military force at its disposal—that of the protecting United States (as it can be said that the British Navy protected the United States in the nineteenth century). But Japan's "power," its "control" of minds and actions around the world, derives from its own economic importance, not from the fact that it can call upon the American armed forces to swing into action to enforce its dictates.

impudence. The Italians were miscalculating the economic statistics, they countered, and besides, the British have far more television sets and telephones per capita. What the British *didn't* do was to point to, or even slyly imply the relevance of, their military superiority—particularly their possession of nuclear weapons.

The Decreasing Importance of Nuclear Weapons as Status Symbols.

In fact, now that nuclear weapons have come up in this narrative, as they do from time to time, it might be interesting to reflect a bit on one of the great curiosities of the postwar era: What ever happened to all those countries that were supposed to have nuclear arsenals by the 1980s? Like Italy, for example.

In 1960, British novelist and pundit C. P. Snow predicted that "within, at the most, six years China and several other nations" would have "a stock of nuclear bombs." Equally prescient was the National Planning Association in Washington, which suggested in 1958 that we would have to plan for "a rapid rise in the number of atomic powers . . . by the mid-1960s." President John Kennedy was alarmed that there might be fifteen to twenty-five nuclear states in the 1970s and called the prospect "the greatest possible danger."[17] At the time, Britain and France had busied themselves with acquiring nuclear weapons as soon as they could afford them, and it was known that China was also seeking to enter the nuclear club. It was widely, if rather casually, assumed that most countries would follow their example as soon as they could manage it.[18] China exploded its first bomb more or less on schedule in 1964; since then India has obtained a "peaceful" bomb, and Israel apparently has outfitted itself with a small stock of secret ones.[19] And that, so far, has been the end of it.

The doomsayers went astray in part because they were extrapolating from the wrong instances; a more pertinent prototype would have been Canada, a country that could easily have had nuclear weapons by the 1960s but declined to make the effort. Moreover, it was assumed that nuclear weapons would continue to be important status—or virility—symbols and therefore that all advanced countries would want to have them in order to show how "powerful" they were. Thus, France's De Gaulle opined in 1965, "No country without an atom bomb could properly consider itself independent."[20]

Countries that have considered acquiring the weapons, however, have come, like Canada, to appreciate several defects: the weapons are dangerous, distasteful, and costly. If a country values economic growth and prosperity above all, the sensible thing is to avoid the weapons unless they seem vital for security. Like military prowess in general, the weapons have *not* proved to be crucial status symbols.[21]

The Prospects for War in the Developed World

From a rational standpoint, then, major war seems to have become unthinkable. It lacks the romantic appeal it once enjoyed, and it has been substantially discredited as a method. Moreover, there has been a shift in values: prosperity has become something of an overriding goal, and war—even inexpensive war—is almost universally seen as an especially counterproductive method for advancing this goal. Finally, prosperity and economic growth have been enshrined as major status, and even power symbols in the international arena, occupying much of the turf previously claimed by military prowess and by success in war.

In composite, these considerations suggest that substantial war in the developed world is highly unlikely, at least in the foreseeable future. The modern state system was built in part on the notion that war was the sort of thing one does from time to time. But now, as the system lurches exhaustedly toward the end of its fifth century, perpetual peace, if not utter tranquility, promises to blanket the developed world. A little dull perhaps, but everyone seems to have come to regard it as distinctly preferable to the most obvious alternative. War has lost its kick.

However, major war is not inconceivable—that is to say, impossible. Given current values and perspectives, major war may be highly improbable, but it could still occur if decision makers become confused or demented and act irrationally or if they undergo a change in values and perspectives so that war once again becomes a seemingly sensible procedure. These concerns are examined next.

Rationality, Uncertainty, War by Accident.

In thinking about war, decision makers are likely to be plagued by misconception, bias, and clouded perspectives, and they also confront enormous problems of uncertainty. What we are entitled to expect of decision makers is not that they be superhuman, but that they be rational—that is, sensible and reasonable in reaching their conclusions.

It must be stressed that there is a great deal of rationality in human behavior. A man who insists that people are irrational—incapable of acting in a reasonable, sensible manner—perjures himself whenever he ventures out into traffic: not only does he assume and predict that other people will behave in a manner he would consider rational, but he stakes his life every minute on the accuracy of that prediction.

And there does seem to be a fair amount of rationality in the way wars begin too. Military historian Michael Howard concludes after a lifelong study of the subject that "the conflicts between states which have usually led to war have normally arisen, not from any irrational and emotive drives, but from almost a superabundance of analytic rationality. . . . Men have fought during the past two hundred years neither because they are aggressive nor because they are acquisitive animals, but because they are reasoning ones." He adds, "Wars begin by conscious and reasoned decisions based on the calculation, made by *both* parties, that they can achieve more by going to war than by remaining at peace."[22]

In assessing such decisions it is useful to separate out two kinds of error: mistakes and blunders. *Mistakes* are errors in judgment that are reasonable and understandable given the enormous problems of uncertainty and imponderability that decision makers very often labor under. *Blunders,* on the other hand, are erroneous judgments that decision makers should reasonably have been able to avoid, even considering those uncertainties and imponderables.

As Carl von Clausewitz stressed in his famous book *On War,* published in 1832, there is in warfare a colossal amount of uncertainty. Clausewitz called it "friction," analogous to the untidy forces in classical mechanics that keep its laws from being precisely true in real life. "No other human activity," Clausewitz concluded, "is so continuously or universally bound up with chance."[23] War is a lethal, improvisatory free-for-all between dedicated and often desperate contestants who are playing for extremely high stakes and who have usually never fought each other before. There are few, if any, rules and no time limits; and although each side is fighting for its own self-interest, that interest may be difficult to assess, and may change as the war progresses. It is often extremely difficult at any point to know what is going on (some, following Clausewitz, have called it the "fog of war"), and each side will do its utmost to confuse and deceive the other. Even small wars involve the command of large, complex organizations, which are difficult to manage even in peacetime; and the course of the war can be crucially determined by such changeable and unmeasureable qualities as morale and leadership, and by such imponderables as weather, evolving technology, the caprices of allies or neutrals, and dumb luck.*

In contemplating war, we can reasonably expect decision makers to try to reduce this uncertainty by careful analysis and assessment; but, as Clausewitz

---

*Apart from any moral concerns, it is probably war's enormous uncertainty that has caused business people over the centuries to dislike war. They would tend to agree with Bernard Brodie: "Peace is better than war not only in being more agreeable but also in being very much more predictable" (1959, p. 408).

would argue, it is wholly unrealistic to expect them to eliminate it. And given the conditions of massive uncertainty, it is unwise to the point of absurdity to judge the soundness of a decision merely by whether it was successful.[24] The Germans lost World War I, but, as noted in chapter 2 (p. 50), that does not necessarily mean their war planning was unreasonably faulty at the war's start in 1914. Since the Germans lost, they were probably mistaken in their decision to enter the war; but their belief that they had a reasonable chance of winning does not seem to have been a blunder. They do seem to have miscalculated—indeed, it could be said that almost all countries that go to war and lose have miscalculated—but they may well have planned and prepared more soundly for war than did the winners.

Decisions to go to war generally seem to be at least somewhat cagey, and usually they do not seem to be the result of erratic flights of irrationality, but they can still be breathtakingly sloppy, even with all due appreciation for the uncertainty under which decision makers usually operate. Very often, in fact, the sloppiness comes from the uncertainty: because an element is difficult to assess, it is simply ignored.

A case in point is the Japanese decision to go to war against the United States in 1941, as discussed in chapter 3 (pp. 73–75). In the short run, Japanese plans seemed reasonable: the Japanese anticipated victory after victory, and they hoped the United States would be demoralized by this process and would decide to let Japan alone while concentrating on the greater threat from Nazi Germany. But the Japanese had no way of guaranteeing that the United States would make this choice, and they knew their long-term prospects for victory were poor: Admiral Yamamoto had warned them, "In the first six months . . . I will show you an uninterrupted succession of victories," but "should the war be prolonged for two or three years, I have no confidence in our ultimate victory."[25]

In deterrence terms (to be discussed more fully in chapter 11) there are at least two ways the Japanese decision for war might be rationalized. It is possible that their estimate of the virtues of peace had sunk so low that even defeat was preferable. (Had they not gone to war, they faced the prospect of gradually weakening into a humiliating second- or third-rate status, because they would be forced by economic circumstances to abandon the cherished empire in East Asia that they had carved out with so much bloodshed over the previous decade.) Second, even if they preferred peace to defeat, and even if their estimate of their likelihood of victory was low, it is still possible to argue that war was rational if they placed an exalted value on victory and if peace was deemed to be only slightly preferable to defeat.

The problem with either rationale is that Japanese leaders seem never to have gone carefully through the exercise of assessing costs, benefits, and risks. In her study of the decision making that led to the Pearl Harbor attack, Roberta Wohlstetter concludes that "war with the United States was not chosen;" rather, it "was forced by the desire to avoid the more terrible alternatives of losing status or abandoning the national objectives."[26] It could be argued, of course, that the Japanese had no need to sort out their values with much care—Wohlstetter's conclusion suggests in fact that the Japanese did have something of an appreciation for how badly the loss of status would feel. And, given the terrific uncertainty of war, it was not entirely unreasonable to hope that they could somehow muddle through and eventually persuade the United States to let them hang onto their precious empire so distant from American shores.[27] Thus, it's not that the Japanese decision departs so far from reality: they probably did have a gut feeling for costs, benefits, and risks. It's just that most of these assessments seem never to have gone much *beyond* the gut level. In particular, the Japanese seem never to have looked carefully at the costs of defeat, comparing them with the costs of maintaining the status quo.[28] Given that they were making what was probably the most important decision in their nation's history, such sloppiness, if not entirely irrational, is, to say the least, remarkable. It's possible that if they thought over the costs and consequences of defeat, they still might have concluded that war was worth the risk; the problem is that they never seem to have bothered to assess the eventuality carefully.

The phenomenon of ignoring important deliberative elements commonly occurs in the real world, even when those elements include human life. If Japanese decision making was sloppy in 1941, how cogent was American decision making at the time? It is not at all clear that the Americans thought carefully about how much it would cost to defeat Japan and to force China from Japanese clutches (and, as it happened, into those of a future American war foe, the Chinese Communists). In fact, well over 100,000 American lives were spent to accomplish that task, a cost one could reasonably have anticipated in 1941. Yet it does not seem that American decision makers ever really attacked the task of determining how much blood and treasure fighting the Japanese would be worth.[29] Had they done so, they might still have come to the conclusion that war was worth it. The concern here is that they seem never to have gone through the effort.*

The conclusion from this is that decision making can often be amazingly sloppy, even when the stakes are high and even when human life is an important consideration in the calculation. Decision makers characteristically do give thought to reality and to what they are doing when important decisions have to be made, and they often have to labor under conditions of tremendous uncertainty and pressure: most leaders can quite honestly say of their decision to go

---

*For an extension of this argument as it might be applied to decisions made—or unmade—about one of the greatest instruments of death ever invented, the automobile, see the Appendix.

to war that it seemed like a good idea at the time. But even giving them full credit for this, important elements in such deliberations often receive far less consideration than they should. The guidance mechanism of the decision process often seems more inertial than reasoned.

For many, considerations like these have led to a concern that a war could somehow be started through an act of irrationality (or of consummate sloppiness) triggered by a weapons accident. Clearly, the existence of nuclear weapons poses peculiar dangers in this regard.[30] No mechanical device can be perfectly safe, and there is always the danger that one or more bombs will go off by sheer accident or will be deliberately launched by an unauthorized, and presumably demented, individual or by an exceptionally well armed terrorist. Before the invention of nuclear weapons, such possibilities were not of great concern, because no weapon or small set of weapons could do enough damage to be truly significant. Each nuclear weapon, however, is capable of destroying in an instant more people than have been killed in an average war, and the weapons continue to exist in the tens of thousands.

Concern about accidents is mitigated somewhat by the remarkable safety record chalked up over the course of the decades. Precisely because the weapons are so dangerous, extraordinary efforts to keep them from going off by accident or by an unauthorized deliberate act have been instituted, and these measures have, so far, been effective: no one has been killed by a nuclear explosion since Nagasaki.

More pertinently, however, even if a bomb, or a few bombs, were to go off, it does not necessarily follow that war would result. For that to happen, it is usually assumed, the accident would have to take place at a time of high war-readiness, as during a crisis, when both sides are poised for action.[31] One side could perhaps be triggered—or panicked—into major action by an explosion mistakenly taken to be part of, or the prelude to, a full attack. This means that the unlikely happening—a nuclear accident—would have to coincide precisely with an event, a major crisis, that is rare to begin with and has become more so as the Cold War has progressed.

Furthermore, even if the accident takes place during a crisis, it does not follow that escalation or hasty response is inevitable or even very likely. During the height of the Cuban missile crisis there were accidents galore. An American spy plane was shot down over Cuba, probably without authorization, and another accidentally went off course and flew threateningly over the Soviet Union. As if that weren't enough, a Soviet military officer spying for the West sent a message, apparently on a whim, warning that the Soviets were about to attack.[32] None of these remarkable events triggered anything in the way of precipitous response. They were duly evaluated and then ignored.

231

In moments of high stress and threat people can be said to have three psychological alternatives: (1) to remain calm and rational, (2) to refuse to believe that the threat is imminent or significant, or (3) to panic, lashing out frantically and incoherently at the threat. Generally, people react in one of the first two ways. Under the severe strain of continued bombing during World War II people did not characteristically panic or revolt; far more common was a sort of passive resignation, and even depression was rather rare. As Jervis points out, "When critics talk of the impact of irrationality, they imply that all such deviations will be in the direction of emotional impulsiveness, of launching an attack, or of taking actions that are terribly risky. But irrationality could also lead a state to passive acquiescence." In her classic study of disaster behavior, Martha Wolfenstein concludes, "The usual reaction is one of being unworried."[33]*

Finally, the historical record suggests that wars simply do not begin by accident. In his extensive survey of wars that have occurred since 1400, Luard concludes, "It is impossible to identify a single case in which it can be said that a war started accidentally; in which it was not, at the time the war broke out, the deliberate intention of at least one party that war should take place."[34]

It does not follow, then, that uncertainty and sloppiness of thought will cause decision makers to choose war in a moment of misguided passion or confusion. Given the widespread assumption that major war would be dramatically catastrophic, even great fools and truly splendid miscalculators are unlikely to topple helplessly into a war. "With the penalty for blundering into a war so great," notes Jervis, "even bold and foolish decision-makers behave cautiously."[35] Given current values and perspectives, it is difficult to see how decision makers—no matter how stupid, inept, miscalculating, and self-deceptive—could grope through the enormous vagaries of major war and accidentally conclude that it might be made to work to their benefit.

Indeed, as discussed more fully at the end of this chapter, in a sense *peace*, not war, has become irrational: Peace in the developed world is persistently being chosen as an option without fully considering the possibility that war might still be useful under some circumstances. The danger of war arises more from the prospect that it will come once again to recommend itself as a viable option than that it will be resorted to, or stumbled into, through an act of unthinking irrationality. If there is to be another major war, it will have to be started by calculation and on purpose, like earlier wars.

*According to the best figures, most people who heard Orson Welles's famous "War of the Worlds" radio broadcast in 1938 were simply not taken in by its portrayal of a Martian invasion, and of those who were, at least a third were not even frightened (Cantril 1940, pp. 57–58, 106–7).

War and the Arms Race.

A number of people have argued that an arms competition could develop in such a way that starting a war might represent a sensible course of action. In particular, many argue, a country that enjoys a substantial superiority of weaponry at a given time—a so-called window of opportunity—might be tempted to launch a war, especially if it seemed that the enemy might close, or even eventually reverse, the gap.

This notion was advocated by the proponents of preventive war who skulked about during the period of American nuclear monopoly after World War II (see pp. 109–10). They based their argument on two assumptions: that war between the USSR and the United States was inevitable, and that American nuclear superiority guaranteed that a war with the Soviet Union would be fairly painless. Both assumptions were roundly refuted at the time, and preventive-war advocates never became more than a tiny fringe group.

Since that time they have essentially vanished from the scene because their premises have progressively become even more implausible. War between the United States and the USSR might conceivably have seemed inevitable during the scariest days of Stalin, but with the rise of Khrushchev and his successors, the idea lost whatever limited cogency it ever had; in the Gorbachev era, it has become positively ludicrous. And when the number of nuclear weapons proliferated, the notion that a U.S.–USSR war might carry tolerable costs became utterly unsupportable—although, as has been noted often in this book, even without the weapons, a credible threat to escalate to a World War II–size war would also be notably sobering, as it was in 1950.[36]

War by Shifts in Values.

A major war is most likely to come about not because of a weapons accident, rampant irrationality, or esoteric arms imbalances, but because countries change their views either about what they most want in the world or about how best to achieve their goals.

As it was pointed out earlier in this chapter, peace in the developed world is currently secure because potential combatants find prosperity to be an especially attractive goal and because they have concluded that a major war would be counterproductive in the quest for prosperity. Conceivably those views could change. A leader somewhere could reverse the verdict of centuries and conclude that war is a sure path to wealth, or one could be impelled by major economic collapse to launch some sort of bizarre war of economic desperation in the belief that war could only improve hopeless conditions. More likely, however, a decision maker might come to lust after goals that, it would seem, could be more effectively gained through war.

Prosperity may be nice, but it is not always an overriding goal even now. In Canada some opponents of free trade with the United States argue that the economic benefits reaped would not be worth it because they would undermine what they term "Canadian identity." That is, it's more important to be Canadian than to be rich. If responsible officials in Canada, a country not noted for rash romanticism, can find an ephemeral thing like "identity" to be more important than prosperity, others could eventually be led once again to come to yearn for values that, it might seem, can be furthered by violence and warfare.

There are certainly plenty of territorial issues in the developed world that remain substantially unresolved, and discontent over these could lead to wars of expansion or territorial readjustment. There are small but violent secessionist movements in Ireland, in Spain, and from time to time even in Canada; and many people under the control of Moscow in Eastern Europe, the Baltic region, and Central Asia regard that control as profoundly illegitimate and repugnant. (A joke in contemporary Poland concerns a woman who waters her flower beds with oil; when queried about this flower-killing process, she replies, "Who cares about the flowers? I'm making sure the guns don't rust.")[37] Japan resents Soviet occupation of some islands in the northwest Pacific, many Koreans find the division of their homeland to be deplorable, and the biggest unsettled territorial issue of all is the divided condition of an important country, Germany.

Part 2 of this book argued that the Cold War ideological contest is in the process of peacefully resolving itself, but there is no firm guarantee that this trend will continue. If Gorbachev's reforms fail to improve visibly the Soviet domestic conditions, or if they encourage or create rebellions and internal schisms that panic Soviet hard-liners, the Soviet leadership might become controlled by fanatical purists yearning for ideological, and possibly territorial, expansion, even if that would temporarily set back the quest for prosperity.[38] Some might convince themselves that external crisis could be productively used to justify internal repression and to distract attention from domestic ills.

Or hot-blooded religious fervor could conceivably rise again in the developed world (possibly even in a post-Communist Russia) and, as in prewar Japan, become associated with romantic territorial expansion.

It is even conceivable that a country wallowing in prosperity might come to find its hedonistic, materialistic, self-indulgent condition unsatisfying and distasteful. The adventure, excitement, and self-sacrifice of war might regain its appeal, bringing a return of war romanticism or even of a pre-1914-style yearning for apocalypse. For example, some wonder whether the war spirit, coupled with a renewed desire for reunification, might again bubble up on one side or the other in Germany, especially if American influence wanes in Europe. Others view Japan with concern, fearing that in time it might match its economic strength with military strength and then romantically seek expansion. Of course, if Japan continues to regard prosperity as its overriding goal, it will not follow such urges unless they seem crucial to maintaining prosperity. The Swiss, after all, have been working on prosperity for centuries now and have made their peace with it. Nevertheless, there is a long military—or militaristic—tradition in Japan (as, however, there once was in Switzerland), and a revival of that spirit is conceivable at least. The noted Japanese novelist-masochist Yukio Mishima committed suicide in 1970 in a demented effort to urge his nation to return to the samurai tradition. The nation, he declaimed, had become "drunk on prosperity" and had fallen into an "emptiness of spirit." At the time, his action was ridiculed by his countrymen as an embarrassing anachronism, but that doesn't mean his perspective could never again come into fashion. (It is worth pointing out, however, that during the main samurai period, Japan stressed isolationist autarky, not militaristic expansion).[39]

If the samurai tradition could be revived, why couldn't another Hitler arise in Japan or elsewhere? As Jervis observes, "Hitlers are very rare," and Hitler's peculiar uniqueness was stressed in chapter 3. But that doesn't mean another such figure could never spring up. Since World War II there have been quite a few leaders who have blended tactical ruthlessness, an adept political sense, enormous popularity, a demagogic charisma, a supreme self-confidence, and a mystical vision of their own and their country's destiny: Stalin, Mao, Sukarno, Nkrumah, Nasser, Khomeini, Castro, Qaddafi. To carry out their visions none of these men has been both willing to risk a major war and capable of starting one the way Hitler was. But some professed to be quite cavalier about the costs of such a war: Mao argued that hundreds of millions of Chinese were expendable, Nasser bellowed that the "path to liberating Palestine" was to send three or four million men into battle "without paying any attention to casualties," and Castro boasted that 10,000 nuclear bombs amount to nothing more than "chicken excrement."[40] Genocide has happened several times since Hitler: another Hitler-style war is certainly not impossible.

The Myth of Escalation

Even if a country were once again to view war in the developed world as potentially desirable, it would be dissuaded, unless it were suicidal, by the fear that the war could escalate to an all-out, counterproductive conflagration like World War II or worse. As noted in chapter 3, even Hitler or the Japanese fanatics of the 1930s might have been deterred had they been convinced that their military ventures would escalate to the kind of costly, multi-front war of attrition they eventually were forced to wage—much less to a nuclear war.

But escalation is not inevitable: limited wars far short of Armageddon could in fact be fought in the developed world. And a major war is most likely to come about because a risk-acceptant disputant becomes aware that the long peace of the post-1945 era is based in part on a dubious assumption: that escalation cannot be controlled.

A central contention of this book is that, insofar as military considerations have been relevant, it is the fear of escalation that has deterred major war, not the ominous presence of nuclear weapons at the end of the escalatory ladder. Fearing escalation to something intolerable, East and West have kept their conflicts under control. However, the lesson of the Cold War era suggests not that escalation is dangerously easy or automatic, but that keeping it contained at a bearable level is quite possible. Nuclear-armed countries may have avoided war with each other partly out of fear of escalation, but where the fear of escalation was absent, they were directly challenged with war: the United States in Korea and Indochina, the Soviet Union in Hungary and Afghanistan, France in Algeria, Britain in the Falklands, China in Vietnam.[41] Moreover, two nuclear countries— the Soviet Union and China—managed to get into a near-war in 1969 but kept things under control.

The experience of the postwar world suggests, then, that the word *escalation* carries misleading connotations. Once on board an escalator, the riders are automatically lofted to the top unless they make strenuous efforts to clamber back down. A more appropriate metaphor would be a ladder: the climber becomes more anxious with each upward step and finds that stopping or retreating requires less effort and is less frightening than continuing the ascent.

War within the developed world could well prove manageable, and self-interested limits of the sort imposed in the Korean War could be applied in other conflicts. Thus, war there could once again become thinkable.

World War III as a Limited Conflict.

In fact, it is conceivable that a major war between the United States and the Soviet Union could be fought entirely with conventional weapons, and that its economic costs and casualty levels could be kept well below those of the first and second world wars.

Chapter 4 included a discussion (pp. 84–86) of a curiosity of World War II: despite the possession by all major combatants of chemical weapons and the means to deliver them, those weapons were never used in the war. This occurred mainly because each side knew that its use of the weapon was likely to trigger retaliation in kind. As World War II remained limited in this respect, it is quite possible that nuclear weapons could be kept out of World War III.

If a major conventional war were to break out today, perhaps escalating from an incident or from a local war fought between friends or allies of the major nuclear countries, leaders on both sides would no doubt issue stern pronouncements about their intention to visit swift and murderous retaliation upon any enemy who violated their tacit agreement about nuclear restraint. Eventually, either a standoff would arise or one side would increasingly come to look like a winner. In either situation, the war could reach a limited, non-nuclear conclusion.

In the case of a standoff, similar perhaps to a large-scale Korea, there would be some incentive for one side or the other to use nuclear weapons in an effort to gain a momentum that might carry it to victory. But such a move might only increase the horror of the war without altering its stalemated condition, and the contestants might well instead work out a negotiated cease-fire, an armistice, or a stand-down like the one accepted by the Chinese and Soviets in 1969.

In the situation where one side began to emerge as a winner, either side might be tempted to use nuclear weapons. In considering escalation, however, the winning side cannot ignore the dangers of retaliation even by the weakened enemy, and the conventional approach, well-tested and thus far successful, would probably seem far wiser. For the losing side most uses of nuclear weapons would probably seem suicidal: the winning side would be in an ideal position to carry out its threat to retaliate murderously. Of course, a rattled, desperate leader could find the risk of national suicide preferable to humiliating defeat and therefore order a nuclear attack; Hitler may have come to this conclusion with respect to chemical warfare in 1945. But it is instructive that such orders, if they were ever actually issued, were effectively sabotaged by underlings who had finally become convinced of Hitler's madness.[42]

As the war progresses, a nuclear weapon might explode somewhere by accident or intent, and this could trigger an escalatory chain reaction among the poised nuclear combatants whose prophesies about the automaticity of escalation would then become self-fulfilling. The history of chemical warfare, how-ever, casts considerable doubt on this thesis. For lethal gases *were* released in World War II, and these incidents triggered no outraged retaliation or escala-tion (see p. 85). Like the unauthorized overflight, shootdown, and war alert during the Cuban missile crisis discussed earlier, these events were simply ig-nored.*

Of course, there are important differences between chemical and nuclear weapons. Nuclear weapons, at least at the strategic level, are considerably more effective weapons. But since the weapon is effective for *both* sides, the horrors of retaliation would be vivid for any side contemplating initiation. If the allies in the last months of World War II had decided to use chemical weapons on Germany, the probability of punishing retaliation was quite low. Had both sides possessed atomic weapons, however, the probability that at least one retaliatory weapon might be lobbed successfully on London would have been disconcertingly high. At the tactical level, the advantages of nuclear over chemical weapons are not nearly so obvious. For both kinds of weapons there are extensive uncertainties of long- and short-term contamination.[43] But because of the World War I experience, chemical warfare was probably much better understood in the 1940s than nuclear warfare is now.

Nuclear weapons are far better assimilated into military planning than chemi-cal weapons were in World War II.[44] Therefore, at any point in a major war the nuclear option is likely to be seriously and informatively argued. But this assimila-tion includes a grim realization of how devastating retaliation by the other side could be, and much of the thinking about nuclear weapons, especially at the strategic level, is grounded on a second-strike mentality. Rather than hasty, spasmodic initiation, this is more likely to generate sophisticated deterrent threats against the other side in intrawar bargaining.†

Thus, it is entirely possible that a major war between East and West could reach a conclusion long before nuclear weapons were used.[45]‡

*Interestingly, the Americans had specifically decided that if a U-2 plane were shot down over Cuba, they would retaliate by destroying the antiaircraft site responsible (Hilsman 1967, p. 220). When the event came to pass, however, the policy was not carried out.

†Nuclear and chemical weapons also differ in that chemical weapons cannot be used to destroy the chemical weapons of the enemy, whereas nuclear weapons can destroy nuclear weapons. Never-theless, the costs of failure remain enormous and may discourage a country from launching a preemptive attack whenever the chances of success drift noticeably away from certainty. Further-more, it might seem wiser to attack nuclear weapons stocks with conventional weapons because the reduced escalatory risks might more than discount the reduced chances of success.

‡It is interesting that two recent popular novels about World War III—John Hackett's *The Third World War, August 1985* (1979) and Tom Clancy's *Red Storm Rising* (1986)—both imagine their wars to end before nuclear weapons receive significant use. Also, war simulations find a "persistent reluctance of war-gamers to resort to the use of nuclear weapons" (Gaddis 1987, p. 8).

Shattering the Escalation Illusion.

All this may suggest a distinctly gloomy conclusion for those who have come to prefer peace to war. The long, pleasant peace in the developed world, it seems, has been partly constructed on a myth—the notion that escalation to a massive war is pretty much inevitable once the major countries become directly involved. Instead, it appears quite likely that they would retain the ability at every level to halt the escalation if they really wanted to, and therefore that they could pull off a war that might be nasty, but still entirely bearable by historic standards. Perhaps the conventional wisdom is as wrong about escalation now as it was about the short war in 1914, and for the same reason: the pundits want the illusion to be true. In 1914 many of those subscribing to the illusion wanted war; today they don't. But if a sufficiently discontented or quarrelsome country in the developed world came to realize, or to believe, that escalation is a myth, might it be tempted eventually to try out a tolerable war or two to advance its interests? Might war in time become a gentlemanly jousting contest again? Politics carried out by other means? A useful arrow in the quiver? A thing of apparent beauty and therefore a curse forever?

A couple of analogies from history may be instructive. If the longest period of peace among the Great Powers has been the era since World War II, the second longest was the thirty-eight-year span following the tumultuous Napoleonic Wars that ended in 1815. The Great Powers of the time gingerly avoided war with one another until France, Britain, and Russia managed to get into a limited contest in 1854. After that there were several other small or smallish Great Power wars—between France and Austria in 1859, between Prussia and Austria in 1866, and between France and Prussia in 1870. These helped create the idea that war among large countries could be kept short and bearable, a bit of wisdom that helped eventually to bring about World War I.

Or consider the aftermath of the Thirty Years War of 1618–48. Europeans continued to engage in war; but because of the huge casualties suffered in that conflict, they kept their wars under control, using cautious and economical fighting methods and often bringing the wars to an end in a draw. After a few decades of this, however, their battles once again began to get larger until, after a century, Prussia fought a war in which perhaps a ninth of its population died.[46]

Might these patterns be repeated? Not necessarily. To begin with, although the chances may be quite good that a war among developed countries could be contained at a tolerable level, there are certainly no guarantees about this. Things could get out of control, rasher heads could prevail, troops could be launched into chaotic and suicidal action, terminal buttons could be pushed. Although one should not discount this very substantial possibility, many prefer not to rest their hopes for perpetual peace on the singularly uninvigorating faith that when the chips are finally down, leaders carefully chosen for their judicious qualities will suddenly turn at once apoplectic and apocalyptic. That, however, is what strategic nuclear deterrence is ultimately all about.

It also could be argued that the danger of repeating previous escalation patterns is low because developed countries have a high stake in the status quo and are basically content with it—even a comparatively small war, like Korea, is too costly, both physically and psychically, by their standards. As discussed in part 2, this is an entirely reasonable observation about the post-1945 world so far. But the dominant countries after 1815 also were basically pleased with the status quo, had no stomach for war, and had a great deal to lose. Yet, in time, they were able to overcome these concerns, and they returned to a pattern where war was a normal course of business.

War Becomes Subrationally Unthinkable

There is, as it happens, another possibility. Perhaps war in the developed world is becoming not only rationally unthinkable, but also subrationally unthinkable. Major war, in other words, may be obsolescent.

War is an idea, and for one to occur a two-step process must be negotiated: first, someone must think of war as a genuine option, and second, when evaluated the war option has to be discovered to be an option worth pursuing. The thought process that leads to war may not always be careful, admirable, dispassionate, judicious, or even very coherent, but it does exist. (As Henry Kissinger suggests, "Despite popular myths, large military units do not fight by accident.")[47]

An idea becomes impossible not when it becomes reprehensible or has been renounced, but when it fails to percolate into one's consciousness as a conceivable option. Thus, two somewhat paradoxical conclusions about the avoidance of war can be drawn. On the one hand, peace is likely to be firm when war's repulsiveness and futility are fully evident—as when its horrors are dramatically and inevitably catastrophic. On the other hand, peace is most secure when it gravitates away from conscious rationality to become a subrational, unexamined mental habit. At first war becomes rationally unthinkable—rejected because it's calculated to be ineffective and/or undesirable. Then it becomes subrationally unthinkable—rejected not because it's a bad idea but because it remains subconscious and never comes up as a coherent possibility. Peace, in other words, can prove to be habit forming, addictive.

Consider a man who is on the fifth floor of a building and is musing over two methods for reaching the ground floor: walking down the stairs (slow) or jumping out the window (fast). While there are uncertainties, the decision is not a terribly difficult one to be "rational" about. If war is like a fifth-floor jump, only someone who is suicidal will start one—or even get close to one. But an important oddity in that little story is in its first sentence: the notion that someone would spend any time at all thinking about whether walking down the stairs is preferable to jumping out the window. The alternative of jumping is not rejected after a balanced, rational decision is made, nor is it even rejected out of hand; rather, it never even comes up as a coherent possibility. Somewhere along the line we learn that jumping out of a fifth-floor window is a really terrible idea, and we live out our lives without ever reassessing the validity of that conclusion. Apparently it becomes a truth so self-evident that it requires no periodic reexamination.

War could be like that. Through rational or semirational calculation of costs, risks, and benefits one might come to believe that war makes no sense—that it is very stupid. Then such reasoned war-avoidance would become so habitual that war never comes up again as a serious option, even when it might have been objectively reasonable at least to consider it as a possibility. The United States refrains from attacking Canada today, but not because American decision makers from time to time examine the option of invading Canada and then soberly and rationally reject it because they decide they prefer the status quo to war. Instead, the option never gets seriously considered, and by now it has slipped so far from the realm of conscious possibility that even to bring it up may seem peculiar if not downright perverse (especially to Canadians). There is also the unexamined and apparently perpetual peace that has evolved between the United States and Britain; either nation now has the technology to annihilate the other, but neither spends much time worrying about that fact. Or, even more strikingly, there is the comfortable neighbor relationship that has developed between Germany and France despite centuries of enmity and despite the fact that France could easily devastate Germany within minutes with its nuclear arsenal.

This process seems to have occurred quite broadly in the developed world. Because of their costly experiences in the Thirty Years War and in the Napoleonic Wars, the surviving combatants were led to avoid war among themselves for a while or to limit its scope. But for the most part they still regarded war in Europe as normal, and they expected that, for better or worse, it would continue to occur. And, as Luard suggests, a "willingness for war . . . may make war almost as inevitable, sooner or later, as a definite intention of war."[48] That attitude, that war willingness, came under concentrated attack in the nineteenth century and has been almost universally rejected in the developed world in the twentieth. Thus, unlike the situation after 1648 or 1815, potential combatants in the developed world have not only come to appreciate the high costs of major war, but they have also come to a considerable consensus that war no longer is something one *does*. Indeed, but for Adolf Hitler, history's supreme atavism, substantial war in Europe, particularly in most advanced areas, might have been expunged in 1918 or so.

If a "willingness for war" can make war nearly inevitable, continues Luard, "a general unwillingness for war" means that "precisely the opposite is the case." That is, to reformulate a famous observation by impresario Sol Hurok, if people don't want to fight, nothing will stop them.

The elimination of major war, therefore, rests in the prospect that there will exist a "general unwillingness" for war—that war will become obsolete, subrationally unthinkable—not that it will become physically impossible or completely extinct. Dueling is still possible, as are foot binding, bearbaiting, slavery, lynching, and the Spanish Inquisition. But like these practices, war in the developed world seems now to be rejected not so much because it's a bad idea, but because it never comes up as a coherent alternative—avoided not because it's stupid, but because it's absurd, ridiculously incongruous. The idea that war is a viable, accepted, and expected way of going about things is a necessary cause of war; if that idea fades, as it has with dueling and slavery, war can't happen.

War can cease to exist without being formally denounced or renounced (actually, to renounce something—like sin or the Devil—implies that it is temptingly seductive and appealing on some presumably base level) and without compulsions administered by some supranational authority. As A. A. Milne once pointed out, "By no compulsion of force is one's wife prevented from removing her shoes and stockings during an afternoon call at the Vicar's. But one has complete moral security against this disaster. Only a fool (or, it may be, a politician just returned from a Peace Conference) would insist on her wearing non-detachable stockings."[49] Thus, war can disappear without a substantial alteration in our condition of international "anarchy" and without fundamental changes in the structure of postwar international politics.[50] (Because there is no effective world government, international affairs can be considered technically to be in a state of anarchy. The word implies, however, desperate chaos and unending violence. It would be at least as accurate to characterize international affairs as "unregulated," a word with milder, and perhaps more instructive, connotations.)

Nor, as the experience of Holland and other war-avoiding states suggests, does war need to be replaced by some sort of moral or practical equivalent—there is no irrepressible energy for war that must be displaced or sublimated, nor does war satisfy a natural impulse that must somehow be serviced. After all, nothing ever really replaced the Hula Hoop or the bustle. If it seems irreverent to compare war to such trivia, it nevertheless does not seem unreasonable to treat war as a fad, like religious conflict or the mystique of colonial expansion. These concerns once seemed urgent to sophisticated Europeans, but the issues have been played out—they have strutted and fretted their hours upon the historical stage and now are heard no more.

In a sense, war can die out, or at least become an endangered species, because one outgrows it. Running through the writings of many of the war opponents over the last two centuries is the notion that war is childish—a thoroughly ridiculous enterprise that ought to embarrass the adults who still embrace it, but, for some utterly unaccountable reason, doesn't. Many of them reach the heights of exasperation when this thought flickers through their minds. Milne, who certainly knew a great deal about children, found war not only evil but also "silly," and there were times, he felt, "when I think its childish silliness is even more heartbreaking than its wickedness." In railing against the war fever that he often saw rise before 1914, Norman Angell sputtered, "Our sense of proportion in these matters approximates to that of a schoolboy."[51]

To Milne, the Fashoda affair of 1898 was an incident in which the British and the French almost got into a war over "a mosquito-ridden swamp" in Africa. When someone soberly countered that "at stake was whether France should be allowed to draw a barrier of French influence across the English area of influence," Milne was catapulted into peak form:[52]

A war about it, costing a million lives, would have seemed quite in order to the two Governments; a defensive war, of course; a struggle for existence, with God fighting on both sides in that encouraging way He has. A pity it didn't come off, when it had been celebrated already in immortal verse.

> Tweedledum and Tweedledee
> Agreed to have a battle,
> For Tweedledum said Tweedledee
> Had spoilt his nice new rattle.

'Only it isn't really a rattle,' said Tweedledum importantly, 'it's an Area of Influence! There's glory for you!'
'I don't think I know what an Area of Influence is,' said Alice doubtfully.
'Silly,' said Tweedledee, 'it's a thing you have a battle about, of course.'
'Like a rattle,' explained Tweedledum.

In 1849, Ralph Waldo Emerson contended that "it is the ignorant and the childish part of mankind that is the fighting part," and he proclaimed it to be plain that "the sympathy with war is a juvenile and temporary state."[53] It has taken far longer than Emerson probably expected, but to a considerable degree the nations of the developed world appear to have begun to put away what he and Angell and Milne would consider to be childish things. A German who today advocated a war for status against France, as many did only a few decades ago, would be treated not merely as wrong-headed but as foolish and childish; so would an American who revived the notion that it was the "manifest destiny" of the United States to invade Canada. Because of that, the ideas no longer even seem to come up as topics for consideration.

As observed in the Introduction, dueling finally died out not so much because it became illegal, but because it became ridiculous—an activity greeted not by admiration or even by grudging acceptance, but by derision and contempt. And today that once-venerable institution has become ludicrously incongruous. When the notion of war chiefly inspires ridicule rather than fear, it will have become obsolete. Within the developed world at least, that condition seems to be gradually emerging. Perhaps we are growing up at last.

11

Implications and Extrapolations

$\mathbb{A}$ CENTRAL THEME of this book holds that nonmilitary elements play an important role in decisions about war. The trend toward obsolescence of war, for example, has been crucially influenced by changing moral and aesthetic values, and weapons, even nuclear weapons, are often far less relevant to issues of war and peace than they seem. In general, it seems, weapons are the effects of war and the war spirit, not their cause. This perspective might seem to undercut the military strategists' concepts of deterrence and stability, but these concepts can easily and fruitfully be recast to incorporate nonmilitary considerations. The first part of this chapter develops this broadened concept.

Much of this book has also been devoted to establishing two specific propositions: (1) that major war is in a state of obsolescence and (2) that the Cold War has never been close to hot war and could well be on the verge of terminal remission as the Soviet Union's enthusiasm for widespread revolution wanes. In time, of course, war might do to this book what it seeks to do to war, in which case these words will be read by people, if any, whose response will be informed by a certain air of wry derision. But if we suppose, until contrary proof is forcefully registered, that the two propositions are correct, they suggest, in combination, some implications about possible future developments. It's possible, although far from certain, that enthusiasm for war will eventually fade in the war-torn areas outside the developed world as it has in those within it. And with a lingering Cold War thaw and a perceived decline in the likelihood of war in the developed world, arms budgets might decrease, the arms race could atrophy, and a viable settlement to the divisions of Europe might be achieved. These prospects are evaluated in the second half of the chapter.

Deterrence

Deterrence is almost always looked at strictly as a military issue. A typical definition characterizes it as "the threat to use force in response as a way of preventing the first use of force by someone else."[1] Starting with a definition like that, most discussions of deterrence quickly get bound up with analyses of various military force levels and postures that make war more or less likely to be successful or profitable. Ideally, the argument characteristically runs, each side should have a secure second-strike capability: it should be able to absorb a surprise attack fully confident that it will be able to respond with an effective counterattack. Thus, each side, rationally fearing costly retaliatory consequences, can be expected to refrain from initiating war. Critics of the notion of deterrence argue that it is inadequate because it simply doesn't explain very well how states actually behave. Sometimes countries start wars even when they have little reason to believe they will be victorious; at other times they remain supremely cautious, refraining from war even though they feel threatened and even though they enjoy a substantial military advantage.[2] But instead of abandoning the notion of deterrence because of these important defects, it can easily be developed to deal with them.

Deterrence can be defined more generally as a state of being—the absence of war between two countries or alliances. If they are not at war, then it is reasonable to conclude that each is currently being deterred from attacking the other. We observe, for example, that the United States and the Soviet Union are not currently at war with each other, and we conclude that the United States is being deterred (by something or other) from attacking the Soviet Union and that the Soviet Union is similarly being deterred from attacking the United States. Then by the same reasoning we can also say that the United States is currently being deterred from attacking Canada, and that Canada is currently being deterred from attacking the United States. And finally, we can observe that Pakistan is currently being deterred from attacking Bolivia, just as Bolivia is similarly being deterred from attacking Pakistan.

This unconventional way of looking at deterrence immediately highlights an important central consideration, one that has attracted remarkably little attention. If countries are principally deterred by military considerations from attacking one another in our chaotic state of international "anarchy," as so many have suggested ("if you desire peace, prepare for war"), why are there so many cases where a militarily superior country lives contentedly alongside a militarily inferior one?* The United States obviously enjoys a massive military advantage over its northern neighbor and could attack with little concern about punishing military retaliation or about the possibility of losing the war. Clearly something is deterring the United States from attacking Canada (a country, as noted in chapter 1, with which the United States has been at war in the past and where, not too long ago, many war-eager Americans felt their "manifest destiny" lay), but obviously this spectacularly successful deterrent has little to do with the Canadians' military might. Similar cases can be found in the Soviet sphere. Despite an overwhelming military superiority, the USSR has been far from anxious to attack such troublesome neighbors as Poland and Rumania. To be complete, a concept of deterrence ought to be able to explain common instances like these, as well as those in which military elements are presumably dominant, such as the considerations that deter Syria from attacking Israel.[3] Indeed, it seems likely that the vast majority of wars that never happen, including most of those that haven't taken place in the developed world since 1945, are caused largely by factors that have little or nothing to do with military considerations.

The Components of the Deterrence Calculation.

In contemplating an attack, a would-be aggressor considers two central conditions and compares them: what its world will probably be like if it goes to war, and what that world will probably be like if it remains at peace. If after making this assessment it finds the war condition preferable to the status quo—that is, if it feels it can profit from war—it will go to war. If it finds the status quo preferable to war, it will remain at peace—that is, it will be deterred from starting a war. (It will be assumed that someone contemplating war does at least a modicum of rational thinking about it before making the plunge. As discussed in chapter 10, this assumption seems a reasonable one.)

A *policy* of deterrence involves a conscious effort by one country to manipulate

---

*For an essay stressing the "anarchy" of international politics where "statesmen are preoccupied with the use of force," where "pure coercion" tends to reign, where "trust is hard to come by," where "statesmen are shortsighted," where states "cannot afford to be moral," where "all states all of the time must make provision for their defense," and where "military power is necessary for survival," see Art and Waltz 1983, pp. 3–8. For the argument that in "anarchy" a "state of war" will exist not only if "all parties lust for power," but also "if all states seek only to ensure their own safety"; that "war is normal"; that "peace is fragile"; and that nuclear weapons are crucial and have been a "great force for peace," see Waltz 1988, pp. 620, 624.

another country's incentives so that the potential aggressor, in thinking things over, finds the virtues of peace to be, on balance, substantially greater than those of starting a war. But of course, two countries may very well be deterred from attacking each other even if neither has anything like a policy of deterrence toward the other. And, more importantly for present considerations, the absence of war—successful deterrence—does not necessarily prove that a *policy* of deterrence has been successful. The United states has a clear and costly policy in which it tries to deter the Soviet Union by threatening nuclear punishment for any major Soviet aggression. But the fact that the Soviet Union has not started a major war cannot necessarily be credited to American policy; indeed, as concluded in chapter 5, the USSR has had little interest in getting into any sort of war, no matter how the United States chooses to array its arsenal.

Peace is most secure when a potential aggressor finds the status quo to be substantially preferable to the value it places on victory. In other words, if the blessings of peace seem to be even greater than those of going to war and winning (much less losing), the potential aggressor will be deterred even if it has a high probability of winning. The persistent American unwillingness to attack Canada is surely principally explained by such reasoning. The United States finds the independent existence of its huge northern neighbor to be highly congenial. Although disagreement on various issues emerges from time to time, on the whole Canada contributes very significantly to the American sense of economic, political, and military well-being. To get invaded, Canada would probably have to do something that dramatically lowered the American pleasure with the status quo. Agreeing to become an outpost for Soviet missiles might do the trick.

A would-be aggressor's sense of the value of the status quo includes estimations of the future. A country may be basically content at present but, fearing a future attack by its opponents, may decide to preempt while in a position of comparative strength. The perceived value of the status quo also varies over time, and it is a quality that can be manipulated by a country trying to deter war. There was a conscious effort to deter by manipulating a would-be aggressor's estimate of the value of the status quo during the Cuban missile crisis. The United States loudly let it be known that its satisfaction with the status quo had just fallen precipitously: it had a severe grievance—the pending implantation of offensive nuclear arms by the Soviet Union in Cuba—and it was apparently prepared to go to war to rectify this grievance. It was deterred from carrying out its threat when the USSR agreed to improve the American evaluation of the status quo by removing the offending arms.

Except in the cases where a country goes to war for the sheer thrill of it, *all* wars can be prevented by raising the potential aggressor's estimation of the status quo. Pearl Harbor could have been prevented by letting the Japanese have Asia,

Hitler's aggression in all probability could have been deterred simply by giving him the territory he wanted, and Israel could send Syria into peaceful contentment by ceasing to exist. As these examples suggest, a policy of deterring war by raising a would-be aggressor's estimate of the status quo closely resembles what is commonly known as *appeasement,* a word that has picked up extremely negative connotations. More neutrally, it can also be called "deterrence by reward" or "positive deterrence."[4] But however labelled, the policy contains both dangers and appeals. Clearly, if the aggressor's price is higher than the deterrer is willing to pay, appeasement is simply not feasible. Furthermore, to apply the central lesson usually drawn from the Munich crisis of 1938, even if the price is bearable, serving the demands of an aggressor may be unwise and ultimately counterproductive because the aggressor's appetite may grow with the feeding, and thus it may be enticed to escalate its demands on the next round, ultimately demanding a price too high to pay. However, the discredit heaped upon appeasement as a result of its apparent misapplication in the 1930s doesn't mean that the policy is always invalid. Obviously, the policy worked in 1962: the Soviet withdrawal of offensive forces in Cuba satiated, not whetted, the American appetite for concession.

Against its estimates of the value of the status quo—the value it finds in remaining at peace—the potential aggressor balances its estimates of what war would most probably bring. Obviously, if it anticipates a severely punishing defeat in the war, it is likely to remain at peace. But it may also be deterred if it anticipates victory. This component of the calculation is rarely discussed, yet it is most important, and a close examination of it helps to explain why there is so much peace in so much of the world. For, simply put, many countries much of the time prefer the status quo to fighting a war and *winning* and thus are comfortably deterred no matter how big their military advantage. Spectacular cases in point, again, are the noninvasion by the United States of Canada, or by the USSR of Rumania or Poland: the big countries believe, probably quite accurately, that they would be *worse* off after the war even if (as seems highly likely) they were to win handily.

There are quite a few policies a country can adopt to deflate the value a would-be aggressor places on victory. It can make threats that either reduce the benefits the aggressor will gain upon victory or increase its costs for achieving victory. The deterrer could announce a scorched-earth policy in which it pledges to burn everything as it retreats, significantly lowering the potential aggressor's anticipated gains.[5] If an invader is interested in taking over a country because it seeks the productive capacity of the people of that country, it might be deterred if the people pledge not to work under its occupation.[6] Like all deterrent threats, policies of scorched earth, economy destruction, passive resistance, and the like will be effective only if the would-be aggressor believes they would be implemented. Because these threats involve a certain amount of self-destruction by the deterring country, there is an inherent problem with credibility. War is more likely to be deterred if high costs are a likely consequence of war itself rather than an imposition upon it. And this is more a matter of escalation than of technology. If a would-be aggressor anticipates that a war is likely to escalate until it becomes intolerably costly (in all, or virtually all cases, this would be well below the nuclear level), it will be deterred. As noted in part 2 and chapter 10, insofar as World War III has been prevented by military considerations, it is this fear that conflict will escalate that has been crucial.

Psychic costs, unlike most physical ones, suffer no problem of credibility; they are self-inflicted. If war is no longer held to be an honorable and invigorating test of manliness but is considered instead to be repulsive and uncivilized, one can only engage in it—win or lose—with a distinctly unpleasant sense of repugnance, and therefore at high cost.[7]

Stability.

This way of looking at deterrence can be used to distinguish between two kinds of stability: crisis stability and general stability. Discussions of deterrence and defense policy have been preoccupied with crisis stability, the notion that it is desirable for disputing countries to be so militarily secure that they could absorb a surprise attack and rebound from it with an effective counteroffensive. If each side were militarily confident in this way, then neither would see much advantage in launching a surprise attack, and thus neither would be tempted to start a war out of fear that the other could get a jump on it. Crises, therefore, would be "stable"—both sides would be able to assess events in a luxuriously slow manner and not feel compelled to act hastily and with incomplete information. In the nuclear period, discussions of crisis stability have centered around the technological and organizational problems of maintaining a secure second-strike capability—that is, developing a retaliatory force so well entrenched that a country can afford to wait out a surprise attack fully confident it will be able to respond with a devastating counterattack. Many have argued that crisis stability is "delicate"—easily upset by technological or economic shifts—and a great deal of thought has gone into assessing whether a given weapons systems or military strategy is "stabilizing" or "destabilizing."[8]

General stability is concerned with broader needs, desires, and concerns. It prevails when two countries, taking all the various costs, benefits, and risks into account, vastly prefer peace to war.[9] It's the sort of thing that prevails between the United States and Canada.

Efforts to improve one form of stability may weaken the other. For example, in an effort to enhance crisis stability a country may try to improve its second-strike capability by building up its military forces, but its opponent may find this provocative, concluding that the buildup is actually a prelude to an attack. On the other hand, generous appeasement concessions, designed to raise a potential aggressor's satisfaction with the status quo by reducing provocation and thus enhancing general stability, may tempt it to attack by giving it reason to believe it could win cheaply in a quick strike.

However, when general stability is high, crisis instability is of little immediate consequence. Thus, many concerns about changes in the arms balance, while valid in their own terms, miss the broader issue. An antimissile defense may increase or decrease crisis stability, but this may not alter the broader picture significantly. It would be like the case of a millionaire who loses or gains $1,000; he is now poorer or richer than before, but his overall status has not changed very much.

Parts 1 and 2 of this book have developed the conclusion that whatever may happen from time to time with crisis stability, general stability has come to prevail broadly in the developed world: the status quo has come to be very substantially preferred to war, even successful war. If that is true, the question of who could fight the most ingenious and effective war becomes irrelevant. Deterrence, and therefore peace, prevails.

The Persistence of War outside the Developed World

Peace, however, does not prevail in many areas outside the developed world, where scores of wars have taken place since 1945. By 1988 some 17 million people had died from these wars, more than perished in all of World War I.[10]

There are no guarantees, but if the recent absence of war in the developed world is truly the result of a long-term trend, rather than a momentary hiatus between conflagrations, war might eventually decline outside the developed world as it has within it.

The Contagion of War-Aversion.

It seems reasonable to consider the developed world as "advanced" in the sense that third world countries are more likely to try to emulate developed countries than vice versa. For example, South Korea over the last twenty years has come to resemble Canada more than Canada has come to resemble South Korea, and Ivory Coast has become more like France than France has become like Ivory Coast. If the developed countries are advanced in that sense, perhaps the rest of the world, as it pursues the luxury and lifestyle of the advanced world, will pick up the developed world's war aversion as well.

It might be fruitful in this regard to think of Japan as the avant garde of the third world. In 1853, Japan discovered that it was substantially less advanced than the West in military technology; it decided to catch up in that area, and did. Next it applied to enter the European Great Power club and went through the approved initiation ceremony in 1904 by defeating one of the weaker Great Powers, Russia, in war. Noticing then that virtually every other Great Power had colonies, it began in the 1930s when Europeans were beginning to tire of their holdings, to establish a vast empire in Asia—something it justified as its duty and natural destiny. Eventually it plunged headily and headlong into a cataclysmic world war and learned, twenty-five years after Europeans had gotten the message, that such wars are a really terrible idea. Since then it has become thoroughly caught up, to say the least, with the trendy notion that war is a bad idea while prosperity is a singularly good one. Whether third-world countries will follow Japan's example by avoiding war and questing after prosperity remains to be seen. Certainly, several Asian states—South Korea, Singapore, Taiwan—are very much on that wavelength (although another Korean war is far from inconceivable); and, as noted in chapter 10, Japan's example has become impressive throughout the world.

Actually, *third* world countries apparently *have* gotten the message. As noted at the outset (p. 3), there have been virtually no wars among the forty-four wealthiest countries—a total that includes quite a few countries outside the first and second worlds. War has taken place almost entirely within the *fourth* world. As countries raise their standard of living, perhaps they will find the prospect of war to be decreasingly attractive because they will have more to lose. The relationship may be a bit spurious, however, because peace has helped to bring relative prosperity to many of these countries, or, to put it another way, they have become relatively prosperous in considerable part *because* they have avoided war. Moreover, the countries that entered into World War I certainly had plenty to lose—and lose it they did. And some of the worst wars in the fourth world have taken place in some of its comparatively prosperous corners: Iran, Iraq, and Lebanon. Nevertheless, "it is not impossible," as Luard puts it carefully, "that prosperity itself has a civilizing influence which increases attachment to peace and inculcates a more widespread and deeply held revulsion from war."[11] A trend toward democracy (pp. 23–24) might also help.

In this regard, it is interesting to note that war outside the developed world has tended to take place among *new* states, not old ones. The oldest collection of less developed—less advanced—states is in Latin America. After freeing themselves from colonial overlordship—which, whatever its defects, did tend to keep local war under control—these countries engaged in a great deal of international warfare for much of the nineteenth century.[12] But eventually they mostly gave it up, or, as H. T. Buckle would have it, they became "civilized" in this respect. Dozens of boundary disputes persisted, but these were almost always settled by negotiation or arbitration. The absence of war is especially notable among the larger countries. Mexico, Brazil, Colombia, and Chile have avoided international war for over a century, and so has Argentina, except for the flareup over the Falklands in 1982. Although it has had boundary disputes with every one of its neighbors, Venezuela, perhaps not incidentally the wealthiest nation south of El Paso, has never gone to war in its entire history. There have been quite a number of civil wars in Latin America (and, of course, the incidence of its elegant equivalent, the coup d'etat, or *golpe de estado*, has been quite spectacular) but even that may be diminishing, especially outside Central America.[13] There may also be something of a wealth effect in this relationship, because Latin American countries are generally better off than their counterparts in Asia and Africa; but, again, cause and effect may be muddled.

Thus, there are resons to anticipate that war-aversion, so popular in the advanced world, will eventually catch on elsewhere. Indeed, that process may already be under way.

The two war analogies suggested in the Introduction may also be partially relevant. Dueling in the United States died out first in its more advanced sections—New England and the North—and then filtered to the less advanced areas, persisting longest in the South and in California.[14] And the intense moral revulsion against slavery and serfdom, together with the movement to abolish these institutions, caught on first in advanced Europe and then spread worldwide. Brazil eventually gave it up in 1888 through the force of embarrassment and ridicule, despite substantial economic costs. Members of the European-oriented Brazilian elite were humiliated because their country, the last bastion in Christendom to tolerate slavery, was constantly being belittled as uncivilized, and the government was "anxious to establish its prestige in Europe."[15] Insofar as slavery still lingers today, it exists only in corners of the world just about everyone would characterize as backward. Eventually war might become as rare and as anachronistic.

The Impact of the Decline of the Cold War.

Some dampening of war outside the developed world may come about if it indeed proves true that the Cold War is dissipating and that the Soviet Union, like China before it, has lost its ideological affection for wars of national liberation. This would also logically lead to a decreased interest by the United States in participating in rollback wars and in opposing wars fomented by Communist or leftist revolutionaries.

However, while this development might reduce the intensity and scope of some of these wars—there would be no more Vietnams or Afghanistans—it would not greatly affect their incidence. The USSR and the United States have only rarely initiated war—the Soviets in Korea, Hungary, and Czechoslovakia; the Americans in Grenada and indirectly in Guatemala in 1954 and at the Bay of Pigs in 1961. Instead, they have generally been drawn into wars that began indigenously.

In a post–Cold War era, it is even conceivable that the advanced countries could work together to officiate over, or to police, unruly situations and incipient or ongoing wars, a role planned for them in the United Nations charter. In 1987, Mikhail Gorbachev proposed as much. There are precedents: the United States and the USSR worked more or less in tandem to bring about an end to the India-Pakistan War of 1965. And major countries, acting on their own, have already done quite a bit of policing since World War II—although generally for self-interested rather than for universalistic reasons. American troop intervention in Lebanon in 1958, in the Dominican Republic in 1965, and in Grenada in 1983 restored order and political stability that in the latter two cases has probably contributed to the substantial long-term economic benefit of the countries policed. At least in their own view, the Soviets accomplished something similar in Hungary in 1956 and in Czechoslovakia in 1968. France has done considerable police work in its former African colonies—its intervention to stabilize the political situation in Gabon in 1964 helped to establish that country as the most prosperous in sub-Saharan Africa.[16]

However, while policing has worked in some cases to stem violence or mitigate its effects in the third world, in others the policing forces have simply become an additional target of the violence—as the United States and the French discovered when they tried to help contain the chaos in Lebanon in 1983. International forces are unlikely to expend much in police efforts unless they feel high stakes are involved (as the British apparently do in Northern Ireland). The remarkable unwillingness of any nation to intervene forcefully to stop the Khmer Rouge genocide in Cambodia testifies to that fact.

Declining Perceptions of the Efficacy and Romanticism of War and Revolution.

The problem in the third (or fourth) world is not that there are severe grievances over turf, nationalism, religion, ideology, and control of the state; grievances on these issues exist in the peaceful developed world as well. The problem is that a fair number of people outside the developed world still think that war and violence can improve the situation.

Moreover, concentrations of romanticism about the violence of war and revolution still linger. The Afghan mujahedeen consider that they are fighting a holy war, as do various groups opposing the state of Israel. This notion has received its most explicit sermonizing in Iran, where Ayatollah Ruhollah Khomeini has interpreted the Koran to encourage, and even to require, war and murder. On the birthday of the Prophet Mohammed in 1984 he declared:

> If one permits an infidel to continue in his role as a corrupter of the earth, his moral suffering will be all the worse. If one kills the infidel and thus stops him from perpetrating his misdeeds, his death will be a blessing to him. For if he remains alive, he will become more and more corrupt. . . . War is a blessing for the world and for all nations. It is God who incites men to fight and to kill. . . . A prophet is all-powerful. Through war he purifies the earth. The mullahs with corrupt hearts who say that all this is contrary to the teachings of the Koran are unworthy of Islam.

Khomeini has even echoed the Spanish religious fanatic who had proclaimed in the 1590s that there was no reason to abandon "God's cause" merely "on grounds of impossibility": regarding Iran's conflict with Iraq, Khomeini announced, "Even our total defeat in this war shall be a blessing from the Almighty and a sign of His Wisdom which we cannot fully understand."[17]

In 1985, Khomeini told a group of radical Moslem leaders that "there are ills that cannot be cured except through burning. The corrupt in every society should be liquidated."[18] Revolutionary Marxists have often come to similar conclusions about people they consider corrupt. Moscow and Beijing have ceased to be spiritual leaders of the movement, having abandoned much of their revolutionary ardor and messianism, but some groups around the world still buy that revolutionary line—in Peru, for example, and in the Philippines.

Indeed, romanticism about revolutionary violence, if not about old-fashioned global war, still lingers even in the developed world and was quite fashionable only a decade or two ago. It motivated various terrorists like the Symbionese Liberation Army in the United States, the Red Brigade in Italy, the Baader-Meinhof gang in Germany, and the Red Army in Japan, and occasionally it flutters into view in the writings of revered leftist writers. Concluding her best-selling and multiple-award-winning 1972 book about Vietnam, *Fire in the Lake*, Frances Fitzgerald looked forward to the day in Vietnam "when 'individualism' and its attendant corruption gives way to the revolutionary community." Then, she enthused, "the narrow flame of revolution" would "cleanse the lake of Vietnamese society from the corruption and disorder of the American war." Cleansing revolution, she proclaimed, was "the only way the Vietnamese of the south can restore their country and their history to themselves."[19]

For war to subside in the fourth world it will be necessary both for such romanticism about war and revolution to die out or at least decline, and for the seeming efficacy of violence to wane. Before 1914, as observed in chapter 2, many Western intellectuals hoped that the violence of war would cleanse and redeem the world of its corruption; in fact, World War I principally cleansed the developed world of the notion that war could be cleansing. Perhaps disillusionment with the cruel, corrupt, and stupendously incompetent postrevolutionary regimes in Vietnam and elsewhere will have a similar impact on revolutionary romantics both within the developed world and outside it.

Moreover, there does seem to be a rising yearning for economic growth and progress and a dawning appreciation for the terrible economic consequences of war. Thus, warfare in Central America since 1979 has brought about declining real per capita income—in both warring *and* nonwarring countries—for the first time since the Great Depression.[20] There are countries in the third and fourth worlds that have never experienced either domestic or international war and have had a high degree of internal political stability—countries like Gabon and Ivory Coast in Africa, or Singapore and Taiwan in Asia. If they, and their relative prosperity, become the model for emulation, war will decline. Certainly, few seem anxious to imitate the fearful mess successful revolutionaries have created in places like Angola, Ethiopia, Iran, Vietnam, and Nicaragua.

However, should the sort of revolution Khomeini leads Iran become endemic, the prospects for war will rise. Not only does he idealize—even sanctify—war and martyrdom, but he specifically rejects the quest for prosperity. Like many war enthusiasts before 1914, he is appalled by "materialism" and by the "greed, prostitution and satanic corruption" that he believes accompany it.[21] On the other hand, Khomeini's reluctant willingness in 1988 to seek an end to the Iran-Iraq war suggests that reality can make inroads even on his consciousness.

The Decline of Conventional War.

Whatever happens with the spirit of revolution, including reactionary revolution in the third and fourth worlds, there may be a decline in the attractiveness of conventional, old-fashioned, set-piece wars where countries send organized armies to battle it out with each other. Israel fought several wars of that sort with its neighbors until 1973, but there have been none since (although there has been a great deal of costly violence in the Middle East anyway). India and Pakistan have fought it out several times, but not since 1971.

It is possible, but only possible, that the terrible Iran-Iraq Idiot War will help to discredit that kind of war further. The war can demonstrate that an application of conventional force to obtain limited ends can dangerously degenerate into a long, costly war of attrition—a lesson well-comprehended in the developed world. Perhaps intrigued by the brevity and decisiveness of the conventional wars between Israel and the Arab states and between India and Pakistan, Iraq started the war against its weakened enemy while laboring under a 1914-style illusion that the war would be a short, successful blitzkrieg. Similar plans for quick, decisive wars went awry in Israel's invasion of Lebanon in 1982, in Vietnam's invasion of Cambodia in 1978, and perhaps in Libya's various ventures into Chad.

The Iran-Iraq War could be used to illustrate the fact that third- and fourth-world countries are now capable of waging long, massively destructive total wars with each other just like Europeans. As development proceeds, more and more countries are going to have that capability. Perhaps they will use it, or perhaps they will learn from the advanced world and decide to skip over that stage of, well, development.

The Impact, If Any, of the Proliferation of Nuclear Weapons.

The consequence of the possible proliferation of nuclear weapons in the third and fourth worlds is not clear. Had Iran possessed a few, it seems unlikely that Iraq would have invaded in 1980, and thus a costly war would have been prevented. On the other hand, the idea that someone like Khomeini might yearn to use the weapon to clean out a hotbed of infidels, and thus bestow a blessing upon them, is a bit unsettling. On the third hand, if the infidels had a retaliatory nuclear capability, even Khomeini might come to prefer milder, less apocalyptic methods.

Nuclear weapons are irrelevant, however, to most of the wars that persist in the third and fourth worlds. Israel's atomic arsenal, if any, is useless against Palestinian uprising and threatening Lebanese chaos; Tibetans seeking independence are not dissuaded by China's big bombs; Afghan rebels have not feared the Soviet nuclear arsenal. And we all remember the Vietcong. Nuclear weapons may have some relevance to the large, set-piece conflict between organized countries—but that kind of war, as noted, is already quite rare.

CONCLUSIONS

Arms Reduction in a World without War

If war is truly in decline in the developed world, it is reasonable to anticipate that there will be downward pressure on arms budgets. The weapons pointed across the Iron Curtain are there to deter war. Given the intense ideological hostility that has characterized the Cold War, concern about direct aggression and war has not been unreasonable, although as part 2 has argued, this concern has probably been substantially overwrought. If, however, the Soviet Union has now abandoned its essentially expansionary ideology and has become a country with an overriding passion for a calm, normal, peaceful, and businesslike international atmosphere, not only would the Cold War become irrelevant, but so would many of the expensive armaments that have become part of it. Thus, arms reduction could be impelled by embarrassment at spending so much money on antiquated and useless relics of a primitive past.

The probability of a major war between the United States and the Soviet Union will never disappear totally, and the potential consequences of such a conflict will always be colossal. But if the probability of catastrophe becomes low enough, it begins to make sense to relax one's concern—and one's guard—over it. A nuclear war between Britain and France, or between either (or both) and the United States, would be far more horrible than any war those countries have ever experienced before. Yet none of those once hostile countries is terribly concerned about it, and if the only worry they had in the international arena was each other, each would no doubt have fewer troops and weapons.

If the probability of war between the United States and the Soviet Union begins to subside to that level—or even to that of a war between the United States and China—a certain degree of arms relaxation would be entirely reasonable.* Total disarmament would hardly be in the offing, of course. The possible reemergence of a dangerous hostility would have to be guarded against, and just to keep abreast of things and to avoid severely unpleasant surprises, both sides would presumably want to maintain active research and development programs. Moreover, there are other concerns that might require military preparedness. The United States would certainly want to retain some military options in the Middle

---

*Contrary to some thinking, the cumulative long-range probabilities are not necessarily in favor of war. If the probability of war in a given year is 1 in 100 (a very high estimate), there would be a fifty-fifty chance war would occur within sixty-nine years. If, however, the probability declines by 20 percent each year, the probability of war over an eternity is less than 5 percent. See Brams and Kilgour 1988, pp. 169–71.

East, the Persian Gulf, Latin America, and elsewhere; and the Soviet Union faces hostility along its border—from Iran, from China, and potentially from a unified religious Afghanistan—and it may also feel it needs troops to keep its factionalized empire intact. Furthermore, neither side would be at all pleased if an arms reduction somehow triggered insecurities that led to the emergence of a vengeful, rearmed Germany or Japan. And both sides would no doubt want to keep some arms around to aid in their quest after "influence" around the globe, because that is apparently part of what they consider their role to be.

It is not clear, however, that these needs call for ships in the hundreds, for thermonuclear weapons in the tens of thousands, or for standing armies in the millions. And neither side is likely to have difficulty envisioning other ways to spend its money. The United States has built up a burdensome deficit, and many are arguing that its overemphasis on arms expenditures has kept it from being able to compete with the crafty Japanese, who, like the Soviets at the end of the 1950s, are increasingly portrayed as being ten feet tall and almost ready to take over the country—not by stealth and subversion like the Soviets, but by purchase. The pressures on the Soviet budget, massively bloated by defense expenditures, are even more severe.*

According to an end-of-column squib in *The New Yorker,* the *Wooster Daily Record* (Ohio) once carried an account in which someone was reported to have argued that "the United States cannot expect a fair agreement on arms limitation with Russia until it achieves military parody." If the threat of major war and localized conflict continues to wane, the weapons designed to deter and wage war will increasingly seem pointless, useless, and wasteful, and the Wooster requirement will have been fulfilled: Mutual and balanced military parody will have been achieved.

However, while the weapons that have been built up during the Cold War may seem increasingly burdensome and parodic, and while there are strong reasons for wanting to reduce the burden and divert the hilarity, the mechanism for doing so may be difficult to engineer. Difficulties will be enhanced if both sides continue to assume that arms reductions must be accomplished through explicit mutual agreement. Arms agreements don't have an impressive history of reducing overall defense spending—reductions in one defense area are characteristically compensated for by increases in another. Moreover, they tend to take forever to consummate: the nonproliferation treaty of 1968, a very mild measure that was clearly in everyone's interest, was argued for five years. Indeed, the existence of arms

---

*Reduced concerns about attack should also lead to enhanced efforts to prevent nuclear weapons accidents. The chief—indeed the only valid—argument against such measures is that they may reduce one's ability to retaliate in the event of war. If tensions decline and war becomes even less probable, accident-prevention measures should become ever more attractive and sensible.

control talks often hampers arms reduction. In 1973, for example, a proposal for a unilateral reduction of U.S. troops in Western Europe failed in Congress because it was felt that this would undercut upcoming arms control negotiations—which have been running on unproductively ever since.[22] Similarly, opponents of the MX missile and of Ronald Reagan's Strategic Defense Initiative have failed in Congress in part because some of those who consider the weapons systems dangerous or valueless nevertheless support them since the weapons appear to be useful as bargaining chips in arms control talks.

If arms are reduced by agreement, both sides are going to strain to make sure that all dangers and contingencies are covered; and they will naturally try, if at all possible, to come out with the better deal. Reduction is certainly possible under those circumstances, but it is likely to be halting, slow, and inflexible. Arms control is essentially a form of centralized regulation, and it carries with it the usual defects of that approach—participants are restricted in their ability to adjust subtly to unanticipated changes, and they are often encouraged, perversely, to follow developments that are unwise. For example, the Strategic Arms agreement of 1972 limited the number of missiles each side could have, but it allowed them to embroider their missiles with multiple warheads and to improve missile accuracy, thereby encouraging them to develop a potentially dangerous first-strike capability (see p. 202).

There is an alternative: just *do* it. The arms buildup, after all, was not accomplished through written agreement; instead, there was a sort of free market in which each side, keeping a wary eye on the other, sought security by purchasing varying amounts of weapons and troops. As requirements and perspectives changed, so did the force structure of each side.

If arms can be built up that way, they can be reduced in the same manner. It would be a sort of negative arms race, and there are historical precedents. A pertinent one was discussed in chapter 1 (pp. 21–23). A half century of cold war followed the hot war between the United States and British Canada that ended in 1814. But finally, more out of economic and psychic exhaustion than anything else, both sides began to let their arms preparations lapse, even though a degree of wariness lingered. "Disarmament became a reality," observes a Canadian student of the era, "not by international agreement, but simply because there was no longer any serious international disagreement."[23]

If the Cold War and the ideological contest have now truly been dampened, a similar arms reduction could come about between West and East. The Soviet Union is under especially severe economic pressure to reduce its arms expenditures. If it does so (or even if it doesn't), there will be substantial pressure on Western governments to reduce as well. Both sides are likely to reduce cautiously, particularly at first out of the sensible—if perhaps overly sensitive—

concern that a severe arms imbalance could inspire the other to contemplate blackmail. But a negative arms race would have been set in motion. The earth is unlikely to be ever completely cleansed of weapons, or of nuclear arms, by this process (or by any other); but the arms race, such as it now stands, will have been reversed.

Since it appears that nuclear weapons have made little difference in the course of history, reducing their number probably won't either. But everyone might at least save a bit of money—even more so if reductions are carried over to conventional arms, which account for most of the military budgets anyway.[24] Such reduction seems most likely to come about not principally by conscious, exquisite design, but by atrophy stemming from a dawning realization that, since preparations for major war are essentially irrelevant, they are profoundly foolish.

Resolving Europe

The Cold War was triggered by disagreement over the fate of Central and Eastern Europe, and that problem remains the chief unresolved issue between East and West. If the Cold War is indeed over, and if the chances of war—particularly major international war—in Europe are diminishing, the possibility of a settlement of the division there becomes real.

As discussed in chapters 5 and 6, NATO was constructed on the assumption that the Soviet Union might be enticed into committing Hitler-style piecemeal aggression unless the tempting morsels of Western Europe clung together with the United States to form an indigestible lump. But by the 1980s few Europeans were still harboring fears of a Soviet attack. In 1984, NATO commander Bernard Rogers observed in some exasperation that "the biggest challenge we face in NATO is getting the message across to our people that there is a threat to their freedom down the road." By 1988, NATO chief Lord Carrington was calmly observing, "I don't think there is a threat in the sense that we're going to get an invasion by the Soviet Union, but . . . the military potential is still there and we have to be prudent."[25]

This attitude in Europe and elsewhere is conditioned in part by the perception that the Soviet Union clearly has its hands so full with its underproductive empire in Eastern Europe and with its domestic difficulties that it hardly needs more territory to control. When concern about war escalated in the early 1980s, the fear in Europe was that Ronald Reagan would start a war, not the Soviets—this despite a fair amount of Soviet rocket rattling in their self-interested "peace offensive" of the period.

There are signs that the Soviet Union could in time tire of its East European empire. Troubles in Poland seem perennial, and conditions in most of the other colonies there aren't much better. By the 1980s, the empire had become not only a headache but probably an economic drain as well. Moreover, its military value as launching pad or as buffer zone had become decreasingly obvious in an age of long-range weapons and of renewed detente. The Soviet defector Arkady Shevchenko had the impression that even Andrei Gromyko, the Soviets' perennial foreign minister in the postwar decades, viewed the East European possessions as a burden and a nuisance.[26] And after Afghanistan the Soviets may have little stomach for maintaining control through military invasion as they did (reluctantly, even then) in Hungary in 1956 and in Czechoslovakia in 1968.

Relieving the Soviets of their anachronistic albatross is not likely to be easy, however. The logical approach would be to fabricate a continental settlement in which both military alliances would be finessed out of effective existence. If war is indeed becoming obsolete in the area, such a solution is perfectly sensible. There would be competitors—rivals in the race for prosperity—but no enemies.

There are quite a few problems, however, not the least of which is the tradition, running back a few millennia now, of warfare, hostility, and suspicion in the area. Although experience leads one to believe that Switzerland will not soon start a war, the same confidence does not surround a prospective independent Germany or Germanies, whether initially armed or not. Thus, there exists a quite understandable if-it-ain't-broke-don't-fix-it syndrome. In Eastern Europe, however, things *are* broke. Discontent and demoralization are widespread, and revolt— even anachronistic armed revolt—is possible. The Soviet Union let Yugoslavia flee the nest, albeit unwillingly, and might in time see wisdom in ceasing to remain the last colonial overlord in the developed world. For a real solution, however, the Soviets would have to be convinced that the Germans would not rise again even in the long term. If the thesis propounded here about the obsolescence of war is correct, the Soviets have little to worry about. That they might have some difficulty swallowing this idea is, however, understandable.

Another problem is that an abandonment of the alliances would leave the Soviet Union as the dominant military entity in the area, even if there were significant arms reductions. The Soviets may now have come to see that their disruptive control over Western Europe would be as harmful to their long-term interests as has been their inept colonizing of East Europe, but there is no guarantee that this point of view is permanent. Clearly, an attractive plan for a lasting resolution of the European situation should guard against the possibility of Soviet domination.

An economic blending of West and East could be part of a solution, but mutual economic dependency has been no guarantee against war in the past; political and military dependency is also necessary. A possibility might be to work to combine the two alliances rather than to abandon them.

It is true that the whole point of the alliances is to oppose each other militarily and that the essential mission of each is to defend against an attack by the other. But it really does seem that such an attack is wildly, almost ludicrously, improbable, and the chief reason the alliances continue to exist is not because they prevent war, but because they exist. Perhaps it is finally time, in Europe at least, to take peace seriously.

The goal would be to create a situation in which every country in the area feels it has some control over the military destiny in the area of every other country and, specifically, one in which both the United States and the Soviet Union maintain control over the military potential of both Germanies. Under that circumstance a relaxation of the Soviet grip on its useless and costly empire in East Europe would be entirely feasible as would an eventual confederation of the two Germanies. Without such a resolution to the German problem the Soviets are likely to want to hang in there, no matter how high the cost, and their colonies will be able to pry themselves free only by causing dangerous unease in Moscow.

Of course if military plans and forces do eventually become intermeshed, strategists might begin to have difficulty figuring out where to point their weapons. Perhaps Switzerland could be a handy target, at least for the purposes of calibration; and a condition where thousands of nuclear weapons and millions of troops are directed at a country that has avoided all warfare since 1798 might serve to highlight the essential absurdity of the military enterprise and to impel a momentum toward judicious, embarrassed, and overdue arms reduction in Europe.

A confederated alliance structure would facilitate further peaceful blending in what has historically been the world's most warlike continent. War would not become impossible in the area, but a confederated alliance would probably be able to help keep conflicts contained, and it could prevent any single member or cluster from possessing undue influence based on military (as opposed to economic, diplomatic, or political) clout. Thus some of the continent's major problems would be resolved and the prospects for major war would be further reduced.

CONCLUSIONS

The Correlates of Peace

Many peace advocates have argued that the problem of war derives from national-ism, the nation-state, or the nation-state system. It has been a central argument of this book that countries have gone to war not because they exist or because of the way they are arrayed, or because of their armaments, but because they have seen appeal in war and advantage in victory: war chiefly arises from the war system itself. Nationalism still persists in the developed world, and there remain major unresolved national issues—such as the division of Germany—that have led to wars in the past. Moreover, the international system, hinged around two colos-sally armed "superpowers"—bipolarity, it's called—remains intact, and we seem no closer than ever to fabricating an effective supernational authority that will bring nations under firm control and benevolent regulation.

The long peace that has enfolded the developed world for so long has been the culminating result of a historic process in which the institution of war has gradually been rejected because of its perceived repulsiveness and futility. In the developed world few, if any, are able to discern either appeal or advantage in war any more; and they have come to value a goal—prosperity—that has long been regarded as incompatible with war. And, as the histories of countries like Holland, Sweden, Switzerland, and Denmark show, once a country drops out of the war system, it can manage for centuries to contain any enthusiasm for reentry.

Thus peace has not come about because the nation-state has begun to wither. However, peace, together with the free-wheeling international economy it has fostered, logically carries with it the potential for the decline, if not the utter demise, of the nation-state: the absence of war and of warlike threat gives national governments much less to do and helps to undermine their reason for existence.[27] But if the history of recent centuries suggests that major war is obsolescent, it suggests at least as strongly that even if governments no longer have wars to fight, worry about, and prepare for, they are likely always to manage to find something to keep them busy—a conclusion some will find deeply (if perhaps refreshingly) pessimistic.

This book began by stressing that in an important sense war is often taken too seriously. War is neither a requirement of human nature nor a cosmic inevitabil-ity; like slavery or dueling, it is merely a social institution, one people can live quite well without. In standard rhetoric there has also been a tendency to take peace too seriously: it is constantly being associated with such misty commodities as harmony, good will, cooperation, love, brotherhood, and justice. To achieve some of those virtues on a truly broad scale would require a change in human nature. Peace, however, can be achieved without such a transformation.

For peace is not some sort of dreamy utopia or fancy condition of perpetual bliss. It is merely what comes about when nations and peoples neglect the institution of war. While peace may sometimes facilitate cooperation and good will, it should not be confused with them. To do so, in fact, can make peace seem hopelessly difficult to achieve: if perfect harmony and justice are necessary for peace, it will never come about.

But peace is neither the necessary cause nor consequence of harmony. There is no reason to believe that the elimination of dueling caused men of the dueling set to become less volatile, self-centered, arrogant, or impetuous. Indeed, by removing a potential punishment for insult and offensive behavior, the demise of dueling may have allowed these natural qualities freer play and to that degree reduced civility and social harmony. And if war becomes as obsolete as dueling there is no reason to believe that national leaders will as a consequence become any less quarrelsome, xenophobic, short-sighted, or willful. They just won't lead their countries into war. Peace can actually decrease apparent international harmony: the recent indecorous behavior of oil-producing countries against the interests of the well-armed West and of East Europeans against the wishes of their well-armed Soviet neighbor has been facilitated by a decline in the fear that big countries will use war to correct antics they find uncivil.

Contentiousness and turmoil would remain in a world without war. Although it would be a better place by the standards of most people, by the standards of none would it be a perfect one.

And perhaps that's just as well. Perfection might be a terminal burden:

HAMLET: What news?
ROSENCRANTZ: None, my lord, but that the world's grown honest.
HAMLET: Then is doomsday near . . .

APPENDIX

War, Death,
and the Automobile

THIS BOOK has dealt with calculations about war. But war is only one social policy in which the loss of human life is an important element, and it may be useful to put decision making about war into a somewhat broader context by comparing it to policy about another instrument of mass destruction.

Suppose an engineering firm came up tomorrow with an amazing new form of transportation. People would step inside a booth, dial a location, and then be taken apart atom by atom and transmitted over wires to the desired location where they would be reassembled. After thoroughly testing the new device for safety, the firm has concluded that the overwhelming majority of trips would be utterly without incident—one could easily emerge from a lifetime of use without a scratch. Unfortunately, in a very tiny percentage of trips, things would go wrong and the traveler would never rematerialize. Injuries, from minor contusions to paralysis, would also occasionally occur. The total: probably not much more per year than 50,000 deaths and 2 million or so disabling injuries—concentrated, for some odd reason, not among the weak and infirm, but among healthy young adults. There would also be considerable death and illness because of atmospheric pollution. Should we install a system with costs like that?

We have, of course. It's known as the private passenger automobile. We often say that there is nothing more important than the value of human life—indeed, a code of ethics for engineers requires them to hold the safety of the public *paramount*. Yet, obviously, we don't really believe this; getting around in cars is far more important than human life: as a society we willingly sacrifice 50,000 lives per year for the privilege.

It is, of course, quite possible to move people without killing them. Engineers have also invented devices for doing that. Large commercial airlines have gone entire years without fatalities; passengers killed on railroads in a year can often be numbered on the fingers of one hand; the New York subway system, regularly maligned for filth, inefficiency, noise, and other indignities, moves millions of people every day and sometimes goes *decades* without a fatality.[1]

War, an important rival to the automobile as an invented means for slaughter, in some respects is surrounded by less hypocrisy. People who plan and conduct wars know lives will be lost, and they often forthrightly, if grimly, build these considerations into their calculations: they estimate how many casualities it will take to capture an objective and consider whether the objective is worth it. The automobile, by contrast, is far less frequently put in that framework; the obvious is too rarely asked: Is having the automobile worth the cost?

It may seem strange to put war and the automobile in the same class, but the moral distinction between them may not be as great as it seems.

For example, war might seem to be worse because the probability of being killed in a war is higher than the probability of being killed in a car crash. This distinction is not terribly useful, because it is quite possible to have wars in which the chance of being killed is very low. Indeed, the probabilities are often within hailing distance: by one calculation, driving a car and being in the army in Vietnam reduced an American's life expectancy on the same order of magnitude. (Actually, in big wars there may be an eerie relation between the two phenomena: World War II probably "saved" over 50,000 American lives because the rationing of gasoline and the drafting of so many dangerous drivers led to a reduction in traffic casualities to levels significantly below pre- and postwar ones.)[2]

Another popular distinction between war and the automobile stresses that the automobile system is voluntary—no one is forced to drive around in a car whereas wars rely on conscription. But many armies (the British in most of World War I, for example) rely entirely on volunteers, and some 15 to 20 percent of those killed in traffic accidents are pedestrians, and it is scarcely realistic to suggest that anyone has a choice about whether to be a pedestrian.

War is most often seen to be morally inferior to other forms of destruction because death is part of its very *intent*. By contrast, no one intends anyone to be killed by automobiles. The distinction is an important one, and it accounts, along with the low probability of injury in a single trip, for the benign acceptance of the automobile system. But suppose there existed two ways to spend $10 billion: one would prevent a war that would kill 1,000 people (by intent); the other would prevent 20,000 accidental deaths. Would it be sensible to prefer the former?

Furthermore, it is a bit disingenuous to suggest that the death and injury automobiles cause are entirely unintentional. Unlike most deaths from cancer and heart disease, they happen because, as a society, we have systematically chosen to encourage the automobile over less dangerous means of transportation. A reduction of the speed limit for private passenger automobiles to ten miles per hour in the United states would, if enforced, save half a million lives by the end of the century; to oppose such a law is to pay this price willingly to get there faster by automobile. But if we are willing to pay this cost, we should also explicitly acknowledge it. Although the engineers' code requires them to hold the safety of the public paramount, neither they nor the country's leaders really believe this; getting around in cars is obviously far more important than human life.

The purpose here, of course, is not to argue that wars are good and automobiles bad, but to suggest that both should be subjected to the same kind of cost–benefit analysis. We might well conclude that few wars have been worth their cost, even as we view 50,000 lives and 2 million disabling injuries per year (plus pollution) as a small price to pay for the blessings of the automobile—the pleasure, the convenience, the personal mobility, the economic benefit, the aesthetic charm, the macho gratification.

Many other social policies involve the same sort of consideration. To take an extreme example: every year a few thousand people die in falls from buildings that are more than one story high. Those lives could be saved by closing off all buildings at the second floor. To reject such a policy is to say tall buildings are worth that cost in lives. As a society, we regularly and inescapably adopt policies in which human lives are part of the price, yet we often casually and opaquely gloss over the issue of the full costs.

NOTES

Introduction: History's Greatest Nonevent

1. Gaddis 1987b. The calculations about eras of peace are by Paul Schroeder (1985, p. 88). The previous record, he notes, was chalked up during the period from the end of the Napoleonic Wars in 1815 to the effective beginning of the Crimean War in 1854. The period between the conclusion of the Franco-Prussian War in 1871 and the outbreak of World War I in 1914—marred by a major war in Asia between Russia and Japan in 1904—was an even longer era of peace among major European countries. That record was broken on November 8, 1988. On some of these issues, see also Nye 1987; Hinsley 1963, ch. 17; Luard 1986, pp. 395–99; Russett and Starr 1981, ch. 15.

2. Said Herman Kahn in 1960: "I have a firm belief that unless we have more serious and sober thought on various aspects of the strategic problem . . . we are not going to reach the year 2000—and maybe not even the year 1965—without a cataclysm" (1960, p. x). Hans J. Morgenthau stated in 1979: "In my opinion the world is moving ineluctably towards a third world war—a strategic nuclear war. I do not believe that anything can be done to prevent it. The international system is too unstable to survive for long" (quoted, Boyle 1985, p. 73). And astronomer Carl Sagan commented in 1983: "I do not think our luck can hold out forever" (quoted, Schroeder 1985, p. 87). On the history of the doomsday clock, see Feld 1978.

3. Churchill: Bartlett 1977, p. 104. Edward Luttwak says, "We have lived since 1945 without another world war precisely because rational minds . . . extracted a durable peace from the very terror of nuclear weapons" (1983b, p. 82). Kenneth Waltz: "Nuclear weapons have banished war from the center of international politics" (1988, p. 627). See also Knorr 1985, p. 79; Mearsheimer 1984/85, pp. 25–26; Art and Waltz 1983, p. 28; Gilpin 1981, pp. 213–19; Betts 1987, pp. 1–2; Joffe 1987, p. 37; F. Lewis 1987.

4. Schell 1982, p. 231. For a discussion of expert opinion concluding that the chances of nuclear war by the year 2000 were at least fifty-fifty, see Russett 1983, pp. 3–4.

5. Wealth is calculated using 1978 data when Iran and Iraq were at their financial peak (World Bank 1980). If later data are used, the figure of forty-four would be greater. Countries like Monaco that have no independent foreign policy are not included in the count. The Soviet invasion of Hungary was in some sense requested by ruling politicians in Hungary and for that reason is sometimes not classified as an international war. On classification issues, see Small and Singer 1982, pp. 55, 305; Luard 1986, pp. 5–7. Small and Singer consider Saudi Arabia to have been a participant in the Yom Kippur War of 1973 because it committed 1,000 troops to the anti-Israeli conflict (p. 306); if one accepts their procedure here, that war would form another example of war among the top forty-four. Some might also include the bloodless "war" between the USSR and Czechoslovakia in 1968.

6. Even as dedicated a foe of the Soviet regime as Aleksandr Solzhenitsyn has said, "I have never advocated physical general revolution. That would entail such destruction of our people's life as would not merit the victory obtained" (quoted, S. Cohen 1985, p. 214).

7. Blainey 1973, p. 3.

8. Thucydides 1934, p. 337.

9. Wedgwood 1938, p. 516. German civilian and military deaths have been estimated at 3,160,000 in World War I and 6,221,000 in World War II (Sivard 1987, p. 29). For the latter-day argument that the losses in the Thirty Years War have been grossly overestimated, see Steinberg 1966, ch. 3. A recent estimate suggests a population decline from 20 million to 16 or 17 million (Parker 1984, p. 211).

10. Luard 1986, p. 51. Small and Singer 1982, pp. 82–99. About 180,000 of the half-million were soldiers (Kennedy 1987, p. 115), giving a battle death rate of about 4 percent.

11. Thirty Years War: Robb 1962. Seven Years War: Kennedy 1987, p. 114; Brodie 1973, pp. 248–49. Milward 1977, p. 3.

12. For other observations of the analogy between war and dueling, see Brodie 1973, p. 275; Angell 1914, pp. 202–3; Gooch 1911, p. 249; Cairnes 1865, p. 650n.

13. Seitz 1929, pp. 98–101; Freeman 1884, pp. 345–48.

14. Stevens 1940, pp. 280–83. See also Cochran 1963, p. 287.

15. Baldick 1965, p. 199.

16. Stowe 1987, p. 15.

17. Clausewitz 1976, p. 75.

18. See Patterson 1982; Engerman 1986, pp. 318–19.

19. Smith 1976, p. 387 (book 3, ch. 2). Engerman 1986, pp. 322–33, 339. Drescher 1987, p. 4; see also Eltis 1987.

Chapter 1   The Rise of Peace Advocacy Before World War I

1. Luard 1986, pp. 330–31, 354, 349, 361, 366–67. See also Schumpeter 1951, pp. 70–71.

2. For a useful discussion, see Levy 1983, ch. 2.

3. Tolstoy 1966, p. 1145. Waltz 1979, p. 72.

4. Morgenthau 1948, p. 21.

5. Roberts 1967, p. 233; see also Lundkvist 1973, pp. 56–57.

6. Lynn Montross, quoted in Levy 1983, p. 45

7. Kennedy 1987, p. 99.

8. See also Blainey 1973, pp. 5–9; Levy and Morgan 1986.

9. A valuable overview of the history of American-Canadian relations is Stacey 1953. See also Winks 1960; Dyson 1979, pp. 152–53.

10. Blainey 1973, p. 106.

11. However, in Canada ritualistic military concerns about an American invasion were still being voiced as late as 1920; see Dyson 1979, p. 153. On groundless American rumors of plans for such an invasion in 1895, see Tuchman 1966, p. 137.

12. Stacey 1953, pp. 13–14.

13. Doyle 1983, 1987. See also Russett and Starr 1981, pp. 439–41; Quester 1982, pp. 253–54; Rummel 1983; and Weede 1984. Doyle (1987, p. 1166n) notes that the earliest observation of this phenomenon in modern writing was by Clarence Streit, who brought it up in a 1939 book advocating a federal union of the fifteen leading democracies.

14. Doyle 1983, pp. 209, 212n, 216, 216n. Streit suggests that the 1830 war in which Belgium seceded from the Netherlands might be an exception (1939, p. 91).

15. As Doyle points out, this is not simply because liberal states are alike. Wars have broken out among fascist states, Communist states, authoritarian states, totalitarian states, and states that are pluralist but not fully liberal (1983, p. 222).

16. Doyle 1983, p. 213.

17. Derived from Doyle 1987, p. 1164. At that rate, extrapolates Doyle, "global peace should be anticipated, at the earliest, in 2113" (1983, p. 352).

18. Brodie argues, however, that it might be "more realistic" to call the play "a dramatic commentary on the limitless penalties of defeat" (1973, p. 232).

19. Howard 1978, p. 13. See also Brodie 1973, pp. 232–33.

20. On these issues, see Brodie 1973, pp. 230–52; Howard 1978, ch. 1; Adams 1962.

21. On Quaker success in business, see Nevaskar 1971. On Quaker values, see Barbour and Roberts 1973, pp. 13–46; Hirst 1923; Russell 1942.

22. For a history of the movement, see Beales 1931; Nurnberger 1987; Chickering 1975, ch. 1; Howard 1978, ch. 2.

23. Buckle 1862, pp. 137–40. Emerson 1904, p. 161; emphasis in the original.

24. In an article on international law published in November 1865 on the heels of several wars, John Elliot Cairnes concluded that "all the leading currents of modern civilization are setting steadily and rapidly towards the formation of a body of international opinion which . . . may

ultimately, and at no remote date, become an effective check on the conduct of nations" (p. 649).

25. Suttner 1914, p. 435. Tolstoy: Lengyel 1975, p. 80. "greatest": Beales 1931, p. 201. Buckle's influence: Suttner 1910, p. 249. The book's impact: Chickering 1975, p. 12. Unusual in treating war realistically: Clarke 1966, pp. 131–32. Suttner's fame: Chickering 1975, p. 79; Lengyel 1975, p. 81.

26. Gooch 1911, pp. 248–49. In that year's edition of the *Encyclopaedia Britannica*, Sir Thomas Barclay concludes the article on "Peace" by observing that "in no distant future, life among nations" would be characterized by "law, order and peace among men" (1911, p. 16). As Blainey points out, the article on "Peace" in the next edition "was a long essay on how the victors punished the vanquished at the Peace Conference of 1919" (1973, p. 24). See also Tuchman 1966, p. 234.

27. Kant 1957, p. 24. See also Hirschman 1977, pp. 79–80, 134–35.

28. Buckle 1862, pp. 146, 151–58. Mill: Howard 1978, p. 37.

29. Angell 1914, p. 31. Angell 1933, pp. 108, 175. See also Schumpeter 1951, p. 75.

30. Angell 1951, pp. 145–49; Miller 1986, pp. 4–8.

31. Mahan 1912, p. 131.

32. Angell 1951, p. 165. Angell 1933, p. 230.

33. Mahan 1912, pp. 126, 131; see also Coulton 1916, pp. 29–30; Osgood 1953, pp. 101–2. See also Miller 1986, pp. 44–45.

34. Angell 1914, p. 36; 1933, pp. 89–92.

35. It is the central contention of Richard Rosecrance's recent *The Rise of the Trading State* that over the course of the last few centuries more and more countries have come to the conclusion that the path to wealth is through trade rather than conquest, and he cites the striking and important examples of two recent converts: "Today West Germany and Japan use international trade to acquire the very raw materials and oil that they aimed to conquer by military force in the 1930s. They have prospered in peaceful consequence." Among trading states, Rosecrance observes, "the incentive to wage war is absent" (1986, pp. 16, 24).

36. Joll 1984, pp. 176–82. On antiwar activities of the French socialists, see Chickering 1975, ch. 8.

37. Clausewitz 1976, pp. 87–88, 605–10. On Clausewitz's thought, see Brodie 1959, pp. 37–38; Brodie 1976.

38. See Chickering 1975, pp. 92–93, 327–28.

39. Angell 1951, pp. 146–47.

40. Angell 1951, p. 178.

41. Twain 1901, p. 328. On this issue, see particularly Osterweis 1949.

42. On Sumter see Swanberg 1957, pp. 328; the only death during the battle itself was of a horse (p. 322). In 1860 dollars, the capital value of all slaves has been estimated at $2.7 billion (Goldin 1973, p. 74). In direct governmental expenditures, the war cost the North $2.3 billion, and the total direct and indirect costs of the war for both sides was about $21 billion (Goldin and Lewis 1975, pp. 304, 309, 317). During the war President Abraham Lincoln was fully aware of the irony: in 1862 he observed that "less than one half day's cost of this war would pay for all the slaves in Delaware at $400 per head . . . [and] 87 days' cost of this war would pay for all in Delaware, Maryland, District of Columbia, Kentucky, and Missouri" (McCarthy 1901, p. 163).

43. Randall and Donald 1961, pp. 192–93. Batty and Parish 1987, pp. 63–64.

44. Lewis 1932, pp. 330, 415, 636. "fine progress": Merrill 1971, p. 230.

45. Lewis 1932, p. 585. "We cannot change": Batty and Parish 1987, p. 180.

46. Twain 1901, p. 328. Linderman 1987, p. 271.

47. See Hirschman 1977, pp. 133–34. "moral equivalent": James 1911, pp. 290–92, 299–301.

48. Chickering 1975, p. 7; Hinsley 1963, p. 108.

49. Kant 1957, pp. 12–13; for an extended discussion of this notion, see Howard 1978. Marx: Hinsley 1963, pp. 108–9.

50. On the level of analysis issue, see also Waltz 1959.

51. Falnes 1938, pp. 8–9; Nobel 1925. For similar reflections from Leo Tolstoy, see Gilpin 1981, p. 216; from Hans Delbrück, a prominent German military historian, in 1899, see Bucholz 1985, pp. 72–76; from a British economist in 1888, see Milward 1977, p. 294. Perhaps with Nobel in mind, Bernard Shaw in a 1905 play characterizes the notion that "the more destructive war becomes, the sooner it will be abolished" as the "usual excuse" arms manufacturers make for their trade (Shaw 1913, p. 70); it may be an indication of the strength of the antiwar movement that such businessmen felt they needed an excuse.

Chapter 2   A Recent Antiquity: War Advocacy Before World War I

1. Gandhi: quoted, Tripp 1976, p. 683.
2. Howard 1984a, p. 9; 1970, p. 102. Stromberg 1982, pp. 1–2. Russell: Stromberg 1982, p. 177. Brodie 1973, p. 268. Angell's lectures: Angell 1951, p. 172; Chickering 1975, pp. 180–81. Suttner: Chickering 1975, p. 91. James 1911, p. 304; emphasis in the original.
3. Linderman 1987, pp. 266–84; Sherman quote: p. 284.
4. Holmes: Lerner 1943, p. 20. Churchill: Weidhorn 1974, p. 20. Tocqueville: Stromberg 1982, p. 186. Frederick: Bernhardi 1914a, p. 27. Smith 1976, p. 697 (book 5, ch. 1). Moltke: Brodie 1973, p. 264. Anthony: May 1977, p. 119. Ryder 1899, p. 727.
5. Treitschke 1916, Vol. 1, pp. 66–67; Vol. 2, pp. 395–96. Youth League: Notestein and Stoll 1917, p. 35.
6. Ruskin 1866, pp. 84, 85, 89. He stresses, however, that "it is not *all* war of which this can be said. . . . The creative or foundational war is that in which the natural restlessness and love of contest among men are disciplined, by consent, into modes of beautiful—though it may be fatal—play," and in which evil is conquered in defense of noble institutions (p. 90). Milne 1935, p. 56.
7. Carpenter: Stromberg 1982, pp. 2, 180. Futurists: Stromberg 1982, p. 28; Miesel 1978, p. 6. Dunne: Linderman 1987, p. 296.
8. James 1911, pp. 267, 282, 288, 290–92, 303. Russell: Stromberg 1982, p. 191.
9. James 1911, pp. 276, 287.
10. Lea 1909, p. 9. Roosevelt 1901, p. 2; on the controversy over giving Roosevelt the Nobel Prize see Falnes 1938, pp. 257–59. Women effeminate: idea from Siegel 1977, p. 119. Ruskin 1866, pp. 91, 96. See also Linderman 1987, pp. 8, 296.
11. Angell 1951, pp. 159–60. German Youth League: Kitchen 1968, p. 141; see also Chickering 1975, pp. 134–35. On the accusation that pacifists were promoting "feminism," see also Chickering 1975, p. 395.
12. Wells 1908, pp. 214–15. Treitschke 1916, Vol. 1, p. 15; Vol. 2, p. 599. Bernhardi 1914a, p. 26; on Bernhardi, see Fischer 1967, pp. 34–35; Tuchman 1962, p. 25. The 1914 war substantially altered Wells's view: "War and the preparation for war, the taxes, the drilling, the interference with every free activity, the arrest and stiffening up of life, the obedience to third-rate people in uniform . . . have become an unbearable nuisance to all humanity." He also came to find Angell's argument that war does not pay to be revolting: "Who cares whether war pays or does not pay. . . . Even if war paid twelve-and-a-half percent per annum for ever on every pound it cost to wage, would it be any the less a sickening abomination to every decent soul?" (1914, p. 99). On these issues, see also Schumpeter 1951, p. 173n7.
13. Bernhardi 1914a, p. 26. Treitschke 1916, Vol. 1, pp. 50, 67. Nietzsche: Barclay 1911, p. 16. Moltke: Chickering 1975, pp. 392–93. Cramb 1915, pp. 128, 146. Kant 1952, p. 113; Kant was in good philosophic company: according to Aristotle "a time of war automatically enforces temperance and justice: a time of the enjoyment of prosperity, and license accompanied by peace, is more apt to make men overbearing" (1958, pp. 321–22). Schiller: Bernhardi 1914a, p. 26. Sumner, Naval War College: Linderman 1987, p. 296.
14. Ruskin 1866, pp. 88–89.
15. Stromberg 1982, p. 11, 189. Belloc: Stromberg 1982, p. 180. Stengel: Chickering 1975, p. 394. Heym: Stromberg 1982, p. 24.
16. See Fischer 1967, pp. 11–12. Bernhardi, of course, saw economic benefit in war: 1914b, p. 116.
17. Wells 1908, pp. 215–16; Wells is quoted approvingly by William James: 1911, p. 294. For the argument that war "was an important stimulus to technological development" in Wells's era, see Milward 1977, p. 2. In the 1936 movie *Things to Come*, for which Wells wrote the screenplay, one pompous character says, "War doesn't stop progress; it *stimulates* progress." That sentiment was clearly an anachronism after World War I, and Wells may have been consciously burlesquing his own earlier view.
18. Treitschke 1916, Vol. 1, pp. 21, 29, 65. Bernhardi 1914a, pp. 18, 20, 111; Van Evera 1986, p. 91.
19. Pearson: Langer 1951, p. 88. Bagehot 1948, p. 46. Russian sociologist: Langer 1951, p. 87. Renan: Langer 1951, p. 89. Wyatt: Langer 1951, p. 90. Zola: Joll 1984, p. 186. Adams, Luce: Linderman 1987, p. 292. "War is the great": Chickering 1975, p. 395. Stravinsky: Stromberg 1982, p. 51. On Admiral Mahan's Social Darwinism, see Brodie 1959, p. 97n.

20. Emerson 1904, pp. 151, 152, 155, 156, 159, 161.
21. Spencer 1909, pp. 664–65. See also Langer 1951, p. 89.
22. Lea 1909, p. 45.
23. Story: Lea 1909, p. xx. Holmes: Lerner 1943, pp. 19–20. James 1911, pp. 300–301. Tolstoy 1966, p. 1372. Cramb 1915, pp. 143, 146.
24. Jervis 1989. Joll 1984, p. 203; see also pp. 167–68, 201–2. Angell 1914, pp. 202–8, 299.
25. Howard 1984a, p. 9. Bernhardi 1914a, p. 43. See also Farrar 1973, pp. 3–7; Brodie 1973, p. 22; Blainey 1973, pp. 35–40.
26. See Tuchman 1962, pp. 142–43; Fischer 1975, p. 462. Reflecting a similar line of thinking, the many fictional accounts of future wars published in the era also portrayed a war that was brief and limited (Clarke 1966, pp. 131–33). Driant: Van Evera 1984, p. 60. "The outcome": Clarke 1966, p. 131n. "brisk and merry": Lebow 1981, p. 251.
27. Van Evera 1984, pp. 59–60. "The best strategy": Howard 1971, p. 106. Also: Quester 1977, chs. 8–10; Van Evera 1986; Snyder 1984a, 1984b; Howard 1984b; Brodie 1959, pp. 42–52.
28. Grey 1925, pp. 71–72; emphasis in the original. Tuchman 1962, pp. 222. Moltke and Joffre: Tuchman 1962, pp. 38–39, 143; Farrar 1973, pp. 4–6.
29. Data from Small and Singer 1982, tables 4.1, 4.2, 13.2. "armed mobs": Esposito 1979, p. 217. On the lessons variously learned and unlearned from these wars, see particularly Howard 1984b. See also Blainey 1973, ch. 14; Luard 1986, pp. 60–61; Brodie 1959, pp. 42–61; Van Evera 1984; Snyder 1984b.
30. Howard 1984b, pp. 41–43. Bloch 1914, pp. ix–x, xxxi.
31. Foch: Howard 1984b, pp. 42–43. Germany: Chickering 1975, pp. 388–92.
32. Howard 1971, p. 107.
33. On this issue see Holborn 1943, p. 199; Brodie 1973, p. 22; S. Sagan 1986, pp. 159–60; Turner 1979, pp. 203–4; Farrar 1973, p. 13. "crushed gloriously": Tuchman 1962, p. 124.
34. Stromberg 1982, pp. 8, 234. In January 1915, Keynes told friends, "German finance is crumbling": Skidelsky 1986, p. 302. See also Howard 1984b, p. 44; Becker 1986. For an 1890 view, however, that "nations seem always to be able to raise money for war," see Wells 1890, p. 323.
35. Quoted, Miller 1986, p. 9. Angell stresses war is futile, but not impossible: Angell 1914, pp. v–vi; 1933, pp. 267–68. See also Tuchman 1962, pp. 24–25; Grey 1925, pp. 20, 71.
36. Treitschke 1916, Vol. 2, p. 443; Vol. 1, p. 70.
37. Brodie 1959, p. 35. See Craig 1964, p. 281; Farrar 1973, p. 4.
38. See, for example, Van Evera 1986, p. 116.
39. Bernhardi thought that a seven-years war would "unify and elevate the people and destroy the diseases which threaten the national health" (1914b, p. 233). For similar sentiments from other Germans, see Chickering 1975, pp. 390–91. On Germany's expansionary war plans, see Fischer 1967; on deterrence issues: Kagan 1987; Glynn 1987. Howard 1971, p. 104.

Chapter 3   World War I: Major War Becomes an Anachronism

1. On the continent wide jubilation and celebration, see Joll 1984, pp. 182–84; Stromberg 1982, p. 233n12; Fischer 1967, p. 98.
2. Brodie 1973, pp. 13, 25.
3. The estimate of battle deaths is from Small and Singer 1982, pp. 89, 302. Sivard estimates 12,599,000 military deaths and 3,041,000 civilian deaths (1985, p. 11).
4. Stromberg 1982, p. 152. Howard: Brodie 1973, p. 15. Tuchman 1966, p. xiii. Toynbee 1969, p. 214; see also p. 239. Brodie 1973, p. 30. See also Fussell 1975, pp. 21–22.
5. On the "meliorist myth", see Fussell 1975, p. 8.
6. Wells 1914, p. 14. "public opinion": Scrugham 1921, pp. 81, 124. "all wars": Wedgwood 1961, p. 8; see also Bialer 1980, p. 43.
7. Bell 1986, p. 12.
8. F. Brown 1968, p. 98; Brodie 1973, pp. 288–90. For a classic examination of the theory, see Noel-Baker 1937.
9. On these developments, see F. Brown 1968, ch. 1; Harris and Paxman 1982, ch. 1; Haber 1986. Quintupled figures: F. Brown 1968, p. 14n.
10. F. Brown 1968, pp. 10–12. See also Harris and Paxman 1982, pp. 34–36.
11. Churchill 1932, pp. 247, 250; F. Brown 1968, pp. 43, 32.

12. F. Brown 1968, pp. 65, 164, 180–81. On Douhet and his exaggerations, see Brodie 1959, ch. 3. On the probable exaggeration of long-range effects, see Haber 1986, p. 258; he concludes, however, that although the cause-and-effect connection between being gassed and later maladies was "tenuous," "it was enough for people to believe that being gassed was the cause of illness years later, and thus the special anxiety created by chemical warfare continued into the peace and was kept alive in the public consciousness." See also Harris and Paxman 1982, ch. 4. For a less alarmist contemporary view of gas bombing, see Dupuy and Eliot 1937, pp. 208–9.

13. Harold Macmillan in Bialer 1980, p. 158.

14. Churchill 1925, pp. 246, 248. Freud 1930, p. 144. Baldwin: Kagan 1987, p. 26. See also Bialer 1980, pp. 46–47; Irwin 1921, pp. 140–41. Worldwide depression: Milward 1977, p. 16.

15. Clarke 1966, pp. 167–76. See also Stromberg 1982, p. 197; Wagar 1982, p. 24.

16. On this thesis, see Fischer 1967 and Fischer 1975. See also Kagan 1987, pp. 22–24; Glynn 1987.

17. In 1918, for example, Britain ordered 250 bombers, each capable of carrying nearly four tons of gas bombs, for use in the battles of 1919 that never took place (F. Brown 1968, pp. 43–46).

18. On these issues, see Bueno de Mesquita 1984, Batchelder 1961.

19. F. Brown 1968, p. 236; Hitler 1939, p. 264.

20. Knox 1984, pp. 8–11, 16–19; 1982, pp. 289–90.

21. Mussolini 1935, p. 7.

22. Knox 1984, pp. 44–45.

23. Knox 1982, pp. 48, 122, 290.

24. Rich 1973, pp. 11, xxxvi–xxxix; Speer 1970, pp. 15–18.

25. "political genius": Rich 1973, p. xxxii; Bullock 1952, p. 735; Trevor–Roper 1953, pp. viii, xiv, xxx. "extrapolating": Jäckel 1972, p. 202. See also Bell 1986, p. 75.

26. Rich 1973, p. xlii; Jäckel 1972; Weinberg 1980, pp. 18, 657; Rich 1974, p. 420; Trevor-Roper 1953, p. xxiii. See also Hitler 1939, pp. 944–53; Bullock 1972; Milward 1977, pp. 6–8; Bluhm 1974, ch. 7. So overwhelming was Hitler's theory that (after blaming international Jewry for starting the war and his generals for losing it) he concluded his last written statement by restating his central objective: "The aim must still be to win territory in the east for the German people" (Bullock 1952, p. 729).

27. Weinberg 1980, p. 670. See also Hitler 1961, pp. 22–23.

28. Hitler 1939, pp. 8, 210, 214–15.

29. Hitler 1961, pp. 9–10. "Good for the German people": Hitler 1953, pp. 23–24, 43. For war-glorifying statements by other Nazis, see V. Van Dyke 1966, p. 133.

30. Weinberg 1980, pp. 657–59; Bullock 1972, pp. 226–29; Rosecrance 1986, pp. 105–6. R. J. Overy argues that an eventual total war was part of Hitler's grand scheme—a scheme he carefully kept from military and industrial leaders who he knew would find it "unthinkable"; the Hitler blitzkrieg, therefore, emerged not so much by plan as "by default" (1982, p. 279 and passim, 1984, chs. 3–8; see also Murray 1984). Hitler apparently recognized that his attack on France in 1940 could lead to a (one-front) struggle of attrition: see Knox 1982, p. 87. On Hitler's procedures for persuading his generals to attack France and the Low Countries in 1940, see Mearsheimer 1983, ch. 4. For Hitler's correct rejection of the popular notion that air power could deliver a quick "knock-out blow," see Bialer 1980, pp. 133–34. On the lack of enthusiasm for a war of conquest by established political and military leaders in Germany, see Bell 1986, p. 44.

31. Knox 1984, pp. 42–43, 49–57; Steinert 1977, pp. 25–102; Rich 1973, p. 211. The 1940 victory: see also Mearsheimer 1983, p. 99.

32. T. Taylor 1979, p. 877; Quester 1977, p. 137; Weinberg 1980, pp. 451–52, 458, 677; Knox 1984, pp. 42, 51, 55; Bell 1986, p. 12; Speer 1970, pp. 166–67; Reck-Malleczewen 1970, pp. 103–9. One analyst of German public opinion characterizes it as "dead set" against major war: Steinert 1977, p. 50.

33. Weinberg 1980, p. 664. "Essentially": Alexandroff and Rosecrance 1977, pp. 416–17. "Irreplaceable": *Documents on German Foreign Policy*, p. 443. See also Knox 1984, p. 54; Mearsheimer 1983, p. 112. Ian Kershaw observes, "There seems little disagreement among historians that Hitler did personally take the 'big' decisions on foreign policy after 1933" (1985, p. 114). P. M. H. Bell concludes in his study of the origins of the European war that "Hitler was out to dominate the Continent. . . . German expansion would not halt unless it was forcibly resisted" (1986, p. 301). John Stoessinger: "If one looks at the outbreak of World War II . . . it was the personality of Hitler that was decisive" (1982, p. 208). Said Hans J. Morgenthau: "The victories which German diplomacy won

from 1933 to 1940 were the victories of one man's mind, and the deterioration of that mind was a direct cause of the disasters which marked the last years of the Nazi regime" (1948, p. 107). For the rare argument that Hitler, though central to the situation, was mainly swept or buffeted into the war by the force of events, see A. J. P. Taylor 1961; for a deft rebuttal, see Hinsley 1963, ch. 15.

34. For a discussion of Hitler's concern about assassination and of the elaborate security measures taken to protect him, see P. Hoffmann 1979.

35. Murray 1984, p. 369. Weinberg 1980, p. 668–70.

36. On this point and on Hitler's idea about attacking France, see Mearsheimer 1983, pp. 95–96, 102, 131–33. Allied plans: Weinberg 1980, pp. 6–7. On the delays in the West on declaring war even after the Germans had invaded Poland, see Moseley 1969, chs. 20–21. "in spite of": T. Taylor 1979, p. 743. "last territorial claim," peaceful proclamations: Hitler 1942, pp. 1517, 1218, 1220, 1235, 1260, 1514, 1639–40, 1661.

37. Weinberg 1980, p. 631.

38. Because Switzerland's last battle had taken place in 1798, it may have been a bit rusty (some of its artillery dated from 1882), but it had no intention of capitulating. Disturbed by the rise of Hitler (whose contempt for the materialistic, democratic Swiss was monumental) and deeply shocked by his expansion in Central Europe, they moved into action. A general was elected (the Swiss army only has one general, and then only in time of war or major threat), and mobilization was ordered. Up to 435,000 men, 21 percent of the entire male population, could be moved into combat positions within twenty-four hours (even on leave each citizen-soldier constantly carried a rifle and forty-eight rounds of ammunition). Building on installations already in place, several lines of resistance were established making use of such natural barriers to invasion as lakes, rivers, and mountainous terrain. If all such efforts failed, plans were formulated for a retreat to a fortress-redoubt deep in the Alpine center of the country. The Swiss were by no means immune to French-style defeatism, and occasionally proposals to send supplicating missions to Berlin surfaced. Moreover, they were willing to allow German materials to pass through the country on efficient Swiss railroads (which they loudly promised to destroy if invaded). And because their lighted cities were serving to guide Allied night bombing, they eventually bowed to German pressure for blackouts (leading to accidental bombings of Swiss territory, which, with interest meticulously added, cost the United States $62 million in 1949). If Hitler had won the war, Switzerland might well have been eventually forced to enter his empire; but while the conflict continued, the Swiss blended subtle appeasement with a grim and credible determination to resist, and this kept the country free of invasion in the midst of history's widest war. On Switzerland, see Schwarz 1980. On Hitler's attitude toward the Swiss ("a pimple on the face of Europe," useful "at the best, as hotel-keepers"), see Hitler 1953, pp. 21, 23–24, 455, 497, 537; and Rich 1974, pp. 401–2, 421.

39. Steinert 1977, p. 118.

40. Vagts 1959, p. 451. On a visit to Japan in 1929, Arnold Toynbee found "the Japanese people still intoxicated by their previous unbroken run of victorious wars" (1969, p. 230).

41. Butow 1961, pp. 24, 46, 79. Luard 1986, p. 368.

42. Butow 1961, pp. 77, 79.

43. Butow 1961, pp. 99–101, 108–9, 254. Rich 1973, pp. 224–25. Battle death figures from Small and Singer 1982, pp. 90–91.

44. Butow 1961, p. 134, 147. The proportion of the Japanese gross national product devoted to military expenditures jumped from 6.8 percent in 1936 to 13.2 percent in 1937 and 17.4 percent in 1938 (Milward 1977, p. 30).

45. Butow 1961, pp. 161–62; Weinberg 1980, p. 661. For 1942 expansions of these ideas with the "ultimate ideal" of placing "the whole world under one roof," see Dower 1986, pp. 273–74.

46. Butow 1961, pp. 192–93.

47. There was substantial sentiment to attack the troublesome Soviet Union first, but instead a neutrality pact was worked out with the Soviets in preference for expansion in the south (the Soviets, now under attack by the Germans, were to be handled later). Butow 1961, pp. 212–20. Oil figures: Milward 1977, p. 31.

48. Butow 1961, pp. 255, 319.

49. Butow 1961, p. 341.

50. Butow 1961, p. 267. Grew: Butow 1961, pp. 245n.

51. Butow 1954, pp. 180, 183. Tojo: Butow 1961, p. 410; see also pp. 167, 330. Support of Japanese people: Butow 1961, pp. 167, 251–52, 332–33.

52. Butow 1961, pp. 321–22.

53. Butow 1961, p. 334.

54. For a similar argument with respect to Hitler's calculations, see Alexandroff and Rosecrance 1977, p. 421.
55. See also Brodie 1973, p. 272.
56. Milne 1935, pp. 4–8.

Chapter 4   Implications of the World War II Experience

1. On Hitler's decision to declare war on the United States, see Rich 1973, ch. 20.
2. Quoted, Lingeman 1970, p. 24; Sherwood: p. 24. Nevins 1946, p. 9.
3. Woito 1987, p. 108. Nevins 1946, p. 23. Milward 1977, pp. 63, 67. Additional information from Harvey De Weerd. As one businessman observed, American war production in 1940 was "virtually nothing"; in 1942 it "equalled that of the three Axis nations combined"; in 1943 it was "one and one half times, and in 1944, more than double" (Nelson 1946, p. 213).
4. Lingeman 1970, pp. 128–29. Milward 1977, p. 74. Kennedy 1987, p. 354.
5. Milward, 1977, pp. 65, 67, 275. Lingeman 1970, p. 129–31.
6. Rosebery 1944, p. xii. Lingeman 1970, pp. 126, 357. Milward 1977, p. 63.
7. Lingeman 1970, p. 121, 132. Rosebery 1944, p. 63. See also Maurice and Smithson 1984, ch. 3. The travel shortage led to a boom for local movie theaters—the slogan in Hollywood was "You can run toilet paper through the projector and people will pay to see it," or as director Vincente Minnelli recalls with more delicacy, "no sensibly budgeted film . . . could fail" (quoted, Mueller 1985b, p. 253). On the 50,000 lives saved by gasoline rationing, see p. 268 of this book.
8. Quoted, Nevins 1946, p. 21.
9. Deane 1947, pp. 93–94. Jones 1969, appendix A, tables 3–5. Additional information from Harvey De Weerd.
10. Werth 1964, p. 627. A 1948 Soviet report understates the deliveries by simply leaving out 1944, the peak year, from its calculations (Werth 1964, p. 627; see also Ulam 1971, p. 4, and Herring 1973, pp. xiv–xv).
11. F. Brown 1968, p. 290.
12. F. Brown 1968, pp. 124–25. Harris and Paxman 1982, p. 32. For lower casualty estimates see Haber 1986, ch. 10. Only 2 percent of American gas casualties in that war died, as contrasted with 26 percent of nongas casualties (Rothschild 1964, p. 3).
13. F. Brown 1968, pp. 154–55.
14. See F. Brown 1968, p. 245.
15. F. Brown 1968, pp. 210–11, 230–31, 264–65; see also pp. 200–201.
16. F. Brown 1968, pp. 229, 237–38. Hitler aide Albert Speer testified after the war, "When rumors reached [me] that gas might be used, I stopped its production in November, 1944. . . . All sensible army people turned gas warfare down as utterly insane, since, in view of [the Allies'] superiority in the air, it would not be long before it would bring the most terrible catastrophe upon German cities" (quoted, Bueno de Mesquita 1984, p. 17). Interestingly, something similar happened in Japan, which actually had been using gas in China even after Roosevelt's stern pledge to retaliate. By 1944, when it was becoming clear that an eventual invasion of the Japanese homeland was likely, the Japanese finally issued a firm pledge not to use gas in the future except in response to the enemy's initiation. The aim, of course, was to deter American use of the weapon in the anticipated invasion. Then the Japanese went even further. Realizing their vulnerability to air attack and apparently trusting the Americans to follow their own declared policy, the Japanese systematically and unilaterally disarmed their capacity to use chemical weapons: beginning in mid-1944, they stopped producing the weapons and recalled all gas munitions from troops already in the field. See F. Brown 1968, pp. 248–49, 260–61.
17. Bueno de Mesquita 1984, pp. 17–18.
18. F. Brown 1968, p. 309.
19. F. Brown 1968, pp. 267–86; Leahy 1950, pp. 439–40. On General George Marshall's support for the use of gas against Japan, see Lilienthal 1964, p. 199.
20. Togo 1956, p. 310. Butow 1954, pp. 145–49. On Truman's overriding desire for an early end to the war, see Brown 1968, pp. 281–82. Like gas in 1915, the atomic bomb was introduced into warfare by the side that enjoyed a monopoly: there was no fear the Japanese would be able to retaliate

in kind. The experience with gas in World War I suggests that had the bomb been used earlier in the war, there would have been a frantic effort by all sides to add the weapon to their arsenals.

21. F. Brown 1968, p. 286n, 198–99. Leahy 1950, p. 440. Lilienthal 1964, p. 198.

22. Compton 1956, p. 237. Dower 1986, pp. 298, 301.

23. See Butow 1954, p. 93, ch. 8; USSBS 1946b; Kase 1950, p. 217. Paul Kecskemeti argues that it was the Soviet declaration of war at the same time as the atomic bombings that was crucial in the timing of Japan's eventual surrender offer: since the Soviet Union could now no longer act as a neutral mediator, the Japanese were forced to meet and to make some new decisions about approaching the United States (Kecskemeti 1958, ch. 6; see also Hoyt 1986, p. 420). On the "strategy" of the last glorious battle, see Ienaga 1978, pp. 229–30.

24. The Potsdam Declaration implied that the Japanese would be allowed to keep their emperor. The Japanese understood the message (Kase 1950, p. 210; Togo 1956, p. 311; Iriye 1981, p. 263), so their public rejection of it, which set the plans for the atomic bombings in motion, proved to be a tragic mistake.

25. Coffey 1970, pp. 518–23; Kase 1950, pp. 254–55; Craig 1967, pp. 212–13.

26. Hoyt 1986, p. 396. Spector 1985, p. 410. See also Craig 1967, p. 13. On the shinyo suicide boats, see Belote 1970, pp. 85–88.

27. On the slogan, see Butow 1954, pp. 49, 68, 93. Premier Suzuki: "Now is the time for every one of the hundred million . . . to become glorious shields for the defense of the national structure" (quoted Belote 1970, p. 323). Saipan: Hoffman 1950, p. 245; Ienaga 1978, pp. 185, 197–98. Okinawa: Ienaga 1978, pp. 185, 198. "stones": Brines 1944, p. 9. "All that remains": Kase 1950, p. 249.

28. De Seversky 1950, pp. 127, 132, 155; 1946, p. 121. Physicist Ralph Lapp, noting that "A-bombs are too big for many military applications," and ignoring isolated targets, concluded it would take seventy-five atomic bombs to duplicate the bomb damage in Germany (Lapp 1949, p. 61). Official estimate: USSBS 1946a, p. 33; on this issue, see also Brodie 1946, pp. 24–25. In a 1946 article, de Seversky declared that an atomic bomb on New York or Chicago would do no more damage than a ten-ton blockbuster (1946, p. 121; for a contemporary refutation, see Littell 1946).

29. De Seversky 1950, chs. 9, 10; USSBS 1946a; Batchelder 1961, p. 123; U.S. Army 1946; Lapp 1949, ch. 7.

30. Brodie 1973, p. 64; Smoke 1987, p. 55.

31. Werth 1964, pp. 1043–44.

32. Rich 1974, pp. 280–81, 292–94. Something somewhat similar happened in the Ukraine; see Rich 1974, p. 375. See also Moseley 1969, pp. 75–88.

33. Rich 1974, p. 423.

34. Milward 1977, pp. 137–41. Rosecrance 1986, pp. 35–36.

35. See Sharp 1973; Lukas 1986, chs. 3–4.

36. Rich 1974, p. 424. Actually, the first of these, the celebrated assassination of Reinhard Heydrich in Czechoslovakia in 1942 (which led to the destruction of the village of Lidice in reprisal) was not carried out by the underground at all but by Czech terrorists trained in Britain and parachuted into the country for the purpose (Rich 1974, pp. 47–48; Mastny 1971, pp. 207–10).

37. The Greek civil war began in 1944, before the end of World War II. For a discussion of definitions, and for a listing of the forty-three wars, see Small and Singer 1982, chs. 12–13.

Chapter 5   Cold War, Containment, and the Irrelevance of Nuclear Weapons

1. Taracouzio 1940, p. 53.

2. Nearly 200,000 people were purged from public activity (Dower 1986, p. 307). For instances of U.S. mistreatment of civilians, see Ienaga 1978, pp. 235–38.

3. Dower 1986, pp. 305–6. See also Gaddis 1987b, pp. 220–21.

4. Waltz 1979, p. 190. For comparative battle statistics, see Rosecrance 1986, p. 112.

5. Ulam suggests 20,000,000 may be low as an estimate of deaths directly or indirectly attributable to the war (1971, p. 6). The estimate for Soviet battle deaths in the war is 7,500,000 (Small and Singer 1982, p. 91); Sivard estimates civilian deaths at an additional 7,500,000 (1987, p. 30).

6.   Wells 1968, p. 67; Wagar 1961, p. 13n. Toynbee 1950, p. 4. In Wells's view, "The occupation and disarmament of Germany will end nothing; it will only inaugurate a scramble of . . . egocentric 'liberators,' . . . of the Roman Catholic Church, of the Communist Party, of the patriotic Polish nationalists in exile, of every silly little intractable patriotism, and of the Big Business and banking systems, with their immense stupid cunning, to gain control of our exhausted world" (Wagar 1961, p. 48).

7.   As always on public opinion surveys, the shape of the question is vital in determining the response. The question "Do you expect the United States will fight in another world war within the next 25 years?" found 30 to 40 percent agreeing in 1944 and 1945, 60 to 75 percent in 1946 and 1947. About half as many responded this way when the question was "Do you think there will probably be another big war during the next 25–30 years, or do you think there is a fairly good chance to avoid it?" For data and analysis, see Mueller 1979, pp. 303–7.

8.   Quoted, Djilas 1962, pp. 114–15.

9.   Einstein 1960, pp. 347, 533, 566. Teller and Russell: Grodzins and Rabinowitch 1963, pp. 101, 124.

10.   Einstein 1960, pp. 382, 417, 482.

11.   See Ulam 1971, pp. 16–18; Weigel 1987, pp. 122–25. Soviet scientists: Einstein 1960, p. 449. Kennedy: Kennedy 1961; Sorensen 1965, p. 246.

12.   Taubman 1982, p. 21. Gaddis 1974, p. 388.

13.   Djilas 1962, p. 187.

14.   Taubman 1982, p. 22. See also Knox 1984, p. 57.

15.   Quoted, Historicus 1949, pp. 191–92. On these issues, see particularly Burin 1963, pp. 337–41. Taracouzio 1940, pp. 45, 142–44. See also Ulam 1971, p. 109.

16.   Taubman 1982, p. 12. On the harvest of revolutions: Historicus 1949, p. 184, 190–91.

17.   Shevchenko 1985, pp. 285–86. Voslensky 1984, pp. 320–30. Pipes 1984, p. 65.

18.   Leites 1953, pp. 46–53. Pipes stresses the Soviet tactical emphasis on "utmost caution," patience, and prudence (1984, pp. 52–53). See also Bluhm 1974, p. 295.

19.   Historicus 1949, p. 198.

20.   Djilas 1962, p. 114; also p. 153. On Stalin's deep aversion to independent Communist parties, see Kennan 1961, pp. 250–51.

21.   On the importance of the Hitler and Munich analogies in American thinking of the time, see May 1973, ch. 2. On the reactive nature of American policy, see Kennedy 1987, p. 360.

22.   Truman 1947, p. 7.

23.   Truman 1947, p. 7.

24.   On these issues, see also Larson 1985, p. 331; May 1984, p. 213; Gaddis 1974, p. 390. For the suggestion that Stalin decided in 1948 to stifle the Greek rebellion largely because of the American intervention, see Djilas 1962, pp. 181–82.

25.   For a discussion, see Weinstein 1978.

26.   Truman 1947, p. 8.

27.   See also Thomas 1986, p. 544.

28.   Quoted, Gaddis 1982, p. 35; see also pp. 366–67, and Gaddis 1987b, p. 41.

29.   Taubman 1982, pp. 169–70. See also Yergin 1977, pp. 350–54. On American Communists and the "bring the boys home" campaign, see Starobin 1972, pp. 4, 276.

30.   Quoted, Gaddis 1982, p. 35. See also Lebow 1981, p. 262n134; Jervis 1980, p. 565.

31.   James Byrnes, quoted in Gaddis 1982, p. 21.

32.   Kennan 1947, pp. 20, 22.

33.   Gaddis 1982, p. 43; Taubman 1982, p. 170. On this issue Kennan liked to quote Edward Gibbon: "There is nothing more contrary to nature than the attempt to hold in obedience distant provinces" (Gaddis 1982, p. 47).

34.   Gaddis 1982, p. 49.

35.   Nevins 1946, pp. 9–10.

36.   Einstein 1960, p. 426. Secretary of Commerce (and former vice president) Henry Wallace declared in a 1946 speech, "The tougher we get, the tougher the Russians will get." He also called upon the Soviets to cooperate with the United Nations and to "stop teaching that their form of communism must, by force of necessity, ultimately triumph over democratic capitalism." If each side meets the other half-way in "peaceful competition," Wallace urged, "the Russian world and the

American world will gradually become more alike. The Russians will be forced to grant more and more of the personal freedoms; and we shall become more and more absorbed with the problems of social-economic justice." Eight days after he gave this speech, Wallace was removed from office (LaFeber 1971, pp. 146–47).

37. For counterargument to rollback, see Kennan 1972, ch. 5, especially pp. 101–2. For the argument that "*strong* and prompt reaction by the West" might have kept Czechoslovakia from sliding into the Soviet camp, see Ulam 1971, p. 137 (emphasis in original); also Mastny 1979, pp. 310–11.

38. For discussions, see Lebow 1984, pp. 168–77; Brodie 1959, pp. 229–41; Fleming 1961, pp. 391–415. Russell's 1946 proposal is reprinted in Grodzins and Rabinowitch 1963, pp. 100–106. For public opinion data on this issue from December 1946, see *Opinion News,* April 15, 1948. Grew: Gaddis 1987b, p. 218n.

39. Stockpile: Smoke 1987, p. 55; see also Gaddis 1987b, p. 109. Lapp 1949, p. 61. See also pp. 89–90 in this book. Russell: Grodzins and Rabinowitch 1963, p. 100. Bradley 1949, p. 169–70; Stalin's view: atomic bombs "are designed to scare those with weak nerves, but they cannot decide wars because there are not enough of them" (Ulam 1971, p. 103). Kennan 1950, p. 3. See also Baldwin 1950: an atomic attack would lead to "a long, hard and vicious struggle, with no holds barred."

40. Gilpin 1981, p. 213.

41. Art and Waltz 1983, p. 28. Churchill: Evangelista 1982/83, p. 110. Truman: Lilienthal 1964, p. 464. See also Brodie 1973, p. 64n8.

42. Kennan 1987, pp. 888–89. Thomas 1986, p. 102. Famine: Khrushchev 1970, ch. 7. Reaction to the Japan declaration: Werth 1964, p. 1039. For an assessment of the difficulties a Soviet attack on Western Europe would entail for the Soviets, see Rosecrance 1986, p. 128.

43. Gaddis 1982, p. 72.

44. Evangelista 1982/83, pp. 110–33. Evangelista also cites American intelligence reports from the middle and late 1940s which concluded that the Soviets would not be ready for major war for at least fifteen years (pp. 133–34). On these issues, see also Mearsheimer 1983, ch. 6.

45. A conventional threat might be more credible than an atomic one even in an era of U.S. nuclear monopoly. The Soviets might be able to counter an American retaliatory threat to destroy Moscow with a threat to level a newly captured Western city like Paris.

46. Ulam 1971, pp. 5, 95. In 1950, the gross national product of the United States was greater than that of the Soviet Union and Western Europe *combined* (Kennedy 1987, p. 369).

47. Quoted, *Newsweek,* March 16, 1953, p. 31. Thomas 1986, p. 548. "If there is any": Huntington 1961, p. 46. According to Ulam, American leaders tended to ignore "the enormous industrial power of their own country as evidenced during World War II and as contrasted with the still unreconstructed state of the Russian economy" (1968, p. 414). See also Millis 1951, pp. 350–51; Jervis 1980, p. 566.

48. Gilpin 1981, p. 218. Gaddis 1986, p. 123. See also Morgan 1977, p. 208; Waltz 1988, p. 628.

49. Thorpe 1978; Bundy 1984, pp. 44–47; Bundy 1988, pp. 232–33. See also Rubinstein 1985, pp. 50–52; Thomas 1986, p. 523.

50. Ulam 1972, p. 82. See also Gaddis 1974, p. 391; 1972, pp. 355–56. Stalin quoted: Djilas 1962, p. 153. For State Department Soviet expert Chip Bohlen's varying assessments on the issue, see Gaddis 1987, p. 115.

51. Schilling 1961, p. 26. Schlesinger 1967, p. 6. Or, Kenneth Waltz: "Nuclear weapons did not cause the condition of bipolarity. . . . Had the atom never been split, [the United States and the USSR] would far surpass others in military strength, and each would remain the greatest threat and source of potential damage to the other" (Waltz 1979, pp. 180–81). See also Gaddis 1987, p. 230n. If nuclear strategy were the major determinant of these alliance patterns, one might well expect the United States and, to a lesser extent, the Soviet Union, to be only lukewarm members. One would also expect the small nations in the two alliances to tie themselves as tightly as possible to the major nuclear country in order to have maximum protection from the core country's nuclear weapons. However, the weakening of the alliances which eventually took place came from the lesser partners, not the major ones.

52. Einstein 1960, p. 376. For further discussion of some of these issues, see Mueller 1988b; for another view, see Jervis 1988.

Chapter 6   Korea and the Demise of Limited War

1.   Ernest May finds it entirely possible that "if forces friendly to the Soviet Union had gained control in Greece and Iran, the consequence would have been to encourage Soviet expansionism" (May 1973, p. 51).

2.   See Lippmann 1947.

3.   See Acheson 1969, pp. 202–10, 304–5; Truman 1956, pp. 89–92.

4.   Simmons 1975, p. 91. On Taiwan: Paige 1968, pp. 62–63; May 1973, p. 65; Acheson 1969, pp. 349–52. But see also Simmons 1975, pp. 88–89. Taiwan's fall: Paige 1968, p. 68; Simmons 1975, p. 87. President Truman prophesied in 1949 that "the Russians will turn out to be the 'foreign devils' in China and that situation will help establish a Chinese government that we can recognize and support" (Gaddis 1974, p. 392).

5.   Mueller 1979, p. 304.

6.   As Shulman puts it, "By the spring of 1950 it was apparent that the contradictory blend of intimidation and blandishment which characterized Soviet policy in this period, as well as that of its foreign instruments, was not effectively decelerating the increase of power and cohesion in the West" (Shulman 1963, p. 138). Harvest of revolutions: Historicus 1949, pp. 191, 212.

7.   Khrushchev 1970, pp. 367–68.

8.   See Taubman 1982, pp. 212–14; Whiting 1960, pp. 37–38; Ulam 1971, p. 171. Joint Chiefs: May 1973, p. 62; see also May 1984, p. 215; Ridgway 1967, p. 12. Connally: Paige 1968, p. 68. Acheson: Kaufman 1986, p. 25. Acheson has pointed out that in defining a "defense perimeter," he was reflecting thoughts expressed in a speech General Douglas MacArthur had made a year earlier; that the Acheson line actually *advanced* the Western commitment in the Pacific; and that his speech specifically noted that, while "no person can guarantee" other Pacific areas "against military attack," if those nations were attacked they could call upon "the commitments of the entire civilized world under the Charter of the United Nations" (Acheson 1969, pp. 356–57).

9.   Khrushchev 1970, p. 370; Simmons 1975, p. 163. Ulam: "One thing remains clear, and that is the extreme reluctance of the Soviets to become involved militarily in any phase of the Korean conflict. The epithet 'peace-loving,' bestowed on herself by Stalin's Russia, was certainly well merited from that point of view" (1968, p. 525). "real Communist": Khrushchev 1970, p. 368.

10.   Shulman 1963, p. 150. See also George 1955, p. 210; Rees 1964, pp. 21–24; Gaddis 1974, p. 396; and Taubman 1982, p. 193.

11.   Truman 1956, p. 333. See also Paige 1968, pp. 137, 174; Taubman 1982, p. 214.

12.   Bradley 1953, p. 62. Speculations: Paige 1968, pp. 171, 173. For a discussion of various American interpretations of the North Korean attack, see George 1955. On Bradley's conviction that Europe was still the "central target," see Paige 1968, p. 166n.

13.   Taubman 1982, pp. 201–2. An August poll found 57 percent of the public opining that the United States was "now actually in World War III," while 28 percent held that the fighting "will stop short of another world war" (Gallup 1972, p. 933). Jessup: Paige 1968, p. 171. War around corner: Brodie 1973, p. 63; Gaddis 1974, p. 396. See also Gati 1974, p. xxii.

14.   Khrushchev 1970, pp. 299–301, 308, 311. Kennan 1961, pp. 250, 386. Djilas 1962, pp. 151–52. Ulam concludes that even in the area of foreign policy, where Stalin most displayed "a sense of realism," his "last phase was one of decline in his powers, of vanity and megalomania increasingly encroaching upon intelligence" (1973, pp. 685–86). Khrushchev remembers being shocked when Stalin said, "to no one in particular," in 1951: "I'm finished. I trust no one, not even myself." "Can you imagine," Khrushchev asks rhetorically, "such a statement coming from a man who decided the fate of his country and influenced the fate of the world?" (1970, p. 307). For contrary speculation about Stalin's mental state, see Taubman 1982, pp. 197–98, 277n23. For a description of the diplomatic atmosphere in Moscow in Stalin's last year, see Kennan 1972, chs. 6–7.

15.   Bluhm 1974, p. 301.

16.   Djilas 1962, p. 190. See also the discussion in Payne 1965, pp. 648–49.

17.   Acheson 1969, p. 478. Matthews: *New York Times*, August 26, 1950, p. 1; Truman 1956, p. 383. Anderson, *Pilot: New York Times*, September 2, 1950, pp. 1, 8. Johnson: Baldwin 1950. Jessup publicly argued that while world war was a "serious" threat, it was not inevitable, and that even if a war against the USSR were successful, "it would leave occupation and reconstruction problems of such complexity as to make our present post-war problems look like child's play" (*New York Times*, August 28, 1950, p. 8).

18.   See Whiting 1960, pp. 158–60; Kaufman 1986, pp. 86–87; Zelman 1967, pp. 3–20. Some American officials also were impressed that, since Chinese "warnings" were usually expressed in private talks with the congenial Indian ambassador, the Chinese were taking "no risk" because the warnings "could be disavowed" (Taubman 1982, p. 218).

19.   Khrushchev 1970, p. 371.

20.   Official conviction: Brodie 1973, pp. 63–64. Public opinion: Mueller 1979, p. 304. For the suggestion that Stalin might have been similarly alarmed in January 1951, see Taubman 1982, pp. 214–15, 224.

21.   On the Chinese assurances, see Khrushchev 1970, p. 372. Robert Simmons concludes that for China, "the conflict was meant to be a limited one, ultimately aimed at convincing the United States that a land war with China would be one of attrition which Washington could not hope to win" (Simmons 1975, p. 167).

22.   Bradley: Brodie 1973, p. 84. On the apparent 1951 near-collapse, see Brodie 1973, pp. 91–97.

23.   Brodie 1973, pp. 64–65. See also Gaddis 1987b, pp. 115–23.

24.   Eisenhower 1963, p. 181.

25.   Gaddis 1987b, p. 128 (emphasis in the original). On the plans, see Foot 1985, ch. 7.

26.   Simmons 1975, pp. 216, 223–35. On the issue of timing, see especially Bundy 1984, pp. 46–47; Bundy 1988, pp. 238–43.

27.   In fact, it appears that at least some of the indirect threats were purely conventional; see Betts 1987, p. 43. For recent Chinese claims that they were not intimidated by the Eisenhower intimations, see Cohen 1987, pp. 288–89. Nixon's conclusion: Nixon 1980, p. 254.

28.   On these international issues, see also Gaddis 1974; Wells 1979, pp. 138–41; May 1984; and especially Jervis 1980, pp. 579–84. The concern about Soviet intentions is suggested by a public opinion trend: in 1946, 58 percent of the American public had said it felt the Soviets were out to become "the ruling power of the world"; by November 1950 this percentage had risen to 81 (Mueller 1973, p. 40).

29.   Relations between the two Communist giants had been rather aloof after the 1949 Communist victory in China. As Chinese Communist leader Mao Zedong recalled in 1962, this was because Stalin feared China would become another Yugoslavia, and "it was only after our resistance to America and support for Korea that Stalin finally came to trust us" (Simmons 1975, p. 59). However, Mao and other Chinese Communist leaders had been proclaiming for decades that one "must either stand on the side of the imperialist front" or on "the anti-imperialist front" and that there is "no third choice" (Whiting 1960, p. 6–7). For Chinese rejection of the notion that Mao might have been cajoled by clever diplomacy to side with the United States rather than with the USSR, see Cohen 1987, pp. 287–88; see also Spanier 1974.

30.   See Weinstein 1978, pp. 476–77, 508.

31.   On these cases, see Radosh and Milton 1983.

32.   Indeed, as Robert Jervis has pointed out, "It was for this reason that the Joint Chiefs of Staff planned to abandon Korea in the event of war. An attack there would form only one small front in the world war and would not be worth the expenditure of scarce military resources" (1950, p. 572). Such thinking is reflected in public opinion polling questionnaires. Before Korea the polling organizations asked questions of the form, "Do you think the U.S. will fight in another war within 10 years?" After June 1950 the question was changed to refer to "another world war" (Mueller 1979, p. 306n). Ridgway 1967, p. 11. Brodie 1959, pp. 307–8. On this issue, see also Halperin 1963.

33.   Brodie 1959, p. 307.

34.   May 1973, p. 83. Taubman 1982, p. 225. In his last address as president, Truman said, "We have averted World War III up to now, and we may have already succeeded in establishing conditions which can keep that war from happening as far as man can see" (Truman 1956, p. xi).

Chapter 7   Khrushchev and the Demise of Crisis

1.   Hudson et al. 1961, p. 44. Among the "forces" in Khrushchev's mind was undoubtedly the growing Soviet nuclear arsenal (for commentary on this point, see Dinerstein 1962 and Zagoria 1962, pp. 302–3); but, as indicated, the basic Soviet position on this issue goes back at least to 1935. "war can be averted": Burin 1963, p. 342.

2. Hudson et al. 1961, p. 154; Zagoria 1962, p. 302. Chinese: Hudson et al. 1961, p. 124. See also Burin 1963, pp. 347–48; Zagoria 1962, pp. 312–13; Lowenthal 1961, p. 13. Malenkov: Dinerstein 1962, p. 71; Burin 1963, p. 347n.

3. Mao 1961, pp. 28–29. "On the debris": Hudson et al. 1961, p. 93–94.

4. Turner and Freedman 1964, p. 250; Hudson et al. 1961, p. 167. Mao: Mao 1961, pp. 28–29. Burin: Burin 1963, p. 350n; see also Zagoria 1962, pp. 312–13, 357.

5. Quoted, Burin 1963, p. 336 (emphasis in original). See also Lenin 1939.

6. Dinerstein 1962, pp. 30–31.

7. Stalin 1973, pp. 471–72. Origins of World War II: Stalin 1973, p. 471; Taracouzio 1940, p. 283.

8. Hudson et al. 1961, pp. 43–44, 210–11. See also Burin 1963, p. 353.

9. Burin 1963, p. 351.

10. Ulam 1973, pp. 512–25. Werth 1964, ch. 66.

11. In addition, the Soviets had several border conflicts with the Japanese in 1938 and 1939. These, however, were largely initiated by the Japanese. See Finch 1951, p. 192. In 1934 two Soviet divisions were ordered to Afghanistan to aid pro-Soviet forces, but the forces were defeated before the Soviet troops could get there (Hosmer and Wolfe 1983, p. 186).

12. Hudson et al. 1961, p. 214.

13. See Starobin 1972, pp. 190–92.

14. See Mueller 1988a; Starobin 1972, p. 213n23; Shannon 1959, pp. 78–81.

15. Khrushchev: Hudson et al. 1961, pp. 45–46, 54, 156. Chinese: Hudson et al. 1961, p. 101; see also Zagoria 1962, p. 314.

16. Estimates for membership in the American Communist party are 80,000 in 1945, 54,000 in early 1950, 25,000 in 1953, 20,000 in 1955, and 3,000 in 1958 (Shannon 1959, pp. 3, 218, 360). The Communist proportion of the vote in France dropped from 26 percent in January 1956 to 19 percent in 1958 (Mackie and Rose 1982, pp. 127–37). See also Medvedev 1983, pp. 87–93; Starobin 1965, p. 47; Starobin 1972, ch. 10. "our inspired leader": Khrushchev 1963, p. 12.

17. Lin 1972, pp. 396, 390. Zagoria 1962, p. 309. Burin: Burin 1983, p. 351.

18. Hudson et al. 1961, pp. 211–13. Similarly, the "Moscow statement" of 1960: "All the socialist countries and the international working-class and Communist movement recognize their duty to render the fullest moral and material assistance to the peoples fighting to free themselves from imperialist and colonial tyranny" (Hudson et al. 1961, p. 196).

19. Wolfe 1970, p. 138; see also Hosmer and Wolfe 1983, p. 22. "rapid stream": Zagoria 1962, pp. 311–12. "heroic Algerian people": Hudson et al. 1961, p. 196; Zagoria 1962, p. 352; Burin 1963, p. 352.

20. Turner and Freedman 1964, p. 252.

21. Schlesinger 1978, p. 465. For samples of contemporary writings, see Greene 1962, and Paret and Shy 1962.

22. On this point see Quandt 1978, pp. 254–57.

23. Bialer 1986, pp. 188–89.

24. Hosmer and Wolfe 1983, p. 4; Ulam 1973, p. 686; Menon 1986, pp. 2–3.

25. MacFarquhar 1961, pp. 40–41; Zagoria 1962, p. 302. Internally, some of Khrushchev's rivals, including the influential Vyacheslav Molotov, apparently felt the cause would be better furthered by working with local Communist parties rather than with bourgeois national leaders, but Khrushchev's approach was the one adopted (Hosmer and Wolfe 1983, p. 9). With either strategy it was important not to push things too fast, because that could alienate leaders who had not yet seen the light; something like that occurred in Iraq in 1959 when "left-wing deviationists" unwisely tried to hurry things up (Zagoria 1962, pp. 307–8). On the alarm Khrushchev's moves caused in the West, see Valkenier 1983, p. 10.

26. Hosmer and Wolfe 1983, p. 13; Betts 1987, pp. 62, 65.

27. Betts 1987, p. 67. Suez: Bundy 1984, p. 49; Hosmer and Wolfe 1983, pp. 12–13. Full credit: Hudson et al. 1961, p. 138, 211–12.

28. Hosmer and Wolfe 1983, p. 17.

29. Valkenier 1983, p. 8.

30. Strumilin 1961, pp. 4–5. Khrushchev: Hudson et al. 1961, p. 214. "power of example": Zagoria 1962, p. 303. To American historian D. F. Fleming in 1961 this all meant that China and the Soviet Union were "now highly organized and marching swiftly into modernity" (1961, p. xiv). On these issues, see also Rubinstein 1985, p. 171.

31. Hudson et al. 1961, p. 179.

32. Rubinstein 1985, p. 319. Ballet: Khrushchev 1963, p. 327.
33. Quoted, Slusser 1978, p. 383n. On the extraordinary impact of the space race, see also Mandelbaum 1981, pp. 218–22; Smoke 1987, pp. 99–103.
34. President's Commission 1960, pp. 1–2. For the 1960–70 decade, the commission anticipated that the economies of the United States and Western Europe would grow only 40 percent and Japan 55 percent, whereas the USSR would grow 70 percent, China 100 percent, and Africa and Latin America 60 percent (p. 369).
35. Mao 1961, pp. 18, 25–27.
36. Hudson et al. 1961, pp. 87, 98; see also Burin 1963, p. 348; Zagoria 1962, pp. 21–22. Soviet view: Hudson et al. 1961, p. 214.
37. Hudson et al. 1961, p. 211.
38. Hudson et al. 1961, pp. 181–82.
39. Shevchenko 1985, p. 103. See also Snyder 1987/88, p. 108.
40. Hudson et al. 1961, pp. 138, 212.
41. Khrushchev's claims: Horelick and Rush 1966, p. 44; Smoke 1987, pp. 101–2. Slusser 1978, p. 392. Visitors to the Soviet Union might be routinely informed that "in Russia the scientists have been working on ballistic rockets since 1946, and the U.S. will never catch up with us" (Novak 1960, p. 265), and a 1960 public opinion analysis concluded that West Europeans were of the opinion "that the United States is not only currently militarily inferior to the USSR but will continue to be so for the next decade or two as well" (Wolfe 1970, p. 86).
42. Morton Halperin argues that "the primary military factors in resolving the crisis" were "American air and naval superiority in the area," not nuclear threats (Halperin 1987, p. 30). See also Betts 1987, pp. 54–62; Chang 1988; Brands 1988.
43. Betts 1987, pp. 71–75, 22. Breaking the siege: George and Smoke 1974, p. 383.
44. Slusser 1978, p. 347. For Khrushchev's frank admission of the problem, see Khrushchev 1970, p. 454.
45. Slusser 1978, pp. 356–57, 367, 375–76. Betts 1987, pp. 85–90.
46. Slusser 1978, p. 387.
47. Betts 1987, p. 93. The notion is repeated in Khrushchev's memoirs: Khrushchev 1970, p. 458.
48. Betts 1987, p. 102, 107; see also Horelick and Rush 1966, pp. 49, 89.
49. Betts 1987, pp. 106–7.
50. Betts 1987, pp. 103, 104, 107; Slusser 1978, pp. 420–32.
51. Slusser 1978, p. 424.
52. Betts 1987, p. 109.
53. Betts 1987, p. 110. For a careful latter-day tally of the missile balance in 1962, see Garthoff 1987, p. 142. In his memoirs, Khrushchev stresses that the missiles were moved to Cuba mainly to "protect Cuba's existence" but admits "in addition" that they "would have equalized what the West likes to call 'the balance of power' " (Khrushchev 1970, pp. 493–94). He suggests that the move was also inspired by something close to pure spite: "The Americans had surrounded our country with military bases and threatened us with nuclear weapons, and now they would learn just what it feels like to have enemy missiles pointing at you; we'd be doing nothing more than giving them a little of their own medicine" (p. 494; Khrushchev discusses Soviet concern in the mid-1950s that the United States was trying to establish bases in Afghanistan on pp. 507–8). This motivation, however petty, should probably be taken seriously; during his visit to America in 1959, Khrushchev spouted, "Let us station our bases in Mexico and Canada, then maybe you will have an understanding" (Khrushchev 1963, p. 338).
54. For the various warnings issued by the Kennedy administration, see Allison 1971, p. 41.
55. Shevchenko 1985, p. 113. Khrushchev's assurances: Allison 1971, pp. 40–42; Medvedev 1983, pp. 186–87. In his memoirs, Khrushchev says his "thinking went like this: if we installed the missiles secretly and then if the United States discovered the missiles were there after they were already poised and ready to strike, the Americans would think twice before trying to liquidate our installations by military means" (1970, pp. 493–94).
56. For debate on this issue, see Orme 1987, pp. 112–16; Lebow 1983, pp. 438–50; Lebow 1987, pp. 202–6. See also Tatu 1969, p. 240.
57. Kennedy 1971, pp. 58, 86–87. The American pledge not to invade required international verification measures; Castro never agreed to this, so the pledge technically does not hold. See Garthoff 1987, pp. 80–83; Kissinger 1979, pp. 633.
58. Betts 1987, pp. 109, 132. Allison 1971, p. 1.
59. Sorensen 1965, p. 705. Khrushchev has left no published probability estimates, but he says

he felt the episode brought the world to the "brink of atomic war" (Khrushchev 1970, p. 504). "war loomed": Sorensen 1965, p. 2. Rusk: Betts 1987, p. 116. "I hope": Sorensen 1965, p. 3. Berlin comparison: Betts 1987, pp. 91–92. See also Bundy 1988, p. 453.

60. Khrushchev 1970, pp. 495–97.

61. Allison 1971, pp. 222–23.

62. Garthoff 1987, p. 51. Shevchenko 1985, p. 118. Khrushchev apparently concluded that an American invasion of Cuba was imminent. The destruction of the Castro regime would have been a profound embarrassment and a major setback to Soviet prestige and to the international Communist movement (see Tatu 1969, pp. 264–65, 269).

63. Kennedy: Kennedy 1971, pp. 40, 105; see also Sorensen 1965, p. 513. McNamara: Blight, Nye, and Welch 1987, pp. 176–77.

64. Ball: Ball 1982, p. 307. McNamara: Trachtenberg 1985, p. 146. Transcripts: Welch and Blight 1987/88, pp. 27–28. Rusk: Irwin 1987; Lukas 1987, p. 58; Blight, Nye, and Welch 1987, pp. 178–79.

65. Welch and Blight 1987/88, p. 27. One in fifty: Blight, Nye, and Welch 1987, p. 184. See also Schlesinger 1978, pp. 528–29.

66. Jervis 1989. Brodie 1973, p. 426. See also Bundy 1988, pp. 453–57, 461–62.

67. Werth 1964, p. xii. "I have participated": Medvedev 1983, p. 190; Allison 1971, p. 221. For an able refutation of the popular notion that it was American nuclear superiority that determined the Soviet backdown, see Lambeth 1972, pp. 230–34; also Bundy 1988, pp. 446–53.

68. Blight, Nye, and Welch 1987, p. 187.

69. Bundy and Blight 1987/88, p. 92. According to one senior member of the British Foreign Office, everyone in the office "expected the Russians would be in West Berlin" on the day following Kennedy's speech (Brodie 1973, p. 431). See also Betts 1987, p. 115.

70. On the absence of crises, see also Mandelbaum 1981, p. 220; Schroeder 1985, p. 88; Adomeit 1986, p. 42; Garthoff 1987, p. 107; Betts 1987, p. 21; Blight, Nye, and Welch 1987, p. 187. For a post-Cuba example of routine Khrushchevian bluster (in January 1964), see Werth 1964, p. xi.

71. Bundy: Bundy 1984, p. 50. In Ball's terms: "By bringing Moscow face to face with the reality of nuclear catastrophe, [the crisis] paved the way for detente" (Ball 1982, p. 309). As Garthoff puts it, the Soviets "drew the lesson that crisis avoidance was better than crisis management" (1987, p. 127). See also Tatu 1969, p. 273; Adomeit 1986, p. 59; Betts 1987, p. 65; Bundy 1988, p. 462.

72. Larson 1963, pp. 193–96; Tatu 1969, p. 352n. Brodie 1973, p. 431.

73. See, for example, Harvard Nuclear Study Group 1983, ch. 3. This issue is discussed more fully in chapter 10.

Chapter 8   Vietnam: China Abandons the Cold War

1. Publication costs were graciously underwritten by the Cuban embassy: Russell 1963, pp. 32–33.

2. On these developments, see also Joffe 1987, pp. 39–40. Origin of CND symbol: Duff 1971, p. 115.

3. Paarlberg 1973, pp. 133, 137. Polls reflect a similar change. Before 1963, the various polling agencies had regularly asked the public if it expected another world war within the foreseeable future. Reflecting declining interest in the issue, the agencies largely abandoned it after 1963, and when they did manage to bring the issue up, they found the public far less concerned about war than earlier. Mueller 1977, pp. 326–27; see also Mueller 1979. Although the time was now seemingly ideal for practical and theoretical discussions of arms control, the *Journal of Arms Control*, launched with great fanfare in 1963, proved to be beyond its time, and it quietly died within the year.

4. Johnson 1971, pp. 297–304; Hosmer and Wolfe 1983, p. 36; Wolfe 1970, p. 271.

5. Bundy 1984, p. 51. Betts 1987, p. 124–28. Kissinger 1982, p. 583. Bundy 1988, pp. 518–25.

6. Hudson et al. 1961, p. 38; trade: pp. 37–38; also Zagoria 1962, p. 10.

7. Zagoria 1962, pp. 4, 9, 22, 403n4.

8. Medvedev 1986, p. 40. "adventurism": Tatu 1969, p. 319. Patch-up efforts: Medvedev 1986, p. 38; Tatu 1969, pp. 319–24. Tiger teeth: Rubinstein 1985, p. 140.

9. Rubinstein 1985, p. 140.

10. Salisbury 1969, pp. 9, 154, emphasis in the original. Trade decline: Perkins 1982, p. 93. Chinese claims: Salisbury 1969, p. 164. Soviets plan strike: Betts 1987, pp. 80–81.

11. See the discussion in Shevchenko 1985, pp. 165–66. Soviet historian Roy Medvedev also mentions the Soviets' "fear of war with a poorly armed but extremely populous and fanatical China" (1986, p. 50). Report of American dismay: Shevchenko 1985, pp. 165–66.

12. During this calamity, the Chinese leadership rejected all offers of outside aid. Ashton et al. 1984, pp. 614, 631.

13. Lin 1972, pp. 396, 398, 402, 410–11.

14. Gallup 1972, pp. 1711, 1811, 1881, 1908–9. Kennedy: Larson 1963, p. 329.

15. Hosmer and Wolfe 1983, pp. 27–28.

16. Hosmer and Wolfe 1983, pp. 40, 61. On the Yemen war of 1962–1970, see Porter 1984, ch. 5.

17. Hosmer and Wolfe 1983, pp. 28, 41.

18. Hosmer and Wolfe 1983, p. 42. On the USSR and Castro, see Jackson 1969, especially pp. 22, 145.

19. Hosmer and Wolfe 1983, p. 42; Nogee and Sloan 1979, pp. 350–65.

20. Lewy 1978, pp. 22, 24. For the argument that these decisions were the most fateful in drawing the United States into Vietnam, see Kattenburg 1980, pp. 108–16.

21. Janis 1982, ch. 5; Tuchman 1984, ch. 5.

22. For a checklist of "symptoms of defective decision-making," none of which apply to the 1965 decisions, see Janis 1982, p. 244. Leslie Gelb and Richard Betts conclude that in 1965 "(1) the core consensual goal of postwar foreign policy (containment of Communism) was pursued consistently; (2) differences of both elite and mass opinion were accommodated by compromise, and policy never strayed very far from the center of opinion both within and outside the government; and (3) virtually all views and recommendations were considered and virtually all important decisions were made without illusions about the odds for success" (Gelb and Betts 1979, p. 2). For other discussions, see Berman 1982, and Sullivan 1985, ch. 3.

23. Halberstam 1972, pp. 810–11.

24. Halberstam 1965, pp. 315, 319. Oddly, none of the passages quoted are included in the 1988 reprint edition of Halberstam's 1965 book. On the issue of changing attitudes toward Vietnam within the American press, see Maitland 1976. On Ball's proposals: Ball 1982, ch. 25; Halberstam 1972, p. 602. Although Ball's proposal shows exceptional insight, it was based in part on the apparently erroneous judgment that escalation would bring about "a serious danger of intervention by the Chinese" (Ball 1982, pp. 400, 505n10).

25. Sheehan 1964. Chinese: Lin 1972, p. 396. North Vietnam: Vo Nguyen Giap quoted by Maxwell Taylor in Fulbright 1966, p. 169. McNamara: Pentagon Papers 1971, Vol. 3, p. 500; see also pp. 50–51.

26. Whiting 1960, pp. 30–33.

27. Lippmann 1965b. Battle deaths: Small and Singer 1982, p. 93. Senator Mike Mansfield, later to become a critic of U.S. policy in Asia, said in 1963 that the Sino-Indian war "makes it clear that it is now necessary for the Southeast Asian nations to reckon with the enlargement of the Chinese role at any time to include the use of military power in a full modern revival of the classic pattern of Chinese imperial techniques in Southeast Asia" (Lewy 1978, p. 421).

28. J. Taylor 1976, pp. 94–97. See also Hilsman 1967, part 8.

29. J. Taylor 1976, pp. 98–101, 104–9; Sulzberger 1966. See also Lippmann 1965a. A White House study of 1964 treats Indonesia as a country that is already all but Communist (Pentagon Papers 1971, Vol. 3, p. 51). For a 1965 assessment that "the odds are" that the Communists "will come to power in Indonesia," see Pauker 1965, p. 285.

30. New York Times, September 7, 1966, p. 5; see also Shaplen 1970, p. 84. Various axes: Pentagon Papers 1971, Vol. 3, p. 267; J. Taylor 1976, ch. 2; Johnson 1971, pp. 136, 606; Shaplen 1970, p. 89.

31. Sulzberger 1966. Johnson 1971, pp. 335, 606; see also Shaplen 1970, p. 84. One of the more dovish of the members of the administration, Michael Forrestal, adapted a culinary image as he expressed concern about "China's swallowing up of Southeast Asia" (Pentagon Papers 1971, Vol. 3, p. 644; see also Gelb and Betts 1979, pp. 149–50).

32. Humphrey 1976, p. 326. Sihanouk: Sheehan 1964. Malaysia: Lewy 1978, p. 422. Others: Pentagon Papers 1971, Vol. 4, pp. 679–80. Laos: Humphrey 1976, pp. 328, 333. Gandhi: Humphrey 1976, p. 333.

33. Khrushchev 1970, p. 474; for similar conclusions by another Soviet commentator, see Henri 1968. "The fall": Sheehan 1964. See also John Kennedy's 1963 observation about the domino theory: "I believe it. . . . China is so large, looms so high just beyond the frontiers, that if South Vietnam

went, it would not only give them an improved geographical position for guerrilla assault on Malaysia, but would also give the impression that the wave of the future in Southeast Asia was China and the Communists" (*Pentagon Papers* 1971, Vol. 2, p. 828). Mao specialist Stuart Schram in 1964: Mao "appears more and more to envisage himself not only as the ruler of China, but also as the undisputed leader of all true revolutionary forces everywhere in the world" (1964, p. 49).

34. *Pentagon Papers* 1971, Vol. 3, pp. 482–83. Or, in 1967: "We'll just go on bleeding them until Hanoi wakes up to the fact that they have bled their country to the point of national disaster for generations" (Lewy 1978, p. 73).

35. Johnson 1971, p. 133. Rusk: Rusk 1971; see also Lippmann 1965a. Limited U.S. goals: see Goodman 1978, p. 37; Berman 1982, p. 146; the North Vietnamese, however, may have feared an American invasion of the north, at least in the early years of the war; see J. Van Dyke 1972, p. 84; McGarvey 1969, pp. 32–39.

36. Rostow: *Pentagon Papers* 1971, Vol. 3, pp. 381–82. Westmoreland 1976, p. 153; see also his comments in Thompson and Frizzell 1977, p. 66. McNamara: *Pentagon Papers* 1971, Vol. 4, p. 624. Some military leaders apparently felt the North Vietnamese supply of fighting-age men could be severely depleted, a calculation Defense Department analysts found to be physically impossible: Lewy 1978, pp. 82–84; Enthoven and Smith 1971, pp. 295–300; Jenkins 1970; Thayer 1977, pp. 85–92.

37. Moyers 1969, p. 270. White House views: *Pentagon Papers* 1971, Vol. 3, p. 215. In 1967, Zagoria observed that the Soviet Union "views the war not as an Armageddon but rather a potentially dangerous, nuisance-like intrusion that only complicates its foreign policy and adds to its dilemma. . . . The best outcome for Russia is a draw. It is for this reason that Russia has been working hard to promote a compromise settlement that falls short of both Chinese and American optimal goals, but which is acceptable to Hanoi" (Zagoria 1967, p. 127). See also Gelb and Betts 1979, p. 188; Goodman 1978, pp. 119–21.

38. Gelb and Betts 1979, p. 343, emphasis in the original.

39. Johnson: Tuchman 1984, p. 321. Moyers: Moyers 1969, p. 262. See also Lewy 1978, pp. 30, 41, 164; Goodman 1978, p. 2. 1964 triumph: see Janis 1982, p. 105.

40. *Pentagon Papers* 1971, Vol. 3, p. 484; Vol. 4, p. 624. Westmoreland: *Pentagon Papers* 1971, Vol. 3, p. 482; Westmoreland argues that this common reading of his 1965 timetable is inaccurate (1976, pp. 142–43). See Janis 1982, ch. 5; Gelb and Betts 1979, pp. 126, 318–22.

41. *Pentagon Papers* 1971, Vol. 4, p. 624. "invariably pessimistic": Janis 1982, p. 106. CIA estimates: see also Epstein 1975, pp. 95–110; *Pentagon Papers* 1971, Vol. 4, p. 26.

42. For a full treatment of this analysis, see Mueller 1980. Rusk: Rusk 1971.

43. Mueller 1980, pp. 505, 509. Near collapse: Khrushchev 1970, p. 482.

44. Quoted in Kinnard 1977, p. 67. As General Maxwell Taylor recalls, "We were inclined to assume . . . that they would behave about like the North Koreans and the Red Chinese a decade before; that is, they would seek an accommodation with us when the cost of pursuing a losing course became excessive. Instead, the North Vietnamese proved to be incredibly tough at accepting losses which, by Western calculation, greatly exceeded the value of the stake involved" (1972, p. 400). Or as Westmoreland put it tersely, "Any American commander who took the same vast losses . . . would have been sacked overnight" (1976, pp. 251–52). On this issue, see also Salisbury 1967, pp. 142–44; Berman 1974; Knoebl 1967; Pike 1966; Leites 1969; Mueller 1980, pp. 511–15; and especially Kellen 1972.

45. Fulbright and Morse: Raskin and Fall 1965, pp. 205–10, 288. Gelb and Betts 1979, p. 150. North Vietnamese: Goodman 1978, p. 6.

46. Polls: Mueller 1973, pp. 53–56. Johnson 1971, p. 153.

47. Interviewed on *Sixty Minutes*, CBS-TV, March 16, 1971.

48. See J. Taylor 1976, pp. 113–19; Shaplen 1970, pp. 91–148. "Living Dangerously": Shaplen 1970, p. 86.

49. Cultural revolution and Indonesia: J. Taylor 1976, pp. 124–25; Dorrill 1971, p. 71; see also Lippmann 1965c; Nogee and Donaldson 1984, p. 186; Mueller 1984b.

50. Kennan did not advocate sudden withdrawal, because this would be "humiliating" and would be "mercilessly exploited" by the Chinese; but he did think the United States should limit its newly overextended commitment and "dig in and wait and see whether possibilities for a solution do not open up," although he acknowledged that this holding action could be costly in lives and money (Fulbright 1966, pp. 109, 121, 133, 135, 140). Bundy 1978, p. 293.

51. Kissinger 1969, pp. 218–19. Test-case justification (Johnson in 1966): *Pentagon Papers* 1971, Vol. 4, pp. 657, 658. Munich (Rusk in 1966): *Pentagon Papers* 1971, Vol. 4, pp. 651, 653.

52. Herring 1986, p. 190; Lewy 1978, pp. 274–75.

53. Clifford 1969, pp. 606–7, emphasis added. McNamara: *Pentagon Papers* 1971, Vol. 4, p. 174.
54. On these decisions, see Schandler 1977.
55. On public opinion and the war, see Mueller 1973, chs. 2–6; for a summary of findings, see Mueller 1984a. On television's limited impact, see Mueller 1973, p. 167; Mandelbaum 1982; Entman and Paletz 1982; Lichty 1984; Mueller 1984a, p. 175; Hallin 1986. On the protesters and Nixon: Mueller 1984a, pp. 151–54.
56. For example, Nixon adviser Kissinger often observed that "North Vietnam could not be the only country in the world without a breaking point" (Goodman 1978, p. 96; see also Karnow 1983, p. 596).
57. Kissinger 1979, pp. 1011, 1039. Public opinion: Mueller 1973, pp. 96–99.
58. J. Taylor 1976, pp. 118–19. Shaplen 1970, p. 91.
59. Rusk 1971. See also Rusk's 1965 assessments in *Pentagon Papers* 1971, Vol. 4, p. 23.
60. See Sharp 1978, p. 255; Goodman 1978, p. 161; Robert Thompson in Thompson and Frizzell 1977, p. 105. See also Mueller 1980, pp. 515–17. Westmoreland: Race 1976, p. 393.
61. For a discussion, see Krepinevich 1986, pp. 261–68. Lewy 1978, pp. 439–40. Gelb and Betts 1979, p. 330.
62. Kellen 1972, p. 106. See also Mueller 1980, pp. 512–15.
63. Even in the mid-1950s when the image of a Communist "monolith" was most prevalent, American decision makers were quite aware of differences within the bloc and sought to exploit them: see the footnote on p. 211; Gaddis 1987b, ch. 6; Chang 1988, pp. 111, 118.
64. Kissinger 1979, p. 684. Hilsman: Turner and Freeman 1964, pp. 245–46.
65. Kissinger 1979, pp. 164, 169, 194, 691; 1950s formula: p. 783.
66. Kissinger 1979, pp. 765, 787. Nixon 1978, pp. 544–45.
67. Lieberthal 1982, p. 15.
68. J. Taylor 1976, pp. 334–37.
69. Kamm 1981.
70. *Policy Review*, Winter 1985, p. 33.

Chapter 9   Soviet Overreach and the Demise of the Cold War

1. Lewy 1978, pp. 202–8. For the argument that Nixon's assurances to the South Vietnamese were not "secret" in any important sense, see Kissinger 1982, pp. 304–6.
2. Lewy 1978, pp. 211–12; Karnow 1983, p. 664.
3. Kissinger 1979, p. 1470. For effective counterargument, see Isaacs 1983, pp. 500–504.
4. For example, polls in 1966 found some 15 to 35 percent of the public favoring withdrawal from Vietnam, but that percentage jumped to 54 percent when the question included the condition "suppose the South Vietnamese start fighting among themselves" and to 72 percent when it included the phrase "if the South Vietnamese government decides to stop fighting." Other poll data suggest that, as in the Korean War, loyalty toward the local anti-Communist ally was a relatively minor motivation among those who supported the American military ventures, and in this the public was in accord with much official thinking: in a 1965 memo Assistant Secretary of Defense John T. McNaughton pointedly excluded "help a friend" as a "U.S. aim" in the Vietnam War (*Pentagon Papers* 1971, Vol. 3, p. 695. Poll data: Mueller 1973, pp. 44, 48, 49, 58, 86–87, 100–101). On the contempt American troops often felt toward their allies, see Frey-Wouters and Laufer 1986, ch. 4.
5. Rescue casualties: E. Becker 1986, pp. 208–10. On these issues, see also Mueller 1984a.
6. Kraus 1979, pp. 538–39.
7. Two polls in 1976 gave respondents lists of twenty or thirty issues and asked them to select those most important to them. The international item that did best on one poll ("The budget for national defense") came in tenth; on the other the comparable item ("Keeping our military and defense forces strong") was eleventh (Mueller 1977, p. 328). Most important problem: Smith 1985, p. 273; see also Smith 1980.
8. Adams and Joblove 1982, p. 217; Sivard 1985, p. 10; E. Becker 1986. Executions in Vietnam: Desbarets and Jackson 1985; see also Canh 1983. Headline: Adams and Joblove 1982, p. 222.
9. Adams and Joblove 1982, pp. 218–19, 224–25.
10. Kissinger 1979, pp. 224–25. McGovern story: Adams and Joblove 1982, p. 219.
11. Breslauer 1987, pp. 436–37. On cautious optimism, see especially Hosmer and Wolfe 1983, ch. 12; Menon 1986, p. 149. See also Kolkowicz 1983, p. 296.

12. Hosmer and Wolfe 1983, pp. 81–84. Porter 1984, pp. 168–69, 177. Menon 1986, p. 136.

13. Hosmer and Wolfe 1983, pp. 86–88; Lescaze 1987. By 1985 Angolan coffee production was down to 5 percent of colonial levels (Brooke 1985).

14. C. May 1986.

15. Hosmer and Wolfe 1983, p. 240. Loss of Soviet credibility: Porter 1984, p. 240. Among the Soviets' more tangible losses was the denial of naval port facilities in Singapore (Hosmer and Wolfe 1983, p. 57).

16. Vance 1983, pp. 350–51, 388–89; Carter 1982, p. 475.

17. For commentary on this issue, see Mueller 1984c and 1987a.

18. Halperin 1987, p. 45.

19. Hosmer and Wolfe 1983, p. 58. See also Valenta 1984.

20. Christian 1986, pp. 55–56; Millett 1988, p. 116.

21. Hosmer and Wolfe 1983, p. 59.

22. Wolf et al. 1983, pp. vi, 20, 26; U.S. comparison: p. 47.

23. Valkenier 1983, pp. 148–49. See also Hough 1986, chs. 8, 9; Hosmer and Wolfe 1983, p. 78.

24. Menon 1986, p. 53. On backsliding, see pp. 166–68, 177–78 above. On Sudan, see Hosmer and Wolfe 1983, pp. 49, 62. Brezhnev doctrine: Wolf et al. 1983, pp. 383–84.

25. Although the new leaders of Grenada's shaky revolution were more ideologically pure than the group they overthrew, Castro was not happy with the change. See Valenta 1984, pp. 15–22.

26. *Congressional Quarterly*, August 25, 1984, p. 2124.

27. Weinberger 1984.

28. On Soviet expansion as United States lapses: Hosmer and Wolfe 1983, pp. 136–38.

29. France's Communist party, once one of the largest in the country, declined to a 20 percent share of the national vote by the mid-1970s, and in 1986 to less than 10 percent while managing to attract only 6 percent of the vote of those under twenty-five. Similarly, in Belgium, where the Communists had once been the third largest party, they failed in 1985 to win a single seat in parliament with their sumptuous 1.2 percent of the vote. See Ricklefs 1986; Markham 1986, 1987. When Khrushchev visited France, the Communist party there was able to organize a tumultuous reception; in the 1980s, Soviet visitors were mostly greeted by protesting dissidents (Markham 1986).

30. American contempt for the Soviet domestic system, however, continued apace: between 1973 and 1982 polls found that the percentage calling Communism the worst kind of government rose from 42 to 57 (Niemi et al. 1990). See also Mueller 1988a.

31. Markham 1986; Rubinstein 1985, pp. 257–60.

32. Bruneau 1985, p. 73; Rubinstein 1985, p. 125; Ferreira and Marshall 1986, pp. 209–11.

33. Bruneau 1985, p. 73. Ford: Ford 1979, p. 285. On NATO assumptions: E. May 1984, p. 219.

34. Markham 1986; Rubinstein 1985, pp. 258–59; Preston 1986, pp. 211–25.

35. Schumacher 1985. Portugal casualties: Bruneau 1985, p. 71.

36. McGlen 1986; see also Kramer et al. 1983.

37. Smoke 1987, ch. 10.

38. Smoke 1987, pp. 197–99.

39. Gwertzman 1981. Reagan on war in Europe: Smoke 1987, p. 232; H. Mueller and Risse-Kappen 1987, p. 83. Prevailing strategy: Smoke 1987, pp. 117, 227–32. U.S. buildup: see Smoke 1987, p. 121.

40. Joffe 1987, pp. 23–24. "Euroshima": H. Mueller and Risse-Kappen 1987, pp. 83–84.

41. Smoke 1987, pp. 234–35; Weigl 1987, p. 140. The resolution failed in the Senate. On public reaction to all this, see McGlen 1986; Schuman et al. 1986. For a deft dissection of the bishops' logic see Wohlstetter 1983.

42. Smoke 1987, pp. 237–39; H. Mueller and Risse-Kappen 1987, p. 87. Much of this "war-scare" propaganda was also directed at the Soviet people, and it may have affected the propagandists themselves as well. See Shlapentokh 1984; MccGwire 1987, pp. 308–10.

43. Before he came to office, 71 percent of West Germans had said they felt only the USSR threatened world peace; but by 1983 this had dropped to 32 percent. Few now felt that the sole country of concern was the United States, but the percentage concluding that both the United States and the USSR threatened peace—a pox on both houses—had risen from 14 to 34. A similar phenomenon took place on a question about which country still felt war was a political instrument

(H. Mueller and Risse-Kappen 1987, p. 58). In Britain during the Carter era those with and without confidence in the American "ability to deal wisely with present world problems" were about equal in numbers, but by 1983, under Reagan, those without confidence outnumbered the confident by 46 percentage points (Joffe 1987, p. 15).

44. Nor, apparently, did it significantly alter public opinion on the issue: in November 1981 nuclear opponents in Amsterdam pulled off the biggest demonstration in Holland's history, yet popular opposition to the new missiles changed hardly at all (De Boer 1985, p. 128; Smoke 1987, p. 234). For the apparent nonimpact in the United States of a widely watched television dramatization about thermonuclear destruction, see Schuman et al. 1986, pp. 528–29.

45. MccGwire 1987, p. 291.

46. Smoke 1987, p. 247.

47. Khrushchev 1974, p. 532. See also Shevchenko: "The men in the Kremlin are absorbed by questions of America's political, military, and economic power, and awed by its technological capacity" (1985, p. 278). On Soviet concerns about a space arms race: Smoke 1987, pp. 277–78.

48. Bialer 1986, pp. 91, 95. For an account suggesting how pathetically incapacitated Brezhnev was as early as 1977, see Shevchenko 1985, pp. 302–3.

49. Kennedy 1987, pp. 488–98, 502; Bialer 1986; Pipes 1984, chs. 3–4; Goldman 1987.

50. Quoted, Kennedy 1987, p. 498.

51. The oil price drop also meant that the Arab states, by far the largest buyers of Soviet arms, were reducing their orders for more. See Kramer 1987, p. 66; Kempe 1986. Defense burden: Kennedy 1987, pp. 498–504.

52. Even if one continues to include China in the camp, there was no relative economic progress: the Soviet camp's share of the gross world product was 22.4 percent in 1960, 22 percent in 1980 (Kennedy 1987, p. 436). Bialer 1986, p. 189. 1961 program: Voslensky 1984, p. 319. Soviet predictions: Strumilin 1961, pp. 4–5; Stephan 1986, p. 636.

53. Bunce 1985; first genuine: p. 32. See also Marer 1986, pp. 594–95.

54. Quoted, Sterba 1985. Vietnam, Cuba costs: Bunce 1985, p. 20. Thai general: Sterba and Lescaze 1985. Flora Lewis: "If Cuba is still anyone's model, it is of how not to run an economy" (1986).

55. For the most part, as Porter notes, "The entry of such weak and poorly developed countries as Angola, Ethiopia, Cambodia, and Afghanistan into the Soviet camp does not amount to more than a minor shift in the global balance" (1984, p. 238).

56. Safire 1988. See also Kontorovich and Rumer 1986; Farnsworth 1988. "policy of accelerating": Gorbachev 1987, p. 10.

57. *Wilson Quarterly*, Autumn 1985, p. 53. See also Treml 1982. After Gorbachev's antialcohol campaign began, home brewing of vodka was sharply up (Clines 1987; Gumbel 1988).

58. D'Anastasio 1987. For higher estimates, see Kontorovich and Rumer 1986, Safire 1988.

59. D'Anastasio 1987.

60. Snyder 1987/88, p. 115. "quiet, normal": Colton 1986, p. 191. 1961 program: Voslensky 1984, p. 319.

61. Fukuyama 1986, p. 715. See also Snyder 1987/88, p. 125; Colton 1986, p. 192; Katz 1986, p. 160. Brezhnev: Rubinstein 1986, p. 358. Andropov: Fukuyama 1986, pp. 718–19.

62. Fukuyama 1987, pp. 4–9; Snyder 1987/88, p. 117. "running sore": Rubinstein 1986, p. 356. Mozambique: Fukuyama 1986, pp. 723–24; Thurow 1987; Valkenier 1986, p. 432. Reduced interest in expansion: Simes 1987, p. 489; Fukuyama 1986, p. 726; Bialer 1986, pp. 337, 343; Colton 1986, p. 192–93; Breslauer 1988, p. 100.

63. Fukuyama suggests that Suslov played "an extremely important role in keeping alive the ideological issue in Soviet foreign policy" (1987, p. 13n). "long-term character": Colton 1986, p. 193; see also Snyder 1987/88, p. 125.

64. Snyder 1987/88, pp. 110–11. Fukuyama 1987, p. 12. For the argument, however, that the Soviet elite "will always find the pursuit of an aggressive foreign policy preferable to coping with internal problems," see Pipes 1984, p. 279. For the argument that the Soviet regime encourages an "imperial consciousness" as a "substitute for the waning ideological appeal of Marxism-Leninism," see Luttwak 1983a, p. 114. For the Leninism-on-its head argument that the elite wishes to maintain its "unrestricted monopoly of power" without a change in the system and "therefore aims at external expansion, the establishment of its rule over foreign countries and the exploitation of their wealth," see Voslensky 1984, p. 320. For the argument that "a Marxist-Leninist regime that actually declared

its intention to live in peace with 'capitalist' powers would inflict a mortal wound on its own legitimacy," see Kristol 1985.

65. See also Colton 1986, p. 191.

66. Shultz 1985.

67. Public opinion shifted in an isolationist direction after 1975 but then shifted back. At the same time, elite attitudes became quite selective—there was renewed interest in defending Western Europe, but apparently lowered enthusiasm for the defense of areas deemed to be less vital. See Mueller 1987b, p. 305.

68. Reagan 1985. On these issues, see also Tonelson 1985–86.

69. On this general argument, see Mueller 1985a, 1986, 1987b. See also Fukuyama 1987, p. 13.

Chapter 10 The Obsolescence of War in the Developed World

1. James 1911, pp. 282, 303.

2. Shaw 1913, p. 70.

3. For a discussion, see Luard 1986, chs. 3, 4, especially pp. 181–82.

4. Lea 1909, p. 45.

5. Snyder 1987/88, p. 113.

6. Luard 1986, pp. 143–44, 167, 180. For a discussion of Hitler's war aims, see pp. 65–66 in this book. On this issue, see also Stoessinger 1982, p. 208; Rosecrance 1986, pp. 9–13.

7. Gooch 1911, p. 248.

8. Britain's continued occupation (as some Irish would see it) of Northern Ireland is motivated primarily by sentiment and by a desire to prevent a bloody civil war there; from an economic point of view it makes little sense. On these issues, see Rosecrance 1986. On Portugal's economy-exhausting efforts to cling to its African colonies for antiquated reasons of status and prestige, see Maxwell 1985. For the argument that colonialism has never been profitable, see Clark 1936.

9. See also Levi 1981, especially ch. 8.

10. Morgenthau 1948, pp. 13, 183; power determinants: pp. 80–108. Similarly, the prominent theorist, Kenneth Waltz, requires that to be a Great Power a country needs to have "immense resources" which enable it to "generate and maintain" military power (1979, p. 183).

11. Waltz 1979, p. 72. Morgenthau on diplomats: 1948, pp. 105–8.

12. On this issue, see Levy 1983, pp. 41–42. Comparative economic and military data: Kennedy 1987, pp. 149, 200, 201.

13. See also Weltman 1974, pp. 407–8; Rosecrance 1986, p. 48.

14. Kennedy 1987, pp. xvi, 461, 539. See also Gilpin 1981.

15. Tolstoy 1966, p. 1145.

16. On this saga, see Revzin 1987; Colby 1987. When Americans were asked in 1988, "Which do you feel is more important in determining a country's influence in the world today—economic power or military power?" economic power was selected by 62 percent, military power by 22 percent (*Wall Street Journal,* May 16, 1988, p. 7).

17. Snow 1961, p. 259. National Planning Association 1958, p. 42. Kennedy: quoted, Joseph Nye in Meyer 1984, p. ix.

18. For example, British defense commentator F. W. Mulley in 1962: "All the arguments which led Britain to decide to develop her own independent nuclear weapons are equally valid . . . for France herself, and there is no reason why other members of NATO should not decide to follow suit" (1962, pp. 79–80). When France exploded its first bomb in 1960, President Charles De Gaulle was jubilant: "Hoorah for France! Since this morning she is stronger and prouder" (De Gaulle 1968, p. 103). See also Kennedy 1987, pp. 370, 401.

19. For the possibility that Indonesia was seeking in 1965 to have a Chinese bomb tested on Indonesian soil for expressive purposes, see p. 171.

20. De Gaulle 1968, p. 103. Robert Gilpin has suggested that "the possession of nuclear weapons largely determines a nation's rank in the hierarchy of international prestige" (1981, p. 215). For a discussion of the relevance of the Canadian case, concluding from it that the issue of nuclear proliferation—then often known as the "Nth country problem"—was approaching "a finite solution," see Mueller 1967. For a more recent analysis of the slow proliferation of nuclear weapons throughout the world, see Meyer 1984.

21. See also Robert Jervis: "India, China, and Israel may have decreased the chance of direct

attack by developing nuclear weapons, but it is hard to argue that they have increased their general prestige or influence" (1989, ch. 1).

22. Howard 1984a, pp. 14–15, 22. See also Blainey 1973, p. 127, ch. 9; Bueno de Mesquita 1981, ch. 2; Luard 1986, ch. 5.

23. Clausewitz 1976, pp. 85, 119–21. Livy said: "Nowhere do events correspond less to men's expectations than in war" (quoted, Linderman 1987, p. ii). See also Tolstoy 1966, p. 701; Gilpin 1981, pp. 202–3.

24. Thus, Sir Edward Creasy commented in 1870: "We thus learn not to judge the wisdom of measures too exclusively by the results. We learn to apply the juster standard of seeing what the circumstances and the probabilities were that surrounded a statesman or a general at the time when he decided on his plan" (p. xiii). See also Tolstoy 1966, p. 876.

25. R. Wohlstetter 1962, p. 350.

26. R. Wohlstetter 1962, p. 353.

27. See Bueno de Mesquita 1981, p. 86; Sagan 1988, pp. 914–17.

28. Thus, as Jervis notes: "Although the Japanese decision to go to war with the United States could be seen as rational, in fact it was based on the assumption that the U.S. would be willing to fight a limited war. This assumption not only proved to be erroneous, but was never analyzed with any care because the Japanese leaders did not want to consider the possibility that their real choice was between giving up China and suffering defeat in an enormously destructive war" (1989). See also Dower 1986, p. 293; Walt 1987, p. 146n19.

29. Schilling 1965, p. 389; Mueller 1968, p. 30. See also Russett 1972; Small 1980, pp. 234–65.

30. For a useful discussion of the ways a major war might begin, see Harvard Nuclear Study Group 1983, ch. 3.

31. See Bracken 1983, pp. 64–65.

32. Plane shot down: Hilsman 1967, pp. 220–21; without authorization: Bernstein 1987. Plane off course: Hilsman 1967, p. 221. Soviet officer: Garthoff 1987, pp. 40–41. Also: Bundy 1988, p. 455.

33. Wolfenstein 1957, p. 17. Jervis 1979, p. 299. Effects of World War II bombing: Brodie 1959, ch. 4. See also Mueller 1968, pp. 3–6.

34. Luard 1986, p. 232. See also Blainey 1973, ch. 9; Hinsley 1963, p. 348. A possible exception is the "football war" between Honduras and El Salvador in 1969 where unintended and undesired hostilities broke out, and where peace was reestablished in a few days (Luard 1986, p. 227n).

35. Jervis 1984, p. 155.

36. For a deft dissection of the "window of opportunity" thesis, see Lebow 1984.

37. Uhlig 1988.

38. For a comparison of "the Russian bear with a cornered tiger," see Weiszacker 1980, pp. 201–3.

39. "drunk on prosperity": Nathan 1974, p. 270. For the arguments that massive Japanese rearmament is "*almost* inevitable," that "the hallowed tradition of self-destruction . . . is at the heart of Japanese culture and history," and that to some Japanese "world wide nuclear holocaust . . . might well be the proper aesthetic response to the death of civility implicit in the idea of a commercialized Japan," see Stokes 1985, p. 63 (emphasis in the original). For a different view, see C. Johnson 1986.

40. Nasser: Lebow 1981, pp. 253–54. Castro: Gonzales and Ronfeldt 1986, p. 7n. Or North Vietnamese general Vo Nguyen Giap: "Throughout the world, a hundred people die every minute. Life and death don't matter" (Fallaci 1969). Compare Adolf Hitler: "Whereas war at the most kills off a fragment of the present, economic warfare murders the future. A single year of birth control in Europe kills more people than all those who fell in battle, from . . . the French Revolution . . . [through] the World War" (Hitler 1961, p. 8). On Mao's apparent military romanticism, see Schram 1964. "Hitlers are rare": Jervis 1984, p. 156.

41. See also Luard 1986, p. 396. For the argument that conventional war could reemerge as a viable possibility under nuclear stalemate, see Luttwak 1988.

42. On Hitler, see p. 85. A more critical time would probably be the "gray period" when one side has just begun to lose: from that point victory would seem increasingly distant, and eventual defeat, although not certain, would become increasingly likely (on this issue, see F. Brown 1968, p. 314). Nuclear weapons under these circumstances might appear to some leaders to be capable of reversing the course of the war before it is too late. The danger and the horror of unrestrained retaliation would remain, however; and more cautious leaders are likely to prefer letting the conventional phase of the war continue, holding nuclear weapons in reserve as a "last resort"—the position British strategists apparently assigned to gas in World War II (F. Brown 1968, p. 229). Thus, by the

time nuclear weapons are again considered by the losing side, when it becomes time to consider "last resorts," their use would have become patently suicidal.

43. See F. Brown 1968, p. 304. When a few unexploded nuclear weapons were lost in Spain and Greenland, incredibly elaborate procedures were found advisable to recover them (Lewis 1967).

44. See also F. Brown 1968, pp. 304–8.

45. Even if nuclear weapons *were* used, the war might well end long before it escalated to a nuclear Armageddon; that is, it is simply not true that "as soon as we use nuclear weapons, there are no limits" (Weiszacker 1980, p. 205). Some analysts hold that with careful planning, a country might be able to keep enough control of its nuclear arsenal so that it was able in a nuclear war to limit damage to itself, to maintain "escalation dominance," and to come out on top—to "prevail," if not exactly to "win"—in the war. (See, for example, Gray and Payne 1980; for an extended critique, see Jervis 1984.) But even those who argue that the war could not be *controlled* do essentially agree that it could be *limited*. Desmond Ball, a prominent proponent of this view, accepts the idea, to begin with, that if nuclear weapons were used very sparingly—for example, for "some clear demonstrative purposes"—escalation could well be avoided. He argues, however, that more extensive use of the weapons would soon bring about the destruction of communication systems which are "inherently relatively vulnerable" and thus that "there can really be no possibility of controlling a nuclear war" (1981, pp. 35–36). It is, of course, possible under conditions of such monumental confusion and chaos that various commanders would panic and start lobbing their bombs at each other without orders or authorization. But while no one could be confident under Ball's scenario that such destructive escalation could be *controlled*, it does not follow, or seem particularly likely, that such uncontrolled escalation would necessarily *happen*. It would obviously be a colossally dangerous situation, but it seems entirely possible that even under such extreme circumstances, well-disciplined commanders would simply lapse into puzzled, even catatonic, inaction as they awaited orders. Paul Bracken, another student of these issues, argues that a surprise attack might succeed because those in charge of retaliating "might be paralyzed into inaction . . . so stunned and disbelieving when told the attack was real that they might also refuse to take immediate action" (1983, p. 71). Thus, the war could well be limited, and escalation contained, because communications collapse or because decision makers react the way many people do when disaster looms: with stunned disbelief. Ball, in fact, eventually reaches the conclusion that even minor nuclear escalation might never take place: because of "the impossibility of developing capabilities for controlling a nuclear exchange," he stresses, "it is likely that decision-makers would be deterred from initiating nuclear strikes no matter how limited or selective the options available to them" (1981, p. 37).

46. Luard 1986, pp. 48–51.

47. Kissinger 1979, p. 885.

48. Luard 1986, p. 231.

49. Milne 1935, pp. 195–96.

50. For a contrary view, see Waltz 1988.

51. Milne 1935, p. 4. Angell 1914, p. 204.

52. Milne 1935, pp. 222–23.

53. Emerson 1904, pp. 155–56.

Chapter 11   Implications and Extrapolations

1. Morgan 1977, p. 9. See also Snyder 1961, ch. 1; Singer 1962, ch. 2; Art and Waltz 1983, p. 10.

2. Jervis 1985, p. 6; Lebow 1985b, p. 204.

3. See also Rosecrance 1975, p. 35.

4. Milburn 1959. See also Baldwin 1971; Jervis 1979, especially pp. 294–96, 304–5.

5. A modern instance: fearing encroachment by the United States during the petroleum crisis of the 1970s, some poorly-armed Arab states pledged to blow up their oil wells if invaded (see Rosecrance 1986, p. 11).

6. See S. Brown 1987, pp. 127–31; Sharp 1973. Switzerland has a large, dedicated, well-trained civilian army ("Switzerland does not have an army," Metternich is reported to have said, "It *is* an army") (Perry 1986). The country does not threaten so much to defeat an invader as to make the

costs of invasion, even successful invasion, very high—and, as noted in chapter 4 (p. 277n38), this threat has apparently been effective even against such devoted aggressors as Adolf Hitler. If defeated in initial battles, the Swiss army has trained to fall back into a network of secluded bases and installations in the Alps; from this bastion it would foray out to harass and obstruct the occupiers (Quester 1977, p. 174; Perry 1986). Moreover, were the Swiss to fight as tenaciously as they threaten, an invader could conquer the country only by destroying it as a productive society, thus lowering the gains of victory.

7. Deterrence can be broken down usefully into four variables—the net values of the status quo, of victory, and of defeat, and the probability of victory—and these variables can be neatly and simply interrelated by means of an expected utility formulation. For a discussion, see Mueller 1968, pp. 15–17, 1969, pp. 283–86; and K. Mueller, 1991.

8. Wohlstetter 1959; see also Snyder 1961, pp. 97–109.

9. See also Rosecrance 1973, pp. 242–51; Brodie 1976b.

10. Sivard 1987, p. 28.

11. Luard 1986, p. 398.

12. Luard 1986, p. 59.

13. See Wood 1966, pp. 3–9; Luard 1986, p. 399.

14. Cochran 1963, p. 287. See also Stevens 1940, especially ch. 15.

15. Graham 1968, p. 166; Drescher 1988.

16. Gorbachev: Lewis 1987; Keller 1987. On the Dominican case, see Lowenthal 1987. On earlier American police work in Nicaragua, see Christian 1986, ch. 1. On American efforts to prevent wars in Latin America between 1932 and 1942, see Wood 1966. On Gabon, see Brooke 1988.

17. "If one permits": Khomeini 1985, pp. 17–18. Spanish fanatic: Luard 1986, p. 338. "Even our": Taheri 1986, p. 295.

18. Taheri 1986, p. 298.

19. Fitzgerald 1972, pp. 589–90. On this issue, see also Stromberg 1982, p. 10.

20. Colburn and Lequizamon 1987, pp. 220–21.

21. Taheri 1986, p. 297. To emulate the West, he finds, would only create "a brothel on a universal scale" (Taheri 1986, p. 298).

22. Smoke 1986, p. 195.

23. Stacey 1953, p. 12.

24. See also Brodie 1976b; Jervis 1984, p. 195n17.

25. Interview on "MacNeil/Lehrer Newshour," May 10, 1988. Rogers: quoted, *U.S. News and World Report,* October 1, 1984, p. 38.

26. Shevchenko, 1985, p. 152; see also Charlton 1984, p. 156. Economic drain: Bunce 1985. Military value: Herspring 1986.

27. For the argument that war has been crucial in the creation and development of the modern state, see Mann 1986, p. 511.

Appendix: War, Death, and the Automobile

1. See *Accident Facts, 1985* (Chicago: National Safety Council), p. 77.

2. Cars and Vietnam: Fischoff et al. 1981, p. 82. Cars and World War II: *Accident Facts, 1985,* p. 13.

REFERENCES

Acheson, Dean. 1969. *Present at the Creation: My Years in the State Department.* New York: Norton.

Adams, Robert P. 1962. *The Better Part of Valor: More, Erasmus, Colet, and Vives, on Humanism, War, and Peace, 1496–1535.* Seattle: University of Washington Press.

Adams, William C., and Michael Joblove. 1982. The Unnewsworthy Holocaust: TV News and Terror in Cambodia. In William C. Adams (ed.), *Televising Coverage of International Affairs.* Norwood, NJ: Ablex, pp. 217–25.

Adomeit, Hannes. 1986. Soviet Crisis Prevention and Management: Why and When Do Soviet Leaders Take Risks? *Orbis,* vol. 30, no. 1 (Spring), pp. 42–64.

Alexandroff, Alan, and Richard Rosecrance. 1977. Deterrence in 1939. *World Politics,* vol. 29, no. 3 (April), pp. 404–24.

Allison, Graham T. 1971. *Essence of Decision: Explaining the Cuban Missile Crisis.* Boston: Little, Brown.

Angell, Norman. 1914. *The Great Illusion: A Study of the Relation of Military Power to National Advantage.* London: Heinemann.

———. 1933. *The Great Illusion 1933.* New York: Putnam's.

———. 1951. *After All: An Autobiography.* New York: Farrar, Straus and Young.

Aristotle. 1958. *The Politics of Aristotle.* New York: Oxford University Press.

Art, Robert J., and Kenneth N. Waltz. 1983. Technology, Strategy, and the Uses of Force. In Robert J. Art and Kenneth N. Waltz (eds.), *The Use of Force.* Lanham, MD: University Press of America.

Ashton, Basil, Kenneth Hill, Alan Piazza, and Robin Zeitz. 1984. Famine in China. *Population and Development Review,* vol. 10, no. 4 (December), pp. 613–45.

Bagehot, Walter. 1948. *Physics and Politics: Thoughts on the Application of the Principles of "Natural Selection" and "Inheritance" to Political Sociology.* New York: Knopf.

Baldick, Robert. 1965. *The Duel: A History of Dueling.* New York: Potter.

Baldwin, David A. 1971. The Power of Positive Sanctions. *World Politics,* vol. 24, no. 1 (October), pp. 19–38.

Baldwin, Hanson W. 1950. War of Prevention: Perils of Proposed Attack on Soviet Now Are Weighed against Alleged Advantage. *New York Times,* September 1, p. 4.

Ball, Desmond. 1981. *Can Nuclear War Be Controlled?* Adelphi Paper 169, Autumn. London: International Institute for Strategic Studies.

Ball, George W. 1982. *The Past Has Another Pattern.* New York: Norton.

Barbour, Hugh, and Arthur O. Roberts. 1973. *Early Quaker Writings, 1650–1700.* Grand Rapids, MI: Eerdmans.

Barclay, Thomas. 1911. Peace. *Encyclopaedia Britannica,* 11th ed., vol. 21, pp. 4–16.

Bartlett, C. J. 1977. *A History of Postwar Britain, 1945–1974.* London: Longman.

Batchelder, Robert C. 1961. *The Irreversible Decision, 1939–1950.* New York: Macmillan.

Batty, Peter, and Peter Parish. 1987. *The Divided Union: The Story of the Great American War, 1861–65.* Topsfield, MA: Salem House.

Beales, A. C. F. 1931. *The History of Peace: A Short Account of the Organized Movements for International Peace.* New York: Dial.

Becker, Elizabeth. 1986. *When the War Was Over: The Voices of Cambodia's Revolution and Its People.* New York: Simon and Schuster.

Becker, Jean-Jacques. 1986. *The Great War and the French People.* New York: St. Martin's.

Bell, P. M. H. 1986. *The Origins of the Second World War in Europe.* London: Longman.

References

Belote, James and William. 1970. *Typhoon of Steel: The Battle for Okinawa.* New York: Harper and Row.

Berman, Larry. 1982. *Planning a Tragedy: The Americanization of the War in Vietnam.* New York: Norton.

Berman, Paul. 1974. *Revolutionary Organization.* Lexington, MA: Lexington.

Bernhardi, Friedrich von. 1914a. *Germany and the Next War.* New York: Longmans, Green.

————. 1914b. *Britain as Germany's Vassal.* New York: Doran.

Bernstein, Richard. 1987. Meeting Sheds New Light on Cuban Missile Crisis. *New York Times,* October 14, p. A10.

Betts, Richard K. 1987. *Nuclear Blackmail and Nuclear Balance.* Washington: Brookings.

Bialer, Seweryn. 1986. *The Soviet Paradox: External Expansion, Internal Decline.* New York: Knopf.

Bialer, Uri. 1980. *Shadow of the Bomber: The Fear of Air Attack and British Politics, 1932–1939.* London: Royal Historical Society.

Blainey, Geoffrey. 1973. *The Causes of Wars.* New York: Free Press.

Blechman, Barry M., and Stephen S. Kaplan. 1978. *Force without War.* Washington: Brookings.

Blight, James G., Joseph S. Nye, Jr., and David A. Welch. 1987. The Cuban Missile Crisis Revisited. *Foreign Affairs,* vol. 66, no. 1 (Fall), pp. 170–88.

Bloch, Jean de. 1914. *The Future of War.* Boston: World Peace Foundation.

Bluhm, William T. 1974. *Ideologies and Attitudes: Modern Political Culture.* Englewood Cliffs, NJ: Prentice-Hall.

Boyle, Francis Anthony. 1985. *World Politics and International Law.* Durham, NC: Duke University Press.

Bracken, Paul. 1983. *The Command and Control of Nuclear Forces.* New Haven, CT: Yale University Press.

Bradley, Omar. 1949. This Way Lies Peace (as told to Beverly Smith). *Saturday Evening Post,* October 15, pp. 33ff.

————. 1953. A Soldier's Farewell (as told to Beverly Smith). *Saturday Evening Post,* August 22, pp. 21ff.

Brams, Steven J., and D. Marc Kilgour. 1988. *Game Theory and National Security.* New York: Basil Blackwood.

Brands, H. W., Jr. 1988. Testing Massive Retaliation: Credibility and Crisis Management in the Taiwan Strait. *International Security,* vol. 12, no. 4 (Spring), pp. 124–51.

Breslauer, George W. 1987. Ideology and Learning in Soviet Third World Policy. *World Politics,* vol. 39, no. 3 (April), pp. 429–48.

————. 1988. All Gorbachev's Men. *National Interest,* Summer, pp. 91–108.

Brines, Russell. 1944. *Until They Eat Stones.* Philadelphia: Lippincott.

Brittain, Vera. 1934. *Testament of Youth: An Autobiographical Study of the Years 1900–1925.* New York: Macmillan.

Brodie, Bernard. 1946. The Weapon. In Bernard Brodie (ed.), *The Absolute Weapon.* New York: Harcourt, Brace, pp. 21–107.

————. 1959. *Strategy in the Missile Age.* Princeton, NJ: Princeton University Press.

————. 1966. *Escalation and the Nuclear Option.* Princeton, NJ: Princeton University Press.

————. 1973. *War and Politics.* New York: Macmillan.

————. 1976a. The Continuing Relevance of *On War,* and A Guide to the Reading of *On War.* In Carl von Clausewitz, *On War.* Princeton, NJ: Princeton University Press, pp. 45–58, 641–711.

————. 1976b. On the Objectives of Arms Control. *International Security,* vol. 1, no. 1 (Summer), pp. 17–36.

Brooke, James. 1985. Angolan Coffee Trade in Shambles. *New York Times,* January 14, sec. 4, p. 4.

————. 1988. Gabon Keeps Strong Links with France, *New York Times,* February 23, p. A9.

Brown, Frederic J. 1968. *Chemical Warfare: A Study in Restraints.* Princeton, NJ: Princeton University Press.

Brown, Seyom. 1987. *The Causes and Prevention of War.* New York: St. Martin's.

Bruneau, Thomas C. 1985. Portugal: Discovering Democracy. *Wilson Quarterly,* vol. 9, no. 1 (New Year's), pp. 67–81.

Bucholz, Arden. 1985. *Hans Delbruck and the German Military Establishment: War Images in Conflict.* Iowa City, IA: University of Iowa Press.

References

Buckle, Henry Thomas. 1862. *History of Civilization in England,* vol. 1. New York: Appleton.

Bueno de Mesquita, Bruce. 1981. *The War Trap.* New Haven, CT: Yale University Press.

———. 1984. Nuclear Peace through Selective Nuclear Proliferation. University of Rochester: Political Science Department (April).

Bullock, Alan. 1952. *Hitler: A Study in Tyranny.* London: Odhams.

———. 1972. Hitler and the Origins of the Second World War. In Henry A. Turner, Jr. (ed.), *Nazism and the Third Reich.* New York: Quadrangle, pp. 219–46.

Bunce, Valerie. 1985. The Empire Strikes Back: The Evolution of the Eastern Bloc from a Soviet Asset to a Soviet Liability. *International Organization,* vol. 39, no. 1 (Winter), pp. 1–46.

Bundy, McGeorge. 1978. The Americans and the World. In Stephen R. Graubard (ed.), *A New America?* New York: Norton, pp. 289–304.

———. 1984. The Unimpressive Record of Atomic Diplomacy. In Gwyn Prins (ed.), *The Nuclear Crisis Reader.* New York: Vantage, pp. 42–54.

———. 1988. *Danger and Survival: Choices About the Bomb in the First Fifty Years.* New York: Random House.

Bundy, McGeorge, and James G. Blight (eds.) 1987/88. October 27, 1962: Transcripts of the Meetings of the ExComm. *International Security,* vol. 12, no. 3 (Winter), pp. 30–92.

Burin, Frederic S. 1963. The Communist Doctrine of the Inevitability of War. *American Political Science Review,* vol. 57, no. 2 (June), pp. 334–54.

Butow, Robert J. C. 1954. *Japan's Decision to Surrender.* Stanford, CA: Stanford University Press.

———. 1961. *Tojo and the Coming of the War.* Stanford, CA: Stanford.

Cairnes, J. E. 1865. International Law. *Fortnightly Review,* vol. 2 (November 1), pp. 641–50.

Canh, Nguyen Van. 1983. *Vietnam under Communism, 1975–1982.* Stanford, CA: Hoover Institution Press.

Cantril, Hadley. 1940. *The Invasion from Mars: A Study in the Psychology of Panic.* Princeton, NJ: Princeton University Press.

Carter, Jimmy. 1982. *Keeping Faith: Memories of a President.* New York: Bantam.

Chang, Gordon H. 1988. To the Nuclear Brink: Eisenhower, Dulles, and the Quemoy-Matsu Crisis. *International Security,* vol. 12, no. 4 (Spring), pp. 96–122.

Charlton, Michael. 1984. *The Eagle and the Small Birds: Crisis in the Soviet Empire from Yalta to Solidarity.* Chicago: University of Chicago Press.

Chickering, Roger. 1975. *Imperial Germany and a World without War: The Peace Movement and German Society, 1892–1914.* Princeton, NJ: Princeton University Press.

Christian, Shirley. 1986. *Nicaragua: Revolution in the Family.* New York: Vintage.

Churchill, Winston S. 1932. *Amid These Storms: Thoughts and Adventures.* New York: Scribner's.

Clancy, Tom. 1986. *Red Storm Rising.* New York: Putnam.

Clark, Grover. 1936. *The Balance Sheets of Imperialism: Facts and Figures on Colonies.* New York: Columbia University Press.

Clarke, I. F. 1966. *Voices Prophesying War, 1763–1984.* London: Oxford.

Clausewitz, Carl von. 1976. *On War* (Edited and translated by Michael Howard and Peter Paret). Princeton, NJ: Princeton University Press.

Clifford, Clark. 1969. A Viet Nam Reappraisal. *Foreign Affairs,* vol. 47 (January), pp. 601–22.

Clines, Frances X. 1987. Moonshine Is Undermining Moscow's Temperance. *New York Times,* November 16.

Cochran, Hamilton. 1963. *Noted American Duels and Hostile Encounters.* Philadelphia: Chilton.

Coffey, Thomas M. 1970. *Imperial Tragedy: Japan in World War II, The First Days and the Last.* New York: World.

Cohen, Stephen F. 1985. *Rethinking the Soviet Experience.* New York: Oxford University Press.

Cohen, Warren J. 1987. Conversations with Chinese Friends: Zhou Enlai's Associates Reflect on Chinese-American Relations in the 1940s and the Korean War. *Diplomatic History,* vol. 11, no. 3 (Summer), pp. 283–89.

Colburn, Forrest D., and Francisco A. Leguizamon. 1987. Deteriorating Public and Private Sector Relations in Central America. *Journal of Policy Analysis and Management,* vol. 6., no. 2 (Winter), pp. 220–29.

Colby, Laura. 1987. Italians' Talk of Surpassing Britain Fades. *Wall Street Journal,* May 21, p. 24.

Colton, Timothy J. 1986. *The Dilemma of Reform in the Soviet Union* (rev. ed.). New York: Council on Foreign Relations.

References

Compton, Arthur H. 1956. *Atomic Quest.* New York: Oxford University Press.

Conquest, Robert. 1986. *The Harvest of Sorrow: Soviet Collectivization and the Terror-Famine.* New York: Oxford University Press.

Coulton, G. G. 1916. *The Main Illusions of Pacifism: A Criticism of Mr. Norman Angell and of the Union of Democratic Control.* Cambridge: Bowes and Bowes.

Craig, Gordon. 1964. *The Politics of the Prussian Army, 1640–1945.* New York: Oxford University Press.

Craig, William. 1967. *The Fall of Japan.* New York: Dial.

Cramb, J. A. 1915. *The Origins and Destiny of Imperial Britain.* London: Murray.

Creasy, Edward. 1870. *The Fifteen Decisive Battles of the World: From Marathon to Waterloo.* London: Richard Bentley.

D'Anastasio, Mark. 1987. Soviet Generals Get Reformist Message. *Wall Street Journal,* May 6, p. 26.

de Seversky, Alexander P. 1946. Atomic Bomb Hysteria. *Reader's Digest,* February, pp. 121–26.

———. 1950. *Air Power: Key to Survival.* New York: Simon and Schuster.

Deane, John R. 1947. *The Strange Alliance.* New York: Viking.

DeBoer, Connie. 1985. The Polls: The European Peace Movement and Development of Nuclear Missiles. *Public Opinion Quarterly,* vol. 49 (Spring), pp. 119–32.

DeGaulle, Charles. 1968. The Thoughts of Charles De Gaulle. *New York Times Magazine,* May 12, pp. 102–3.

Desbarats, Jacqueline, and Karl D. Jackson. 1985. Research among Vietnam Refugees Reveals a Blood Bath. *Wall Street Journal,* April 22, p. 29.

Dinerstein, Herbert S. 1962. *War and the Soviet Union: Nuclear Weapons and the Revolution in Soviet Military and Political Thinking.* New York: Praeger.

Djilas, Milovan. 1962. *Conversations with Stalin.* New York: Harcourt, Brace.

Documents on German Foreign Policy, 1918–1945, Series D, Vol. 8. 1954. Washington: U.S. Government Printing Office.

Dorrill, William F. 1971. Power, Policy, and Ideology in the Making of the Chinese Cultural Revolution. In Thomas W. Robinson (ed.), *The Cultural Revolution in China.* Berkeley and Los Angeles: University of California Press, pp. 21–112.

Dower, John W. 1986. *War without Mercy: Race and Power in the Pacific War.* New York: Pantheon.

Doyle, Michael W. 1983. Kant, Liberal Legacies, and Foreign Affairs. *Philosophy and Public Affairs,* vol. 12 (Summer and Fall), pp. 205–35, 323–53.

———. 1987. Liberalism and World Politics. *Americam Political Science Review,* vol. 80. no. 4 (December), pp. 1151–69.

Drescher, Seymour. 1987. *Capitalism and Antislavery: British Mobilization in Comparative Perspective.* New York: Oxford University Press.

———. 1988. Brazilian Abolition in Comparative Perspective. *Hispanic American Historical Review,* vol. 68, no. 3 (August), pp. 429–60.

Duff, Peggy. 1971. *Left, Left, Left: A Personal Account of Six Protest Campaigns.* London: Allison and Busby.

Dupuy, R. Ernest, and George Fielding Eliot. 1937. *If War Comes.* New York: Macmillan.

Dyson, Freeman. 1979. *Disturbing the Universe.* New York: Harper and Row.

Earle, Edward Mead. 1943. Lenin, Trotsky, Stalin: Soviet Concepts of War. In Edward Mead Earle (ed.), *Makers of Modern Strategy: Military Thought from Machiavelli to Hitler.* Princeton, NJ: Princeton University Press, pp. 322–64.

Einstein, Albert. 1960. *Einstein on Peace* (Edited by Otto Nathan and Heinz Norden). New York: Simon and Schuster.

Eisenhower, Dwight D. 1963. *Mandate for Change: 1953–1956.* Garden City: Doubleday.

Ellsberg, Daniel. 1969. The Crude Analysis of Strategic Choice. In John Mueller (ed.), *Approaches to Measurement in International Relations: A Non-Evangelical Survey.* New York: Appleton-Century-Crofts, pp. 288–94.

Eltis, David. 1987. *Economic Growth and the Ending of the Transatlantic Slave Trade.* New York: Oxford University Press.

Emerson, Ralph Waldo. 1904. War. In *Miscellanies.* Cambridge: Riverside, pp. 150–76.

Engerman, Stanley L. 1986. Slavery and Emancipation in Comparative Perspective: A Look at Some Recent Debates. *Journal of Economic History,* vol. 46, no. 2 (June), pp. 317–39.

References

Enthoven, Alain C., and K. Wayne Smith. 1971. *How Much Is Enough? Shaping the Defense Program 1961–1969*. New York: Harper Colophon.

Entman, Robert M., and David Paletz. 1982. The War in Southeast Asia: Tunnel Vision on Television. In William C. Adams (ed.), *Televising Coverage of International Affairs*. Norwood, NJ: Ablex, pp. 181–201.

Epstein, Edward Jay. 1975. *Between Fact and Fiction: The Problem of Journalism*. New York: Vintage.

Esposito, Vincent J. 1979. World War I. In *Encyclopedia Americana*, Vol. 29. Danbury, CT: Americana, pp. 216–363.

Evangelista, Matthew A. 1982/83. Stalin's Postwar Army Reappraised. *International Security*, vol. 7, no. 3 (Winter), pp. 110–38.

Fallaci, Oriana. 1969. Interview with General Giap. *Washington Post*, April 6, p. B1.

Falnes, Oscar J. 1938. *Norway and the Nobel Peace Prize*. New York: Columbia University Press.

Farnsworth, Clyde H. 1988. Study Finds Soviet Output Is Stagnant. *New York Times*, April 25, p. D1.

Farrar, L. L., Jr. 1973. *The Short-War Illusion: German Policy, Strategy and Domestic Affairs, August–December 1914*. Santa Barbara, CA: ABC-Clio.

Feld, Bernard T. 1978. To Move or Not to Move the Clock. *Bulletin of Atomic Scientists*, January, pp. 8–9.

Ferreira, Hugo Gil, and Michael W. Marshall. 1986. *Portugal's Revolution: Ten Years On*. Cambridge: Cambridge University Press.

Finch, Clark W. 1951. Quasi-War between Japan and the USSR, 1937–1939. *World Politics*, vol. 2, no. 2 (January), pp. 174–99.

Fischer, Fritz. 1967. *Germany's Aims in the First World War*. New York: Norton.

———. 1975. *War of Illusions: German Policies from 1911 to 1914*. New York: Norton.

Fischoff, Baruch, Sarah Lichtenstein, Paul Slovic, Stephen L. Derby, and Ralph L. Keeney. 1981. *Acceptable Risk*. Cambridge: Cambridge University Press.

Fitzgerald, Frances. 1972. *Fire in the Lake: The Vietnamese and the Americans in Vietnam*. New York: Vintage.

Fleming, D. F. 1961. *The Cold War and Its Origins 1917–1960*. Vol. I: 1917–1950. Garden City, NY: Doubleday.

Foot, Rosemary. 1985. *The Wrong War: American Policy and the Dimensions of the Korean Conflict, 1950–1953*. Ithaca, NY: Cornell University Press.

Ford, Gerald R. 1979. *A Time to Heal*. New York: Harper and Row.

Freeman, Major Ben C. 1884. *The Field of Honor: Being a Complete and Comprehensive History of Dueling in All Countries*. New York: Fords, Howard, and Hulbert.

Freud, Sigmund. 1930. *Civilization and Its Discontents*. London: Hogarth.

Frey-Wouters, Ellen, and Robert S. Laufer. 1986. *Legacy of a War: The American Soldier in Vietnam*. Armonk, NY: Sharpe.

Fukuyama, Francis. 1986. Gorbachev and the Third World. *Foreign Affairs*, vol. 64, no. 4 (Spring), pp. 715–31.

———. 1987. Patterns of Soviet Third World Policy. *Problems of Communism*, vol. 36, no. 5 (September–October), pp. 1–13.

Fulbright, J. William. 1966. *The Vietnam Hearings*. New York: Vintage.

Fussell, Paul. 1975. *The Great War and Modern Memory*. New York: Oxford University Press.

Gaddis, John Lewis. 1972. *The United States and the Origins of the Cold War, 1941–1947*. New York: Columbia University Press.

———. 1974. Was the Truman Doctrine a Real Turning Point? *Foreign Affairs*, vol. 52, no. 2 (January), pp. 386–401.

———. 1982. *Strategies of Containment: A Critical Appraisal of Postwar American National Security Policy*. New York: Oxford University Press.

———. 1987a. Expanding the Data Base: Historians, Political Scientists, and the Enrichment of Security Studies. *International Security*, vol. 12, no. 1 (Summer), pp. 3–21.

———. 1987b. *The Long Peace: Inquiries into the History of the Cold War*. New York: Oxford University Press.

Gallup, George H. (ed.). 1972. *The Gallup Poll: Public Opinion 1935–1971*. New York: Random House.

References

———. 1978. *The Gallup Poll: Public Opinion 1972–1977.* Wilmington, DE: Scholarly Resources.

Garthoff, Raymond L. 1987. *Reflections on the Cuban Missile Crisis.* Washington: Brookings.

Gati, Charles. 1974. Introduction: But Was the Cold War Really Necessary? In Charles Gati (ed.), *Caging the Bear: Containment and the Cold War.* Indianapolis, IN: Bobbs-Merrill, pp. xiii–xxvi.

Gelb, Leslie H., with Richard K. Betts. 1979. *The Irony of Vietnam: The System Worked.* Washington: Brookings.

George, Alexander L. 1955. American Policy-Making and the North Korean Aggression. *World Politics,* vol. 7, no. 2 (January), pp. 209–32.

George, Alexander L., and Richard Smoke. 1974. *Deterrence in American Foreign Policy: Theory and Practice.* New York: Columbia University Press.

Gilpin, Robert. 1981. *War and Change in World Politics.* Cambridge: Cambridge University Press.

Glynn, Patrick. 1987. The Sarajevo Fallacy: The History and Intellectual Origins of Arms Control Theology. *The National Interest,* Fall, pp. 3–32.

Goldin, Claudia D. 1973. The Economics of Emancipation. *Journal of Economic History,* vol. 33, no. 1 (March), pp. 66–85.

Goldin, Claudia D., and Frank D. Lewis. 1975. The Economic Costs of the American Civil War: Estimates and Implications. *Journal of Economic History,* vol. 35, no. 2 (June), pp. 299–326.

Goldman, Marshall I. 1987. *Gorbachev Challenge: Economic Reform in the Age of High Technology.* New York: Norton.

Gonzales, Edward, and David Ronfeldt. 1986. *Castro, Cuba, and the World: Executive Summary.* R-3420/1, April. Santa Monica, CA: Rand Corporation.

Gooch, B. P. 1911. *History of Our Time, 1885–1911.* London: Williams and Norgate.

Goodman, Allan E. 1978. *The Lost Peace: America's Search for a Negotiated Settlement of the Vietnam War.* Stanford, CA: Hoover Institution Press.

Gorbachev, Mikhail. 1987. *Perestroika: New Thinking for Our Country and the World.* New York: Harper and Row.

Graham, Richard. 1968. *Britain and the Onset of Modernization in Brazil, 1850–1914.* London: Cambridge University Press.

Gray, Colin S., and Keith Payne. 1980. Victory Is Possible. *Foreign Policy,* no. 39 (Summer), pp. 14–27.

Greene, T. N. (ed.). 1962. *The Guerrilla—And How to Fight Him: Selections from the Marine Corps Gazette.* New York: Praeger.

Greenhouse, Steven. 1988. Zaire, The Manager's Nightmare: So Much Potential, So Poorly Harnessed. *New York Times,* May 23, p. 48. See also correction, May 26, p. A3.

Grey, Edward. 1925. *Twenty-Five Years, 1892–1916,* Vol. 2. New York: Stokes.

Grodzins, Morton, and Eugene Rabinowitch (eds.). 1963. *The Atomic Age: Scientists in National and World Affairs.* New York: Basic Books.

Gumbel, Peter. 1988. Moscow Buzzes with Talk that Dry Laws May Be Eased to Placate Lovers of Vodka. *Wall Street Journal,* June 1, p. 23.

Gwertzman, Bernard. 1981. Allied Contingency Plan Envisions a Warning Shot, Says Haig. *New York Times,* November 5, p. A1.

Haas, Ernst. 1983. On Hedging Our Bets: Selective Engagement with the Soviet Union. In Aaron Wildavsky (ed.), *Beyond Containment.* San Francisco: Institute for Contemporary Studies, pp. 93–124.

Haber, L. F. 1986. *The Poisonous Cloud: Chemical Warfare in the First World War.* Oxford: Clarendon.

Hackett, John. 1979. *The Third World War: August 1985.* New York: Macmillan.

Halberstam, David. 1965. *The Making of a Quagmire.* New York: Random House.

———. 1972. *The Best and the Brightest.* New York: Penguin.

———. 1988. *The Making of a Quagmire* (rev. ed.). New York: Knopf.

Hallin, Daniel C. 1986. *The "Uncensored War": The Media and Vietnam.* New York: Oxford University Press.

Halperin, Morton H. 1963. *Limited War in the Nuclear Age.* New York: Wiley.

———. 1987. *Nuclear Fallacy: Dispelling the Myth of Nuclear Strategy.* Cambridge, MA: Ballinger.

Harris, Robert, and Jeremy Paxman. 1982. *A Higher Form of Killing: The Secret Story of Chemical and Biological Warfare.* New York: Hill and Wang.

References

Harvard Nuclear Study Group. 1983. *Living with Nuclear Weapons.* New York: Bantam.

Henri, Ernst. 1968. The View from the Pamirs. *Survival,* vol. 10, no. 1 (January), pp. 28–30.

Herring, George C. 1973. *Aid to Russia 1941–1946.* New York: Columbia University Press.

———. 1986. *America's Longest War: The United States and Vietnam, 1950–1975* (2d ed.). New York: Knopf.

Herspring, Dale R. 1986. The Soviet Union and the East European Militaries: The Diminishing Asset. In Roman Kolkowicz and Ellen Propper Mickiewicz (eds.), *The Soviet Calculus of Nuclear War.* Lexington, MA: Lexington Books, pp. 243–65.

Hilsman, Roger. 1967. *To Move a Nation: The Politics of Foreign Policy in the Administration of John F. Kennedy.* New York: Delta.

Hinsley, F. H. 1963. *Power and the Pursuit of Peace: Theory and Practice in the History of Relations between States.* London: Cambridge University Press.

Hirschman, Albert O. 1977. *The Passions and the Interests: Political Arguments for Capitalism before Its Triumph.* Princeton, NJ: Princeton University Press.

Hirst, Margaret E. 1923. *The Quakers in Peace and War: An Account of Their Peace Principles and Practice.* New York: Doran.

Historicus [George Allen Morgan]. 1949. Stalin on Revolution. *Foreign Affairs,* vol. 27, no. 2 (January), pp. 175–214.

Hitler, Adolf. 1939. *Mein Kampf.* New York: Reynal and Hitchcock.

———. 1942. *The Speeches of Adolf Hitler.* London: Oxford University Press.

———. 1953. *Hitler's Secret Conversations 1941–1944.* New York: Farrar, Straus and Young.

———. 1961. *Hitler's Secret Book.* New York: Grove Press.

Hoffman, Carl W. 1950. *Saipan: The Beginning of the End.* Washington, DC: Historical Division, U.S. Marine Corps.

Hoffmann, Peter. 1979. *Hitler's Personal Security.* Cambridge, MA: MIT Press.

Holborn, Hajo. 1943. Moltke and Schlieffen: The Prussian-German School. In Edward Mead Earle (ed.), *Makers of Modern Strategy: Military Thought from Machiavelli to Hitler.* Princeton, NJ: Princeton University Press, pp. 172–205.

Horelick, Arnold L., and Myron Rush. 1966. *Strategic Power and Soviet Foreign Policy.* Chicago: University of Chicago Press.

Hosmer, Stephen T., and Thomas W. Wolfe. 1983. *Soviet Policy and Practice toward Third World Countries.* Lexington, MA: Lexington.

Hough, Jerry F. 1986. *The Struggle for the Third World: Soviet Debates and American Options.* Washington: Brookings.

Howard, Michael. 1971. *Studies in War and Peace.* New York: Viking.

———. 1978. *War and the Liberal Conscience.* New Brunswick, NJ: Rutgers University Press.

———. 1984a. *The Causes of Wars and Other Essays* (2d ed.). Cambridge, MA: Harvard University Press.

———. 1984b. Men against Fire: Expectations of War in 1914. *International Security,* vol. 9, no. 1 (Summer), pp. 41–57.

Hoyt, Edwin P. 1986. *Japan's War: The Great Pacific Conflict 1853 to 1952.* New York: McGraw-Hill.

Hudson, G. F., Richard Lowenthal, and Roderick MacFarquhar (eds.). 1961. *The Sino-Soviet Dispute.* New York: Praeger.

Huldermann, Bernhard. 1922. *Albert Ballin.* London: Cassell.

Humphrey, Hubert. 1976. *The Education of a Public Man.* Garden City, NY: Doubleday.

Huntington, Samuel P. 1961. *The Common Defense.* New York: Columbia University Press.

Ienaga, Saburo. 1978. *The Pacific War: World War II and the Japanese, 1931–1945.* New York: Pantheon.

Iriye, Akira. 1981. *Power and Culture: The Japanese-American War, 1941–1945.* Cambridge, MA: Harvard University Press.

Irwin, Don. 1987. Kennedy Plan for Missile Deal Told. *Los Angeles Times,* August 29, p. I–2.

Irwin, Will. 1921. *"The Next War": An Appeal to Common Sense.* New York: Dutton.

Isaacs, Arnold R. 1983. *Without Honor: Defeat in Vietnam and Cambodia.* New York: Vintage.

Jäckel, Eberhard. 1972. The Evolution of Hitler's Foreign Policy Aims. In Henry A. Turner, Jr. (ed.), *Nazism and the Third Reich.* New York: Quadrangle, pp. 201–17.

References

Jackson, D. Bruce. 1969. *Castro, The Kremlin and Communism in Latin America.* Baltimore, MD: Johns Hopkins University Press.

James, William. 1911. *Memories and Studies.* New York: Longmans, Green.

Janis, Irving L. 1982. *Groupthink: Psychological Studies of Policy Decisions and Fiascos.* Boston: Houghton Mifflin.

Jenkins, Brian M. 1970. *Why the North Vietnamese Keep Fighting,* P–4395 (August). Santa Monica, CA: Rand Corporation.

Jervis, Robert, Richard Ned Lebow, and Janice Gross Stein (eds.). 1985. *Psychology and Deterrence.* Baltimore: Johns Hopkins University Press.

Jervis, Robert. 1979. Deterrence Theory Revisited. *World Politics,* vol. 31, no. 2 (January), pp. 289–324.

———. 1980. The Impact of the Korean War on the Cold War. *Journal of Conflict Resolution,* vol. 24, no. 4 (December), pp. 563–92.

———. 1984. *The Illogic of American Nuclear Strategy.* Ithaca, NY: Cornell University Press.

———. 1985. Introduction. In Robert Jervis, Richard Ned Lebow, and Janice Gross Stein (eds.), *Psychology and Deterrence.* Baltimore: Johns Hopkins University Press, pp. 1–12.

———. 1988. The Political Effects of Nuclear Weapons: A Comment. *International Security,* vol. 13, no. 2 (Fall), pp. 80–90.

———. 1989. *Implications of the Nuclear Revolution.* Ithaca, NY: Cornell University Press.

Joffe, Josef. 1987. Peace and Populism: Why the European Anti-Nuclear Movement Failed. *International Security,* vol. 11, no. 4 (Spring), pp. 3–40.

Johnson, Chalmers. 1986. Reflections on the Dilemma of Japanese Defense. *Asian Survey,* vol. 26, no. 5 (May), pp. 557–72.

Johnson, Lyndon Baines. 1971. *The Vantage Point: Perspectives of the Presidency 1963–1969.* New York: Holt, Rinehart and Winston.

Joll, James. 1984. *The Origins of the First World War.* New York: Longman.

Jones, Robert Huhn. 1969. *The Roads to Russia.* Norman, OK: University of Oklahoma Press.

Kagan, Donald. 1987. World War I, World War II, World War III. *Commentary,* March, pp. 21–40.

Kahn, Herman. 1960. *On Thermonuclear War.* Princeton, NJ: Princeton University Press.

———. 1970. Issues of Thermonuclear War Termination. *Annals of the American Academy of Political and Social Science,* vol. 390 (November), pp. 133–72.

Kamm, Henry. 1981. China Plays Down Support of Asian Rebels. *New York Times,* February 2, p. A3.

Kant, Immanuel. 1952. *The Critique of Judgement.* London: Oxford University Press.

———. 1957. *Perpetual Peace.* Indianapolis, IN: Bobbs-Merrill.

Karnow, Stanley. 1983. *Vietnam: A History.* New York: Viking.

Kase, Toshikazu. 1950. *Journey to the Missouri.* New Haven, CT: Yale University Press.

Kattenburg, Paul M. 1980. *The Vietnam Trauma in American Foreign Policy, 1945–75.* New Brunswick, NJ: Transaction.

Katz, Mark N. 1986. Soviet Military Policy toward the Third World. *Washington Quarterly,* Fall, pp. 159–63.

Kaufman, Burton I. 1986. *The Korean War: Challenges in Crisis, Credibility, and Command.* New York: Knopf.

Kecskemeti, Paul. 1958. *Strategic Surrender: The Politics of Victory and Defeat.* New York: Atheneum.

Kellen, Konrad. 1972. 1971 and Beyond: The View from Hanoi. In J. J. Zasloff and Ellen E. Goodman (eds.), *Indochina in Conflict.* Lexington, MA: Heath, pp. 99–112.

Keller, Bill. 1987. Russians Urging U.N. Be Given Greater Powers. *New York Times,* October 3, p. A1.

Kempe, Frederick. 1986. Gorbachev Task: Revamping Economy in the Face of Declining Soviet Exports. *Wall Street Journal,* February 25, p. 34.

Kennan, George F. 1947. The Sources of Soviet Conduct. In Charles Gati (ed.), *Caging the Bear: Containment and the Cold War.* Indianapolis, IN: Bobbs-Merrill, 1974, pp. 9–24.

———. 1950. Is War with Russia Inevitable? *Reader's Digest,* March, pp. 1–9.

———. 1961. *Russia and the West under Lenin and Stalin.* Boston: Little, Brown.

———. 1972. *Memoirs 1950–1963.* Boston: Little, Brown.

References

———. 1987. Containment Then and Now. *Foreign Affairs,* vol. 65, no. 4 (Spring), pp. 885–90.

Kennedy, John F. 1961. Address to the United Nations General Assembly. *New York Times,* September 26, p. 14.

Kennedy, Paul. 1987. *The Rise and Fall of the Great Powers.* New York: Random House.

Kennedy, Robert F. 1971. *Thirteen Days: A Memoir of the Cuban Missile Crisis.* New York: Norton.

Keohane, Robert. 1984. *Beyond Hegemony.* Princeton, NJ: Princeton University Press.

Kershaw, Ian. 1985. *The Nazi Dictatorship: Problems and Perspectives of Interpretation.* London: Edward Arnold.

Khomeini, Ruhollah. 1986. Speech given on December 12, 1985. *Harper's,* April 1985, pp. 17–18.

Khrushchev, Nikita. 1963. *Khrushchev Speaks: Selected Speeches, Articles, and Press Conferences 1949–1961.* (Edited by Thomas P. Whitney). Ann Arbor, MI: University of Michigan Press.

———. 1970. *Khrushchev Remembers* (Edited by Edward Crankshaw and Strobe Talbott). Boston: Little, Brown.

———. 1974. *Khrushchev Remembers: The Last Testament.* (Edited by Strobe Talbott). Boston: Little, Brown.

Kinnard, Douglas. 1977. *The War Managers.* Hanover, NH: University Press of New England.

Kissinger, Henry A. 1969. The Viet Nam Negotiations. *Foreign Affairs,* vol. 47, no. 2 (January), pp. 211–34.

———. 1979. *White House Years.* Boston: Little, Brown.

———. 1982. *Years of Upheaval.* Boston: Little, Brown.

Kitchen, Martin. 1968. *The German Officer Corps, 1890–1914.* London: Oxford University Press.

Knoebl, K. 1967. *Victor Charlie.* New York: Praeger.

Knorr, Klaus. 1966. *On the Uses of Military Power in the Nuclear Age.* Princeton, NJ: Princeton University Press.

———. 1985. Controlling Nuclear War. *International Security,* vol. 9, no. 4 (Spring), pp. 79–98.

Knox, MacGregor. 1982. *Mussolini Unleashed 1939–1941: Politics and Strategy in Fascist Italy's Last War.* New York: Cambridge University Press.

———. 1984. Conquest, Foreign and Domestic, in Fascist Italy and Nazi Germany. *Journal of Modern History,* vol. 56 (March), pp. 1–57.

Kolkowicz, Roman. 1983. Military Strategy and Political Interests: The Soviet Union and the United States. In Bernard Brodie, Michael D. Intriligator, and Roman Kolkowicz (eds.), *National Security and International Stability.* Cambridge, MA: Oelgenschlager, Bunn and Hain, pp. 273–99.

Kontorovich, Vladimir, and Boris Rumer. 1986. Recalculations Put Gorbachev and Co. Deeper in Hole. *Wall Street Journal,* February 27, p. 24.

Kramer, Bernard M., S. Michael Kalick, and Michael A. Milburn. 1983. Attitudes toward Nuclear Weapons and Nuclear War: 1945–1982. *Journal of Social Issues,* vol. 39, no. 1, pp. 7–24.

Kramer, Mark N. 1987. Soviet Arms Transfers to the Third World. *Problems of Communism,* vol. 36, no. 5 (September–October), pp. 52–68.

Kraus, Sidney, 1979. *The Great Debates: Carter vs. Ford, 1976.* Bloomington, IN: Indiana University Press.

Krepinevich, Andrew F., Jr. 1986. *The Army and Vietnam.* Baltimore, MD: Johns Hopkins University Press.

Kristol, Irving. 1985. Coping with an 'Evil Empire.' *Wall Street Journal,* December 17, p. 32.

LaFeber, Walter (ed.). 1971. *The Origins of the Cold War: 1941–1947.* New York: Wiley.

Lambeth, Benjamin S. 1972. Deterrence in the MIRV Era. *World Politics,* vol. 24, no. 2 (January), pp. 221–42.

Langer, William. 1951. *The Diplomacy of Imperialism, 1890–1902.* New York: Knopf.

Lapp, Ralph E. 1949. *Must We Hide?* Cambridge, MA: Addison-Wesley.

Larson, David C. (ed.). 1963. *The "Cuban Crisis" of 1962: Selected Documents and Chronology.* Boston: Houghton Mifflin.

Larson, Deborah Welch. 1985. *Origins of Containment: A Psychological Explanation.* Princeton, NJ: Princeton University Press.

Lea, Homer. 1909. *The Valor of Ignorance.* New York: Harper.

Leahy, William D. 1950. *I Was There: The Personal Story of the Chief of Staff to Presidents Roosevelt and Truman Based on His Notes and Diaries Made at the Time.* New York: Whittlesey House.

Lebow, Richard Ned. 1981. *Between Peace and War: The Nature of International Crisis.* Baltimore: Johns Hopkins University Press.

References

——. 1983. The Cuban Missile Crisis: Reading the Lessons Correctly. *Political Science Quarterly*, vol. 98, no. 3 (Fall), pp. 431–58.

——. 1984. Windows of Opportunity: Do States Jump through Them? *International Security*, vol. 9, no. 1 (Summer), pp. 147–86.

——. 1985a. Deterrence Reconsidered. *Survival*, vol. 27, no. 1 (January–February), pp. 20–28.

——. 1985b. The Deterrence Deadlock: Is There a Way Out? and Conclusions. In Robert Jervis, Richard Ned Lebow, and Janice Gross Stein (eds.), *Psychology and Deterrence*. Baltimore: Johns Hopkins University Press, pp. 153–232.

——. 1987. Deterrence Failure Revisited. *International Security*, vol. 12, no. 1 (Summer), pp. 197–213.

Leites, Nathan. 1953. *A Study of Bolshevism*. Glencoe, IL: Free Press.

——. 1969. *The Viet Cong Style of Politics*, RM-5487-1-ISA/ARPA (May). Santa Monica, CA: Rand Corporation.

Lengyel, Emil. 1975. *And All Her Paths Were Peace: The Life of Bertha von Suttner*. Nashville, TN: Thomas Nelson.

Lenin, V. I. 1939. *Imperialism: The Highest Stage of Capitalism*. New York: International.

Lerner, Max (ed.). 1943. *The Mind and Faith of Justice Holmes*. Boston: Little, Brown.

Lescaze, Lee. 1987. A Land of Oil, War and Paradoxes, Angola Ranks Second in Misery Index. *Wall Street Journal*, April 14, 1987, p. 16.

Levi, Werner. 1981. *The Coming End of War*. Beverly Hills, CA: Sage.

Levy, Jack S. 1983. *War in the Modern Great Power System, 1495–1975*. Lexington, KY: University Press of Kentucky.

Levy, Jack S., and T. Clifton Morgan. 1986. The War-Weariness Hypothesis. *American Journal of Political Science*, vol. 30, no. 1 (February), pp. 26–49.

Lewis, Flora. 1986. Step Back from Folly. *New York Times*, November 7, p. A35.

——. 1987. Don't Be Afraid of 'Da.' *New York Times*, April 17, p. A31.

Lewis, Lloyd. 1932. *Sherman, Fighting Prophet*. New York: Harcourt, Brace.

Lewis, Paul. 1987. New Soviet Interest in U.N. Broadens. *New York Times*, September 25, p. A8.

Lewy, Gunther. 1978. *American in Vietnam*. New York: Oxford University Press.

Lichty, Lawrence W. 1984. Comments on the Influence of Television on Public Opinion. In Peter Braestrup (ed.), *Vietnam as History*. Lanham, MD: University Press of America, pp. 158–60.

Lieberthal, Kenneth. 1982. The Background in Chinese Politics. In Herbert J. Ellison (ed.), *The Sino-Soviet Conflict: A Global Perspective*. Seattle: University of Washington Press, pp. 3–28.

Lilienthal, David E. 1964. *The Atomic Energy Years 1945–1950* (The Journals of David E. Lilienthal, Vol. 2). New York: Harper and Row.

Lin Biao. 1972. Long Live the Victory of People's War! September 3, 1965. In K. Fan (ed.), *Mao Tse-Tung and Lin Piao: Post Revolutionary Writings*. Garden City, NY: Anchor, pp. 357–412.

Linderman, Gerald F. 1987. *Embattled Courage: The Experience of Combat in the Civil War*. New York: Free Press.

Lingeman, Richard R. 1970. *Don't You Know There's a War On? The American Home Front, 1941–1945*. New York: Putnam.

Lippmann, Walter. 1947. *The Cold War: A Study in U.S. Foreign Policy*. New York: Harper.

——. 1965a. The Vietnamese War Today. *Newsweek*, September 13, p. 17.

——. 1965b. The Power Politics of Asia. *Newsweek*, September 27, p. 23.

——. 1965c. The Light at the End of the Tunnel. *Newsweek*, November 8, p. 29.

Littell, Robert. 1946. What the Atomic Bomb Would Do to Us. *Reader's Digest*, May, pp. 125–28.

Lowenthal, Abraham F. 1987. *Partners in Conflict: The United States and Latin American*. Baltimore, MD: Johns Hopkins University Press.

Lowenthal, Richard. 1961. *Diplomacy and Revolution: The Dialectics of a Dispute*. In G. F. Hudson, Richard Lowenthal, and Roderick MacFarquhar (eds.), *The Sino-Soviet Dispute*. New York: Praeger, pp. 9–34.

Luard, Evan. 1986. *War in International Society: A Study in International Sociology*. New Haven, CT: Yale University Press.

Lukas, J. Anthony. 1987. Class Reunion: Kennedy's Men Relive the Cuban Missile Crisis. *New York Times Magazine*, August 30, pp. 22–27, 51, 58, 61.

Lukas, Richard C. 1986. *The Forgotten Holocaust: The Poles under German Occupation 1939–1944*. Lexington, KY: University Press of Kentucky.

References

Lundkvist, Sven. 1973. Experience of Empire: Sweden as a Great Power. In Michael Roberts (ed.), *Sweden's Age of Greatness.* New York: St. Martin's, pp. 20–57.

Luttwak, Edward N. 1983a. *The Grand Strategy of the Soviet Union.* New York: St. Martin's.

———. 1983b. Of Bombs and Men. *Commentary,* August, pp. 77–82.

———. 1988. An Emerging Postnuclear Era? *Washington Quarterly,* vol. 11, no. 1 (Winter), pp. 5–15.

MacFarquhar, Roderick. 1961. Points of Departure. In G. F. Hudson, Richard Lowenthal, and Roderick MacFarquhar (eds.), *The Sino-Soviet Dispute.* New York: Praeger, pp. 39–41.

Mackie, Thomas T., and Richard Rose. 1982. *The International Almanac of Electoral History.* New York: Facts on File.

Mahan, Alfred Thayer. 1912. *Armaments and Arbitration: The Place of Force in the International Relations of States.* New York: Harper.

Mailer, Norman. 1968. *Miami and the Siege of Chicago: An Informal History of the Republican and Democratic Conventions of 1968.* New York: World.

Maitland, Ian. 1976. Only the Best and the Brightest? *Asian Affairs,* vol. 3 (March–April), pp. 263–72.

Mandelbaum, Michael. 1981. *The Nuclear Revolution.* Cambridge: Cambridge University Press.

———. 1982. Vietnam: The Television War. *Daedalus,* Fall, pp. 157–69.

Mann, Michael. 1986. *The Sources of Social Power: A History of Power from the Beginning to A.D. 1760,* Vol. 1. Cambridge: Cambridge University Press.

Mao Zedong. 1961. *Comrade Mao Tse-tung on "Imperialism and All Reactionaries Are Paper Tigers."* Beijing: Foreign Languages Press.

Marer, Paul. 1986. The Political Economy of Soviet Relations with Eastern Europe. In Robbin F. Laird and Erik P. Hoffmann (eds.), *Soviet Foreign Policy in a Changing World.* Hawthorne, NY: Aldine, pp. 570–600.

Markham, James M. 1986. Crisis for Western Communists: Once-Powerful Parties Stagnate. *New York Times,* February 3, p. A1.

———. 1987. Let Them Eat Glasnost, French Communists Say. *New York Times,* November 11.

Mastny, Vojtech. 1971. *The Czechs under Nazi Rule: The Failure of National Resistance, 1939–1942.* New York: Columbia University Press.

———. 1979. *Russia's Road to the Cold War: Diplomacy, Warfare, and the Politics of Communism, 1941–1945.* New York: Columbia University Press.

Maurice, Charles, and Charles W. Smithson. 1984. *The Doomsday Myth: 10,000 Years of Economic Crises.* Stanford, CA: Hoover Institution Press.

Maxwell, Kenneth. 1985. Prisoners of Glory. *Wilson Quarterly,* vol. 9, no. 1 (New Year's), pp. 49–66.

May, Arthur J. 1977. *A History of the University of Rochester 1850–1962.* Rochester, NY: University of Rochester Press.

May, Clifford D. 1986. Ethiopian Policies Blamed in Famine. *New York Times,* May 21.

May, Ernest R. 1973. *"Lessons" of the Past: The Use and Misuse of History in American Foreign Policy.* New York: Oxford University Press.

———. 1984. The Cold War. In Joseph S. Nye, Jr. (ed.), *The Making of America's Soviet Policy.* New Haven and London: Yale University Press, pp. 209–30.

McCarthy, Charles H. 1901. *Lincoln's Plan of Reconstruction.* New York: McClure, Phillips.

MccGwire, Michael. 1985. Deterrence: The Problem, Not the Solution. *SAIS Review,* vol. 5, no. 2 (Summer–Fall), pp. 105–124.

———. 1987. *Military Objectives in Soviet Foreign Policy.* Washington, DC: Brookings.

McGarvey, P. I. 1969. *Visions of Victory: Selected Communist Military Writing, 1964–1969.* Stanford, CA: Hoover Institution Press.

McGlen, Nancy E. 1986. The Sources of Support of the Freeze Movement. Niagara Falls, NY: Niagara University, Department of Political Science.

Mearsheimer, John J. 1983. *Conventional Deterrence.* Ithaca, NY: Cornell University Press.

———. 1984/85. Nuclear Weapons and Deterrence in Europe. *International Security,* vol. 9, no. 3 (Winter), pp. 19–47.

Medvedev, Roy. 1983. *Khrushchev.* Garden City, NY: Doubleday.

———. 1986. *China and the Superpowers.* New York: Basil Blackwell.

Menon, Rajan. 1986. *Soviet Power and the Third World.* New Haven, CT: Yale University Press.

Merrill, James M. 1971. *William Tecumseh Sherman.* Chicago: Rand McNally.

Meyer, Stephen M. 1984. *The Dynamics of Nuclear Proliferation.* Chicago: University of Chicago Press.

References

Miesel, Victor H. 1978. Ludwig Meidner. In *Ludwig Meidner: An Expressionist Master.* Ann Arbor, MI: University of Michigan Museum of Art, pp. 1–23.

Milburn, Thomas W. 1959. What Constitutes Effective U.S. Deterrence? *Journal of Conflict Resolution,* vol. 3, no. 2 (June), pp. 138–45.

Miller, J. D. B. 1986. *Norman Angell and the Futility of War.* New York: St. Martin's.

Millett, Richard L. 1988. Nicaragua: "Patria Libre". *Wilson Quarterly,* vol. 12, no. 1 (New Year's), pp. 98–118.

Millis, Walter (ed.). 1951. *The Forrestal Diaries.* New York: Viking.

Milne, Alan Alexander. 1935. *Peace with Honour.* New York: Dutton.

Milward, Alan S. 1977. *War, Economy and Society, 1939–1945.* Berkeley, CA: University of California Press.

Morgan, Patrick. 1977. *Deterrence: A Conceptual Analysis.* Beverly Hills, CA: Sage.

Morgenthau, Hans J. 1948. *Politics among Nations: The Struggle for Power and Peace.* New York: Knopf.

Moseley, Leonard. 1969. *On Borrowed Time: How World War II Began.* New York: Random House.

Mosley, Nicholas. 1976. *Julian Grenfell: His Life and the Times of His Death, 1888–1915.* London: Weidenfeld and Nicolson.

Moyers, Bill. 1969. Bill Moyers Talks about the War and LBJ. In Robert Manning and M. Janeway (eds.), *Who We Are.* Boston: Little, Brown, pp. 261–71.

Mueller, Harold, and Thomas Risse-Kappen. 1987. Origins of Estrangement: The Peace Movement and the Changed Image of America in West Germany. *International Security,* vol. 12, no. 1 (Summer), pp. 52–88.

Mueller, John. 1967. Incentives for Restraint: Canada as a Non-Nuclear Power. *Orbis,* vol. 11, no. 3 (Fall), pp. 864–84.

———. 1968. *Deterrence, Numbers, and History.* Los Angeles: University of California, Security Studies Project.

———. (ed.). 1969. *Approaches to Measurement in International Relations: A Non-Evangelical Survey.* New York: Appleton-Century-Crofts.

———. 1973. *War, Presidents and Public Opinion.* New York: Wiley. (Reprinted by University Press of America, Lanham, MD, 1985).

———. 1977. Changes in American Public Attitudes toward International Involvement. In Ellen Stern (ed.), *The Limits of Military Intervention.* Beverly Hills, CA: Sage, pp. 323–44.

———. 1979. Public Expectations of War during the Cold War. *American Journal of Political Science,* vol. 23, no. 2 (May), pp. 301–29.

———. 1980. The Search for the 'Breaking Point' in Vietnam: The Statistics of a Deadly Quarrel. *International Studies Quarterly,* vol. 24, no. 4 (December), pp. 497–519.

———. 1984a. Some Reflections on the Vietnam Protest Movement and on the Curious Calm at the War's End; and A Summary of Public Opinion and the Vietnam War. In Peter Braestrup (ed.), *Vietnam as History.* Lanham, MD: University Press of America, pp. 151–57, 171–77.

———. 1984b. Reassessment of American Policy, 1965–1968. In Harrison E. Salisbury (ed.), *Vietnam Reconsidered: Lessons from a War.* New York: Harper and Row, pp. 48–52.

———. 1984c. Lessons Learned Five Years After the Hostage Nightmares. *Wall Street Journal,* November 6, p. 28.

———. 1985a. The Cold War Consensus: From Fearful Hostility to Wary Contempt. In Richard A. Melanson and Kenneth W. Thompson (eds.), *Foreign Policy and Domestic Consensus.* Lanham, MD: University Press of America, pp. 7–18.

———. 1985b. *Astaire Dancing: The Musical Films.* New York: Knopf.

———. 1986. Containment and the Decline of the Soviet Empire: Some Tentative Reflections on the End of the World as We Know It. Paper presented at the National Convention of the International Studies Association, Anaheim, CA, March 25–29.

———. 1987a. Presidents and Terrorists Should Not Mix. *Wall Street Journal,* March 31, p. 36.

———. 1987b. Vietnam and the Mellowing of Containment: Implications for U.S. Foreign Policy Attitudes. In George K. Osborn, Asa A. Clark IV, Daniel J. Kaufman, and Douglas E. Lute (eds.), *Democracy, Strategy, and Vietnam: Implications for American Policymaking.* Lexington, MA: Lexington, pp. 297–310.

———. 1988a. Trends in Political Tolerance. *Public Opinion Quarterly,* vol. 52, no. 1 (Spring), pp. 1–25.

References

————. 1988b. The Essential Irrelevance of Nuclear Weapons. *International Security,* vol. 13, no. 2 (Fall), pp. 55–79.

Mueller, Karl P. 1991. Asymmetric Deterrence and Grand Strategy. Ph.D. dissertation, Princeton University.

Mulley, F. W. 1962. *The Politics of Western Defense.* New York: Praeger.

Murray, Williamson. 1984. *The Change in the European Balance of Power, 1938–1939.* Princeton, NJ: Princeton University Press.

Mussolini, Benito. 1935. The Political and Social Doctrine of Fascism. *International Conciliation,* no. 306 (January), pp. 5–17.

Nathan, John. 1974. *Mishima: A Biography.* Boston: Little, Brown.

National Planning Association. *1970 without Arms Control.* Washington, DC: National Planning Association.

NBC (National Broadcasting Company). 1982. Bataan: The Forgotten Hell. Telecast December 5.

Nelson, Donald M. 1946. What Industry Did. In Jack Goodman (ed.), *While You Were Gone: A Report on Wartime Life in the United States.* New York: Simon and Schuster, pp. 213–29.

Nevaskar, Balwant. 1971. *Capitalists without Capitalism: The Jains of India and the Quakers of the West.* Westport, CT: Greenwood.

Nevins, Allan. 1946. How We Felt about the War. In Jack Goodman (ed.), *While You Were Gone: A Report on Wartime Life in the United States.* New York: Simon and Schuster, pp. 3–27.

Niemi, Richard G., John Mueller, and Tom W. Smith. 1990. *Trends in Public Opinion: A Compendium.* Greenwood, CT: Greenwood.

Nixon, Richard. 1978. *RN: The Memoirs of Richard Nixon.* New York: Grosset and Dunlap.

————. 1980. *The Real War.* New York: Warner.

Nobel, Alfred. 1925. How Wars Will Come to an End. *The Forum* (NY), vol. 74, no. 1 (July), pp. 194–98. (As recorded from notes made in 1890 by E. Schneider-Bonnet.)

Noel-Baker, Philip. 1937. *The Private Manufacture of Armaments.* New York: Oxford University Press.

Nogee, Joseph L., and John W. Sloan. 1979. Allende's Chile and the Soviet Union: A Policy Lesson for Latin American Nations Seeking Autonomy. *Journal of Interamerican Studies and World Affairs,* vol. 20, no. 3 (August), pp. 339–68.

Nogee, Joseph L., and Robert H. Donaldson. 1984. *Soviet Foreign Policy Since World War II* (2d ed.). New York: Pergamon.

Notestein, Wallace, and Elmer E. Stoll (eds.). 1917. *Conquest and Kultur: Aims of the Germans in Their Own Words.* Washington, DC: U.S. Government, Committee on Public Information.

Novak, Joseph. 1960. *The Future Is Ours, Comrade: Conversations with the Russians.* Garden City, NY: Doubleday.

Nurnberger, Ralph D. 1987. 'Bridling the Passions.' *Wilson Quarterly,* vol. 11, no. 1 (New Year's), pp. 96–107.

Nye, Joseph S., Jr. 1987. Nuclear Learning and U.S.–Soviet Security Regimes. *International Organization,* vol. 41, no. 3 (Summer), pp. 371–402.

Orme, John. 1987. Deterrence Failures: A Second Look. *International Security,* vol. 11, no. 4 (Spring), pp. 96–124.

Osgood, Robert E. 1953. *Ideals and Self-Interest in America's Foreign Relations.* Chicago: University of Chicago Press.

Osterweis, Rollin G. 1949. *Romanticism and Nationalism in the Old South.* New Haven, CT: Yale University Press.

Overy, R. J. 1982. Hitler's War and the German Economy: A Reinterpretation. *Economic History Review,* vol. 35, no. 2 (May), pp. 272–91.

————. 1984. *Goering: The 'Iron Man.'* London: Routledge and Kegan Paul.

Paarlberg, Rob. 1973. Forgetting about the Unthinkable. *Foreign Policy,* no. 10 (Spring), pp. 132–40.

Paige, Glenn D. 1968. *The Korean Decision, June 24–30, 1950.* New York: Free Press.

Panikkar, K. M. 1955. *In Two Chinas: Memoirs of a Diplomat.* London: Allen and Unwin.

Paret, Peter, and John W. Shy. 1962. *Guerrillas in the 1960s.* New York: Praeger.

Parker, Geoffrey. 1984. *The Thirty Years War.* London: Routledge and Kegan Paul.

Patchen, Martin. 1966. The American Public's View of U.S. Policy toward China. In A. T. Steel, *The American People and China.* New York: McGraw-Hill, pp. 251–313.

References

Patterson, Orlando. 1982. *Slavery and Social Death: A Comparative Study.* Cambridge, MA: Harvard University Press.

Pauker, Guy J. 1965. Indonesia: The PKI's "Road to Power." In Robert A. Scalapino (ed.), *The Communist Revolution in Asia: Tactics, Goals, and Achievements.* Englewood Cliffs, NJ: Prentice-Hall, pp. 256–89.

Payne, Robert. 1965. *The Rise and Fall of Stalin.* New York: Simon and Schuster.

Pentagon Papers. 1971. (Senator Gravel ed.). Boston: Beacon.

Perkins, Dwight. 1982. The Economic Background and Implications for China. In Herbert J. Ellison (ed.), *The Sino-Soviet Conflict: A Global Perspective.* Seattle: University of Washington Press, pp. 91–111.

Perry, James M. 1986. They May Poke Fun at the Swiss Navy, but Not at the Army. *Wall Street Journal,* December 8, p. 1.

Pike, Douglas. 1966. *Viet Cong.* Cambridge, MA: MIT Press.

Pipes, Richard. 1984. *Survival Is Not Enough.* New York: Simon and Schuster.

Porter, Bruce D. 1984. *The USSR in Third World Conflicts: Soviet Arms and Diplomacy in Local War 1945–1980.* New York: Cambridge University Press.

Posen, Barry R. 1984. *The Sources of Military Doctrine.* Ithaca, NY: Cornell University Press.

———. 1984/85. Measuring the European Conventional Balance. *International Security,* vol. 9, no. 3 (Winter), pp. 47–88.

Powers, Thomas. 1984. What Is It About? *Atlantic,* January, pp. 35–55.

President's Commission on National Goals. 1960. *Goals for Americans.* New York: Prentice-Hall.

Preston, Paul. 1986. *The Triumph of Democracy in Spain.* London: Methuen.

Quandt, William B. 1978. Lebanon, 1958, and Jordan, 1970. In Barry M. Blechman and Stephen S. Kaplan (eds.), *Force Without War.* Washington: Brookings, pp. 222–88.

Quester, George H. 1977. *Offense and Defense in the International System.* New York: Wiley.

———. 1982. *American Foreign Policy: The Lost Consensus.* New York: Praeger.

Race, Jeffrey. 1976. Vietnam Intervention: Systematic Distortion in Policy-Making. *Armed Forces and Society,* vol. 2 (Spring), pp. 377–96.

Radosh, Ronald, and Joyce Milton. 1983. *The Rosenberg File: A Search for the Truth.* New York: Holt, Rinehart and Winston.

Randall, J. G., and David Donald. 1961. *The Civil War and Reconstruction* (2d ed.). Boston: Heath.

Raskin, Marcus G., and Bernard B. Fall (eds). 1965. *The Viet-Nam Reader.* New York: Vintage.

Reagan, Ronald. 1985. Excerpts from the President's Address. *New York Times,* April 16, p. A8

Reck-Malleczewen, Friedrich Percyval. 1970. *Diary of a Man in Despair.* New York: Macmillan.

Rees, David. 1964. *Korea: The Limited War.* New York: St. Martin's.

Reporter. 1963. The Press: A Week of Cuba. *Encounter,* January, pp. 84–95.

Revzin, Philip. 1987. Italy Boasts It Deserves Britain's Place in Rich Nations' Club. *Wall Street Journal,* February 27, p. 42.

Rich, Norman. 1973. *Hitler's War Aims: Ideology, the Nazi State, and the Course of Expansion.* New York: Norton.

———. 1974. *Hitler's War Aims: The Establishment of the New Order.* New York: Norton.

Ricklefs, Roger. 1986. French Twist: America's Image Improves. *Wall Street Journal,* July 1, p. 30.

Ridgway, Matthew R. 1967. *The Korean War.* Garden City, NY: Doubleday.

Rielly, John E. 1975. *American Public Opinion and U.S. Foreign Policy 1975.* Chicago: Chicago Council on Foreign Relations.

Robb, Theodore K. 1962. The Effects of the Thirty Years' War. *Journal of Modern History,* vol. 34 (March), pp. 40–51.

Roberts, Michael. 1967. *Essays in Swedish History.* London: Weidenfeld and Nicholson.

Roosevelt, Theodore. 1901. *The Strenuous Life.* New York: Century.

Rosebery, Mercedes. 1944. *This Day's Madness.* New York: Macmillan.

Rosecrance, Richard. 1963. *Action and Reaction in World Politics.* Boston: Little, Brown.

———. 1975. *Strategic Deterrence Reconsidered.* London: International Institute for Strategic Studies, Adelphi Paper No. 116 (Spring).

———. 1986. *The Rise of the Trading State: Commerce and Conquest in the Modern World.* New York: Basic Books.

Rothschild, J. H. 1964. *Tomorrow's Weapons: Chemical and Biological.* New York: McGraw-Hill.

References

Rubinstein, Alvin Z. 1985. *Soviet Foreign Policy since World War II: Imperial and Global* (2nd ed.). Boston: Little, Brown.

———. 1986. A Third World Policy Waits for Gorbachev. *Orbis*, vol. 30, no. 2 (Summer), pp. 355–64.

Rummel, Rudolph J. 1983. Libertarianism and International Violence. *Journal of Conflict Resolution*, vol. 27, no. 1 (March), pp. 27–71.

———. 1986. War Isn't This Century's Biggest Killer. *Wall Street Journal*, July 7, p. 12.

Rusk, Dean. 1971. Interview on NBC-TV, July 2.

Ruskin, John. 1866. War. In *The Crown of Wild Olives: Three Lectures on Work, Traffic, and War*. New York: Wiley, pp. 83–127.

Russell, Bertrand. 1963. *Unarmed Victory*. Baltimore, MD: Penguin.

Russell, Elbert. 1942. *The History of Quakerism*. New York: Macmillan.

Russett, Bruce. 1963. The Calculus of Deterrence. *Journal of Conflict Resolution*, vol. 7 (June), pp. 97–109.

———. 1972. *No Clear and Present Danger: A Skeptical View of the United States' Entry into World War II*. New York: Harper and Row.

———. 1983. *The Prisoners of Insecurity: Nuclear Deterrence, the Arms Race, and Arms Control*. San Francisco: Freeman.

Russett, Bruce, and Harvey Starr. 1981. *World Politics: The Menu for Choice*. San Francisco: Freeman.

Ryder, H. I. D. 1899. The Ethics of War. *Nineteenth Century*, May, pp. 716–28.

Safire, William. 1984. Only the 'Fun' Wars. *New York Times*, December 3, p. A23.

———. 1988. Bailing out Moscow. *New York Times*, February 25, p. A31.

Sagan, Carl. 1983/84. Nuclear War and Climatic Catastrophe: Some Policy Implications. *Foreign Affairs*, vol. 62, no. 2 (Winter), pp. 257–92.

Sagan, Scott D. 1985. Nuclear Alerts and Crisis Management. *International Security*, vol. 9, no. 4 (Spring) pp. 99–139.

———. 1986. 1914 Revisited: Allies, Offense, and Instability. *International Security*, vol. 11, no. 2 (Fall), pp. 151–75.

———. 1988. The Origin of the Pacific War. *Journal of Interdisciplinary History*, vol. 18, no. 4 (Spring), pp. 893–922.

Salisbury, Harrison E. 1967. *Behind the Lines: Hanoi*. New York: Harper and Row.

———. 1969. *War between Russia and China*. New York: Norton.

Sarkesian, Sam C. 1984. *America's Forgotten Wars: The Counterrevolutionary Past and Lessons for the Future*. Westport, CT: Greenwood.

Schandler, Herbert Y. 1977. *The Unmaking of a President: Lyndon Johnson and Vietnam*. Princeton, NJ: Princeton University Press.

Schell, Jonathan. 1982. *The Fate of the Earth*. New York: Knopf.

Schelling, Thomas C. 1966. *Arms and Influence*. New Haven, CT: Yale University Press.

Schilling, Warner R. 1961. The H-Bomb Decision. *Political Science Quarterly*, vol. 76, no. 1 (March), pp. 24–46.

———. 1965. Surprise Attack, Death, and War. *Journal of Conflict Resolution*, vol. 9 (September), pp. 285–90.

Schlesinger, Arthur M., Jr. 1978. *Robert Kennedy and His Times*. Boston: Houghton Mifflin.

Schlesinger, James. 1967. *On Relating Non-technical Elements to Systems Studies*, P–3545 (February). Santa Monica, CA: Rand Corporation.

Schram, Stuart R. 1964. The 'Military Deviation' of Mao Tse-tung. *Problems of Communism*, vol. 13, no. 1 (January–February), pp. 49–56.

Schroeder, Paul. 1985. Does Murphy's Law Apply to History? *Wilson Quarterly*, vol. 9, no. 1 (New Year's), pp. 84–93.

Schumaker, Edward. 1985. Spain Insists U.S. Cut Troops There. *New York Times*, November 20.

Schuman, Howard, Jacob Ludwig, and Jon A. Krosnick. 1986. The Perceived Threat of Nuclear War, Salience, and Open Questions. *Public Opinion Quarterly*, vol. 50, no. 4 (Winter), pp. 519–36.

Schumpeter, Joseph. 1955. *Imperialism and Social Classes*. New York: Meridian.

Schwarz, Urs. 1980. *The Eye of the Hurricane: Switzerland in World War Two*. Boulder, CO: Westview.

References

Scrugham, Mary. 1921. *The Peaceable Americans of 1860–1861: A Study of Public Opinion.* New York: Columbia University Press.

Seitz, Don C. 1929. *Famous American Duels.* New York: Crowell.

Shannon, David A. 1959. *The Decline of American Communism: A History of the Communist Party of the United States since 1945.* New York: Harcourt, Brace.

Shaplen, Robert. 1970. *Time Out of Hand.* New York: Harper Colophon.

Sharp, Gene. 1973. *The Politics of Nonviolent Action.* Boston: Porter Sargent.

Sharp, U. S. G. 1978. *Strategy for Defeat.* San Rafael, CA: Presidio.

Shaw, Bernard. 1913. *Major Barbara.* Baltimore, MD: Penguin.

Sheehan, Neil. 1964. Much Is at Stake in Southeast Asian Struggle. *New York Times,* August 16, p. E4.

Shevchenko, Arkady N. 1985. *Breaking with Moscow.* New York: Knopf.

Shlapentokh, Vladimir E. 1984. Moscow's War Propaganda and Soviet Public Opinion. *Problems of Communism,* vol. 38, no. 5 (September–October), pp. 88–94.

Shulman, Marshall D. 1963. *Stalin's Foreign Policy Reappraised.* New York: Atheneum.

Shultz, George. 1985. Excerpts from Shultz's Speech to Policy Group. *New York Times,* October 3, p. A10.

Siegel, Marcia B. 1977. *Watching the Dance Go By.* Boston: Houghton Mifflin.

Simes, Dimitri K. 1987. Gorbachev: A New Foreign Policy? *Foreign Affairs: America and the World 1986,* vol. 65, no. 3, pp. 477–500.

Simmons, Robert R. 1975. *The Strained Alliance: Peking, Pyongyang, Moscow and the Politics of the Korean Civil War.* New York: Free Press.

Singer, J. David. 1962. *Deterrence, Arms Control, and Disarmament.* Columbus, OH: Ohio State University Press.

Sivard, Ruth Leger. 1985. *World Military and Social Expenditures 1985.* Washington: World Priorities.

———. 1987. *World Military and Social Expenditures 1987/88.* Washington: World Priorities.

Skidelsky, Robert. 1986. *John Maynard Keynes: Hopes Betrayed 1883–1920.* New York: Viking.

Slusser, Robert M. 1978. The Berlin Crises of 1958–59 and 1961. In Barry M. Blechman and Stephen S. Kaplan (eds.), *Force without War.* Washington: Brookings, pp. 343–439.

Small, Melvin. 1980. *Was War Necessary? National Security and U.S. Entry into War.* Beverly Hills, CA: Sage.

Small, Melvin, and J. David Singer. 1982. *Resort to Arms: International Civil Wars, 1816–1980.* Beverly Hills, CA: Sage.

Smith, Adam. 1976. *An Inquiry into the Nature and Causes of the Wealth of Nations.* New York: Oxford University Press.

Smith, Tom W. 1980. America's Most Important Problem: A Trend Analysis, 1946–1976. *Public Opinion Quarterly,* vol. 44, no. 2 (Summer), pp. 164–80.

———. 1985. The Polls: America's Most Important Problem, Part 1: National and International. *Public Opinion Quarterly,* vol. 49, no. 2 (Summer), pp. 264–74.

Smoke, Richard. 1987. *National Security and the Nuclear Dilemma: An Introduction to the American Experience.* New York: Random House.

Snow, C. P. 1961. The Moral Un-Neutrality of Science. *Science,* January 27, pp. 255–62.

Snyder, Glenn H. 1961. *Deterrence and Defense.* Princeton, NJ: Princeton University Press.

Snyder, Jack. 1984a. Civil-Military Relations and the Cult of the Offensive, 1914 and 1984. *International Security,* vol. 9, no. 1 (Summer), pp. 108–46.

———. 1984b. *The Ideology of the Offensive.* Ithaca, NY: Cornell University Press.

———. 1987/88. The Gorbachev Revolution: A Waning of Soviet Expansionism? *International Security,* vol. 12, no. 3 (Winter), pp. 93–131.

Sorensen, Theodore C. 1965. *Kennedy.* New York: Harper and Row.

Spanier, John. 1974. The Choices We Did Not Have: In Defense of Containment. In Charles Gati (ed.), *Caging the Bear: Containment and the Cold War.* Indianapolis, IN: Bobbs-Merrill, pp. 128–53.

Spector, Ivan. 1959. *The Soviet Union and the Muslim World, 1917–1958.* Seattle: University of Washington Press.

Spector, Ronald H. 1985. *Eagle against the Sun: The American War with Japan.* New York: Vintage.

Speer, Albert. 1970. *Inside the Third Reich.* New York: Macmillan.

References

Spencer, Herbert. 1909. *The Principles of Sociology,* Vol. 2. New York: Appleton.

Stacey, C. P. 1953. *The Undefended Border: The Myth and the Reality.* Ottawa: Canadian Historical Association.

Stalin, Joseph V. 1954. *Works,* Vol. 7, 1925. Moscow: Foreign Language Publishing House.

———. 1973. *The Essential Stalin* (Edited by Bruce Franklin). London: Croom Helm.

Starobin, Joseph R. 1965. The State of the Parties: North America. In Leopold Labedz (ed.), *International Communism after Khrushchev.* Cambridge, MA: MIT Press, pp. 144–53.

———. 1972. *American Communism in Crisis, 1943–1957.* Cambridge, MA: Harvard University Press.

Stein, Janice Gross. 1985. Calculation, Miscalculation, and Conventional Deterrence: The View from Cairo. In Robert Jervis, Richard Ned Lebow, and Janice Gross Stein (eds.), *Psychology and Deterrence.* Baltimore, MD: Johns Hopkins University Press, pp. 34–59.

Steinberg, S. H. 1966. *The Thirty Years War and the Conflict for European Hegemony 1600–1660.* New York: Norton.

Steinert, Marlis G. 1977. *Hitler's War and the Germans: Public Mood and Attitude during the Second World War.* Athens, OH: Ohio University Press.

Stephan, John S. 1986. Asia in the Soviet Conception. In Robbin F. Laird and Erik P. Hoffmann (eds.), *Soviet Foreign Policy in a Changing World.* Hawthorne, NY: Aldine, pp. 623–47.

Sterba, James P. 1985. Bandung Anniversary Spurs Some to Suggest Communism Is Losing Appeal in Third World. *Wall Street Journal,* April 23, p. 34.

Sterba, James P., and Lee Lescaze. 1985. Vietnam's Legacy: Of the Asian Dominoes that Haven't Fallen, Several Are Thriving. *Wall Street Journal,* March 14, p. 1.

Stevens, William Oliver. 1940. *Pistols at Ten Paces: The Story of the Code of Honor in America.* Boston: Houghton Mifflin.

Stoessinger, John G. 1982. *Why Nations Go to War* (3d ed.). New York: St. Martin's.

Stokes, Henry Scott. 1985. Lost Samurai: The Withered Soul of Postwar Japan. *Harper's,* October, pp. 55–63.

Stowe, Steven M. 1987. *Intimacy and Power in the Old South: Ritual in the Lives of the Planters.* Baltimore, MD: Johns Hopkins University Press.

Streit, Clarence. 1939. *Union Now: A Proposal for a Federal Union of Democracies.* New York: Harper.

Stromberg, Roland N. 1982. *Redemption by War: The Intellectuals and 1914.* Lawrence, KS: Regents Press of Kansas.

Strumilin, S. 1961. The World 20 Years from Now. *Soviet Digest of the Soviet Press,* October 18, pp. 3–7.

Sullivan, Michael P. 1985. *The Vietnam War: A Study in the Making of American Policy.* Lexington, KY: University Press of Kentucky.

Sulzberger, C. L. 1966. Foreign Affairs: The Nutcracker Suite. *New York Times,* April 10, p. E8.

Suttner, Bertha von. 1910. *Memoirs of Bertha von Suttner: The Records of an Eventful Life.* Boston and London: Ginn.

———. 1914. *Lay Down Your Arms.* New York: Longmans, Green.

Swanberg, W. A. 1957. *First Blood: The Story of Fort Sumter.* New York: Scribner's.

Taheri, Amir. 1986. *The Spirit of Allah: Khomeini and the Islamic Revolution.* Bethesda, MD: Adler and Adler.

Taracouzio, T. A. 1940. *War and Peace in Soviet Diplomacy.* New York: Macmillan.

Tatu, Michel. 1969. *Power in the Kremlin: From Khrushchev to Kosygin.* New York: Viking.

Taubman, William. 1982. *Stalin's American Policy.* New York: Norton.

Taylor, A. J. P. 1961. *The Origins of the Second World War* (2d ed.). New York: Fawcett.

Taylor, Jay. 1976. *China and Southeast Asia: Peking's Relations with Revolutionary Movements.* New York: Praeger.

Taylor, Maxwell. 1972. *Swords and Plowshares.* New York: Norton.

Taylor, Telford. 1979. *Munich: The Price of Peace.* New York: Doubleday.

Thayer, Thomas C. 1977. We Could Not Win the War of Attrition We Tried to Fight. In W. Scott Thompson and Donaldson D. Frizzell (eds.), *The Lessons of Vietnam.* New York: Crane and Russak, pp. 85–92.

Thomas, Hugh. 1986. *Armed Truce: The Beginnings of the Cold War, 1945–46.* New York: Antheneum.

References

Thompson, W. Scott, and Donaldson D. Frizzell (eds.). 1977. *The Lessons of Vietnam*. New York: Crane and Russak.

Thorpe, James A. 1978. Truman's Ultimatum to Stalin on the 1946 Azerbaijan Crisis: The Making of a Myth. *Journal of Politics*, vol. 40. no. 1 (February), pp. 188–95.

Thucydides. 1934. *The Peloponnesian War*. New York: Modern Library.

Thurow, Roger. 1987. Impoverished Mozambique Rolls out Red Carpet for Both East and West. *Wall Street Journal*, April 20, p. 18.

Togo, Shigenori. 1956. *The Cause of Japan*. New York: Simon and Schuster.

Tolstoy, Leo. 1966. *War and Peace*. New York: Norton.

Tonelson, Alan. 1985–86. The Real National Interest. *Foreign Policy*, no. 61 (Winter), pp. 49–72.

Toynbee, Arnold J. 1950. *War and Civilization*. New York: Oxford University Press.

———. 1969. *Experiences*. New York: Oxford University Press.

Trachtenberg, Marc. 1985. Nuclear Weapons and the Cuban Missile Crisis. *International Security*, vol. 10, no. 1 (Summer), pp. 156–63.

Treitschke, Heinrich von. 1916. *Politics*. New York: Macmillan.

Treml, Vladimir G. 1982. *Alcohol in the USSR: A Statistical Study*. Durham, NC: Duke University Press.

Trevor-Roper, H. R. 1953. The Mind of Adolf Hitler. In *Hitler's Secret Conversations 1941–1944*. New York: Farrar, Straus and Young, pp. vii–xxx.

Tripp, Rhoda Thomas. 1976. *The International Thesaurus of Quotations*. New York: Penguin.

Truman, Harry S. 1947. The Truman Doctrine. In Charles Gati (ed.), *Caging the Bear: Containment and the Cold War*. Indianapolis, IN: Bobbs-Merrill, 1974, pp. 3–8.

———. 1956. *Years of Trial and Hope*. Garden City: Doubleday.

Tuchman, Barbara. 1962. *The Guns of August*. New York: Dell.

———. 1966. *The Proud Tower: A Portrait of the World Before the War, 1890–1940*. New York: Macmillan.

———. 1984. *The March of Folly: From Troy to Vietnam*. New York: Knopf.

Turner, Arthur C., and Leonard Freedman (eds.). 1964. *Tension Areas in World Affairs*. Belmont, CA: Wadsworth.

Turner, L. C. F. 1979. The Significance of the Schlieffen Plan. In Paul M. Kennedy (ed.), *The War Plans of the Great Powers, 1880–1914*. London: Allen & Unwin, pp. 199–221.

Twain, Mark. 1901. *Life on the Mississippi*. New York: Harper.

Uhlig, Mark A. 1988. Barbs of a Polish Comedian Bring Cheers on U.S. Tour. *New York Times*, April 4, p. B1.

Ulam, Adam S. 1968. *Expansion and Coexistence*. New York: Praeger.

———. 1971. *The Rivals: America and Russia since World War II*. New York: Penguin.

———. 1973. *Stalin: The Man and His Era*. New York: Viking.

U.S. Army, Manhattan Engineer District. 1946. *The Atomic Bombings of Hiroshima and Nagasaki*. Washington, DC.

U.S. Strategic Bombing Survey (USSBS). 1946a. *The Effect of Atomic Bombs on Hiroshima and Nagasaki*. New York: Garland.

———. 1946b. *Japan's Struggle to End the War*. New York: Garland.

Vagts, Alfred. 1959. *A History of Militarism*. London: Hollis and Carter.

Valenta, Jiri and Virginia. 1984. Leninism in Grenada. *Problems of Communism*, vol. 33, no. 4 (July–August), pp. 1–23.

Valkenier, Elizabeth Krindl. 1983. *The Soviet and the Third World: An Economic Bind*. New York: Praeger.

———. 1986. Revolutionary Change in the Third World. *World Politics*, vol. 38, no. 3 (April), pp. 415–34.

Van Dyke, Jon M. 1972. *North Vietnam's Strategy for Survival*. Palo Alto, CA: Pacific Books.

Van Dyke, Vernon. 1966. *International Politics*. New York: Appleton-Century-Crofts.

Van Evera, Stephen. 1984. The Cult of the Offensive and the Origins of the First World War. *International Security*, vol. 9, no. 1 (Summer), pp. 58–107.

———. 1986. Why Cooperation Failed in 1914. In Kenneth Oye (ed.), *Cooperation under Anarchy*. Princeton, NJ: Princeton University Press, pp. 80–117.

Vance, Cyrus. 1983. *Hard Choices: Critical Years in America's Foreign Policy*. New York: Simon and Schuster.

References

Voslensky, Michael. 1984. *Nomenklatura: The New Soviet Ruling Class.* Garden City, NY: Double-day.

Wagar, W. Warren. 1961. *H. G. Wells and the World State.* New Haven, CT: Yale University Press.

————. 1982. *Terminal Visions: The Literature of Last Things.* Bloomington, IN: Indiana University Press.

Walt, Stephen M. 1987. The Search for a Science of Strategy: A Review Essay. *International Security,* vol. 12, no. 1 (Summer), pp. 140–65.

Waltz, Kenneth. 1959. *Man, the State, and War.* New York: Columbia University Press.

————. 1979. *Theory of International Politics.* Reading, MA: Addison-Wesley.

————. 1988. The Origins of War in Neorealist Theory. *Journal of Interdisciplinary History,* vol. 18, no. 4 (Spring), pp. 615–28.

Wedgwood, C. V. 1938. *The Thirty Years War.* London: Jonathan Cape.

————. 1961. *The Thirty Years War.* Garden City, NY: Anchor.

Weede, Erich. 1984. Democracy and War Involvement. *Journal of Conflict Resolution,* vol. 28, no. 4 (December), pp. 649–64.

Weidhorn, Manfred. 1974. *Sword and Pen: A Survey of the Writings of Sir Winston Churchill.* Albuquerque, NM: University of New Mexico Press.

Weigel, George. 1987. A Long March. *Wilson Quarterly,* vol. 11, no. 1 (New Year's), pp. 122–43.

Weigley, Russell F. 1984. Reflections on "Lessons" from Vietnam. In Peter Braestrup (ed.), *Vietnam as History.* Lanham, MD: University Press of America, pp. 115–24.

Weinberg, Gerhard L. 1980. *The Foreign Policy of Hitler's Germany: Starting World War II, 1937–1939.* Chicago: University of Chicago Press.

Weinberger, Casper W. 1984. Excerpts from Address of Weinberger. *New York Times,* November 29.

Weinstein, Allen. 1978. *Perjury: The Hiss-Chambers Case.* New York: Knopf.

Weiszacher, Carl-Friedrich. 1980. Can a Third World War Be Prevented? *International Security,* vol. 5, no. 1 (Summer), pp. 198–205.

Welch, David A., and James G. Blight. 1987/88. The Eleventh Hour of the Cuban Missile Crisis: An Introduction to the ExComm Transcripts. *International Security,* vol. 12, no. 3 (Winter), pp. 5–29.

Wells, David A. 1890. *Recent Economic Changes and Their Effect on the Production and Distribution of Wealth and the Well-Being of Society.* New York: Appleton.

Wells, H. G. 1908. *First and Last Things: A Confession of Faith and a Rule of Life.* New York: Putnam's Sons.

————. 1914. *The War That Will End War.* New York: Duffield.

————. 1968. *The Last Books of H. G. Wells.* London: H. G. Wells Society.

Wells, Samuel F., Jr. 1979. Sounding the Tocsin: NSC 68 and the Soviet Threat. *International Security,* vol. 4, no. 2 (Fall), pp. 116–58.

Weltman, John S. 1974. On the Obsolescence of War. *International Studies Quarterly,* vol. 18, no. 4 (December), pp. 395–416.

Werth, Alexander. 1964. *Russia at War, 1941–1945.* New York: Dutton.

Westmoreland, William. 1976. *A Soldier Reports.* Garden City, NY: Doubleday.

Whiting, Allen S. 1960. *China Crosses the Yalu: The Decision to Enter the Korean War.* New York: Macmillan.

Winks, Robin W. 1960. *Canada and the United States: The Civil War Years.* Baltimore, MD: John Hopkins University Press.

Wohlstetter, Albert. 1959. The Delicate Balance of Terror. *Foreign Affairs,* vol. 27, no. 2 (January), pp. 211–34.

————. 1983. Bishops, Statesmen, and Other Strategists on the Bombing of Innocents. *Commentary,* June, pp. 14–44.

Wohlstetter, Roberta. 1962. *Pearl Harbor: Warning and Decision.* Stanford, CA: Stanford University Press.

Woito, Robert. 1987. Between the Wars. *Wilson Quarterly,* vol. 11, no. 1 (New Year's), pp. 108–21.

Wolf, Charles, Jr., K. C. Yeh, Edmund Brunner, Jr., Aaron Gurwitz, and Marilee Lawrence. 1983. *The Costs of the Soviet Empire.* Santa Monica, CA: Rand Corporation.

References

Wolfe, Thomas W. 1970. *Soviet Power and Europe, 1945–1970*. Baltimore, MD: Johns Hopkins University Press.

Wolfenstein, Martha. 1957. *Disaster: A Psychological Study*. London: Routledge and Kegan Paul.

Wood, Bryce. 1966. *The United States and Latin American Wars, 1932–1942*. New York: Columbia University Press.

World Bank. 1980. *World Development Report, 1980*. New York: Oxford University Press.

Yergin, Daniel. 1977. *Shattered Peace: The Origins of the Cold War and the National Security State*. Boston: Houghton Mifflin.

Zagoria, Donald S. 1962. *The Sino-Soviet Conflict, 1956–1961*. Princeton, NJ: Princeton University Press.

———. 1967. *Vietnam Triangle*. New York: Triangle.

Zelman, Walter A. 1967. *Chinese Intervention in the Korean War: A Bilateral Failure of Deterrence*. Los Angeles: University of California, Security Studies Project.

INDEX

Index

Berlin, Irving, 52
Berlin blockade, 106, 119, 149–151
Berlin wall, 151
Bernhardi, Friedrich, 42, 44, 46–47, 275n39
Betts, Richard, 151–152, 162n, 175, 177, 182–183, 287n22
Bialer, Seweryn, 207
Blainey, Geoffrey, 5
Bloch, Ivan, 48–51, 55
Blunders, 228, 232
Bluster, in international relations, 148–152, 188, 202–205, 211
Boer War, 29, 48
Bracken, Paul, 294n45
Bradley, Omar, 110, 122, 125
Brandt, Willy, 161
Brezhnev, Leonid, 188, 202, 205–206, 210
Brezhnev Doctrine, 197–198
Bright, John, 27
Brittain, Vera, 54n
Brodie, Bernard, 38, 51, 54, 126, 155, 157, 228n
Brogan, Denis, 83
Brooke, Rupert, 54n
Brown, Frederic, 84, 85, 293n42
Buckle, H. T., 26, 32–34, 44, 93, 253
Bulletin of Atomic Scientists, 3–4, 98
Bullock, Allan, 65, 68n
Bunce, Valerie, 207
Bundy, McGeorge, 114, 157, 178
Burin, Frederic, 135, 141
Burma, 120
Burr, Aaron, 9–10, 11
Butow, Robert, 75

Caesar, Julius, 18
Cairnes, John Elliot, 272n24
Cambodia, 168, 173, 189, 190–191, 197, 254, 257
Campaign for Nuclear Disarmament (CND), 160
Canada, 226, 234; U.S. relations with, 241, 244, 246–247, 249
Capitalism, as cause of war, 33
Capitalist world: intracapitalist rivalries and, 135–137; revolution in, 138–140, 199–200
Carnegie, Andrew, 27, 32n, 50
Carnegie Endowment for International Peace, 27
Carpenter, Edward, 40
Carrington, Lord, 261
Carter, Jimmy, 190, 193–196, 203
Carter Doctrine, 195
Carthage, 8
Castro, Fidel, 145, 166–167, 235
Casualties, 84, 271n9. *see also* Costs of war
Cataclysmic war, 7–8, 12, 59–60, 77. *see also* Escalation; Major war; World War III

Causes of war, elimination of, 33–34
Central America. *see* Latin America; *specific countries*
Central Intelligence Agency (CIA), 106, 123, 154n, 175
Chad, 257
Chamberlain, Neville, 68, 69–70, 181
Character, peace as detrimental to, 42–43
Chemical weapons: decontamination from, 84; as deterrent, 60–61; doomsday visions and, 57–58; escalation and, 237; Germany and, 57–58, 278n16; public opinion and, 276n12; World War II and, 84, 237, 278n16
Chernenko, Konstantin, 206
Chile, 167–168, 253
China: abandons Cold War 184–186; Cold War and, 159, 184–186, 211; Japanese war on, 73; Korean War and, 123, 124–125, 133; man-made famine in, 8n, 165; military action by, 138; non-expansionist Communism and, 6, 160, 184–186, 219; nuclear weapons and, 126–127, 226; response to *Sputnik* in, 147; Sino-Soviet split and, 163, 184; U.S. policy before Korea in, 119–120; Vietnam and, 170–173, 178, 182; view of major war in, 134–135
Churchill, Winston, 4, 39, 59, 69–71, 111; on poison gas, 58, 85
CIA. *see* Central Intelligence Agency
Civilians: killing of, 61; mass suicide among, 88
Civilization: peace and, 26; war and, 44
Civil war: between *1945* and *1980,* 92; China and, 119, 140–141; Communism and, 118, 139; in developed world, 5, 91–92; in Greece, 104; in Laos, 143; in Latin America, 140, 253; in Spain, 61, 91, 201; in USSR, 101. *see also* Civil War, U.S.; Wars of national liberation
Civil War, U.S., 23, 30–32, 48, 220
Clarke, I.F., 59
Clausewitz, Carl von, 11, 29, 228–229
Clifford, Clark, 179
CND. *see* Campaign for Nuclear Disarmament
Cobden, Richard, 27
Cold War: after Korean War, 132; alliance patterns of, 115; China and, 159, 184–186, 211; demise of, 211–213, 253–254; escalation and, 236; impact of decline of, 253–254; prospects for major war and, 6, 213–214; Sino-Soviet split and, 165–168; Soviet ideology and, 99–102, 105; stakes in Vietnam and, 168–173, 177–178. *see also* Containment; Crisis; Korean War; Vietnam War
Colet, John, 24
Colombia, 167, 253
Colonialism, decline of, 120, 140–141, 148
Communism: capitalist-Communist conflict and, 134–135; history and, 133–134; intracapitalist wars and, 135–137; military probes and, 137–138; revolutionary ideology and, 138–140, 255; Sino-Soviet split and, 159,

Index

Index

Index

Grey, Edward, 47–48, 48*n*
Gromyko, Andrei, 262
Gross National Product (GNP): costs of empire as percentage of, in USSR, 197; defense as percentage of, 8; defense costs as percentage of, in USSR, 206
Guatemala, 167

Haas, Ernst B., 212*n*
Haber, L.F., 276*n*12
Haig, Alexander, 203
Halberstam, David, 169–170, 175*n*, 287*n*24
Halperin, Morton, 285*n*42
Hamilton, Alexander, 9–11, 13
Harmony, and peace, 264–265
Harriman, Averell, 113–114
Hatred, 87*n*, 88
Hegel, Georg, 42
Helsinki Accords, 162, 197
Heroism. *see* War romanticism
Heydrich, Reinhard, 279*n*36
Heym, Georg, 43
Hilsman, Roger, 184
Hiroshima, 87, 90
Hiss, Alger, 128
Hitler: claims of peaceful intentions by, 69; military strategy of, 66–67
Hitler, Adolf, 73, 77, 88, 96, 106, 122, 213; atomic bomb and, 89; centrality of, 64–65, 68–69, 71; chemical warfare and, 61, 237; comparison of Stalin to, 100, 117, 205; deterrence of, 236, 249; instigation of World War II and, 6, 64–68, 217–218, 242; invasion of Poland, 18, 109; invasion of USSR, 71, 81; military strategy of, 66–67, 72; opposition to, 68–71, 212; profit in war and, 91–92, 223; rise of another, 182, 235; Spanish civil war and, 91; successes of, 67–68; suicide of, 95; on Swiss, 277*n*38; total war and, 94, 276*n*30; on value of life, 293*n*40
Ho Chi Minh, 120
Holland. *see* Netherlands
Hollandization, 19–21, 96, 218
Holmes, Oliver Wendell, Jr., 39, 46
Honduras, 293*n*34
Honor. *see* War romanticism
Horror of war: atomic bomb and, 89–90; in interwar Europe, 64; restraint in crisis behavior and, 114; as solution to war, 35–36
Hot-line, 162
Howard, Michael, 24, 38, 47, 52, 54, 228
Humanism, and war as repulsive, 25–26
Human life, value of, 267–269
Human nature: alternatives to war and, 33; war as endemic to, 21, 22, 41, 46, 264; war as fad and, 242–243

Human rights, 199–200
Humphrey, Hubert, 173, 180
Hungary, 4, 5, 92, 138, 140, 254, 262, 271*n*5
Hurok, Sol, 242

Imperialism, as cause of war, 33
India, 162, 173, 226
India-Pakistan conflicts, 162, 254, 256, 257
Indochina, 120, 128, 140, 142
Indonesia: anticolonial war in, 140; French experience in, 175*n*, 176; and U.S. policy before Korea, 120; Vietnam War and, 171–173, 177–178, 181–182
Injustice, as cause of war, 33
Intellectual left, 203*n*
Intercontinental ballistic missiles, 146, 149, 202
International arbitration, 34. *see also* World government
Internationalism, 108–109
International Monetary Fund (IMF), 209
Iran, 114, 195, 255, 256
Iran-Iraq war, 255, 256–257
Iraq, 255, 256–257
Ireland. *see* Northern Ireland
Isolationism, 108, 292*n*67
Israel, 21, 226, 256, 257
Italy: acquiescence of, after World War II, 95–96; Communist party in, 139, 200; economic strength and, 225–226; nongreatpowers and, 20; nuclear weapons and, 226; as reluctant, in World War II, 62–63
Ivory Coast, 256

Jains (religion), 24
James, William, 33, 38, 41, 46, 220
Japan, 6, 21; acquiescence of, after World War II, 95–96; decision for war in, 74–75, 229–230; as Great Power, 19; Hollandization of, 77; invasion of China by, 18; potential for war and, 234, 235; pre-World War II expansion of, 72–73, 74; pre-World War II opposition to, 75–77; prosperity and, 223–226, 259, 273*n*35; rearmament of, 259, 293*n*39; romance of war and, 217; Soviet border conflicts with, 284*n*11; surrender of, 87–89, 279*n*23; third world war-aversion and, 252
Jervis, Robert, 46, 155, 232, 235, 283*n*32, 292*n*21, 293*n*28
Jessup, Phillip, 123, 282*n*17
Joffre, Joseph, 47
Johnson, Louis, 124
Johnson, Lyndon B., 167–173, 175, 177, 180
Joll, James, 46
Jordan, David Starr, 50

Index

Index

Mansfield, Mike, 287*n*27
Mao Zedong, 185; ambition of, 173, 182, 288*n*33; costs of war and, 235; progress of Communism and, 135, 147; Sino-Soviet relations and, 164, 283*n*29; Vietnam War and, 171, 181; widow of, 222
Marshall, George, 87
Marx, Karl, 33, 99, 137, 139, 199
Master race, Germans as, 65–66
Materialism, and peace as immoral, 42–43, 46
Matthews, Francis P., 124
May, Ernest, 282*n*1
Mayaguez incident, 190
Mazzini, Giuseppe, 33
Medical care, wartime, 8–9
Melos, destruction in, 8
Mendel, 123
Mexican War, 29
Military establishment: chemical weapons and, 61, 84; in Hitler's Germany, 68*n;* Mussolini's war and, 63
Military parody, 259
Military probes, Communist, 137–138, 211
Mill, John Stuart, 27
Milne, A.A., 40, 55*n*, 77, 242, 243
Milward, Alan, 8, 274*n*17
Minnelli, Vincente, 278*n*7
Miracle of Marne, 49–50
Mishima, Yukio, 235
Missile gap, 149, 151
Mistakes, 228
Molotov, Vyacheslav, 284*n*25
Moltke, Helmuth von, 40
Montesquieu, 27
More, Sir Thomas, 24
Morgenthau, Hans J., 19–20, 110–111; on Hitler, 277*n*33; on power, 224–225; on World War III, 271*n*2
Morse, Wayne, 177
"Moscow statement" of *1960*, 284*n*18
Movie theaters, in World War II, 278*n*3
Moyers, Bill, 175
Mozambique, 192, 197
Mulley, F. W., 292*n*18
Munitions-maker theory, 57, 273*n*51
Murray, Williamson, 69
Mussolini, Benito, 66, 72, 77, 91, 122; invasion of Albania, 18, 63; war against Ethopia, 62–63; World War II and, 62–63, 81, 95

Nagasaki, 87, 90
Napoleonic Wars, 21, 25, 55, 241
Nasser, Gamal Abdel, 144, 167, 235
National honor, and Vietnam War, 178–179
National identity, 234
National policy: costs and, 269; deterrence in, 247–248; war as instrument of, 30

Nation-state system, 33–34, 264
NATO. *see* North Atlantic Treaty Organization
Nature, control of, and Stalin, 123
Nazi Germany: centrality of Hitler to, 65; civil warfare under occupation by, 91–92; contemporary awareness of death camps and, 86–87; profitability of occupation by, 91–92; public opinion in, 67–68
Netherlands, 5, 20, 70, 203, 224, 242, 264
Neutrality, and Hitler's expansion, 70
Nevins, Allan, 82
New York Times, 190, 191
Nicaragua, 196–197, 197, 198, 256
Nietzsche, Friedrich, 42
Nixon, Richard, 127, 203; China and, 184–185; Vietnam and, 180–181, 187, 189
Nixon Doctrine of *1969,* 191, 195, 198
Nkrumah, Kwame, 166
Nobel, Alfred, 36
Nobel Peace Prize, 27
Nobility. *see* War romanticism
Nonwars, 4–5, 241, 243–244
North Atlantic Treaty Organization (NATO): containment and, 106; Korean War and, 128; Portuguese Communism in, 201; rationale behind, 115, 261; rearmed West Germany and, 133; Soviet intermediate-range missiles and, 202–205, 209
Northern Ireland, 5, 92, 234, 292*n*8
North Vietnam, 21
Norway, 70
Novels about doomsday, 59, 238*n*
Nuclear weapons: accidents and, 231, 237–238, 259*n;* alliances and, 281*n*51; China and, 164, 171; Cold War alliance patterns and, 115; as deterrent, 4, 6, 76; European development of, 292*n*18; freezing levels of, 204, 205; irrelevance of, 110–115, 127, 155–156, 161, 165, 257, 261; Japan's decision to surrender and, 87–89; Korea and, 126–127; last resort use of, 293*n*42; likelihood of escalation and, 218–219, 294*n*45; military planning and, 238; moderation of crisis behavior and, 114–115; Soviet buildup in, 188; Soviet noninvasion of Western Europe and, 111–114; as status symbols, 226; underdeveloped countries and, 142, 257; U.S. buildup in, 202–203; U.S. decision to use, 86–87; Vietnam War and, 180*n*, 183; as weapons, 89–90; World War II experience with gas and, 85–86
Nuclear weapons testing, 151, 157–158, 164, 202

Obsolescence: of nuclear weapons, 205; of war in developed world, 6–7, 217–244
Offensive syndrome, 47–50
Overy, R.J., 276*n*30

323

Index

Index

Index